MEDIEVAL POLITICAL IDEAS

MEDIEVAL POLITICAL IDEAS

by

EWART LEWIS

VOLUME ONE

NEW YORK
COOPER SQUARE
PUBLISHERS, INC.
1974

Originally Published 1954 by Alfred A. Knopf, Inc.
Reprinted by Permission of Alfred A. Knopf, Inc.
Published 1974 by Cooper Square Publishers, Inc.
59 Fourth Avenue, New York, New York 10003
International Standard Book Number 0-8154-0485-9
Library of Congress Catalog Card Number 73-82907

Printed in the United States of America

CONTENTS

v

CONTENTS

PREFACE

THIS book was planned in the hope that it might be useful to teachers and advanced students of political theory and of medieval history who feel the need of a more intimate acquaintance with the political ideas of the Middle Ages but find considerable difficulties in their way.

The source material is voluminous, and a great deal of it is inaccessible to the non-specialist. Only a small fraction of the important writings of medieval publicists can be found in English translation; modern editions even of Latin texts are lacking in many instances, so that firsthand acquaintance with such well-reputed works as, for example, the *De Regimine Principum* of Aegidius Romanus, the *Dialogus* of Occam, or the conciliarist pamphlets of Gerson can be pursued only under the rather forbidding auspices of the rare book rooms of the largest university libraries. Some progress, indeed, is being steadily made, especially in the modern publication of Latin texts. But much remains to be done; and the barriers imposed by language and sheer extent do not yield readily to attack. It is hard to imagine a day when the average professor of political theory, preparing his lecture on the conciliar movement, will be able to dip into his well-underlined copy of Cusa's *De Concordantia Catholica* with the same facility as that with which, earlier in the semester, he had turned to the *Politics* of Aristotle or that with which he will later turn, with a sigh of relief, to the *Second Treatise on Civil Government*. If ever a book of 'readings' is justified, it would seem to be justified in the field of medieval political thought.

PREFACE

This assumes, of course, that the field is one worth knowing. Its significance for the medieval historian need not be argued; he is, presumably, already committed to the proposition that what happened in the Middle Ages is interesting and important, though he may question whether the thoughts that happened then are as interesting and important as certain other phenomena. My remarks are addressed primarily to the political theorist, who tends to be much more comfortable among ideas more directly related to the values and problems of the modern world, and who often, no doubt, surreptitiously wishes that merciful oblivion would again blot out those teeming centuries that intervene between, shall we say, Cicero and Machiavelli. Of course, as a historian of theory, he is well aware that the ideas of those centuries were links in an intellectual chain, so that some understanding of medieval patterns of thought helps in the precise recognition of what Bodin, or Hooker, or Locke was driving at. He also knows that modern Catholic thought is self-consciously continuous with constructions developed in the Middle Ages. But he is less likely to appreciate that medieval political thought has some significance besides its significance as a background.

A good deal of it was directed upon problems that remain the central problems of any political theory; and some of the minds that worked on those problems were excellent ones, highly trained in sharp definition and logical analysis. True, their frames of reference, both practical and ideological, were different from ours; but for that very reason acquaintance with their ways of handling the eternal questions can be an illuminating experience, revealing new dimensions for conceptual problems that we tend to treat within the perspectives of our own world. In a sense, knowledge of medieval thought helps to make the study of political theory a really comparative study. There were, moreover, points at which medieval political thought reached, it seems to me, a definitive statement in the sense that it pursued the implications of a certain point of view about as far as they could be pursued. The explorations of the problem of political obligation by Aquinas and by Occam, for example, are remarkable achievements in clarification on normative, rationalist premises and are, accordingly, an absolute contribution to discussion. In this general context, the points at which medieval thought bogged down are quite as suggestive as the points at which it pushed through to lucid and comprehensive statement.

PREFACE

Medieval political thought has another kind of interest. It is common, and in a sense correct, to refer to the unity of medieval civilization, but there is a sense in which one could as plausibly refer to its exceptional dichotomy. The medieval centuries were, roughly speaking, an age in which the conceptual frameworks used by the intellectuals were much more remote from the shape of contemporary institutions than is usually the case. Accordingly, a great part of medieval thought developed from its inherited intellectual chromosomes with comparatively little influence from its environment; and a great part of what seem to us the obviously salient characteristics of that environment were only gradually, painfully, and incompletely formulated into usable conceptual schemes. This is one reason, of course, why the field of medieval political theory is so baffling to the novice, who expects to find in any system of thought some kind of rationalization or, at any rate, some evident reflection of contemporary life. But, if one starts by recognizing the fact of dichotomy, even a superficial acquaintance with medieval political thought can be a fascinating experience. It is a case study in the remarkable vitality of ideas uprooted from the soil in which they had grown; it is a case study in the extreme difficulty which men find, without the help of a continuous and relevant intellectual tradition, in defining the terms of their own daily life and work; it is a case study in the slow and devious ways in which the culture of one civilization can meet and blend with the routine patterns of a civilization that is very different. For the process of assimilation did go on throughout the Middle Ages: concept and custom interacted and finally merged. Perhaps the process was completed, so far as such a process is ever completed, in the sixteenth century.

It seemed, then, worth while to ease the terms on which modern students can gain access to the world of medieval political thought, through making a collection of translated passages, numerous enough to plot out the variety of opinion, long enough to indicate the process of thought as well as its conclusions. It also seemed desirable to orient the reader in this material through introductory essays which would trace the development of thought, point out the interrelated influences that shaped it, and attempt to suggest its ultimate significance.

The period covered by this book begins with the investiture struggle and goes through the fifteenth century. Earlier political thought, less systematically explicit, did not seem to lend itself to the projected treatment. The temptation to carry the story into the sixteenth century, when, as I have suggested, many trends of medieval thought reached a kind of culmination, was a strong temptation; but one must stop somewhere, and the century of Machiavelli and the Protestant Reformation presented not only some culminations, but also some very fresh starts. The reader will notice that I have often found it convenient to divide my period into an 'earlier' and 'later' Middle Ages, with a rather wobbly dividing line somewhere around the latter part of the thirteenth century.

I have followed a topical organization in the hope that it might make for a clearer and more significant presentation than I could manage if I tried to follow a single chronological line. It also seemed possible that a topical organization might be of use to readers particularly curious about particular topics, whose history is often obscured by the dominance of the theme of church *versus* state. For that reason, the separate essays have been written so as to be fairly independent of one another. This has entailed some repetition and gerrymandering, for which I ask everybody's forgiveness. Of course, as frequent cross-references testify, no theme of discussion really developed in isolation from the others. But perhaps the more complex and more variously debated themes may become more meaningful, and more readily intelligible, if they are approached by way of the more basic concepts which served as premises to the great debates.

In choosing selections, I have tried, on the one hand, to cover the characteristic features of the systems of the most original publicists and, on the other hand, to provide clear statements of viewpoints typical of all medieval thought or of important schools of medieval thought. Recent research has revealed the importance of civilists and canonists in first developing many medieval concepts; I have, however, given preference to the less technical, more generalized statements of these ideas by philosophical publicists, which may be more directly intelligible to the non-specialist reader. The translations have been made from the best published texts I could lay my hands on. Where they have been abridged, the fact has been indicated. My goal in translation has been to keep as close to the original as possible rather than to achieve a graceful English style. A number of medieval publicists wrote well, in the sense that they wrote in a clear and orderly fashion, but few of them wrote gracefully; on the other hand, the way they said things had meaning to them and may well have meaning to us. I have changed references to the *Corpus Juris Civilis* and the *Corpus Juris Canonici* to brief modern forms of citation. References to Aristotle's *Politics* have been given in terms of the system of books and chapters established by Schneider and followed in, for example, the Loeb Classical Library edition. Biographical data on each medieval author introduce the first selection from his works.

The introductory essays have been written on the assumption that they will be read in connection with the selections they introduce. They have been written also on the assumption that the reader will have no more than a text-book knowledge of medieval history, but will have that. Medievalists and political scientists will both, I hope, forgive me. I must also ask their respective forgivenesses for sweeping generalizations about medieval institutions, which seemed desirable, and for technicalities in the discussion of medieval ideas, which seemed unavoidable. A good deal of medieval political thought was technical, and its meaning is most accurately described in its own technical terms. I have continually tried to suggest the long-range significance of medieval ideas, but I have also tried to keep such suggestion distinct from analysis of the ideas as they were held by those who held them. The implications of an idea are certainly part of its interest, but the first problem is to define the idea itself.

Accurate presentation of the thought of medieval publicists is no easy task. The study of medieval political theory is still a developing field of specialized scholarship. Many conclusions of scholars of previous generations have become suspect; many conclusions of present-day scholars remain tentative and controversial. A great deal of rigorous and sensitive work still remains to be done to help us to define with certainty what a medieval publicist meant by what he said and whether he was the first to say it. I trust that this book may claim some originality of statement and comment, but it has no pretensions to be a contribution to the intensive sort of scholarship. It rests—I hope—on the best of present-day opinion. So far as it treats of the ideas of lawyers, it rests almost exclusively on secondary writings. I have, however, read substantially in the writings of medieval publicists other than the lawyers, and my own reading has inevitably affected my interpretation or my choice among interpretations. Where reputable scholars disagree with one another, or where I disagree with a reputable scholar, foot-notes will indicate.

I know that errors must have got into this book; I hope, not so many as to undermine its usefulness. Like William of Occam, 'I beg and en-treat that whoever reads the things to be written here, if he thinks that I have erred in any way, may deign to show me my error. . . .'

I hope this book may serve as a partial payment on my large and pleasant debt to George Sellery, a great teacher, who knew how to communicate to his students, among many valuable things, something of his own friendliness with medieval minds. I owe a good deal also to John Gaus, whose teaching of the history of political thought continu-ally suggested the bearing of the past upon the present and of the present upon the past. Charles Howard McIlwain encouraged me in the early planning of the book and gave generous and very useful advice, for which I thank him heartily and humbly. I also warmly thank all who read parts of the manuscript and helped me with detailed criticism: in particular, Jane Ruby and Gaines Post. I am glad to acknowledge the kindness of the libraries where I have worked: especially Oberlin College Library, which was most cooperative in arranging interlibrary loans, and Widener Library, the excellence of whose hospitality is happily combined with the excellence of its resources in this field. I am very glad to record my reverent admiration of Miss June Wright, a typist without a fault. Finally, I am grateful to my husband, John D. Lewis, not only for judicious support and counsel in the preparation of this book, but also for diligent and expert instruction in various branches of the science of politics.

EWART LEWIS

Oberlin, Ohio
October 1953

Chapter One

THE IDEA OF LAW

NOWADAYS, most people think of law as the command of a definite will or group of wills endowed with legislative authority. The authority that a legislator exercises may be regarded as its own, as in the case of an absolute monarchy or a dictatorship, or it may be considered a delegated authority, as in the case of a democracy; but, in either case, law appears as the product of human will. So it is with the limitations set to legislative authority: sometimes these are formally expressed in a constitution, sometimes there exist only the uncharted but real limitations of public consent, but both these limits are conceived as limits set by the volition of men.

This is the conventional modern view, whose origins, however, can be traced back far behind Austin, who gave it its definitive statement. Yet there are those who attack it; and even the common man's thinking on law—to say nothing of the pronouncements of judges—bears traces of an older, different approach. May not one look behind a constitution and find it a reflection of certain necessary relationships based upon the very nature of social life? Does law really proceed from will, or from a recognition of norms of right that are independent of human will? If it is true that the government makes the law, is it not equally true that law makes the government? Are there not higher standards by which enacted law may be measured—standards which sometimes sanction disobedience to the legislative will?

In the Middle Ages, laymen and experts would have had no doubt about the answers to such questions; and their answers would not have been the Austinian answers. While the role of human will in the formulation of law was not unnoticed, a great body of thought concerned itself with a kind of law whose existence and content were independent of human decision; and, while modern thought subordinates law to government as its expression, medieval thought subordinated government to this kind of law as its corollary and instrument. 'Whereas the modern democrat is prepared to respect a law in so far as he can regard himself as its author, medieval obedience was founded on the opposite sentiment, that laws were respectable in so far as they were not made by man.'[1] While modern thought regards legislation as the highest activity of the state, to which judicial enforcement is logically subordinate, medieval thought typically admitted legislation only as 'a part of the judicial procedure—a more or less surreptitious incident of "*jus dicere*."'[2]

The study of medieval political theory, therefore, must begin with the medieval idea of law—or, better, medieval ideas of law. For the common man of the Middle Ages and the feudal lawyers who spoke for him did not think of fundamental law in quite the same way as the scholars and philosophers.

The law in which medieval institutions were actually enmeshed was largely customary law. Its content was miscellaneous: rights and practices which came into play with the growth of feudalism were combined with age-old Germanic customs and, particularly in southern Europe, with a body of modified Roman law that had become traditional, its origin forgotten. The origin of customary law had no significance for its validity: it was valid simply because it existed and had long existed as the law by which a particular region was accustomed to be judged. And although, till it came to be congealed in written codes, custom actually underwent continual gradual change, it was conceived as theoretically changeless.

In a society which had few techniques for controlling its human lords, the customary law was naturally regarded as a precious possession of the community. It had the dignity of age, and the intimacy of communal experience. It seemed just because it was old, and also because it was familiar: it was not locked away in the books of specialists, but rather was immediately present in the common usage of those whom it affected. It was the cherished safeguard of personal rights and of property, the immutable authority to which men could appeal against innovation, which too often meant new exploitation. For a man to be deprived of the right to live under the law of his group—to be 'outlawed'—was naturally considered a penalty harsh enough for the gravest crime.[3]

Now this customary law, although or perhaps because its validity was so completely accepted, was never given a thorough basis of systematic theory. Living and known through the customs of its users (*moribus utentium*), it was not even systematically recorded till the thirteenth century, and then not completely, though here and there partial codes were promulgated by royal authority before that time. But the early development of governmental institutions and the academic study of Roman law, whose orderliness was a grave challenge to the defenders of local custom, did result in the more or less precise definition of certain facets of custom-law theory. Among the thirteenth-century compilers of customary law, there are some whose comments illuminate the doctrine of the law that they record. Otherwise, medieval thought about customary law must be gleaned from scattered phrases in the recorded law itself or deduced from the typical patterns of medieval practice.

From these sources it is evident that the development of governmental institutions and familiarity with Roman law did not at once alter the medieval concept of the immutability and supremacy of tradition. But that development did carry with it an increasing emphasis on the importance of authoritative promulgation in the 'establishing' of law—a process which was not conceived as the making of law, but as the formal finding of a law that already existed, and as the formal declaration of what the law already was. It was generally agreed that in the promulgation of law the king should be assisted by a council of magnates to represent, not the law-making will of the community, but the community's best knowledge of the law. A naive description of the ideal process is to be found in Jean d'Ibelin's narrative of the method by which he assumed the Assizes of the Kingdom of Jerusalem to have been formulated. A briefer description of the elements which enter into the authoritative promulgation of law is found in Bracton. And some combination of 'the authority of the king, the advice and agreement of the magnates, and the general guaranty of the community' —however expressed—was the typical medieval procedure.

As a matter of fact, the promulgation of customary law often

3

involved an actual modification, whether through misunderstanding of the original meaning, or through a deliberate attempt to apply old custom to new circumstances. But this practical modification of custom proceeded without a theory of legislation. It was rather assumed that the law, recently distorted and abused, was being restored to its original purity, or that the bearing of old law on new conditions was now being clearly defined. The extent to which this fiction might be stretched is vividly illustrated in the case of the English statute of *Quia Emptores*,[4] which actually made a radical change in the land law in the guise of the removal of an abuse. Even after the development of estates, popular thought still tended to find in past custom rather than present will the ultimate authority of law.

Indeed, the promulgation of fundamental law in the Middle Ages was more like an act of jurisdiction (*juris dictio*) than an act of legislation. The king with his council or the king with his parliament declared the law as a court declares it, except that it was declared in general terms rather than applied to the settlement of a particular dispute. The authority given to custom by such formal declaration was parallel in its significance to the authority which, according to Beaumanoir, a custom received through its 'proving' in a successful lawsuit.

Custom was not the only kind of law the Middle Ages knew. The growth of effective royal government gave increasing prominence to a type of law which did proceed from the authority and discretion of the king as the administrative and judicial head of the realm, responsible for the enforcement and maintenance of the fundamental law and the security of the public peace. Such ordinances were not always clearly distinguished from customary law. Beaumanoir, for example, speaks of the king of France as making 'new customs' when his obvious reference is to administrative orders rather than to an alteration of basic legal relationships. In the early days of the medieval monarchy, the promulgation of such ordinances, like the formal promulgation of customary law, was often done with the advice and consent of a great council of magnates. But as time went on, the growing pressure of governmental business made such formalities impossible, while the growing prestige of the king made them unnecessary. The great bulk of such ordinances in France tended to be made simply in the king's regular council; and English practice and terminology in the fourteenth century distinguished between the statute, which involved basic custom

4

and therefore needed the consent of Parliament, and the ordinance, which did not affect fundamental relationships and therefore needed no authorization beyond the king's will.[5]

But long before differences in procedure had developed, some feudalists had grasped the logical distinction between the law which was changeless custom, defining a permanent structure of rights and obligations, and the laws of the king, which were mere administrative orders, temporary and changeable, designed to supplement and enforce the permanent law itself. And in their definitions they had blocked out one pattern for medieval legal thought: a pattern controlled by the network of changeless custom, but in which the limited though important areas of policy and administration, procedural and penal law, were left to the legislative discretion of the king.[6] They made it clear that they regarded custom as the higher law. The royal edict must conform to its principles; if the royal edict conflicted with custom, it was invalid— unless, as Beaumanoir indicated, a special emergency might make the customs of normal times temporarily inapplicable.

This conviction was forcibly though variously expressed by feudal lawyers in their solutions to the problem of terminology forced on them by acquaintance with Roman jurisprudence. Custom, in the Roman system, was the lowest variety of law; it was considered as an expression of the popular will, and there was much debate among students of the civil law as to whether the popular will, having transferred its authority to the emperor, was competent to make law at all; its competence to make law that should take precedence over imperial legislation was even more dubious. The term *lex*, in the civilists' vocabulary, was reserved for law, substantive as well as procedural, enacted by government; custom (*consuetudo*) was definitely inferior in prestige. The feudalists were obliged to deal with this conflict of terminology, confused further by a tendency to stress the accident of writing as a distinguishing characteristic of a *lex*. Their solutions varied: the Norman author of the *Summa de Legibus* employed the term *lex* for the administrative and procedural enactments of the ruler; the Lombard author of the *Libri Feudorum* thought of *lex* as written law, particularly Roman law, and frankly subordinated it to custom; Glanville and, following him, Bracton saw *leges* as the term implying the highest prestige and attempted to show that the customs of England corresponded to the *leges* of other nations and deserved to be so called.[7] In this attempt, both were led to stress the importance of formal promulgation as a factor in the authority of the law, but they saw it as only one of several factors. They were not assimilating the Roman theory but under its pressure were attempting to formulate their own.

Thus the great feudal lawyers set down their conception of law. But when we inquire what was the ultimate basis of the customary law which they revered, the feudalists have no answer to give us. They may have felt that custom could be equated with reason; but they made no search for general rational principles underlying its details, nor had they any theory to describe how reason is transmuted into law. They were not trained philosophers and did not easily think in abstract terms.

It is evident that such an approach to law would, if consistently applied, keep human institutions in an eternal and untidy stagnation. But the naive feudal belief in the supremacy of custom as the touchstone of right did not satisfy philosophical and scholarly minds, which, even if they were not troubled by its lack of flexibility, did demand a rational and uniform standard by which human laws and institutions might be measured. For such minds the obvious point of departure was the natural-law doctrine of the Stoics, which was transmitted to the Middle Ages through the Roman juristic writings collected in the *Corpus Juris Civilis* of Justinian and through the discussions of the church Fathers. The organization, analysis, and assimilation of the antique theories of law became an important intellectual exercise, which ultimately reacted on medieval thought about medieval problems. But, since natural-law theory had originally developed in an environment very unlike that of the Middle Ages, scholarly discussion of law was inevitably somewhat formal and abstruse; and the application of the scholars' concepts to the medieval scene was a process never completely carried out.

Three groups of scholars contributed to the medieval philosophy of law: the students of the Roman civil law, the students of the canon law, and the students whose first concern was theology and whose second concern was the philosophic structure of man's world.

With the twelfth-century recovery of the complete text of the *Corpus Juris Civilis* and the development of the University of Bologna and of civil-law faculties in other universities, Roman law became a field of intensive critical study. This study included the study of Roman legal theory as it might be reconstructed from the fragmentary and often contradictory texts of Roman jurists preserved by Justinian's compilers. Simultaneously, the canon law became the object of study, beginning with Gratian's codification of the canon law in the middle of the twelfth century, and continuing with papal additions to the canons and with expert glosses and commentaries on Gratian's *Decretum* and on the later collections. The canonists were generally familiar with the ideas of their civilist contemporaries and their thought likewise stemmed from Stoic sources, but they departed in several significant ways from the thought of the civilists. This was partly because their notion of natural law came to them in a form already modified by patristic thought, and partly because, unlike the civilists, the canonists were from the beginning concerned with the living law of a living institution, and were thus forced to more decisive positions than the civilists, commenting on dead texts, had to assume.

From their early sources, the civilists and canonists learned to think that positive law was based on the human recognition of norms of right not dependent on human construction but rooted in the very nature of the world. This conviction was expressed in various ways in the sources and therefore by medieval scholars. Sometimes they traced positive law to justice, that quality of the human will which 'wishes to assign to each his right,'[8]—and thus they assumed the existence of a system of rights which positive law does not create. Or the rights which human law does not create could be conceived as resting on a higher law, the law of nature itself.

What was this 'natural law' and what was its content? The Roman lawyers and philosophers had given various interpretations, and the medieval scholars inherited their perplexities. Underlying all the definitions was the thought that natural law was more universal in its validity than the civil, or positive, law of individual states,[9] and that, in Cicero's phrase, it was the product 'not of opinion' but of 'a certain innate force.'[10] To Cicero, this force was the reason native to all men which grasped the rational harmonies of the universe itself and embodied them in changeless principles for the guidance of all human life. Similarly, the second-century jurist Gaius defined natural law as 'what natural reason has established among all men.'[11] Starting from this approach, it was possible to see in propositions that satisfied a taste for symmetry the very laws of nature itself. It was also possible—and here

7

dispute began—to assume that one could find natural law by gathering together all those legal relations which seemed to appear in the law of every human society. The Roman lawyers noticed many such uniformities and grouped them under the title *jus gentium*—the law of peoples—and Gaius thought that this law of peoples was the same as natural law. By this test, the right to acquire property by taking possession of things without an owner, the right to make slaves of prisoners, and slavery in general became institutions of natural law;[12] and the same dignity might be applied to Hermogenian's longer list of *jus gentium* institutions: 'By this law of peoples wars were introduced, nations separated, kingdoms founded, lordships distinguished, the boundaries of lands marked out, buildings erected, commerce, buying, selling, leasing, hiring, and mortgaging instituted—with the exception of some things which were introduced by civil law.'[13]

But it was also possible to distinguish between these uniformities of organized human society and natural law itself. The innate force which produced natural law might be identified, as Ulpian in the third century identified it, with the natural instincts of animals, of whom man is one. The law 'which nature has taught all animals' would include 'the union of male and female . . . , the procreation and nurture of the young'[14]; slavery, sanctioned by the conventional law of peoples, must be contrasted with the freedom of the instinctive natural law.[15]

Another distinction between natural law and the law of peoples was born of Seneca's dream of a primitive golden age and of a natural man, stripped of all the distinctions and artificialities of organized life, possessed of no property, no rights over his fellows, only the dignity of a rational and moral soul.[16] The Stoic's dream fitted the Christian theory of the age of innocence which preceded the Fall of Man, and the early Fathers of the church elaborated the distinction between the natural-law principles that would have guided the lives of sinless men and the law of peoples which developed after the Fall to meet the unhappy fact of human imperfection. 'The common possession of all things and the one liberty of all men'[17] were contrasted with the *jus gentium* institutions of government, property, and slavery; and thus a fourth definition of natural law was prepared for the confusion of the medieval mind.

To these four definitions of natural law Gratian added yet a fifth, when he identified natural law with divine law and thus with the precepts of the Holy Scriptures. This definition substituted for reason or instinct a series of objective—and not always mutually compatible—commands.

Scholars of the twelfth and thirteenth centuries were thus at once confronted with the problem of listing and analysing the various senses in which the term 'natural law' might be used. The civilists scarcely went further,[18] but the canonists who glossed the *Decretum* made some effort to choose among the varying definitions or to reconcile one with another, while the theologians tried to adjust the concept of natural law to their broader view of the universe.

The very nature of the canonists' material made Ulpian's definition uninteresting to them; the instincts of animals seemed to them no promising basis for morality or law; for them, the most important foundation of right was the rationality that distinguished man from the brute beasts, modifying and restraining the impulses of his lower nature. But they were inhibited from a full analysis of the relation between natural law and human reason by the force of Gratian's identification of natural law with Scriptural commands. Several of the decretists forbore to choose between natural law as natural reason and natural law as God's command; Rufinus, however, with some ingenuity explained the Mosaic and Evangelic law as an external substitute for the internal light of reason, which was clouded, though not quite extinguished, by the appearance of sin.[19] In searching the Scriptures for the essential elements of divine law, the canonists moved toward consistency by making a distinction between the 'moral' precepts of the Scriptures, which had eternal validity, and the 'mystic' or ceremonial precepts, which applied only to particular historical settings. Later canonists recognized the possibility of change even in some precepts of the moral law.

The theologians of the same period, owing no special courtesies to Gratian, took their stand firmly on the idea of natural law as innate in man himself and thus were able to explore its place in the human mind. William of Auxerre opened a promising line of thought when he compared the first principles of natural law with the first principles which guide the operations of 'the speculative reason'; both alike were directly known, immutable, independent of sense-experience. This idea, further developed by Albert the Great, was to be elaborately set forth by Aquinas. But while the theologians were even more eager than the

9

canonists to tie natural law to human reason, their richer analysis of the place of man in the universe enabled them to find room for Ulpian's definition as well. For William of Auxerre, the first principles of natural law included principles of good for the three levels of man's nature: for man as substance, for man as animal, for man as human—that is, as a rational creature. Alexander of Hales saw natural law prescribing what is good for man as animal, for man as specifically human, for man as the object of God's grace.[20]

When they turned to examination of the content of natural law, canonists and theologians alike were confronted by a problem with which earlier thought had already grappled: the problem of the relationship between the principles appropriate to a state of innocence and the present institutions of men. Such a relationship must be found, unless one was willing to say that natural law had been left behind in the Garden of Eden, and that the universally prevalent institutions of government and property were opposed to nature and therefore bad. Stoic and patristic thought had refused to accept this conclusion. It was thus driven unavoidably to the alternative solution of the problem: that some at least of the precepts of natural law were changed by the appearance of sin in the world, and that natural law now sanctioned, as expedient to sinful men, institutions that it would not have sanctioned had men continued in perfection.

The institutions of the *jus gentium*, in Seneca's thought, were conventional and artificial; they were unnatural in that they were not based on man's primitive innocent nature. But they could not be directly contrary to natural law, since they sprang from man's rational and moral nature. The Fathers were able to take over this theory. Natural law could apply directly only to man before the Fall, but sinful man needed a different system, a system of restraints. Whether this conventional social system which was 'the penalty and remedy for sin' was in itself evil, they disagreed; but most of them thought that coercive government, private property, slavery, and so forth were good institutions approved by God for the discipline of His erring children, and therefore could not be flatly contradictory to natural law, since natural law was God's law too.

Rufinus met the same problem by dividing natural law into eternal and varying precepts. The commands and prohibitions of natural law always applied; but natural law also contained precepts which simply pointed out what was expedient under varying circumstances. Thus, as circumstances changed with the Fall, what had been expedient once was expedient no longer; and the law of peoples made by man after the Fall was inspired by this change in the variable part of natural law. Theologians offered other solutions. Natural law, said Alexander of Hales, is immutable in itself, variable in its applications. 'Even as the art of medicine often dictates that wine is healthful, and the same art denies wine to the sick man, so natural law says that to a healthy nature all things are common and that they ought to be so, and yet the same natural law will give property to a sick nature.'[21] Albert the Great saw a variety of rules for different situations flowing from the first principles of natural law. Slavery, for instance, was not in nature *per se*; it was the result of sin; but the justification of slavery could be traced to the immutable natural-law principle that the sinner must be punished; similarly, natural reason commanded common property for innocence, private property for sin.[22] Thus medieval scholars came to terms with the idea that changing circumstances might demand changing institutions, and associated the notion of expediency with a doctrine of fundamental law. The flexibility of medieval natural-law theory, which contrasts sharply with the rigidity of natural law in eighteenth-century thought, can be directly traced to the challenge of this fundamental problem.[23]

The great medieval systematization of natural-law theory was, of course, Aquinas's masterly treatise in his *Summa Theologiae*. Here traditions used by previous scholars were organized and harmonized within themselves and firmly woven into the pattern of an entire philosophical system. Here we have a clear-cut classification of law into its four great branches: the eternal law, which is God's plan for the governing of the whole universe to its ultimate ends; natural law, which is the rational human apprehension of those principles of the eternal law that concern human nature and its natural ends; human law, which is the detailed application of these natural-law principles by man to specific questions; and divine law, which is a supplement to natural law, known by revelation rather than by reason, composed of the principles appropriate to man's search for supernatural beatitude.

This classification provided a skeleton for articulating the natural-law tradition with Aristotelian metaphysics. Basic to that metaphysics was the idea that the supreme good, the final cause, of every member of a species was the fulfilment of the capacities inherent in its species. In Aquinas's theory the idea of the multiple goal to which the universe is ordained and of the paths by which each species may attain its goal is the eternal law of God. But, among species, there is a sharp cleavage in the means by which the eternal law is fulfilled. Irrational beings are passive creatures of the law: they move toward self-fulfilment under the impetus of forces acting in them and upon them, which they do not understand and in which they have no choice. But man, the rational animal, knows his own end and the first principles directing him to that end. It is his responsibility to shape his own life rationally in accordance with those principles. 'And this participation of the rational creature in the eternal law is called natural law.'

As Aquinas stated the self-evident first principles of natural law, it is obvious that for him natural law had become a system of norms rather than a group of specific rules. It defined the goals to which human institutions were ordained and by which they must be measured, but it did not prescribe the means by which those goals might be reached.[24] This does not mean that natural law had lost all definite content. The norms expressed in natural law were conceived as specific, permanent, and universally valid for the judgment of human institutions because they were rooted in the specific, permanent, and universal tendencies which scholastic philosophy conceived to be characteristic of human nature itself. But, as Aquinas saw, this definition of natural law logically reduced all specific rules to an ancillary position.

Thus the institutions of the *jus gentium* appeared in Aquinas's system neither as identical with natural law nor as contrasted with it but as 'conclusions' drawn from the premises of natural law—secondary principles added by human reason to natural law because of their demonstrable usefulness in fulfilling its general ends. As secondary conclusions, they partook to some extent of the variability of specific circumstances, and thus, although they were generally valid as means to the constant ends which natural law proclaimed, there would be exceptional circumstances in which their usefulness would fail. By eliminating from his system any definition of natural law as the law which ruled the state of innocence, Aquinas was able to maintain the immutability of natural law.[25]

No other philosopher of the Middle Ages wrote so elaborate a treatise on law as that of Aquinas, and those who did discuss legal theory at some length did not directly borrow all his solutions to the problems involved. Aegidius Romanus, for instance, followed him in equating natural law with the constant norms of human nature; but Aegidius advocated a different terminology, in which natural law in the broad sense was subdivided into the law of peoples, the law of animals, and a third branch which seemed to him particularly to deserve the name of natural law—these three divisions corresponding respectively to the norms of man as human, as animal, and as substance. Aegidius seems to have regarded property, contracts, and so forth as following directly from man's human nature, although initiated by human ingenuity, and thus to occupy the same intermediate position between positive and natural law as Aquinas had assigned to them as 'conclusions' from the first principles of natural law. His difference from Aquinas was rather a difference of terminology than of essential meaning.

Minds less steeped in Aristotelianism, more responsive to the pressure of earlier interpretations, found it hard to accept such a system. The patristic definition of natural law as the law which had applied before the Fall continued to echo in later writings, and with this went the traditional treatment of the law of peoples as a law fabricated by men in response to the fact of sin, whose precepts significantly departed from those which had governed man's vanished innocence. The lingering of this definition had some importance. No medieval writer suggested as remotely possible or desirable a general return to paradisal anarchy and communism. But the doctrine of the original freedom of man buttressed resistance to despotism and, in the hands of Nicholas of Cusa, ultimately flowered into the principle that no coercive government could be legitimate unless based on the consent of the subjects.[26] The doctrine that all property had once been held in common was generally transmuted into the principle of communion of goods in time of necessity, while the Spiritual Franciscans gave it a special application in their argument that, while ownership might be appropriate to sinful men, a primitive abnegation of proprietary rights should characterize those who had devoted themselves to the religious life. Finally, the contrast between nature and convention could be used to throw a faint bar sinister upon secular titles to property and power—a flaw of which the church, securely resting on the revealed law of God, could safely claim to be the beneficiary.[27]

Far more important in the political thought of the Middle Ages was that broader definition that equated natural law with the prescriptions of reason. The most interesting example of the potentialities of this approach is found in the natural-law theory of William of Occam.[28] His first two definitions of natural law echoed old traditions. In one sense, natural law was composed of a list of immutable and specific dictates of natural reason.[29] In a second sense, it was the law that ought to be followed by men who used 'natural equity alone, without any human custom or statute'—the law of the Garden of Eden, no longer binding on mankind. But there was a third kind of natural law, developed by inference: a body of fluent principles, changing with changing circumstances, and constant only in that all were shaped by reason for the same unwavering end, the common utility of men. The rules of this third kind of natural law, Occam said, might be set aside through the consent of those whose interests were protected by them. Thus, although they had the cogency of their reasonableness, they were not so deeply rooted in necessary right as were the rules in the first category of natural law.

Occam defined the *jus gentium* as the law 'proper to the whole community of mortals' and placed it between natural law and the civil laws 'of emperors and other persons and of particular countries.' When he used the term *jus gentium*, Occam sometimes seems to have been thinking of the concrete system of legal institutions traditionally classified as belonging to it; at other times, he seems to have been thinking of the rational principles which these institutions embodied, and with this latter emphasis the category of *jus gentium* merged into 'natural law in the third sense.' At any rate, Occam spoke of the *jus gentium* as a law 'which in a sense is natural and in a sense human or positive.'[30] It was not for him what it was for Aquinas, a series of direct and inescapable and only exceptionally invalid deductions from natural law, but rather an extension of natural law in which human agreement had played a considerable part.[31] He 'really regards *ius gentium* much more as human law than as natural law.'[32] His interpretation allowed an unlimited possibility of variation, in accordance with circumstances, to the rules of the law of peoples, and made their binding power finally contingent on the consent of 'the whole community of mortals.'

But Occam was by no means a positivist. Reason was for him at least as necessary as consent to the making and unmaking of the *jus gentium*. The universality of its acceptance was as much the consequence as the cause of its binding power; for the fact that 'all peoples, and particularly all rational peoples, use such law'[33] must be the result of its intrinsic rationality and usefulness. When he examined the possibility of change in the *jus gentium*, his procedure shows that he regarded such change as legitimized not by the arbitrary fiat of men's wills but by an actual change in the circumstances to which those wills responded. This is admirably illustrated in his handling of the vexed question of universal empire.[34]

The appeal to natural law or evident reason runs through all Occam's political writings. In his hands, traditional principles of natural law were turned to novel uses. His assumption that reason and revelation were harmonized in the will of God enabled him to apply reason to the interpretation of divine law and test the institutions of the church by rational principles. He boldly justified the deposition of a criminous and incorrigible pope through the argument that natural reason dictated the amputation of a hopelessly diseased and ineffective member for the sake of the body's health[35]; the emperor's right to intervene in papal elections, if pope and cardinals were notorious heretics, was ingeniously traced to the natural-law principle that every community could elect its own superior, a principle which reposed a latent right of election in the clergy and people of Rome, including the emperor as an indispensable member of the citizen body.[36]

While no one, perhaps, equalled Occam in the daring and subtlety with which standards of natural reason were applied to vexed questions, the belief in the existence of fundamental natural standards of legal right was the visible or concealed warp of all the political theorizing of the Middle Ages.[37] Natural law could be applied to all questions left open by the silence or ambiguity of revelation: 'it might furnish a rule where no rule had been declared, or might guide interpretation where the application of the rule was not certain.'[38] The doctrine that natural law prescribed whatever reason revealed as just or as beneficial to human ends was constantly applied by the canonists in their interpretation of the law of the church and in their resolution of conflicting laws. Civilists appealed to natural law as they faced the task of harmonizing the Roman code and adapting it to the medieval scene. A distaste for canonist terminology induced the English framers of the common law before the Reformation to avoid references to the law of nature; but, as Pollock points out,[39] the common-law concept of 'reasonableness' played precisely the same role and was part of the same structure of ideas.

The assumption that what reason could prove to be useful was *ipso facto* blessed by nature itself supported political philosophers in their search for the principles of legitimate government; with its help they surmounted or reinterpreted claims based on fiat or tradition. In particular, the appeal to reason provided the basis for the doctrine, widely maintained, that in cases where the rules of positive law conflicted with the ends they were meant to serve they should be set aside, no matter what authority of custom or command was thereby flouted. For many minds the rational proof that government or property was necessary to human welfare seemed sufficient evidence of its rightful independence from the determinations of the church, and natural law in turn protected property from government even while it provided a basis for the slowly-developing doctrine of expropriation or taxation on behalf of the common good. Natural reason supported the slow emergence of a clear-cut royal absolutism from the maze of traditional lordships which confused the early medieval scene; but political theorists also learned to argue that by the law of peoples all authority ultimately came from popular consent. Finally, in the conciliar struggle, the principles which reason had composed for temporal affairs were turned upon the sacred structure of the church.[40]

To the extent that natural law was equated with the reasonable and the useful it lost, of course, a definite, permanent content of its own; for in the name of reason and utility a variety of conflicting principles could be defended. It was 'inevitable that the appeal to the Law of Nature . . . should often become indistinguishable . . . from a pretty frank appeal to expediency.'[41] On the other hand, 'when the authority of natural law was universally allowed, every disputant strove to make out that it was on his side. But such an endeavour would have been idle if the Law of Nature had meant nothing but individual opinions.'[42] Only the belief that an objective common standard existed in nature could have freed medieval dispute from the sterility and confusion of appeals to custom and precedent. And even those controversialists who were most sharply opposed had so many premises in common that their debates never sounded like the clash of discordant systems, but like a range of increasingly complex variations on a single theme; thus medieval men, even when they disagreed on specific questions of right, were not led thereby to doubt the existence of common norms. That underlying unity of key was of course possible only because medieval minds (like modern minds) easily assumed the intrinsic rationality of many principles which in fact they simply borrowed from authority: phrases from the Bible, the *Corpus Juris*, and Aristotle,[43] asserted as rules of natural law, came to be persistent themes for a variety of thinkers, and those who challenged conclusions drawn from them were obliged to proceed to solution by distinction rather than by denial of the premise.

It has frequently been claimed that the thought of Marsiglio of Padua decisively broke with this whole natural-law tradition. He has been called a 'positivist'[44] and a 'voluntarist' and compared with Hobbes and Austin.[45] Marsiglio had, it would seem, no regular training in law or in theology. His interest in legal theory was motivated directly by his eagerness to destroy the claim of the canon law to legal status. He was accordingly not much interested in the substantive content of law or its substantive origins; to him the most important element of law was formal: its enactment by an authoritative will, which could embody 'true concepts of justice and civil good' in the form of a coercive command. His rather amateurish formalism was perhaps re-enforced by the influence of Averroist thought, with its fundamental doubt as to whether there necessarily existed an ultimate harmony between the spheres of reason and of revelation; and it was perhaps impossible for him to conceive such a structure as the Thomist pattern of the relationships between eternal, divine, natural, and human law. It is, however, scarcely accurate to say that his conception of law was 'certainly the exact reverse of the Thomist conception.'[46] His definition of law 'in its most proper sense' was not purely formal: not merely 'the proper form: namely, a coercive command of observance,' but also 'the proper condition: namely, a proper and true ordination of just things' were essential to perfect law. Thus, although he had no theory to explain what such norms might be or whence derived, and though he did not regard such norms as themselves inherently law, he shared the general medieval belief in the existence of objective, rational norms behind positive law, and the general medieval belief that the making of positive law was essentially a rational process.

Every scheme of classification inherited by the medieval scholars contrasted with the universally valid law of nature a category of law which varied from one country to another and rested immediately on human determinations. The Roman jurists referred to this kind of law as civil law; and the *jus civile* of Gaius and Ulpian was easily identified with the 'positive right' of Aristotle and with the 'human law' which Isidore contrasted with divine law.

The relation of positive to natural law was a complex one. On the one hand, it was generally agreed that positive law was in some way derived from natural law; that its specific rules were an application and an embodiment of more abstract principles. This was the Stoic conception of positive law, transmitted by the Roman jurists and the church Fathers. It was easily harmonized with Aristotle's teachings.[47] Thus medieval thought emphasized the role of reason in the making of law. 'Law consists of reason,' said the *Decretum*, quoting Isidore. 'It makes no difference whether it consists of writing or reason, since it is reason that recommends law.' 'Law is a certain ordinance of reason . . . ,' said Aquinas. 'It is necessary that the will be regulated by some reason in regard to the things that are commanded, if volition is to have the character of law.' Perfect law, said Marsiglio, necessarily involves 'a true concept of justice and civil good.'

On the other hand, the embodiment of natural law in civil codes was no mere process of conclusion from premises. Much must be added, much adjusted, and the resulting laws might in certain instances deviate widely from the prescriptions of reason and equity. Aquinas defined the relationship with his usual care. Simple deduction, he thought, added the secondary rules of the law of peoples to the primary rules of natural law itself[48]; but the civil law proceeded from natural law by particularization—as the craftsman particularizes the general idea of *house* in his plans for a specific house. 'For instance, the law of nature holds that he who sins is punished; but the specific penalty that he should undergo is a particular determination of the law of nature.'[49] Aegidius compared the relation of positive and natural law to the relation between speech, which is natural to all men, and language, which is a matter of choice. 'Positive right,' he said, 'begins where natural right ends'; it 'presupposes natural right even as those things that are of art presuppose those things that are of nature.' But, as Aristotle said, the prescriptions of positive right were matters of indifference until they had been enacted. Like Aquinas, he cited the determination of specific penalties as an illustration.

Thus the framing of positive laws involved an element of discretion. The general tendency of such laws was fixed by natural law, but there was always a possibility of choice among means to ends; moreover, laws must be adapted to the circumstances to which they were applied. In Isidore's often-quoted words, law should be not only 'virtuous, just, necessary, useful' but also 'possible according to nature and the custom of the country' and 'suitable to time and place.'[50] The particularization of natural law was a rational process, but a synthetic and creative one. The reason of the legislator did not simply move from one abstraction to another; it moved from the general to the particular, and constructed a specific rule in the light of specific facts. In this sense, positive law was 'made' rather than 'found'; legislation was not a science, but an art; but positive law was not 'made' by arbitrary will in the modern, Austinian sense.

It was generally recognized that positive law, so much more specific in its content than natural law, could not be expected to apply to all situations with equal justice. Aristotle had pointed this out, and had shown that in the enforcement of law the judge must often return to first principles, supplementing positive law with equity.[51] Roman magistrates had developed the recourse to equity into a regularized procedure. The 'failure' of positive law in many instances was conspicuously forced on medieval attention through the fact that medieval laws were in general far more detailed than modern laws, and constantly needed flexible interpretation in order to prevent obvious injustices. Aquinas found a theoretical explanation for this inevitable flaw in the validity of positive law; and medieval thinkers were virtually unanimous in drawing the practical conclusion that in those exceptional cases where the literal enforcement of positive laws would clash with natural right the laws enjoyed no force. Thus the dispensing power appeared to medieval minds as an essential part of judicial authority; and many thinkers, including Aquinas, also recognized a right of private individuals to violate the letter of the law in emergency situations.

Other elements appeared in the definition of law. Medieval writers agreed that law was focused on the *common* utility; it was not the instrument of the ruler's private advantage, nor even of the welfare or moral development of different individuals as such. Moreover, as Aquinas in particular pointed out, law must be made known if it was to serve as a measure of human actions; as natural law was promulgated by God through being instilled into the minds of all men, so human law needed formal promulgation. Finally, the idea of coercive force was inseparable from the idea of law. For Aquinas, coercive force was a precondition of the utility of law; thus, although it does not appear immediately in his definition of law, it is logically a part of it. Marsiglio made the idea of coercive force a *sine qua non* in his working definition of law: 'not all true concepts of justice and civil good are laws, unless a coercive command concerning their observance has been given, or unless they have been expressed in the form of a command.'[52] This emphasis on the coercive character of true law became the premise of much of Marsiglio's most original thought, since it led ultimately to his denial of the character of law to the whole system of church law except that which had been endorsed by the politically-organized community. But what was unique in Marsiglio was his insistence that coercive force on earth was the monopoly of the political community. He was not far from Aquinas and the whole medieval scholarly tradition in regarding coercion as an essential aspect of human law.

All these considerations—the discretionary element involved in particularization, the social purpose of law, the necessity of its formal promulgation, and its coercive character—supported a conclusion sharply diverse from early medieval presuppositions: the conclusion that human law must be produced by a will endowed with public authority. The wisdom of private minds could not make law, nor could age-old tradition; reason was the metal of which law was made, the passage of time would help to make it familiar currency, but it must be stamped with the seal of authoritative will.

The idea that human law always proceeded from an authoritative will was, of course, familiar to the civilists from the beginning, since it was one of the assumptions of Roman jurisprudence, and innumerable phrases of the *Corpus Juris* led the civilists always to stress the authoritarian conception of the origin of law. Custom itself, they assumed, proceeded from a legislative will in the people, and the only question was whether the will of the people was able to make law without the emperor's at least tacit approval. Gratian, on the other hand, had set the canonists off on a different track by incorporating in the

Decretum Isidore's identification of human law with custom, and by his assumption that only the accident of writing distinguished *constitutio* from *consuetudo*. Here was a direct reflection of the naive medieval attitude. But later canonists turned away from the implication of this identification. For various reasons, they retained a special tenderness toward long-established custom, but like the civilists they defined custom itself as the product of the popular will and construed the antiquity of custom as simply an index to the existence of a public intention to create customary law.[53] With less sharpness of concept, writers on political theory tended also to speak of custom as made by the people. Aquinas pointed out that the reason and will of men could be expressed by deeds as well as by words, and interpreted custom as such an expression.

Medieval theorists differed widely in their answers as to the location of the will that could make law. Certain elements in the actual and academic environments made the prince the obvious claimant for the position. In the medieval kingdom, up to the development of estates, the people enjoyed no formal organ for expressing a legislative intention, while the king appeared as the authoritative promulgator of custom and as the maker of ordinances which derived their force solely from his authority. In the contemporary church a more matured monarchic legislation was appearing, although, even as the king was hemmed in by custom, so the pope was supposedly hemmed in by a body of church law which was considered immutable[54]; and the church knew varieties of law from other sources—local and general customs, and the enactments of general councils over which the pope presided. Again, the *Corpus Juris Civilis* presented the emperor as the supreme source of law—basing his right, however, on the legal fiction that the Roman people had originally possessed complete legislative authority but for reasons of expediency had concentrated this authority in various hands and finally in those of the emperor. A frequently-quoted sentence from the *Digest* summed up the situation: 'What has pleased the prince has the force of law, since by the *lex regia* which was enacted concerning his empire the people confers upon him all its authority and power.'[55] Finally, as political theory developed, appreciation of the need for unity of will in government was a factor obviously recommending the concentration of legislative authority in the prince. And the will of the prince alone seemed able to guarantee the flexibility of adjustment to changing conditions which abstract theory and practical experience both indicated as desirable in law. Aristotle himself, although the balance of his argument swung in favour of a popular legislature, had underlined the advantage of the flexibility which a single will could give, and had referred to a monarch as 'a living law.'[56]

The prince's monopoly of secular legislative authority was maintained by a group of civilist lawyers, first for the emperor, later for other kings who were 'emperors in their own kingdoms.' It was defended in general terms by the thirteenth-century publicist Aegidius Romanus and strongly stated for the emperor by the fifteenth-century treatise of Aeneas Sylvius.[57] An important group of canon lawyers and ecclesiastical publicists of the fourteenth century gave the pope the same position, construing custom as resting on his permission and interpreting the validity of conciliar decrees as due to his presidency of the council. Aquinas offered an alternative: 'To establish law belongs either to the whole people, or to the public person who has the care of the whole people.'[58] While he did not choose decisively between ruler and community as the holder of legislative power, it seems evident from the rest of his writing that he thought of the prince as the normal maker of positive law in his own time.[59] Explaining custom as popular legislation, he found that its validity must depend on the assumed consent of the ruler in the states in which the ruler controlled the legislative power.

The argument by which Aquinas demonstrated that the right to choose decisively among the prescriptions of reason must be reposed in the will that controlled the public instruments of coercion is in sharp contrast with our own political thinking. We sharply distinguish between the 'three branches' of government, and tend to construe the executive and judicial branches as servants to the legislative branch. For Aquinas the authority to formulate laws and the authority to enforce them were inseparable; and this fusion was the natural consequence of the difference between his conception of legislation and ours. When legislation is conceived as a choice made not by an arbitrary will, but by a will governed by a higher law, the modern distinction between legislative and judicial activity tends to disappear. Legislation appears as a phase of jurisdiction; the authority to apply the law easily includes the authority to define it. The prince has 'the care of the multitude' and a general power to do whatever is necessary for the care of the multitude. And *because* he has power, his rational decisions on the best means of attaining the common good differ from the similar decisions of private persons in being law.[60]

The range of positive law subject to legislative control is not clear in the theory of Aquinas or that of Aegidius. It is possible that both were thinking only of the sphere of legislation which was generally submitted to the medieval king: roughly, that of administration and policy, procedural and penal law. It may be significant that Aquinas, copied by Aegidius, cited the definition of penalties as his example of particularization. But this may be an accident. If Aquinas actually meant to limit the ruler's control over human law to the area controlled by the medieval king, there would seem to be no place at all in his system for the whole body of substantive law, including the law of real property, which medieval practice immunized from legislative control as changeless custom. He could scarcely have assumed that all this law was included in his *jus gentium*; simple deduction from natural law could scarcely have produced rules so various and so detailed. If, as seems more likely, he thought of this kind of law as part of 'the custom of the country,' then, as we shall see, he specifically admitted it to the possibility of cautious legislative change. The conclusion seems inescapable that in his system the boundary between the temporary executive order and 'the law' itself disappeared, and that his prince, although perhaps chiefly interested in crime, enjoyed a potential legislative control over the entire area of human law. Aegidius's case is less clear; while he said flatly that the king 'is above positive law because he constitutes it by his authority,' he granted that some positive law might be above the ruler 'not in proportion as it is positive, but in proportion as there is preserved in it the virtue of natural law.'[61] I incline to class him with Aquinas; but his discussion is too vague to support a decisive interpretation.

Other elements in the background of medieval thought furthered the idea that an ultimate legislative authority rested in the people, which they might exercise either apart from the prince or in combination with him. As we have seen, the customary law, regarded as the law *par excellence* by the common man, was conceived as the law of the community as a whole; and though originally there was no notion that such law had been deliberately *made* by the community, the *finding* of custom by popular representatives could easily shade into a public right to confirm or amend, and this in turn would be only a short step from a public right to make and abrogate. When the public organized itself into estates taking a regularized part in the formulation of law, the path was opened for an ultimate recognition that these representative bodies were actually making the law that they claimed to find. And even before the maturation of the estates, examples of corporate legislation had appeared. The rules of the guild and the university, the constitutions and codes of the town acquainted medieval men with the cooperative making of laws, and demonstrated that unity of legislative decision need not be rooted in the single will of a ruler.

In the traditions and institutions of the church, in spite of its monarchic tendency, there was much that kept alive the idea of a legislating people. Gratian's famous statement that 'laws are instituted when they are promulgated, they are confirmed when they are approved by the custom of the users' recognized a popular role in the validation of law. The canon law included a mass of general and local custom and of the enactments of representative councils, whose status as law would be hard to explain if the legislative power were construed as the monopoly of the pope. Gratian himself accepted custom as valid law only in the absence of papal or conciliar enactments, but later canonists were kinder. Gregory IX allowed a rational custom, fulfilling certain technical requirements, to abrogate a general church law; Boniface VIII ruled that old customs, if rational, remained valid against new papal decrees unless their abrogation was explictly declared; these papal pronouncements became the basis of the general canonist position. This favourable attitude toward custom was rather a concession to local diversity than to a theory of popular supremacy: in each case, the consent of the pope was assumed.[62] Yet here were materials which could be used, and were used during the conciliar movement, to support the idea of popular participation in the making even of church law.

As we have seen, civilist studies introduced the idea that the Roman people had originally enjoyed the legislative authority which the emperor later exercised by their grant. The civilists differed as to whether this grant was revocable and as to whether the people remained possessed of a residual authority which they could express in the making of custom with legal validity; all agreed that custom might supplement or support imperial legislation, but the majority argued that custom which clashed with the emperor's decree could have validity only through the emperor's tacit consent.[63] At all events, civilist theory presented the *populus Romanus* as the original source of the Roman law; and, as the medieval theory of the law of peoples took form, the Roman experience could be construed as a single instance of a general principle. 'By the law of peoples . . . ,' Hermogenian had said, 'kingdoms were founded. . . .' On the basis of this phrase in particular there developed in the later Middle Ages the conception of the law of peoples as a body of pre-governmental law, stemming from the people themselves, from which law the authority of kings was itself derived and which also controlled and safeguarded private property, contracts, constitutions, and the rules of international relations. Thus the *jus gentium* was assimilated to the traditional customary law of the Middle Ages, and this scholars' conception, which begins to appear in Occam's writings, led to a view of divided legislative authority not unlike that which appeared in the actual medieval kingdom, if one assumed that in founding kingdoms the people had granted their prince only a restricted right of legislation, encasing him in a body of its own law which his will could not affect.

Two other important influences shaped the medieval theories of popular participation in legislation. Aristotle's defence of cooperative judgment[64] offered an important argument from the point of view of expediency; and, when the coercive aspect of law was stressed, it could be argued that 'since by nature all are free,' men could not be submitted to such coercion save through their own consent. The latter argument was to be used particularly by Nicholas of Cusa.

The most vigorous assertion of the legislative right of the community was that presented in the *Defensor Pacis*. More precisely, its thesis was that the monopoly of all human legislative authority was originally vested in the 'more weighty part' (*valentior pars*) of the community organized as 'the legislator.' An elected committee of 'prudent and expert' men should formulate the laws to be submitted to the legislator for ratification; or the legislator might delegate its own authority to one man or a smaller group. But no valid law, ecclesiastical or temporal, could be made except by virtue of the ultimate authority of the community of citizens, however that authority might, in practice, be exercised.

25

A particular interest attaches to the arguments by which Marsiglio, so often regarded as 'the first modern man,'[65] supported his thesis. He did not appeal to the natural right of each individual to participate in the determining of his own destiny; the right which he asserted was the right of a corporate group in which the 'quality' (the word seems to have connoted both status and personal characteristics) of different members gave different weights to their voices; and that right was mainly derived, with the help of Aristotle, from practical considerations. Such a legislator was most likely to produce the most reasonable, most just, and most enforceable laws. The Aristotelian idea that 'the state is a community of free men' and a variant of the Roman-law maxim that what touched all should be approved by all do indeed appear in Marsiglio's discussion; but they are given no basic significance: freedom is treated as a fact affecting the probability of obedience; the desirability of consensus on common concerns is defended as a means of securing 'what is beneficial.' Marsiglio's answers to possible objections show the same practical bias. To the argument that the depraved and ignorant members of the community might produce unwise and unjust laws, he answered that it was for that very reason that unanimity was not demanded but the voice of the 'more weighty part' taken as the voice of the community—men so depraved as to seek the evil rather than the good of the state ought to be considered slaves rather than citizens and not counted. However, the natural impetus of men toward civil life guaranteed that most men would not be depraved nor stupid—they would be, at any rate, wise enough to judge and to suggest modifications of laws originally drafted by the more expert. Marsiglio was also concerned over the problem of securing agreement in a large group and admitted that unity of opinion was more easily secured among a few than among many; but he pointed out that the agreement of the few might be far from agreement on the *common* good, and thus the untaught multitude might be a useful check on the learned minority.[66]

Ironically enough, in view of Marsiglio's emphasis on coercive authority as essential to the making of law, his case included no explanation of how or why the political community, and only the political community, should happen to have coercive authority; that premise was simply assumed. The arguments that he used tended to demonstrate the superior rationality and justice of the collective mind rather than the superior force of the collective will. Such arguments are convincing only if they are used, as Aristotle originally used them, to support an actual, active participation of the community in the legislative process.[67] This consideration raises the question of the actual role which the legislator of the *Defensor Pacis* was expected to play; and this, in turn, unfortunately raises the question of the authorship of the *Defensor Pacis*.

We have been assuming, in common with the preponderance of scholarly opinion, including that of the two modern editors of the treatise, that the whole of the *Defensor Pacis* was substantially the work of Marsiglio of Padua. John of Jandun, who shared both the papal censures and the imperial favours that resulted from its writing, doubtless had some share in the authorship, but most modern scholars feel that it is impossible to define his contribution precisely, unless it is apparent in some particular passages where Averroist thought is conspicuous, and that, at all events, his contribution was small; but it has been argued that the greater part of *dictio* 1—that is, the general theory of political institutions—was originally written by him, and merely adapted by Marsiglio to serve as an introduction to the theory of the church which is the theme of *dictio* 2.[68]

One of the arguments for assigning the disputed section to the Italian Marsiglio has been the apparently close parallels between the institutions there described and the structures and practices of contemporary Italian communes.[69] If one takes these at their face value, one readily comes to the conclusion that, while writing this section, the chief influence on the author, aside from his reading of Aristotle, was his experience of Italy. In that case, the author must be Marsiglio, and the legislator of *dictio* 1 may plausibly be taken to correspond to the popular assembly of the Italian communes, which was not merely a constituent and elective body, but also gave consent to the making and modifying of codes of very specific law, by which its rulers were supposed to be rather narrowly bound. On the other hand, if John of Jandun was the author of these chapters, the apparent parallels to Italian institutions must be discounted or traced to other sources, and the legislator may be reinterpreted as equivalent to the constituent *populus* of the transalpine kingdom, which did not itself exercise a legislative authority except as it might be supposed to have established in the remote past a framework of fundamental law and to have constituted the kings who would thenceforth act, with wide discretion, on its behalf.[70]

No solution that has yet been proposed for the question of authorship is entirely satisfactory, but with some discomfort I range myself among those who feel that the weight of the evidence supports Marsiglio's authorship of *dictio* 1 and that the remarkable unity of overall plan and interlocking of detail that bind *dictio* 1 with *dictio* 2 would have been impossible if a single mind had not been dominant in the conception and writing of the entire work. But even if we continue to assume that Marsiglio was responsible for the constitutional theory of *dictio* 1, and that, in describing his legislator, he naturally thought of it in the familiar terms of his own Italian background, we must nevertheless recognize that in the Italian city the role of the people was no more than a shouted approval of laws formulated by a smaller group. The advocacy of actual popular participation in legislation was by no means Marsiglio's primary purpose. His essential interest was in juristic relations rather than in political processes: the one point on which he really insisted was the principle that the politically organized people was fundamentally the source of all legislative authority, and therefore of every kind of authority, regardless of how that authority might, in practice, be delegated or divided. What he needed as preparation for the arguments of *dictio* 2 was a structure of formal principles that could be applied to every variety of state, and in particular to the empire, whose ruler he was to present as juristically equivalent to the legislator itself. Thus, as Scholz says, his concept of the legislator is a many-faceted concept, 'wavering between the notions of an abstract state-personality, of an Italian association of burghers, of the head of a state, and finally of the Christian Emperor as overlord of Christendom.'[71] That, in the course of these metamorphoses, the premises on which the authority of his legislator had originally been based were quietly evaporating he —not unnaturally—did not notice.

In summing up medieval thought on positive law, it is important to point out that while it is perhaps true that no complete theory of legislative sovereignty appeared in the Middle Ages, there were strong tendencies in this direction, which sometimes issued in positions that fell short of that taken by Bodin only in clarity of definition.[72] The scholars' definition of law in terms of reason and will undermined the sway of tradition and opened men's minds to the idea that laws could and should be changed to keep pace with changing conditions and with the growth of human wisdom. Aquinas, who set forth the theory of change in laws, urged with characteristic caution that they be changed only when the advantage to the common good clearly outweighed the damage done by breaking the bonds of established usage; but usage appeared in his system simply as a factor in the utility of law, which the lawgiver must take into consideration, but by which he was by no means bound. The idea that the right to make law carried with it the right to alter and abrogate it ran through all scholarly theory. Marsiglio specified it for his popular legislator; the civilists claimed it for the emperor; the canonists claimed it for the pope. It was agreed that no ruler could bind his successor by his legislation and that no prescriptive rights were finally valid against him in whom the supreme legislative authority was based.

However, no medieval thinker envisaged the abrogation and amendment of substantive law as occurring very frequently. And those who limited the legislative power of the prince by a concrete *jus gentium* or by popular law did not expect that that encircling law would undergo much change. Occam, who perhaps conceived the *jus gentium* more flexibly than any one else, remarked that it could never 'be fully abrogated, but only for a time.'[73] And even while theorists defended legislative change, popular thought remained conservative, preferring that innovation should always wear the mask, at least, of restoration.

No complete theory of legislative sovereignty could appear while theorists thought of legislation as a process controlled and guided by natural law standards and maintained that all positive law could be tested for validity by those standards. It is true that theorists differed widely in their willingness to enforce the higher law against the lower. On the one hand, Aquinas asserted that law which ran counter to reason and justice was a 'perversion of law,' imposing no burden on men's consciences unless for the sake of avoiding scandal; and Occam insisted that 'any civil law whatsoever which is repugnant to divine law or evident reason is not law' and was not to be observed.[74] Such doctrines were logical conclusions from the premises that natural law was the supreme law and that it was generally instilled in human minds. But other thinkers were not always so willing to risk the potential anarchy involved in setting up the private mind as the judge of the validity of law that seemed to clash with reason. Canonists and civilists were quick to disallow mere customs on the grounds of irrationality, but as time went on they increasingly argued that enacted law could be anulled only by a regular magistrate, or perhaps only by the pope or emperor himself, whose law should be presumed to be reasonable. This position did not necessarily involve a full conception of sovereignty, but when the maker of law was presented as its only competent judge, the practical result might be indistinguishable.

Of all medieval writers, Marsiglio perhaps came closest to a theory of sovereignty. He asserted the primacy of law-making over all other expressions of state power; he insisted on the indivisibility of ultimate legislative authority; his legislator was restrained by no laws.[75] One might say that he had the essential elements of a theory of sovereignty; only the theory itself was lacking. Marsiglio had no interest in theoretical definition except as it served his controversial purpose. But, beyond that, he was prevented from developing fully the implications of his most radical ideas by the fact that he was still enmeshed in the rationalist traditions of medieval scholarship. Thus, as we have seen, he did not define law as anything whatever that his legislator chose to command: 'a proper and true ordination of just things' was also essential. He never resolved the duality of his fundamental definition of law —as, in the main stream of medieval thought, a similar duality was resolved by doctrines of the right of resistance and nullification; he did not even say that the decisions of his legislator must be presumed to be just; he simply took it for granted that in a perfect, Christian community they would be just; and he offered no alternative to obedience. One can scarcely, I think, in reading the *Defensor Pacis* avoid the conclusion that Marsiglio did not really leave his legislator free to establish whatever its sovereign will might dictate: its decisions are preordained by reason and defended by syllogisms. The prudent and expert 'find' the law, regarded as 'the science of just and beneficial civil actions.' Thus Marsiglio may, indeed, 'stand at the beginning of the road that leads to Machiavelli,'[76] and to Bodin and Hobbes and Austin; but his feet are still planted on medieval ground.

Later progress along that path was determined by social and political developments which made existing customs increasingly anachronistic and demanded more and more legislation in the interstices of custom or in direct opposition to its provisions. The Protestant Reformation, especially, involved in the countries concerned an overturning of traditional patterns of right so revolutionary that it could only be construed as deliberate change by an authoritative legislator. When toward the end of the sixteenth century Bodin sharply defined the concept of legislative sovereignty, seeing the free making and unmaking of law rather than its enforcement as the prime characteristic of government, political theory was responding to the pressure of facts that had become too conspicuous to be longer concealed under medieval concepts.

Bodin still regarded the legislative sovereign as limited by natural law. But thinkers of succeeding periods gradually transformed the concept of natural law. For the social contract theorists, it appeared as the system of principles that determined the form and powers of the state and bounded it with the natural rights of individuals; it was not expected to guide the decisions of the sovereign within those boundaries. Then the idea of natural law was itself attacked by the relativist and empirical spirit of modern social science; and at the same time, as popular legislatures took the place of kings, intellectual resistance to the notion of arbitrary legislation died away. The way was open for the Austinian definition of law as the mere will of the sovereign.

Yet the medieval ideas of law have played an important part in the modern world. Much of modern law rests on medieval rules. Courts, always interested in the continuity and self-consistency of law—and sometimes hostile to the policies of legislative majorities—have constantly reinterpreted enacted law to conform with the law of the past, and at times have also called on natural law to strengthen their decisions. The social and political teachings of the Catholic Church have continuously rested on the foundations of the natural-law theory constructed by Aquinas and others in the Middle Ages. And throughout the modern centuries common men, stirred to resistance against laws that do not satisfy their sense of right, have justified their resistance in the name of a higher law than any made by man.

Gratian

[Gratian was a monk of a Bolognese convent, where he taught canon law; practically nothing else is known of his life. His *Concordantium Discordantium Canonum*, or *Decretum* (ca. 1148) was by far the most important of twelfth-century attempts to collect and systematize the law of the church. It superseded all previous compilations and enjoyed an immense and continuing prestige; it was the basic text used in the universities for the study of canon law; it was glossed and commented on by illustrious canonists and quoted for innumerable purposes; it came to be regarded as the first part of the *Corpus Juris Canonici*. In form, the *Decretum* is a legal treatise, in which quotations from a wide variety of authorities were pieced together under various headings and interspersed with Gratian's own summaries or comments; where authorities disagreed, Gratian lined them up in opposing groups and attempted a reconciling solution. The following selections are from pt. 1, distinctions 1, 4, and 8.]

DISTINCTION I

GRATIAN: *Mankind is ruled in two ways: namely, by natural law and by customs. The law of nature is that contained in the Law and the Gospels, by which each is ordered to do to another what he wishes to be done to himself, and is prohibited from inflicting on another what he does not wish done to himself. Wherefore Christ said in the Gospel: 'All things whatsoever ye would that men should do unto you, do ye also to them. For this is the law and the prophets.'*

Whence Isidore says (Etymol., bk. 5, [ch. 2]):

CANON I. *Divine laws consist of nature, human laws of customs.*

All laws are either divine or human. The divine laws consist of nature, human laws of customs, and therefore these are different, because different peoples are pleased by different things. 1. Divine law is *fas*; human law is *jus*. To cross through another's field is *fas*, and not *jus*.

GRATIAN: *From the words of this authority it is evidently given to be understood in what divine and human law differ among themselves, since everything that is fas is covered by the name of divine or natural law; and by the name of human law we understand customs written as law and handed down. 1. Moreover, jus is a general name, containing many species under it.*

Whence Isidore says in the same book [ch. 3]:

CANON II. *Jus is the genus, law is its species.*

Jus is the general name; moreover, law is a species of *jus*. *Jus*, moreover, is so called because it is just. Moreover, all *jus* is composed of laws and customs.

CANON III. *What a law* (lex) *is.* [*Ibid.*]

A law is a written decree (*constitutio*).

CANON IV. *What custom* (mos) *is.* [*Ibid.*, and bk. 2, ch. 10.]

Moreover custom (*mos*) is a *consuetudo* of long standing, which, similarly, is derived from customs.

CANON V. *What a custom* (consuetudo) *is.* [*Ibid.*]

A custom is a kind of law instituted by customs, which is accepted as

THE IDEA OF LAW

law when law is lacking. 1. Nor does it make any difference whether it consists of writing or reason, since it is reason that recommends law. 2. Further, if law consists of reason, everything which consists of reason will be law, provided that it is in harmony with religion, is suitable for discipline, and furthers welfare. 3. Moreover, it is called a custom, because it is in common use.

GRATIAN: *Therefore, when it is said, 'it makes no difference whether it consists of writing or reason,' it appears that customary law is partly redacted into writing, partly preserved only by the customs of the users. What is redacted into writing is called a decree or law; but what is not redacted into writing is called by the general name, custom. 1. There is another division of law, as Isidore testifies in the same book [bk. 5, ch. 4], saying as follows:*

CANON VI. *What are the species of law.*

Law is either natural law, or civil law, or the law of peoples.

CANON VII. *What is natural law. [Ibid.]*

Natural law is the law common to all peoples, in that it is everywhere held by the instinct of nature, not by any enactment: as, for instance, the union of man and woman, the generation and rearing of children, the common possession of all things and the one liberty of all men, the acquisition of those things which are taken from air and sky and sea; also, the restitution of an article given in trust or money loaned, and the repelling of force with force. 1. For this, or whatever is similar to this, is never considered unjust, but natural and equitable.

CANON VIII. *What is civil law. [Ibid., ch. 5.]*

Civil law is that which each people or state has established as proper to itself in accordance with a divine or human cause.

CANON IX. *What is the law of peoples. [Ibid., ch. 6.]*

The law of peoples is the occupation of territory, building, fortifying, wars, captivities, slaveries, rights of restoration, alliances of peace, armistices, the inviolability of ambassadors, the prohibition of marriage with an alien. 1. This is called the law of peoples for this reason: that this law is used by nearly all peoples.

DISTINCTION IV

GRATIAN: PART I. *The cause for which laws are made is to curb human wilfulness and to restrain the capacity to harm, as Isidore testifies (bk. 5, ch. 20), saying:*

CANON I. *Wherefore laws are made.*

M.P.I.—3
33

Moreover, laws are made that by fear of them human wilfulness may be curbed, innocence be safe among the wicked, and, among the wicked themselves, the capacity to harm be restrained by the dread of punishment.

GRATIAN: PART II. *Besides this, while laws are being framed, the kind of laws to be framed should be particularly considered, that they may contain in themselves honour, justice, possibility, suitability, and so forth, which Isidore enumerates in the same book [ch. 21], saying:*

CANON II. *What the attributes of law should be.*

Moreover, law will be virtuous, just, possible according to nature and according to the custom of the country, appropriate to time and place, necessary, useful, and of manifest clarity, lest through obscurity it should contain something unsuitable, written not for private advantage, but for the common utility of the citizens.

GRATIAN: PART III. *Therefore, moreover, these things should be considered while the law is being framed, because, when laws have been established, one is no longer free to judge concerning them, but should judge according to them.*

Whence Augustine says in his book Of True Religion [ch. 31]:

CANON III. *The time to judge concerning laws is while they are being framed, not when they have been established.*

In regard to those temporal laws, although men may judge concerning them when they are framing them, yet when they have been framed and confirmed it will not be fitting to judge concerning them, but according to them.

GRATIAN: *Laws are instituted when they are promulgated; they are confirmed when they are approved by the customs of the users. For even as some laws are today abrogated by the contrary customs of the users, so by the customs of the users laws are confirmed. . . .*

DISTINCTION VIII

GRATIAN: PART I. *The law of nature differs also from custom and statute. For by the law of nature all things are common to all men; and not only is this believed to have been observed among those of whom we read, 'Moreover the multitude of believers had one heart and one mind,' etc. [Acts 4:32], but also it is found to have been taught by the philosophers from an earlier time. Whence Plato taught that that state was most justly ordained, in which each man was ignorant of private desires. But by the law of custom or statute, this is mine, and that belongs to someone else.*

THE IDEA OF LAW

Whence Augustine says [*Tract.* VI on John 1:25]:

CANON I. *By divine law all things are common to all men; but by statute law this is mine, and that belongs to someone else.*

By what law do you claim the lands of the church, by divine law, or human? We have divine law in the divine scriptures, human law in the laws of kings. Whence does each man possess what he possesses? Is it not by human law? For by the divine law, 'The earth is the Lord's, and the fulness thereof.' Of one clay God made rich and poor, and one earth supports rich and poor. Therefore, it is by human law that one says: this is my farm, this is my house, this is my slave. Moreover human laws are laws of emperors: wherefore? Because God assigned to the human race the human laws themselves through emperors and secular kings. *Again.* 1. Take away the laws of the emperor, and who dares to say: this is my farm, that slave is mine, this is my home? If, however, those things are held from men and the laws of kings have made them, do you intend that we should set aside the laws that you may enjoy them? etc. *Again.* 2. The laws are collected, where manifestly the emperors have laid down, that those who outside the communion of the catholic church usurp for themselves the name of Christians, and do not wish to worship in peace the author of peace, dare possess nothing in the name of the church. 3. But you say, 'What have we to do with the emperor?' But I have already said that this is a matter concerning human law. The apostle wished that kings should be served and honoured, and he said, 'Reverence the king.' 'What have I to do with the king?' Then what have you to do with possessions? Through the laws of kings, possessions are possessed. You have said, 'What have we to do with the king?' Then do not call them your possessions, since you have renounced those very human laws by which possessions are possessed.

GRATIAN: PART II. *In dignity the natural law prevails absolutely over custom and statute. For, if it is opposed to natural law, anything accepted by custom or contained in writing should be held null and void.*

Whence Augustine says [*Confessions*, bk. 3, ch. 8]:

CANON II. *It is permitted to no one to do anything contrary to natural law.*

Those things which are outrages against the customs of men ought to be avoided for the sake of the diversity of customs, in order that no wantonness of citizen or wayfarer may violate the compact of a people among themselves, whether it be confirmed by the custom of the state

35

or by law. For shameful is the part which is not congruous with its whole. 1. However, when God orders anything against the custom or compact of any, whoever they may be, although it was never done there, it should be done; and if it was neglected, it should be resumed; and if it was not instituted, it should be instituted. 2. For if it is permitted to a king, in the state in which he reigns, to order something which no one before him nor he himself had ever ordered, and it is obeyed even if it is against the association of the state, nay rather, not to obey it is against the association (since there is a general compact of human society to obey its kings): how much more ought God, who reigns over the universe His creature, to be obeyed without hesitation in those things which He has commanded? For even as, among the powers of a human association, the greater power is set above the lesser to be obeyed, so God is set above all.

CANON IV. *Custom ought to be considered of less weight than truth and reason.* [Augustine, *De Baptismo, contra Donatistas,* bk. 3, ch. 6]

'When truth is manifest, let custom yield to truth': obviously, who would doubt that custom yields to manifest truth? *Again,* 'Let no one set custom before reason and truth, because reason and truth for ever overcome custom.'

CANON V. *Any custom whatever ought to be considered of less weight than truth.* [Gregory VII, to Wimund, Bishop of Aversa]

If, perchance, you offer in opposition the authority of custom, you should consider that the Lord said: 'I am the Truth.' He did not say, 'I am custom,' but 'truth.' 1. And certainly (to use the expression of the Blessed Cyprian) any custom whatever, however old, however popular, is to be altogether less esteemed than truth, and a usage which is contrary to truth should be abolished. . . .

GRATIAN: *Therefore it clearly appears, that custom is of less weight than natural law.*

Rufinus

[Rufinus, French by birth, studied civil law at Bologna, and wrote an important early commentary on the *Decretum* (1170). The following selections are taken from his preface and from his discussion of pt. 1, distinction 1, Gratian, pt. 1: *Summa Decretorum,* ed. Heinrich Singer (Paderborn, 1902), pp. 4; 6–7.]

The dignity of man before sin was lofty, hanging as if on cords on these two qualities: namely, rectitude of justice and clarity of knowledge; through the one he controlled human affairs, through the other he approached divine matters. However, as the wickedness of the devil grew within him, the rectitude of justice was depressed by the weight of perverse malice and by the mist of error the light of knowledge was made dim. Therefore, since through the lameness of ill-will he came to the blindness of ignorance, yet still retained the natural order imprinted on his mind, it was necessary that the integrity of knowledge be repaired through the exercise of justice. And therefore, since the natural force deep within him had not been extinguished, he began to bestir himself that in some way he might differ from the brute beasts, as by his prerogative of knowing and of living by law. And when man resolved to join with his neighbours and consult with them for mutual advantages, then, as if from dying embers, appeared the sparks of justice: namely, the precepts of moderation and temperance, teaching men to change their rude and fierce ways to those that are decent and honourable, and to submit to bonds of concord, and to make fixed contracts; and these are called the law of peoples, because nearly all peoples use them: for instance, sales, leases, barters, and the like. However, since our weakness could not be transformed by these means to the fulness of good, God in His mercy came to our aid and set forth, in the letters of the Ten Commandments given through Moses, that law of life which from of old He had written on the hearts of men; and we call this the Old Law, or the Law of the Synagogue. But because, as the Apostle bears witness [Hebrews 7:19], the Law brings no one to perfection, when the fulness of time came God sent His Son, through Whom He established for us the law of life, the law immaculate, converting souls, to which we give that happy name, the Gospel.

Gratian, about to treat of canon law as drawn from the net of a higher law, broadens the scope of his work, beginning with natural law, which is indeed older in time and more excellent in dignity. Now the tradition of the legists most generally defined this law in these words: 'Natural law is that which nature has taught all animals' [Digest, 1, 1, 1; Inst., 1, 2]. But let us briefly look at natural law—not caring for a generality of that sort, which includes all animals—according as it is ascribed to the human race alone, examining what it is and in what it consists and whence it proceeds, and in what respect anything has been added to or subtracted from it. Therefore, natural law is a certain force implanted in the human creature by nature, for doing good and avoiding the contrary. Moreover natural law consists of three parts: namely, commands, prohibitions, and indications. It commands what is good, as 'Thou shalt love the Lord thy God'; it prohibits what is harmful, as 'Thou shalt not kill'; it indicates what is expedient, as 'Let all goods be held in common,' or 'Let there be one liberty for all,' and the like. Therefore this natural law at the first sinning of man was so confused that thenceforth men thought that nothing would be unlawful; whence the Apostle says: 'Sin was not imputed, since there was no law' [Romans 5:13]. Afterwards the natural law was re-established through the Ten Commandments inscribed on two tables, but not restored in all its fulness, because in them unlawful acts were altogether condemned, but not the will so to act. And for this reason the Gospel was substituted, where natural law is restored in all its fulness, and in that restoration is perfected. Moreover, since natural law follows the naked nature of things, showing that one thing is by its nature right, but another wrong, it was necessary that good customs should follow after, for the modification and adornment of natural law, by which customs a fitting and proper order might be preserved in it. For instance: the union of man and woman belongs to natural law, but in order that men should not use that good thing casually and precipitantly like beasts, this natural law has been modified through the order of wise and honourable custom: namely, that only certain persons, and only after a certain celebration of marriage, may be united. Behold, it is now clear what is added to natural law from without: namely, the manner and order of customs. Moreover, there has been subtraction from natural law, not in regard to the commands and prohibitions, which can undergo no derogation, but in regard to the indications (those things, that is, which nature neither forbids nor commands, but shows to be good), and especially in regard to the one liberty of all men and common possession: for now, by civil law, this is my slave, that is your field. Yet all these things which seem contrary to natural law are finally related to it. For example: because certain men had begun to be unbridled, and lived, as it were, headless without a ruler, committing all conceivable crimes with impunity, it was established that those who pertinaciously rebelled against those who had authority over them would be perpetually slaves when defeated and captured in war. What is the purpose of this, except that those who formerly were wild, haughty, and harmful through free licence, should thereafter become gentle, humble, and harmless through the discipline of servile necessity? And no one doubts that these things, namely, to shrink from pride and ill-will and to prefer harmlessness and humility, belong to natural law; and in this way the rivers of human virtue return to the sea of natural law, which, all but lost in the first man, has been restored in the Mosaic Law, perfected in the Gospel, and adorned in customs. Moreover, these customs are partly set forth in writing and called statute law; partly they are preserved unwritten in the pleas of the users, and this is called simply custom.

Bracton

[Henry de Bracton (d. 1268) was for many years one of those travelling royal justices who through their decisions gradually shaped the customs of England into the English common law. He also held various ecclesiastical offices, including the chancellorship of the cathedral of Exeter. But his fame rests on his *De Legibus et Consuetudinibus Angliae*. In this 'large and noble book,' as Maitland called it, Bracton attempted a systematic compilation of the living English law of his period, borrowing from the civilists little more than their form and method and a scattering of axioms. The greater part of the book appears to have been compiled between 1250 and 1256; it is unfinished. Appearing just as the common law was nearing the close of its period of rapid growth, it became a basic text for English legal studies in the Middle Ages and thereafter and played an important part in fortifying the English common law against the pressure of the revived law of Rome.

I have used the text edited by George E. Woodbine (New Haven, 1915 ff.). The following selections are taken from Bracton's Introduction, folios 1–2 (vol. II, pp. 19, 21–22).]

What things are necessary in a king

In the king who rightly rules these two are the necessary things: namely, arms and laws, by which both the time of war and the time of peace may be rightly governed. For each of these needs the aid of the other, whereby not only military affairs can be safe, but also the laws themselves may be preserved by support of arms. Moreover, if arms fail against enemies, rebels and unconquered, the kingdom will be defenceless; and if the laws fail, then justice will be exterminated, nor will there be anyone to make just judgment. Moreover, although in nearly all regions the written law is used, England alone uses within her bounds unwritten law and custom. Here indeed right is based upon unwritten law, which use has proven. But it will not be absurd to speak of the English laws, although unwritten, as laws, since whatsoever has been justly defined and approved, with the advice and consent of the magnates and the general guaranty of the commonwealth, with the authority of the king or prince presiding, has the force of law. Also, there are in England many and diverse customs, according to the diversity of places. For the English hold many things by custom which they do not hold by law, as in various counties, cities, towns, and villages, where it must always be inquired what the custom of that place is and in what way those who allege custom use the custom.

Laws order and forbid

Now the English laws and customs by the authority of kings sometimes order, sometimes forbid, sometimes sentence and punish transgressors. And these laws, indeed, when they have been approved by the consent of the users and confirmed by the oath of kings, cannot be changed nor destroyed without the common consent of all those by whose counsel and consent they were promulgated. Yet, without their consent, the laws can be altered for the better, because what is altered for the better is not destroyed. Moreover, if new and unaccustomed things emerge which were not previously used in the kingdom, they may be judged by similar things, if similar things have occurred, and when there is a good opportunity to proceed from like to like. Now if such things never happened before, and the judgment of them is obscure and difficult, then the judgments may be brought even before the great court, and there through the counsel of the court they may be settled; although there are some who, presuming on their own knowledge, knowing nothing of the law, as it were, do not wish to seek the counsel of anyone. And in such a case, it would be more honourable and more prudent to have advice from those men rather than to define anything rashly, since it is not useless to deliberate over individual cases.

What law is, and what custom is

We should also consider what law is. And it should be known that law is the common precept of men, the decision of the wise, the coercion of crimes which proceed either from will or from ignorance, and the general guaranty of the commonwealth. Now the author of justice is God, and thus justice is in the creator. And accordingly, *ius* and *lex* mean the same. And although in the broadest sense one may define *lex* as anything that is read, yet it especially signifies a just command which orders honourable deeds and prohibits the contrary. Custom, indeed, is sometimes observed instead of law in regions where it has been approved by the custom of the users, and it takes the place of law. For the authority of long usage and custom is no mean authority.

Jean d'Ibelin

[Jean d'Ibelin d'Arsur (1215–1266), Count of Jaffa and Ascalon, was a member of one of the most important noble families of the Latin Orient. As warrior and statesman, he played a leading part in the affairs of a region in which a transplanted feudalism flourished in a purer form than ever in the West. His *Livre des Assises de la Haute Cour* (1265 or 1266), designed for the instruction of the king and the great barons, became an important reference-book. The following selection, while of no value as an account of actual events, is a significant illustration of the way in which a feudal magnate assumed that the laws of his kingdom would naturally have originated: *Livre des Assises de la Haute Cour*, chs. 1 and 3, in *Assises de Jérusalem*, ed. A. A. Beugnot (Paris, 1841–1843), vol. II.]

CHAPTER I

When the Holy City of Jerusalem was conquered from the enemies of the Cross and restored to the power of the faithful of Jesus Christ, in the year of the Incarnation of our Lord Jesus Christ 1099, . . . and when the princes and the barons who had conquered it had elected for king and lord of the Kingdom of Jerusalem Duke Godfrey of Bouillon, and when he had received the lordship, since he was very attentive and eager that this kingdom should be put in good order and good condition and that his men and his people and all kinds of people going and coming and dwelling in the said kingdom should be guarded and governed, kept and maintained, ruled and judged by law and by reason, he chose by the advice of the Patriarch of the Holy City and Church of Jerusalem, and by the advice of the princes and barons, and of the wisest men that he could have there, wise men to inquire and know from the people of various lands who were there the usages of their lands; and as soon as those whom he had chosen to do this could know and learn these usages, they had them put into writing; and they brought this writing before Duke Godfrey; and he assembled the patriarch and the others aforementioned, and showed them the writing, and had it read before them; and then, with their advice and consent, he collected from those writings what seemed good to him; and he made thereof assizes and usages that should be held and maintained and used in the Kingdom of Jerusalem, by which he and his men and his people and all other kinds of people going and coming and dwelling in his kingdom should be governed, guarded, kept and maintained, ruled and judged, by law and by reason in the said kingdom.

CHAPTER III

After the aforesaid assizes were made and the usages established, Duke Godfrey and the kings and lords who succeeded him in that kingdom amended them several times; for when they saw and knew some change which seemed good to them, they added to the assizes, or enlarged them, or subtracted from them, with the counsel and consent of the Patriarch of Jerusalem and of the barons and of the magnates of the said kingdom, and of the most wise that were there available, knights and clerks and laymen. And whenever pilgrims passed through, the king of the kingdom, as he had leisure, assembled at Acre the patriarch and the others aforesaid, and had inquiry made of the wise men who came from diverse parts of the world concerning the usages of their lands; and all those things which he had established in this way were put into writing, and those writings were brought to the king; and he showed them to the patriarch and the others aforesaid, and with their counsel and consent he enlarged or added to or subtracted from the assizes and usages of the kingdom what seemed to them to be good or otherwise as an amendment to the said writings. And some of the kings of the said kingdom sent messengers several times into various parts of the world to inquire and learn the usages of those lands, that they might by their skill and knowledge amend the assizes and usages of the said kingdom; and they amended them, with the counsel of the aforesaid, in whatever

42

ways seemed good to them. And this they did several times in several years, until they had made the assizes and usages the best and most suitable they could or would be for lords and men, for knights and pilgrims, and for every other kind of people going and coming and dwelling in the said kingdom, to govern, guard, hold and maintain, rule and judge them well and truly and lawfully, according to the status of every man and every woman.

Beaumanoir

[Little is known of the life of Philippe de Rémi, Sieur de Beaumanoir (ca. 1250–1296). In 1273, he was *bailli* at Senlis, in 1280 at Clermont; documents occasionally mention him as presiding at assizes held in various towns. His collection of the customs of Beauvais is in general a straightforward compilation of the feudal law with which such a judge would have to deal; it is distinguished from similar collections of provincial customs by some Roman law influences and a tendency to exalt the special position of the king. The following selections are from his *Coutumes de Beauvaisis*, ed. A. Salmon (Paris, 1899–1900), ch. 24, secs. 682–684; ch. 34, sec. 1043; ch. 49, secs. 1510–1512.]

CHAPTER XXIV

682. Because all pleas are determined in accordance with customs . . . we shall tell briefly in this chapter what custom is, and what one should hold for custom. . . . And we shall speak of usages, and which usages are valid and which are not, and of the difference between usage and custom.

683. Custom is proved in one of two ways. One of these ways is: when it is general throughout the whole county and has been maintained without dispute so long as man can remember; for instance, when any freeman acknowledges a debt, he is commanded to pay it within a week, and a gentleman within a fortnight; this custom is so clear that I never saw it disputed. And the other way that one may know it and hold it for a custom is when there has been a dispute, and one of the parties wished to support his case with a custom, and was approved by judgment, as has often occurred in the case of the sharing of inheritances or other quarrels. And by these two methods one may prove custom, and these customs the count is bound to preserve, and to make his subjects preserve them so that no one may corrupt them.

43

And if the count himself wished to corrupt them or to allow them to be corrupted, the king should not permit it, for he is bound to preserve and to make others preserve the customs of his realm.

684. The difference between custom and usage is that all customs are to be maintained, but there are usages such that if anyone should plead the contrary and bring the case to judgment the usages would not be maintained.

CHAPTER XXXIV

1043. It is true that the king is sovereign above all and has by his own right the general care of the kingdom, by which he can make such edicts as he pleases for the common advantage, and what he establishes should be held.

CHAPTER XLIX

1510. There are some exceptional times when one neither can nor ought to do what has been used and accustomed as law for a long time: for instance, everyone must know that there are two kinds of times—those of peace and those of war. It is reasonable that the time of peace should be ruled by the usages and customs which have long been used and accustomed for living in peace: for instance, in such times, one may do as he likes with his own, give or sell or spend it, in accordance with what several chapters of this book teach. But in the time of war and in the time when war is expected, it is fitting that kings and princes, barons and other lords, do many things which, if they did them in time of peace, would wrong their subjects; but the time of necessity excuses them; by which the king may make new decrees for the common profit of his realm: for instance, he may command, when he thinks he must do so to defend his land or attack someone who has done him wrong, that squires and gentlemen be knights, and that rich men and poor men be furnished with arms each according to his estate, that the chartered towns prepare their services and their fortresses and that everyone be prepared to move when the king shall command it. All such decrees and others which seem suitable to him and to his council the king can make for time of war or in expectation of war to come; and every baron also in his land, provided that it be not for an enterprise against the king.

1511. There are other times when it is appropriate to do things other than those that customs allow in time of peace: for instance, in time of famine when there is a scarcity of the things needed to sustain the common people, as a lack of grain or of wine. In such a time one may well set limits, that each man may not deal at his pleasure in the things that are scarce; for if one allowed the rich man to buy them in order to put them in granaries and then hold them without selling, to raise the price, it would be unendurable. Thus, when it happens to be such a time, the lords of the lands can order their subjects to retain, of the goods that are scarce, only so much as is fitting for them and their households for the year, and to sell the rest at the just price that the goods are worth when they are on sale in open market; for it is better to pursue the common profit than to follow the will of those who want time to raise the price.

1512. No one except the king in the Kingdom of France can make a new decree which is to run as law, nor new contracts, nor new customs, save in time of necessity; for every baron in time of necessity can advance the dues of his subjects, as we have said above; but they cannot make new contracts, nor new customs, without the permission of the king. But the king can do it when it pleases him, and when he sees that it is for the common profit: as one sees every day that the king gives a new custom to some towns or barons who belong to him or are his subjects: for instance, to repair bridges, or roads, or churches, or other common conveniences; in such cases the king can do it, and no one else. . . .

While the king may thus make new decrees, he should take great care that he makes them for a reasonable cause and for the common profit and with the great council, and especially that he does not make them against God nor against good morals; for if he did . . . his subjects should not permit it. . . .

Thomas Aquinas

[Thomas Aquinas was born in 1224 or 1225 of a noble family in the Kingdom of Naples. In 1244 he entered the Dominican Order, and was sent to the University of Paris to study theology. Here and at Cologne, he studied under Albert the Great, who was a pioneer in a cause which Thomas later made his own, the assimilation of Aristotle's science and philosophy into the Christian theological tradition. From 1252 to 1259 he lectured on theology

45

at the University of Paris, meeting frequent opposition from older teachers who resented the new prestige of the regulars, but impressing his students by his intellectual dignity, his mastery of his subject, and the vigour and freshness of his approach. In this period his commentary on the *Sentences of Peter Lombard* (1253-1255) was written. In the next few years, we find the Dominican Order making particular use of his capacities: he helped to organize a curriculum for the Dominican schools—including secular as well as spiritual studies; he wrote his *Summa contra Gentes* (1259-1264) as a basic theological text for Dominican missionaries to the Arabs in Spain. After 1261, he spent some years in Italy, partly at the papal court in Orvieto and Viterbo, partly in Rome, where he was sent to supervise Dominican studies; he was offered the archbishopric of Naples, but refused it. In the course of these years, he wrote several commentaries on works of Aristotle, which William of Moerbeke at his instigation had translated directly from the Greek, including the *Ethics* (1261-1264); he also wrote his little, unfinished *De Regimine Principum* (ca. 1266) for the King of Naples, and the first part of his vast *Summa Theologiae* (1266 ff.). In 1268, the Dominicans sent him back to Paris, and for the next few years he was occupied in teaching, in academic and intellectual controversy, and in continuing the never-to-be completed *Summa*. In 1272 he wrote a commentary on part of the *Politics* of Aristotle, and in the same year he was recalled to Italy by the Dominicans, to organize a general theological curriculum for the Roman province of the Order. In 1274, he died while travelling to the Council of Lyons, to which Gregory X had summoned him as an expert on the doctrines of the Greek Church.

There is a story that once, sitting at the table of Louis IX of France, Thomas was lost in thought, and emerged at last to exclaim in triumph, 'I have just thought of a new argument against the Manichaeans!' True or not, the story may carry a lesson for those who persistently attempt to explain his political writings in terms of the political issues of the period. The career that we have outlined was that of a scholar, not that of a statesman. Thomas Aquinas's overwhelming concern was what he himself specified as the chief end of natural man: through the use of reason he sought an understanding of God. He believed profoundly in the rational order of a universe whose being was derived from the reason of God; he believed profoundly that through study of that order man could attain to a rational knowledge of God which would necessarily be harmonious with the more direct and fuller knowledge granted by revelation; and he believed profoundly that through the rational ordering of his own concerns and the fulfilment of his own nature man could share in the fulfilment of the divine plan and attain positive values which might fittingly be crowned and perfected by the gifts of grace. Thus he welcomed the wisdom of the pagan Aristotle, feared by many of his colleagues,

46

and used it confidently to strengthen and clarify Christian thought. And thus, when he came to write on law and government, he was able to reorient the medieval tradition by treating them as positive means to the good life. For the rest, he had a wide range of scholarship; a magnificent logical mind, of the sort that does not lose itself in detail but strikes at fundamentals; a genius for systematic and forthright statement; and a good deal of sturdy common sense.

The following selection is a drastic condensation of the treatise on law which forms part of the *Summa Theologiae* (2a 2ae, qs. 90–97. I have used the Leonine edition). I have tried to follow the main line of Aquinas's own thought, reluctantly omitting his presentation of conflicting views and most of his specific answers to objections; the reader should remember that, voluminous as his works are, Aquinas suffers more than most medieval writers by condensation.]

QUESTION XC. OF THE ESSENCE OF LAW

Article 1. Whether law is something pertaining to reason

. . . . Law is a certain rule and measure of actions, according to which someone is induced to action or restrained from action. . . . Moreover, the rule and measure of human actions is reason, which is the first principle of human actions . . . for it is proper to reason to ordain to an end, which, according to the Philosopher [*Ethics*, bk. 7, ch. 4], is the first principle in actions. . . .

. . . . Reason has its power of moving from the will . . . ; for it is due to the fact that someone wills the end that reason makes commands concerning those things which serve the end. But it is necessary that the will be regulated by some reason in regard to those things that are commanded, if this volition is to have the character of law. And in this sense it is understood that the will of the ruler has the force of law; otherwise the will of the prince would be rather iniquity than law.

Article 2. Whether law is always ordained to the common good

. . . . Now the first principle in practical matters . . . is the ultimate end. Moreover, the ultimate end of human life is happiness or beatitude. . . Whence it follows that law must above all concern the order which leads to beatitude. And again, since every part is ordained to the whole as the imperfect is to the perfect, and the individual is a part of the perfect community, the law necessarily concerns that order which leads to the common happiness. . . .

. . . Actions are indeed concerned with particular cases; but these particular cases can be related to the common good—not, indeed, as their common genus or species, but as their final cause, according to · which the common good is said to be the common end.

Article 3. Whether the reason of anyone may be the maker of law

. . . . It is proper to law that it first and principally concerns the order leading to the common good. Now, to ordain something for the common good belongs either to the whole people, or to someone who represents the whole people. Thus to establish law belongs to the whole people, or to the public person who has the care of the whole people. Because, in all other cases, to ordain to an end is the business of him whose end it is.

. . . . A private person cannot effectively induce to virtue. For he can.only advise, but if his advice be not accepted, he has no coercive power, which law should have, that it may effectively induce to virtue, as the Philosopher says in X *Ethics*, [ch. 9]. However, the people, or a public person to whom belongs the infliction of penalties, has this coercive power, as will be shown below. And therefore it or he alone can make laws.

Article 4. Whether promulgation is essential to law

. . . . As has been said, a law is imposed on others as a rule or measure. Moreover, a rule or measure is imposed by being applied to those things which are ruled and measured. Whence, in order that law may obtain the binding force that is proper to it, it must be applied to the men who are to be ruled by it. Moreover, such application is made in this way: by being brought to their knowledge through promulgation. Therefore promulgation is essential, if law is to have its force.

And so from the four preceding articles, this definition of law can be collected: that it is nothing other than a certain ordinance of reason for the common good, [made] by him who has the care of the community, [and] promulgated.

QUESTION XCI. OF THE VARIOUS KINDS OF LAW

Article 1. Whether there is any eternal law

. . . . As was said above, law is nothing other than a certain dictate of the practical reason in the prince who governs some perfect

48

community. But it is evident . . . that the whole community of the universe is governed by divine reason. And therefore the principle by which things are governed, which exists in God as the ruler of the whole, has the nature of law. And because the divine reason conceives nothing in time, but has eternally conceived, . . . this kind of law must be called eternal.

Article 2. Whether there is in us any natural law

. . . . It is evident that all things participate in the eternal law, inasmuch, namely, as from its impression upon them they have inclinations to their proper acts and ends. Moreover, compared with others, the rational creature is subjected to the divine providence in a rather more excellent way, inasmuch as, being provident for itself and for others, it shares itself in providence. Therefore it shares in the eternal reason, through which it has a natural inclination to its due act and end. And such participation of the rational creature in the eternal law is called natural law. . . .

Article 3. Whether there is any human law

. . . . As was said above, law is a certain dictate of the practical reason. Moreover, the procedure of the practical reason and that of the speculative reason are found to be similar, for each proceeds from principles to conclusions. . . . Therefore, accordingly, it should be said that, even as in the case of the speculative reason the conclusions of the diverse sciences not naturally known but found through the industry of the reason are produced from the indemonstrable principles naturally known, so also, from the precepts of natural law, as if from certain general and indemonstrable principles, the human reason necessarily proceeds to more particular determinations. These particular determinations, discovered through human reason, are called human laws, if the other conditions which pertain to the nature of law, as described above, are fulfilled. Wherefore Tully also says, in his *Rhetoric* [bk. 2, ch. 53], that 'the beginning of law comes from nature; then certain things became customary because of their reasonableness and utility; then reverence for law sanctioned those things that proceeded from nature and were approved by custom.'

. . . . The human reason cannot participate fully in the dictate of the divine reason, but does so in its own way, and imperfectly. And therefore, as in the case of the speculative reason, through natural participation in the divine wisdom, there is in us a knowledge of certain general principles, but not a particular knowledge of each truth, such as is contained in the divine wisdom: so also, in the case of the practical reason, man naturally participates in the eternal law in regard to certain general principles, but not, however, in regard to particular rules for particular cases, which yet are contained in the eternal law. And therefore it is necessary that the human reason proceed further to certain particular commands of law.

. . . . The practical reason deals with practical affairs, which are individual and contingent, but not with necessary things, as does the speculative reason. And therefore human laws cannot have that infallibility which the demonstrable conclusions of the sciences possess. Nor is it necessary that every measure be in every way infallible and certain, except in so far as is possible for its own genus.

Article 4. Whether a divine law was necessary

. . . . Because man is ordained to the end of eternal beatitude, which is beyond the attainment of his natural faculty, . . . it was necessary that he should be directed to his goal by a law divinely given, in addition to natural and human law.

Secondly, as a result of the uncertainty of human judgment especially in regard to contingent and particular things, it happens that different judgments about human acts are formed by different men, and from these proceed different and contrary laws. Therefore, that man may know without any doubt what is to be done and what avoided, it was necessary that in regard to particular actions he should be directed by a law divinely given, which assuredly cannot err.

Thirdly, man can make law for those things of which he can judge. But man cannot judge of inner happenings, which are hidden, but only of external acts, which are apparent. And yet, for the perfection of virtue, righteousness is required in both kinds of actions. Therefore human law could not sufficiently control and ordain internal acts, but it was necessary that a divine law should supervene for this purpose.

Fourthly, as Augustine says in *De Libero Arbitrio*, bk. 1, [ch. 5] human law cannot punish or prohibit all evil deeds, because, while it was seeking to remove all evils, it would also cause the loss of many good things, and would prevent them from serving the common good as is necessary for human intercourse. Therefore, in order that no evil should remain unforbidden and unpunished, it was necessary that a divine law should supervene, by which all sins are prohibited.

QUESTION XCII. OF THE EFFECTS OF LAW

Article 1. Whether an effect of law is to make men good

As stated above, law is nothing other than a dictate of reason in the ruler, by which his subjects are governed. Now the virtue of any subordinate is to be well subjected to that by which it is governed. . . . Moreover, every human law is ordained to be obeyed by those subjected to it. Thus it is clear that it is proper to law to lead those subjected to it to their appropriate virtue. Therefore, since virtue is 'what makes him who has it good' [*Ethics*, bk. 2, ch. 6] it follows that the proper effect of law is to make those to whom it is given good, either in an absolute or in a relative sense. For if the intention of the maker of law is directed toward the true good, that is, the common good regulated according to divine justice, it follows that through his law men become good in an absolute sense. But if the intention of the legislator is turned toward that which is not good absolutely, but useful or pleasant to himself, or opposed to divine justice, then the law does not make men good absolutely, but in relation to something, namely, to such a government. And thus good is found even in things bad in themselves: as one speaks of a good thief, because his actions are adapted to his end.

. . . . The goodness of any part is considered in proportion to its whole, whence Augustine says in the third book of the *Confessions*, [ch. 8], that 'shameful is that part that is not congruous to its whole.' Since, therefore, each man is a part of the state, it is impossible that any man be good unless he is well proportioned to the common good; nor is any whole well composed unless it is composed of parts congruous to itself. Thus it is impossible that the common good of a city be well maintained unless the citizens are virtuous, or at least those who rule it. So far as the good of the community is concerned, it is sufficient that the others be virtuous to the extent that they obey the commands of the prince. And therefore the Philosopher says in III *Politics*, [ch. 2] that 'the virtue of a prince and that of a good man are the same, but the virtue of a citizen and that of a good man are not the same.'

. . . . A tyrannical law, since it is not in accord with reason, is not a law in the absolute sense, but rather a kind of perversion of law. And

51

yet in so far as it has something of the nature of law, it tends to this: that the citizens shall be good. For it has none of the nature of law except that it proceeds from the dictate of a ruler laid upon his subjects, and that it aims at their obedience: that is, that they shall be good, not in the absolute sense but in relation to this particular government.

QUESTION XCIII. CONCERNING THE ETERNAL LAW

Article 3. Whether every law is derived from the eternal law

As stated above, law means a certain plan of reason directing acts toward an end. Now in every system of motion, the power of the second mover must be derived from the power of the first mover, because the second mover does not move except in so far as it is moved by the first. Thus we see the same thing in all who govern: that the plan of governing is derived from the chief governor by the subordinates; thus the plan of the things to be done in a state is derived from the king through his instructions to his subordinate administrators; and in craftsmanship the plan of the work is derived from the architect by the inferior craftsmen, who work with their hands. Therefore, since the eternal law is the supreme governor's plan of governing, all plans of governing that the subordinates have are necessarily derived from the eternal law. Now these plans of the subordinate governors consist of all other laws except the eternal law. Therefore all laws, in so far as they participate in right reason, are derived from the eternal law. And therefore Augustine says in *De Libero Arbitrio*, bk. 1, [ch. 6], that 'in temporal law nothing is just and lawful which men have not derived for themselves from the eternal law.'

. . . . Human law has the nature of law in so far as it accords with right reason; and in this it is clear that it is derived from the eternal law. But, to the extent that it departs from reason, it is called unjust law, and thus it has not the nature of law, but rather of violence. —And yet, in so far as this unjust law preserves some likeness to law through the authority of him who makes it, it too is derived from eternal law; for 'all power is from the Lord God,' as Romans 13:[1] says.

QUESTION XCIV. CONCERNING THE LAW OF NATURE

Article 2. Whether the law of nature has several precepts or only one

. . . . The first principle for the practical reason is that which is based on the nature of good, which is: 'good is that which all things seek.' This is therefore the first precept of law: that 'good is to be done and to be followed, and evil is to be avoided.' And upon this are based all other precepts of the natural law, so that all those things which the practical reason naturally apprehends as human goods [or evils] belong to the precepts of the law of nature as things to be done or to be avoided.

But, because good has the nature of an end, but evil the nature of an opposite, it follows that all those things to which man has a natural inclination the reason naturally apprehends as good, and therefore to be actively pursued; and their opposites as evils to be avoided. So the order of the precepts of the law of nature corresponds to the order of natural inclinations. For, in the first place, there is in man an inclination to what is good according to the nature which he shares with all substances: for instance, every substance, according to its nature, seeks self-preservation. And according to this inclination those things which preserve the life of man and ward off its adversaries belong to natural law. Secondly, there is in man an inclination to some more particular things, in accordance with the nature which he shares with other animals. And, in keeping with this, those things 'which nature has taught all animals' [*Digest*, 1, 1, 1] belong to natural law: for instance, the union of husband and wife, the nurture of the young, and so forth. In the third place, there is in man an inclination toward that which is good according to the nature of reason, which is proper to him: for instance, man has a natural inclination to know the truth concerning God, and to live in society. And accordingly, those things pertain to natural law which concern an inclination of this sort: for instance, that a man should avoid ignorance, that he should not offend others with whom he holds converse, and other things which fall under this heading.

Article 3. Whether all acts of virtue are prescribed in the law of nature

We can speak of virtuous acts in two ways, according to whether they are considered as virtuous or as belonging to a particular species. If we are speaking of virtuous acts with regard to their virtue, then all virtuous acts belong to natural law. For it has been said that everything to which a man is inclined in accordance with his nature belongs to natural law. Now everything is naturally inclined to the behaviour that is appropriate for it according to its form: for example, fire is inclined to give heat. Therefore, since a rational soul is the proper form of man, every man has a natural inclination to act in accordance with reason. And this is to act in accordance with virtue. From this point of view, all virtuous acts are prescribed in the law of nature, for each man's reason naturally dictates to him that he should act virtuously. But if we are speaking of virtuous acts in themselves, considered as belonging to their own species, not all virtuous acts are prescribed in the natural law. For many things are done virtuously, to which nature does not at first incline; but men have discovered, through the inquiry of reason, that they are useful to the good life.

Article 4. Whether the natural law is the same among all men

As has been said above, those things to which man is naturally inclined belong to natural law; among these, it is proper to man that he is inclined to act in accordance with reason. Now reason, as such, proceeds from the general to the particular, as is stated in I *Physics*, [ch. 1]. But in this process the speculative reason differs from the practical reason. For the speculative reason deals chiefly with necessary facts, which cannot be otherwise than as they are, and flawless truth is found in the particular deductions as in the general principles. But the practical reason deals with contingencies, among which are human actions; and therefore, although there is necessity in the general principles, the more we descend to particulars, the more defect is found. Thus in speculative problems truth is the same for all men, in the principles and conclusions alike, though the truth of the conclusions is not known to everyone, but only that of the premises, which are called 'common concepts.' In problems of action, however, although the truth, or practical rectitude, of the general principles, is the same for all men, the truth of the particular conclusions is not; and those for whom the same particular conclusions are right are not equally aware of their validity.

Thus it appears that, in regard to the general principles of the speculative and the practical reason, the truth is the same for all men, and equally known to them. And in regard to the particular conclusions of the speculative reason, the truth is the same for all men, yet not equally known to all: for it is true for all men that the three angles of a triangle are equal to two right angles, although not everyone knows this. But in regard to the particular conclusions of the practical reason, there is not the same truth or validity for all men, nor is the truth equally known to those for whom it is the same. For all men this is right and true: that they should act in accordance with reason. Moreover, from this principle there follows as a proper conclusion, that things given in trust should be restored to their owner. And this indeed is true in most cases, but in a particular case it may happen to be injurious and therefore irrational to restore goods held in trust: for instance, if they are wanted for the purpose of fighting against one's country. And the proposition is found to be more and more at fault, as we descend further to particulars: for instance, if we should say that goods held in trust should be restored with a specific guarantee, or in a specific way, for, as more and more particular conditions are added, there are more and more ways in which the principle may fail, so that it may not be right either to restore or not to restore.

Therefore it must be said that the law of nature, in its first principles, is the same among all men, both in validity and in being known. But in its particular details, which are, as it were, conclusions from the general principles, the law of nature is the same among all in most cases, both in validity and in being known; but in a few cases it may fail of validity on account of some particular obstacles . . . , and also it may fail of being known, since the reason of some men is perverted by passion, or a bad habit, or a natural evil disposition: for instance, theft, which is expressly contrary to natural law, was once not considered wrong among the Germans, as Julius Caesar tells us in his book *De Bello Gallico* [bk. 6, ch. 23].

Article 5. Whether the law of nature can be changed

. . . . Change in the law of nature can be understood in two senses. One of these is the addition of something to it. And, in this sense, nothing prevents natural law from being changed; for many things useful to human life have been added over and above the natural law, not only by divine law, but also by human laws.

Or by a change in natural law we may understand a change through subtraction: that is, that something that was once according to natural law should cease to be so. In this sense, the first principles of natural law are absolutely unchangeable; but the secondary precepts, which, we have said, are certain particular proximate conclusions from the first principles, cannot be changed in such a way that what the natural law contains shall not always be right for most cases. Yet, in some particular respect, and in a few cases, these can be changed on account of some special causes which hinder the observance of the precept in question, as was said above.

Article 1. Whether it was useful that laws should be established by man

. . . . As appears from what has been said above, there is naturally in man a certain aptitude to virtue, but the very perfection of virtue must come to man through some training. Similarly, we see that through his industry man is assisted in meeting his needs, for example, of food and clothing; some initial aids to this he has from nature, namely, his reason and his hands, but he has not the full complement, as have other animals to whom nature has given sufficient covering and food. Now it is not easy to find a man who is sufficient to himself in regard to this training, because the perfection of virtue chiefly consists in restraint from undue pleasures, to which man is especially prone, and above all the young, upon whom discipline is the more effective. And therefore this training by which virtue is attained must be received from someone else. It is true that there are some young people who are inclined to acts of virtue by their good natural disposition, or by custom, or rather by a gift from God: in their case, paternal training, through admonitions, may be enough. But since there are some who are depraved and prone to vice and not easily moved by words, it is necessary for them to be restrained from evil by force and fear, in order that, by desisting from evil-doing, they may at least give others a quiet life, and also that by habitual practice of this sort, they themselves may finally be led to doing voluntarily what once they did from fear, and so become virtuous. Now this sort of discipline, which compels through fear of punishment, is the discipline of laws. . . .

Article 2. Whether all positive human law is derived from the law of nature

. . . . As Augustine says, in *De Libero Arbitrio*, bk. 1, [ch. 5], 'that which is not just does not seem to be law.' Therefore, it has the force of law only in so far as it has justice. Now in human affairs something is said to be just if it is right according to the rule of reason. Now the first rule of reason is the law of nature, as appears from what has been said above. Therefore every law made by man has the nature of law

56

in so far as it is derived from the law of nature. But if in any respect it is not in harmony with the law of nature, then it is not law, but a corruption of law.

But it should be known that something can be derived from the law of nature in two ways: in one way, as a conclusion from premises; in the other way, as a kind of determination of generalities. The first way is like that of the sciences, when demonstrated conclusions are deduced from premises. But the second way is like what happens in craftsmanship, when general forms are particularized to a specific case: for instance, the craftsman must particularize the general form of *house* to this or that shape of house. So from the general principles of the law of nature, some laws are derived as conclusions: for example, that 'one should not kill' can be derived as a kind of conclusion from the proposition that 'one should do evil to no one.' On the other hand, some laws are derived as particular determinations: for instance, the law of nature holds that he who sins is punished, but the specific penalty that he should undergo is a particular determination of the law of nature.

Thus both kinds of derivation are found in positive human law. But instances of the first kind, when they are included in human law, derive their force not only from it but also from natural law. But those of the second kind have their force from human law alone.

Article 3. Whether Isidore suitably describes the quality of positive law

. . . . The form of everything that exists for the sake of an end must be determined in proportion to that end: for instance, the form of a saw is such as is suitable for cutting; as appears in the *Physics* [bk. 2, ch. 9]. Moreover, anything that is ruled and measured must have a form proportioned to its rule and measure. Now, human law has both, because it is something ordained to an end, and because it is a rule or measure which is ruled or measured by a superior measure; and this again is twofold: namely, the divine law and the law of nature, as appears from what has been said above. Now the end of human law is usefulness to men, as the Jurist says [*Digest*, 1, 3, 24]. And therefore Isidore [*Etymologies*, bk. 5, ch. 3], setting conditions for law, lays down three in particular: namely, 'it should be in harmony with religion,' inasmuch as it is proportioned to the divine law; ' it should be suitable for discipline,' inasmuch as it is proportioned to the law of nature;

and 'it should further welfare,' inasmuch as it is proportioned to human utility.·

And all those conditions which he afterwards sets [ch. 21] reduce to these three. For when he says 'virtuous' he refers to harmony with religion. Moreover, when he continues 'just, possible according to nature and according to the custom of the country, appropriate to place and time,' he means that it should be suitable for discipline. For human discipline depends, in the first place, on rationality, which is implied in the word 'just.' Secondly, it depends on the ability of the doers. For a discipline ought to be suitable to each individual according to his capacity, with consideration both of natural possibility (for the same demands should not be laid upon children as upon grown men), and also of possibility according to human custom, for a man cannot live alone in society and pay no heed to others. In the third place, it depends on due circumstances, and therefore he says, 'appropriate to place and time.' And when he adds, 'necessary, useful, [and of manifest clarity],' he refers to the furtherance of welfare; for necessity refers to the removal of evils; usefulness, to the attainment of good; and clarity, to the avoidance of that harm which might come from the law itself. And because, as has been said above, law is ordained to the common good, this itself appears in the last part of his definition: ['written not for private advantage, but for the common utility of the citizens'].

Article 4. Whether Isidore [bk. 5, chs. 4 ff.] sets forth a suitable classification of human laws

. . . . Anything whatever can be classified in accordance with that which is contained in its nature. . . . Now there are many things in the nature of human law, in accordance with which we can properly classify the subdivisions of human law. In the first place, it pertains to the nature of human law that it is derived from natural law, as appears from what has been said above. And accordingly positive law can be divided into the law of peoples and the civil law, in accordance with the two ways by which it is derived from natural law, which were discussed above. For to the law of peoples belong those things that are derived from the law of nature as conclusions from premises: for instance, just buying and selling, and other things of this sort, without which men could not live together in mutual relationships; which are derived from the law of nature, because man is naturally a social animal, as is proved in the *Politics*, [bk. 1, ch. 1]. And those things that are derived from the law of nature by the method of particular determination belong to the civil law, in accordance with the fact that each state determines what is suitable to itself. . . .

QUESTION XCVI

Article 3. Whether human law prescribes all acts of virtue

. . . . The kinds of virtue are distinguished according to their objects. . . . Now all objects of the virtues can be referred either to the private good of each person or to the common good of a people: for instance, one can achieve fortitude either for the preservation of the state or the preservation of the right of a friend, and so with the other virtues. Now law, as has been said, is ordained to the common good. And therefore there is no virtue concerning whose actions the law cannot prescribe. Yet human law does not prescribe all acts of all the virtues, but only those which are ordainable to the common good, either immediately, as when certain things are done directly for the sake of the common good, or mediately, as when things are ordained by the legislator which pertain to good discipline, through which the citizens are trained that they may preserve the common good of justice and peace.

Article 4. Whether human law is binding in the court of conscience

. . . . Laws established by men are either just or unjust. If, indeed, they are just, they possess the power of binding the conscience from the eternal law, from which they are derived, according to Proverbs 8: [15]: 'Through Me kings reign, and the makers of laws decree just things.' Moreover, laws are called just both in regard to their end, that is, when they are ordained to the common good, and in regard to their author, that is, when the law that is made does not exceed the competence of its maker, and in regard to their form, that is, when burdens are laid upon the subjects in accordance with an equality of proportion and with a view to the common good. For, since one man is a part of the many, each man, what he has and what he is, belongs to the many, even as any part, whatever it is, belongs to a whole. Therefore, nature also lays injury on a part that the whole may be safe. And, accordingly, laws of this sort, laying burdens proportionately, are just, and are binding in the court of conscience, and are lawful laws.

Moreover, laws are unjust in two ways. On the one hand, they may be opposed to human good, being contrary to the conditions mentioned above: either in regard to the end, as when someone in authority lays on his subjects burdensome laws which do not pertain to the common utility, but rather to his own greed and glory; or in regard to the author, as when one makes a law that exceeds the power entrusted to him; or in regard to the form, as when burdens are unequally distributed over the people, even though they are ordained to the common good. And laws of this sort are rather acts of violence than laws: because, as Augustine says in his book *De Libero Arbitrio*, [bk. 1, ch. 5], 'What is not just does not seem to be law.' Wherefore such laws lay no obligation upon man's conscience, unless, perhaps, for the sake of avoiding scandal or disturbance, a purpose to which a man should yield his right, according to Matthew 5: [40, 41], 'If a man force thee one mile, go with him also two; and whoever would steal thy coat, give to him the cloak also.'

On the other hand, laws may be unjust through opposition to divine good: such are the laws of tyrants inducing to idolatry, or to whatever else may be against the divine law. And such laws one is not permitted to observe at all, because, as Acts 5: [29] declares, 'one must obey God rather than man.'

Article 5. Whether all men are subject to the law

. . . . As appears from the above, law is essentially twofold: first, it is a rule of human actions; second, it has coercive force. Thus a man can be subject to a law in two ways. In one way, as that which is ruled is subject to a rule. And in this way all who are subject to any authority are subject to the law that proceeds from that authority. . . . But in another way, one is called subject to a law as that which is coerced is subject to the coercer. And in this way virtuous and just men are not subject to the law, but the wicked only. For coercion and force act against one's will. However, the will of good men is in harmony with the law, from which the will of the wicked is discordant. So in this sense the good are not under the law, but the bad only.

. . . . A prince is said to be released from the law, in regard to its coercive force; for no one can properly be constrained by himself, and law derives its coercive force only from the authority of the ruler.

Therefore, the prince is said to be released from the law in the sense that no one can bring a condemnatory judgment against him for an action contrary to the law. Whence the Gloss on Psalms 50:[6], 'Against Thee only have I sinned,' says that 'there is no man who can judge the actions of a king.' But in regard to the directive force of the law the prince is subjected to the law by his own will. . . . Thus . . . the prince is not released from the directive force of the law but ought to fulfil it voluntarily, without coercion. . . .

Article 6. Whether he who is subject to law can act outside the letter of the law

. . . . As was said above, law is ordained to the common welfare of men, and in so far it obtains the force and nature of law; and in so far as it fails of this, it has not obligatory force. Whence the Jurist [*Digest*, 1, 3, 25] says that 'no reason of law or kindness of equity permits that by harshness of interpretation against the interest of men we should pervert to severity those things that were introduced for the welfare and utility of men.' Now it often happens that the observance of some law is, in most cases, useful to the common good and yet in some cases is most harmful. Therefore, since the legislator cannot take care of every individual case, he establishes the law in accordance with what usually occurs, directing his intention upon the common good. Therefore, if a case arises in which the observance of such a law would be dangerous to the general welfare, it is not to be observed. For instance, if in a besieged city there exists a law that the gates of the city should remain closed, this is useful for the common welfare in most cases; but if it happens that the enemies are pursuing some citizens who are defenders of the city, it would be most dangerous to the city if the gates were not opened; thus, against the letter of the law, the common utility would be protected, as the legislator intended.

It should, however, be considered that, if the observation of the letter of the law does not involve a sudden danger which needs instant action, it is not appropriate that anyone at random should interpret what is useful to the state and what is not; but this is in the competence of rulers only, who have the power of dispensing from the laws for cases of this sort. But if there be a sudden emergency which does not allow the delay of referring to a superior, the necessity itself brings its own dispensation, for necessity is not subject to law.

THE IDEA OF LAW

Article 1. Whether human law can be changed in any way

.... As was said above, human law is a certain dictate of reason, by which human activities are directed. Accordingly human law can justly be changed for two causes: on the part of reason, or on the part of the men whose acts are regulated by law. On the part of reason, because it seems to be natural to human reason that it gradually advances from the imperfect to the perfect. Therefore, we see in the speculative sciences that the first philosophers taught certain imperfect doctrines, which were later made more nearly perfect by their successors. So it is in practical affairs also. For those who first attempted to discover something useful to the community of men, being unable to take everything into consideration themselves, set up certain imperfect institutions which were in many ways defective; these their successors have changed, instituting others which might be less deficient in common utility.

On the part of men, whose acts are regulated by law, law can rightly be changed on account of change in the conditions of men, for whom different things are expedient in accordance with different conditions. Augustine gives as an example, in *De Libero Arbitrio*, bk. 1, [ch. 6], that 'if the people is truly moderate and earnest, and most carefully guards the common utility, a law may rightly be enacted to allow such a people to create their own magistrates to govern the commonwealth. But if the same people should gradually become so depraved as to sell their votes and entrust the government to scoundrels and criminals, the power of giving honours is rightly withdrawn from such a people, and returned to the decision of a few good men.'

Article 2. Whether human law should always be changed when something better offers itself

.... As has been said, human law is rightly changed only in so far as its change is conducive to the common utility. Now the changing of law is in itself a certain detriment to the general welfare, because custom is the greatest aid to the observance of laws: inasmuch as those things which are done contrary to common custom, even if they are trivial in themselves, seem serious matters. Thus when law is changed, the binding power of law is lessened, inasmuch as custom is absent. And therefore, human law should never be changed unless the advantage to the common welfare compensates for the disadvantage entailed by this loss. And this occurs either when a very great and very evident utility proceeds from the new statute or when there exists a very great necessity: either because the accustomed law involves a manifest injustice or because its observance is exceedingly harmful. Therefore, it is said by the Jurist [*Digest*, 1, 4, 2] that 'in establishing new laws, the utility ought to be evident, if one is to depart from a law which has long seemed to be fair.'

Article 3. Whether custom can obtain the force of law

.... Every law proceeds from the reason and will of the legislator: divine law and natural law from the reason and will of God, and every human law from the human will regulated by reason. Now as the reason and will of men in practical affairs are manifested in words, so also they are manifested in deeds: for what one carries out is apparently what is chosen as good. Now it is manifest that law can be changed and also expounded by human words inasmuch as they manifest the inner movement and concept of the human reason. And therefore law may also be changed and expounded by actions, especially by repeated actions, which build up a custom; and also something can be caused which obtains the effect of law: inasmuch as through the repetition of external acts the inner motion of the will and the concept of the reason are very effectively declared; for when something is done many times, it seems to proceed from a deliberate judgment of the reason. And accordingly custom has the force of law, and abolishes law, and is the interpreter of law.

.... As has been said above, there are some cases for which human laws are faulty, whence it is possible sometimes to act outside the law: namely, in that case in which the law is deficient; and yet the act will not be evil. And when such cases are multiplied, on account of some change in man, then through custom it is made manifest that the law is no longer useful, even as would be shown by the verbal promulgation of a contrary law. Now, if there still remains the same reason for whose sake the first law was useful, then custom does not conquer law, but law is victor over custom; unless, perhaps, the law seems useless simply on this account, that it is not 'possible according to the custom of the country,' which was one of the conditions of law. For it is difficult to abolish the custom of a people.

. . . . The people among whom a custom is introduced may be of two conditions. For if there is a free people which can make law for itself, the consent of the whole people expressed in custom is of more weight in regard to some observance than is the authority of the ruler who has not the power of making law except in so far as he bears the person of the people. Therefore, although single persons cannot establish law, yet the whole people can do so. But if the people has not the free power of making its own law, or of abrogating the law issued by a higher power, yet custom itself, prevailing in such a people, obtains the force of law, to the extent that it is tolerated by those to whom belongs the right of laying down the law for the people, for by this very tolerance they seem to approve what custom has introduced.

Aegidius Romanus

[Aegidius of Rome, possibly a member of the important Colonna family, was born ca. 1246 or 1247. He became a member of the Order of Hermits of St. Augustine, and was sent by his order to Paris, where he studied under Aquinas and became a zealous champion of his master's teachings. His theological writings made him one of the most noted scholars of the University of Paris. Philip III of France entrusted to him the education of his son, later to succeed him as Philip IV; Aegidius wrote his *De Regimine Principum* in 1285 as a text-book for his royal pupil. In 1292, he was elected superior-general of his order; in 1295, Boniface VIII and Philip IV agreed in elevating him to one of the most important archbishoprics in France, that of Bourges. Thereafter, he spent most of his time at the papal court, and the great controversy between Boniface and Philip found him an ardent supporter of the papal claims. His *De Potestate Ecclesiastica*, written in 1302 and dedicated to Boniface VIII, was a brilliant attempt to provide a systematic philosophical basis for direct papal overlordship over all temporal lordships. After the death of Boniface VIII, he was taken into favour once more by his former pupil and was active in Philip's campaign against the Order of Templars. He died at Avignon in 1316.

The *De Regimine Principum* does not anticipate Aegidius's theories of 1302. Its first two books deal with the moral principles that should govern royal behaviour, and with the king's family and household. The third is a general treatise on government, following Aristotle's *Politics* closely, though with some important deviations, and revealing the influence of Aquinas in many of its comments. Widely read through the Middle Ages, the *De Regimine Principum* was regarded as the most authoritative work of its type.

There is no modern edition of the *De Regimine Principum*. I have used an edition printed at Rome in 1482 for the following translation from bk. 3, pt. 2, chapters 24 and 25.]

CHAPTER XXIV. *That there are various kinds of law and various sorts of justice, and that all may be reduced to the two categories of natural and positive law*

Since laws are rules of right through which our actions are regulated, judging through themselves which of our deeds is just and which not just, it plainly appears that we can classify laws as we classify right or justice, and *vice versa*. Now we can make five classifications of right and likewise of justice: two of these are mentioned in I *Rhetoric*, the third is set forth in V *Ethics*, [ch. 7], the fourth is taken from the Jurists, and the fifth we can add ourselves. For right is divided into written and unwritten, common and private, natural and legal or positive: moreover, these three classifications of right are given us by the Philosopher, but the Jurists have classified right in a fourth way, saying that there is a natural right and a right of peoples and a civil right. Accordingly, in the same way as the Jurists distinguish natural right from the right of peoples we can distinguish natural right from the right of animals and make a fifth classification of right, saying that there are four categories of right: namely, natural right, the right of animals, the right of peoples, and civil right.

Therefore these five classifications which we have made of right or justice can be applied to law itself, in order that all these matters may be made more clear and that we may reduce these diversities to concord. It should be known that justice, or law, is of two kinds: natural and positive. For those things which are equated and proportioned by their own nature are called naturally just; or those things which natural reason designates as just, or to which we have a natural impetus and inclination, are called naturally just. But those things which are judged to be right, not from their own nature, but from human compact or institution, are called positively just. For the nature of things is the same everywhere, because what is fire in one place, as in France, is fire in another, as in Italy; for things are the same everywhere, even though they are not called by the same names. But the statutes of a people and the compacts of citizens and the edicts of a prince are not the same everywhere. Thence it is that natural right is said to differ from positive: because natural right, as is taught in V *Ethics*, [ch. 7], has the same force everywhere, but positive right, originally, before it is established, is a matter of indifference, but after it has been enacted, it begins to have binding force. Moreover, the reason why positive law must be added to natural law is that many things are naturally just, even as it is natural to man to speak; for we have a natural impetus and natural inclination to speak and to manifest to one another through speech what we have conceived in the mind; but that we speak one language or another is not natural but a matter of choice. Thus all men speak, but all do not choose the same language. For this reason also the Philosopher says in the *Perihermenias*, [ch. 1], that words and expressions are a matter of choice, although in the *Politics* [bk. 1, ch. 1] he says that speech was given us by nature. Therefore, among all those who wish to live civilly evil deeds are punished, but the same evil deeds are not everywhere corrected with the same penalties; therefore, positive right begins where natural right ends. For those things that are discovered through the art of men are always founded in those that have been given by nature; and thus positive right, discovered through the art and industry of men, presupposes natural right even as those things that are of art presuppose those things that are of nature. Wherefore, if natural right dictates that thieves and criminals are to be punished, this principle, presupposed by positive right, precedes those things that are further determined: namely, by what punishment they are to be punished. This being understood, so far as concerns the present problem, we are able to mark out a twofold distinction between natural and positive right. The first is that natural right presents itself immediately to the intellect; positive right does not reveal itself at once, but only after it has been discovered through the industry of men. And because it presents itself to our intellect thus, it is said that natural law and whatever things belong to natural law in the strict sense are written in our hearts: 'For the peoples which have not the law naturally do those things which are of the law and show the work of the law written in their hearts' [Romans 2:14–15]. But because positive right is not written in our hearts, it needs to be written on some exterior substance lest it escape our memory. Therefore, both laws, natural and positive, can be written on some exterior substance,

66

but natural law does not, like positive law, need to be written thus, for it cannot, like positive law, escape our memory.

The second difference is that natural right is the same among all men; therefore it is called common right; but positive right is diversified among diverse states; therefore, it is called particular right. . . .

CHAPTER XXV. *That the right of peoples and positive right must be distinguished from natural right*

All the classifications of right made by the Philosopher, which we have treated in the preceding chapter, consisted of two members: one of which was contained under natural right and the other under civil or positive right. Yet the Jurists, as was said, have added a third category, the right of peoples, and according to this way of speaking there can be added a fourth category, the right of animals. To show this, it should be known that, considered from the viewpoint of reason which is proper to him, man differs from other animals, but as an animal, subsumed in a common category with them, he agrees with other animals. If, therefore, those things to which we have a natural impetus or inclination belong to natural right, such a natural impetus may, on the one hand, proceed from our nature as men and as different from other animals, and the right so derived is called the right of peoples. But if that inclination proceeds from our nature as it agrees with other animals, the right so derived is called natural right. Therefore, according to the *Institutes*, [bk. 1, ch. 2], as they have been handed down to us, natural right is defined as that which nature has taught all animals. For, as is written there, all right is not peculiar to mankind but some belongs to all animals which are born in the sky or on the land or in the sea. These things, therefore, belong to natural right: the union of male and female, the procreation of offspring and the nurture of children; for if man naturally is inclined to these things by such an impetus, it proceeds from human nature not as human but as animal and as shared with other animals; for animals also are naturally inclined so that males unite with females to generate sons and to nourish and foster them. But that which is not common to other animals is called the right of peoples, according as it is common to the whole human race. Therefore from this right nearly all contracts were introduced, such as buying, selling, leasing, hiring, etc., without which human society could scarcely be sufficient for life. It is for this reason, therefore, that loan and deposit, which also serve human life and in which other animals do not share, are included in the right of peoples. The right of peoples is, therefore, a kind of restricted natural right. Therefore that right which nature taught all animals and which proceeds from the natural inclination which we share with other animals is called natural in comparison with the right of peoples. For if the things said in the preceding chapter are considered, natural right is that common right which is known and which is immutable. To the extent, therefore, that any right is more common than the right of peoples, so much the more it merits the name of natural right; therefore that right which nature has taught all animals and in which all animals share is more common than the right of peoples, and consequently is more known, because things that are more widespread are more known to us, for the more universal something is, the more it is known to our intellect and the earlier it enters our apprehension. Also, right of this sort is the more immutable because, in proportion as rules of right are applied to more special matter, they take on more defects and in more cases ought not to be observed and undergo greater mutation. Therefore, right of this sort is correctly called natural in comparison with the right of peoples.

Now that we have seen how the right of peoples differs from natural right, it easily becomes apparent how the right of animals differs from natural right; for as human nature agrees with the nature of other animals to the extent that man is animal, so in as much as man lives and is a kind of being he agrees with plants and with other substances and with all beings. For man naturally desires to be conserved in existence, which all beings also desire; he naturally desires to produce sons and to nurture his offspring, which other animals also desire; and he naturally desires to live in society in accordance with suitable conventions and compacts, which is proper to man alone among animals. If, therefore, the rules of things to be done are founded on the fact that man naturally desires to exist, rules of this sort can belong to natural right according as human nature is a certain entity and agrees with all entities. But if these rules are based on the fact that man naturally desires to produce and nurture sons, they can belong to natural right according as what nature has taught all animals is called natural right. But if they are based on the fact that man naturally desires to live in society in accordance with suitable conventions and compacts, they will belong to natural right as natural right is restricted to the right of peoples, which is proper to mankind alone.

From this, therefore, it manifestly appears that, even as the right of peoples is not considered so natural as the right which nature has taught all animals, so this right which nature has taught all animals is not so natural as the right which follows the inclination of our nature which we share not merely with other animals but with all beings. For the latter kind of right is more known and more common than the former; for to desire good and existence and to shun evil and non-existence belong to natural right more than to desire to procreate sons and to nourish offspring. Therefore there will be this order: that the right which proceeds from our nature according as we desire existence is natural in comparison with the right of animals, or the right which nature has taught all animals, even as that right is natural in comparison with civil right, which is merely positive. Therefore, these three belong to natural law, each in its own way, according as the inclination proceeds from our nature: for, if it proceeds from our nature as human, the right of peoples is derived; if it proceeds from our nature as it agrees with other animals, there arises that right which nature has taught all animals; but if it proceeds from our nature as it agrees with all beings, there arises that right which, by autonomasy, is called natural; for to desire existence and the good and to shun non-existence and the bad, which we naturally desire according as our nature agrees with all beings, belongs to natural law so that all other rules and other laws, whether natural or civil, originate in this and are based on this; for in all things we seek either the attainment of good or the avoidance of evil. . . .

Marsiglio of Padua

[Many of the facts of the life of Marsiglio de Mainardino are obscure. He was born in Padua, then still a free commune, sometime between 1270 and 1280; his father was a notary attached to the University of Padua. Marsiglio studied arts and medicine at the University of Padua, later moved on to Paris, where for a few months in 1312–1313 he was Rector of the University. In 1316 he seems to have expected the grant of a canonry at Padua from the newly-elected John XXII; he may have actually received this appointment. There is some evidence that he went to Avignon and, like Luther later, was deeply impressed by the worldly tone of the papal court. In 1318, he received from the pope the reservation of the first vacant benefice at Padua. In 1318–1319, or perhaps earlier, he appears to have been in the service of Cam Grande of Verona and to have been active in Ghibelline diplomacy. By 1320, at all events, we find him established at Paris, where he practised medicine and perhaps began the study of theology.

The *Defensor Pacis* was completed on 24 June 1324. In 1326 Marsiglio went to Germany and attached himself to Lewis of Bavaria, to whom the *Defensor Pacis* had been dedicated. His flight was shared by his friend John of Jandun, who had been a noted leader of the Averroists in the arts faculty at Paris, and who had been associated with Marsiglio to an undetermined degree in the composition of the *Defensor Pacis*. Lewis, then in the thick of his struggle with John XXII, took both men under his protection. Marsiglio became his influential adviser and accompanied him on the Italian campaign of 1327–1328. In ceremonies suggesting the theory of the *Defensor Pacis*, Lewis had John XXII deposed by an anti-pope elected by a parliament representing the Roman people and had himself crowned emperor with popular consent. He appointed Marsiglio his spiritual vicar for the city of Rome. When the Roman triumph collapsed in 1328, Marsiglio returned to Germany with Lewis. He and John of Jandun had been excommunicated in April 1327, and six of the main theses of the *Defensor Pacis* were decisively labelled as heretical in a papal bull later in that year. John of Jandun died in 1328; little is known of Marsiglio's later life, except that he continued to live under the Emperor's precarious protection and in 1342 produced the *Defensor Minor* and a treatise on the imperial jurisdiction in matrimonial cases. By April 1343 he was dead—'the worst heretic,' said Clement VI, that he had ever read.

A few of the influences that shaped his thought are clearly apparent. The evidence of the *Defensor Pacis* shows that he was intensely moved by the unhappy condition of Italy, which he attributed to papal intervention in its affairs; the memory of the struggle between Boniface VIII and Philip the Fair also affected him, teaching him to see the problem of Italy as one instance of the general problem of Europe. From his Italian background, also, he presumably derived the concept of a functioning community of citizens which became a foundation stone of his theory. In Padua and in Paris he is known to have associated with Averroists; the influence of Averroism shows itself in his work not so much in specific principles as in the general tone of scepticism and positivism and in the sharpness with which he contrasts the areas of secular knowledge and of revelation. In the New Testament, which he read with a literal spirit and a critical historical sense, he found a basis for his theories of church government; and he was able to support them with the help of Pseudo-Isidore, the letters of St. Jerome, and a few other miscellaneous works. Finally, he was deeply influenced by Aristotle, in particular by the *Ethics* and the *Politics*; he also found congenial material in Cicero's *De Officiis*. Attempts to trace his thought to other specific influences—to contacts with Occam and the Spiritual Franciscans, with the circle of Nogaret, or with the Waldensians—have been unsatisfactory or inconclusive.

His aloofness from some of the main streams of medieval intellectual life was, perhaps, as significant for the character of his thought as the few positive influences that have been established. Important as Aristotle was to him, the Aristotle that he knew was the scientist, not the metaphysician. His mind had a legalistic bent, but he had practically no acquaintance with the civil law and only a haphazard and elementary knowledge of the canon law. His knowledge of theology was fragmentary. His fresh approach to the New Testament was perhaps not entirely unconnected with the fact that he had little knowledge of the patristic writings or later commentaries. He was untouched by the recent great systematizations of scholastic thought, like that of Aquinas, which were the glory of advanced theological studies at Paris. Thus he had almost no share in the intellectual disciplines which might have taught him to qualify his assertions or to relate them to a more general view of the universe. His great political treatise—like that of Rousseau—owes some of its most conspicuous merits and defects to the intellectual characteristics of the inspired amateur—original, vigorous, penetrating, absolute, arrogant, doctrinaire. Like the author of the *Social Contract*, the author of the *Defensor Pacis* proceeds with brilliant assurance to draw startling conclusions from startling premises never critically examined or quite clearly conceived; and in both works, an apparently firm structure of tightly-articulated logic only half-conceals an ultimate vagueness and inconsistency which continually baffle interpreters and set them quarrelling.

The following selection from *dictio* 1 of the *Defensor Pacis*, chs. 10, 12, 13, presents Marsiglio's radical theories of law and the legislator, which prepare the way for his radical theories of church government in *dictio* 2. I have used both modern editions of the *Defensor Pacis*: that edited by C. W. Prévité-Orton (Cambridge, 1928), and that edited by Richard Scholz (Hanover, 1932–33).]

CHAPTER X. *Concerning the distinction and assignation of the meanings of this word 'law,' and its most proper sense, in which we use it*

3. . . . . Lest difficulty arise because of the many senses of the word, it is well to distinguish the meanings or senses of the word 'law.' For this word means in one sense a natural sensitive inclination to any action or passion; and in this sense it was used by the Apostle in Romans

7: [23], when he said: 'Moreover, I see one law in my members, warring against the law of my mind.' But in another sense this word 'law' is used of some operative quality, and generally of every form of an operable thing existing in the mind, from which as type or measure the forms of artifacts proceed, as is said in Ezekiel 43: [12–13]: 'Therefore this is the law of the house; that is the measure of the altar.' But in a third sense law means a rule containing admonitions to prescribed human actions, according to which they are ordained to glory or punishment in the world to come; and in this sense the Mosaic Law is called law in regard to any of its parts, and similarly the Evangelic Law as a whole is called law. Whence the Apostle, in the Epistle to the Hebrews, says of these matters [7:12]: 'For since the priesthood has been changed, there is made of necessity a change also of the law.' Thus the Evangelic discipline is also called law in James 1: [25]: 'But whoso looketh into the perfect law of liberty, and continueth therein,' etc., 'this man shall be blessed in his doing.' In this sense the term is also applied to all the laws of sects, as wholes or as parts: for instance, of Mahomet or of the Persians; although the Mosaic and Evangelic Law, that is, the Christian law, alone of all these contain the truth. . . . Moreover, in the fourth and best-known sense this word 'law' means the science or doctrine or universal judgment of just and beneficial civil actions, and their opposites.

4. And, taken in this sense, law can be considered in two ways: in one way substantively, as in itself it shows what is just or unjust, beneficial or harmful; and in this way we speak of the science or doctrine of this sort of law. In another way, it can be considered in accordance with the fact that in regard to its observance a command is given, which is coercive through a penalty or reward to be assigned in our present life, or in accordance with the fact that it is transmitted by means of such a command; and considered in this way it is most properly called, and is, law. And in this sense Aristotle also defined it, in X Ethics, ch. 10, when he said: 'Moreover law has coercive force, being the utterance of a certain prudence and intelligence'; an utterance or saying, therefore, of a certain prudence and intelligence, namely, the political: that is, law is an ordinance concerning just and beneficial deeds and their opposites, made by political prudence, having coercive force: that is, concerning the observance of which there is given a command that one is compelled to observe, or which is expressed in the form of a command.

5. Wherefore not all true concepts of just and beneficial civil actions are laws, unless a coercive command concerning their observance has been given, or unless they have been expressed in the form of a command; a true concept of these things is necessarily requisite for perfect law. Nevertheless sometimes false concepts of just and beneficial things are made laws, when their observance is commanded or they are expressed in the form of a command, as appears in the countries of certain barbarians, who cause it to be observed as just that a murderer is absolved from guilt and civil penalty if he pays some real price for his crime, although this is, in the strict sense, unjust and consequently their laws are not, in the strict sense, perfect. For while they may have the proper form, namely, a coercive command of observance, yet they lack the proper condition, namely, a proper and true ordination of just things.

6. Moreover, under law in this sense are included all rules of just and beneficial civil actions instituted by human authority, as customs, statutes, plebiscites, decretals, and all the like. . . .

7. We ought also to recognize that the Law of the Gospels, as well as the Mosaic Law, and perhaps the other laws of particular sects . . . sometimes come, or have formerly come, or will come, under the third sense of law, and sometimes under the last. . . .

CHAPTER XII. *Concerning the demonstrable efficient cause of human laws, and also concerning that which cannot be proved by demonstration: that is, to seek the legislator. Whence it also appears that by election alone, without any other confirmation, authority is given to that which is established by election*

1. We must now discuss the efficient cause of law, so far as this can be done by demonstration; for I do not intend to discuss here the institution of those laws which may be, or once might be, made by the act of God or through His immediate mouthpiece, without the intervention of human decision: such as the institution of the Mosaic Law. Nor do I intend to discuss here even such of its precepts as apply to the present life. But I shall speak only of the institution of such laws and governments as proceed immediately from the decision of the human mind.

2. And, as we approach this question, let us say that if law is considered, as it were, substantively and in accordance with the third sense [more accurately, the first subdivision of the fourth] defined above (namely, as the science of just and beneficial civil actions), such law

THE IDEA OF LAW

can be discovered by any citizen whatever, although the search for law in this sense can more expediently and more thoroughly be carried out by the observations of those who have opportunity for leisure, the elders and those more experienced in practical affairs who are called 'the prudent,' rather than by the opinions of artisans, who have to direct their activity toward acquiring the necessities of life. But the true knowledge or discovery of just and beneficial things is not law in its last and most proper sense, according to which it is a measure of human civil actions, unless it is combined with a coercive command enjoining its observation or is expressed in the form of a coercive command by him by whose authority transgressors can and should be restrained. Therefore it is fitting to tell what person or persons have the authority to issue such a command and to restrain its transgressors; and this is to seek out the legislator, or maker of law.

3. Let us moreover say, truly and in accordance with the opinion of Aristotle in III *Politics*, ch. 11, that the legislator, or prime and proper effective cause of law, is the people or body of citizens, or its more weighty part, through its choice or will orally expressed in the general assembly of citizens, commanding or determining, in regard to the civil actions of men, that something be done or not done, under penalty of temporal punishment. The more weighty part, I say, taking into consideration the number and the quality of persons in that community for which the law is enacted. The whole corporation of citizens, or its weightier part, either makes law itself, directly, or entrusts this task to some person or persons, who are not and cannot be the legislator in the absolute sense, but only for specific matters, and temporarily, and by virtue of the authority of the prime legislator. And I say in consequence that laws and anything whatever that is established by choice ought to receive the necessary approval by none other than that same prime legislator, with whatever solemnities may be appropriate. . . . And I further say that by that same authority laws, and other things that are established by choice, ought to undergo addition or diminution or total change, interpretation, and suspension, in accordance with the exigency of times or places or other circumstances which make such change expedient for the sake of the common welfare. Also, by that same authority laws ought to be promulgated or proclaimed after their institution, so that no delinquent citizen or sojourner can plead ignorance of the law as his excuse.

4. Moreover, following Aristotle's opinion in III *Politics*, chs. 1, 3, 13, I mean by citizen any man who participates in the civil community, in the principate or the council or the jury, according to his rank. By this definition boys, slaves, sojourners, and women are excluded from the category of citizens, though in different ways. For the sons of citizens are potentially citizens, lacking only the qualification of age. And the weightier part should be discovered in accordance with the opinion of Aristotle in VI *Politics*, ch. 3.

5. Now that we have defined the citizen and the more weighty multitude of citizens, let us return to our announced purpose: namely, to demonstrate that the human authority of legislation belongs only to the corporation of citizens or to its more weighty part. And we shall attempt to prove this as follows. The primary human authority, in an absolute sense, to make or institute laws, belongs only to him from whom alone the best laws can proceed. Now this is the corporation of citizens, or its more weighty part, which represents the whole corporation, because it is not easy or possible to bring all persons to one opinion on account of the deficient nature of some, who through individual perversity or ignorance dissent from the common opinion but whose irrational protestations or contradictions ought not to impede or frustrate the common benefit. Therefore the authority to make or institute laws belongs only to the corporation of citizens, or to its more weighty part.

The major premise of this syllogism is very nearly self-evident. . . . I prove the minor premise (namely, that the best law is made only by the knowledge and command of the whole multitude) by agreeing with what Aristotle says in III *Politics*, ch. 7, that the best law is that which is made for the common benefit of the citizens. . . . And that this can best be attained only through the corporation of citizens, or its more weighty part, which in any matter acts on behalf of the corporation, I show thus: because the truth of anything is more certainly judged and its common utility more diligently studied, when the whole corporation of citizens directs upon it its intellect and desire. For a greater number can give more attention to a defect in a proposed law than can any part of that number, since the whole of any body is at least greater in mass and in virtues than is any of its parts separately. Also, the common utility of a law is given more attention by a whole multitude, since no one knowingly harms himself. Moreover, under

75

such circumstances everyone can see for himself whether the proposed law tends to the advantage of some one man or group of men rather than to that of the others or of the community, and can protest against it; which would not be done if the law were made by one man only or by some few, looking rather to their own than to the common good. . . .

6. We may also prove the principal conclusion in this way. The authority of legislation belongs only to him whose making of the laws results in their being better or more directly observed. Now this is none other than the corporation of citizens; therefore to it belongs the authority of legislation. The first premise of this syllogism is very nearly self-evident, for a law would be idle if it were not observed. Whence Aristotle says in IV *Politics*, ch. 6, 'Moreover, to have good laws enacted and yet not to obey them does not constitute a good disposition of laws.' And he also says in VI *Politics*, ch. 5, 'There is no advantage if judgments concerning just things have been made and yet do not attain their end.' The minor premise I prove thus. Any one of the citizens will better observe that law which he seems to have imposed upon himself; such is the law laid down by the knowledge and command of the whole multitude of citizens. The first premise of this auxiliary syllogism is almost self-evident: for, since 'the state is a community of free men,' as it is written in III *Politics*, ch. 4, every citizen ought to be free and not bear the despotism—that is, the lordship over slaves—of another. Now this would not be the case if some one or some few of the citizens should lay down the law by their own authority for the corporation of citizens; for thus those who made the law would be the despots of the others. And therefore the rest of the citizens—namely, the larger part—would bear such a law, however good it might be, with vexation or not at all, and would protest against it on the grounds that they had been treated with contempt, and, not having been summoned to its making, they would in no way observe it. But if it were made by the knowledge and consent of all the multitude, even if it were less useful, each of the citizens would easily observe and endure it; because each would seem to have established it for himself, and therefore would have no protest against it, but would rather endure it with a calm mind. I also prove the minor premise of the primary syllogism in another way, as follows. The power to cause laws to be observed belongs to the one who alone has coercive power

over transgressors; now this is the corporation or its more weighty part; therefore it alone has the authority of legislation.

7. We may also proceed to the principal conclusion as follows. That doable thing, in whose due institution consists the greatest part of the common sufficiency of citizens in this life, and in whose wrong institution there threatens a common detriment, ought to be instituted only by the corporation of citizens; now this is a law; therefore the institution of a law belongs to the corporation of citizens. The major premise of this syllogism is nearly self-evident, and has been established in the immediate truths which were set forth in the fourth and fifth chapters of this book. For men have joined into a civil community for the sake of attaining their advantage and a sufficient life, and in order to avoid the opposite. Those things, therefore, which can affect the benefit and disadvantage of all ought to be known and heard by all, so that they may follow what is beneficial and reject what is not. But such things are laws, as was stated in the minor premise. For in these, rightly set forth, a great part of the total and common human sufficiency consists; but under unfair laws, servitude and oppression and the misery of the citizens may be introduced, by which at last the polity may be dissolved.

8. Again—and this is a kind of abbreviation and summary of the former proofs: the authority of legislation belongs either to the corporation of citizens alone, as we have said, or to a single man, or to a few; it cannot belong to a single man on account of those things which were said in chapter XI above and those which we have added in our first syllogism; for he would be able to make a bad law through ignorance or perversity or both: specifically, through having regard rather to his own than to the common advantage; whence it would be tyrannical. For the same reason, it does not belong to a few: for they could err in the same way in making a law for the benefit of a few—that is, of themselves—and not for the common good; as can be seen in oligarchies. This authority, therefore, belongs to the corporation of citizens or to its more weighty part; for another, opposite reason applies to them. For since all citizens ought to be measured by the law in accordance with due proportion, and no one knowingly injures himself or wishes injustice for himself, therefore all or most will desire a law that agrees with the common advantage of the citizens.

9. From these syllogisms also, with only the minor premise changed,

it can be proved that the approval, interpretation, and suspension of laws, and the other things listed in the third section of this chapter, belong to the authority of the legislator alone. And the same conclusion should apply to everything that is established through choice. . . .

CHAPTER XIII

8. . . . . It is suitable and very useful that the search for, or the discovery and examination of the rules of just and beneficial civil actions . . . which are to be made laws or statutes should be entrusted by the corporation of citizens to prudent and expert men: either each of the primary parts of the state . . . should elect some of these prudent and expert men, in accordance with the proportion of each, or all the citizens assembled together should elect them all. And this will be a suitable and useful way of coming together for the discovery of laws without injury to the rest of the multitude, namely, of the less learned, who would be of little help in seeking out rules of this sort and would be disturbed from their other work and other necessary things, which would be harmful both to them as individuals and to the community.

But when these rules . . . have been discovered and diligently examined, they ought to be submitted for approval or rejection to the assembled corporation of citizens, in order that, if it seems to any of the citizens that something ought to be added to them, or subtracted, or if something should be altered or totally rejected, he may say so; because in this way the law can be more usefully ordained. For, as we have already said, the less learned citizens can sometimes notice something to be corrected in regard to the proposed law, although they would not have known how to discover the law. Also, because laws thus passed by the hearing and consent of the whole multitude will be better observed, and no one will have an occasion of protest against them.

Now when the said rules . . . have been made public and those citizens who wish to say anything rationally against them have been heard, such men as we have described ought again to be chosen in the way described, or the aforesaid confirmed, who, representing the name and authority of the corporation of citizens, will approve or reject the aforesaid rules in whole or in part; or, if it so wishes, the whole corporation of citizens or its weightier part may do this. And after this approval, and not before, the aforesaid rules are laws. . . .

William of Occam

[William of Occam was born in England between 1290 and 1300. He joined the Franciscans and was educated at Oxford, where he wrote the incisive logical and theological works that founded the medieval school of nominalism. In 1324, he was summoned to Avignon because of some dubious theological doctrines he had promulgated; here he spent the next four years in contact with Michael of Cesena, the minister-general of the Franciscan Order, and with Bonagratia of Bergamo, its procurator. The group were excommunicated in 1328 for their defence of the doctrine of apostolic poverty; shortly before the sentence was delivered they escaped to the protection of Lewis of Bavaria, who was then returning from his anti-papal expedition to Rome. Between 1330 and 1338, Occam remained at Munich under the emperor's protection, writing voluminously. He defended the doctrine of apostolic poverty, attacked the heresies of John XXII, and gradually broadened his thought to include searching analyses of papal authority and of the bases and limitations of authority in general. The enormous *Dialogus*, in which his political principles are most elaborately set forth, was begun ca. 1334, and what we have of it was finished by 1343, though it was still far from complete, and apparently never completed, in terms of Occam's original design. Occam's location and activities after 1338 are not definitely known. After Cesena's death in 1342, he became reconciled with the Franciscan faction which had remained loyal to the pope, but there is no evidence that he ever made peace with the church. In view of the vigorous tone of his *De Imperatorum et Pontificum Potestate* (written in 1346 or 1347), it is most probable that, like Marsiglio, he remained under its ban till his death, in 1349 or 1350.

The same temper which led Occam to raise fundamental doubts about traditional principles of medieval theology and epistemology appears in the questions and qualifications characteristic of his political thought. His philosophical innovations, however, affected the ultimate premises of his political theory rather than its proximate assumptions or its conclusions. Since he was, very profoundly, a believing Christian, close to the orthodox tradition of medieval Catholicism except at certain points, his faith restored as known through revelation much that his reason defined as unprovable; his immediate premises for the rational analysis of institutions owed much to Aristotle and Aquinas and to the analyses of civilists and canonists; nothing was further from his intentions than a radical reconstruction of traditional institutions in church and state. Thus his political theory was, on the whole, continuous with established medieval patterns. It was distinguished by the boldness with

THE IDEA OF LAW

which he refused to submit his mind to any coercion save that of 'evident reason or an authority of Holy Scripture reasonably understood,' as he wrote in the preface to his last treatise; by his unwavering opposition to absolute authority in church or state; by his amazing grasp of logical complexities; and by his willingness to accept the variability of earthly institutions. In his writing, the medieval habit of analysing a problem from all aspects, with arguments and counter-arguments, rebuttals and surrebuttals, reaches a bewildering extreme; whether from caution or from his mental temper, he was often so reluctant to state his own position that one can find the victorious thesis only, if at all, by examining the casualty-lists for the many-sided battle of ideas that he arranged. This method of writing has led a few commentators to assert that Occam was certain of nothing but his doubts. But in spite of many loose ends, ambiguities, and inconsistencies, especially on topics at the periphery of his interests, there is a core of firm and passionate conviction in Occam's thought, and a general consistency of theory underlies his most academic writings and rises sharply to the surface in his polemical works.

Occam's theory of natural law is imbedded in an argument that the right to elect the pope belongs ultimately to the Roman people: *Dialogus*, ed. M. Goldast, *Monarchia . . .* , vol. II (Frankfort, 1668), pt. 3, tr. 2, bk. 3, ch. 6 (pp. 393–395). The whole passage illustrates the way in which Occam's theory of 'natural law in the third sense' blends the notions of reason and consent; it also illustrates his characteristic boldness in subjecting questions of ecclesiastical organization to the criteria of natural law.]

PUPIL: Tell me how they answer the argument . . . that neither by divine law nor by human law do the Romans have the right of electing the supreme pontiff.

TEACHER: They answer that, if one extends the concept of divine law to cover all kinds of natural law, the Romans have by divine law the right of electing the supreme pontiff.

PUPIL: That answer seems obscure to me, and therefore I should like to have it explained; . . . but first tell me why they say, 'if one extends the concept of divine law to cover all kinds of natural law'; second, why all kinds of natural law can be called divine law.

TEACHER: First, they make a distinction between three senses of the term *natural law*. For in one sense natural law means that which conforms to natural reason, which in no case fails: for instance, 'thou shalt not commit adultery,' 'thou shalt not deceive,' and the like. In another sense, natural law is that which ought to be kept by those who use natural equity alone, without any human custom or statute, which is natural because it is [not] contrary to the original state of nature, and because it ought [Goldast inserts 'not'] to be followed or observed if all men lived according to natural reason or divine law. In the second sense and not the first, all things are common by natural law; for in the original state of nature all things would have been common, and if after the Fall all men were living in accordance with reason, all things would still be common and nothing private, for property was introduced on account of sin (*Decretum*, c. 2, C. 12, q. 1). It is in this sense that Isidore speaks when he says in the fifth book of the *Etymologies*, as quoted in the *Decretum* (c. 7, di. 1), that according to natural law all possession of all things is common and there is one liberty of all men; for the common possession of all things and the one liberty of all men do not belong to natural law in the first sense—for if that were the case no one could licitly appropriate anything for himself, nor could anyone be made a slave by the law of peoples and the civil law, since natural law in the first sense is immutable and invariable and indispensable (§1, di. 5 and §1, c. 3, di. 6). It is clear, however, that some men are licitly slaves by the law of peoples, as the blessed Gregory bears witness when he says (as quoted in c. 68, C. 12, q. 2): 'It is well done if men, whom nature originally brought forth free, and whom the law of peoples brought under the yoke of slavery, are, by the beneficence of a manumittor, restored to liberty as to the nature in which they were born.' These words imply that by natural law all men are free and yet by the law of peoples some are slaves. From this one can infer that natural law, in the sense in which the term is used here, is not immutable; but rather it is permissible to establish that something be done contrary to that law.

In the third sense, the term *natural law* applies to that which is inferred from the law of peoples or some human fact by evident reason, unless the contrary is established by the consent of those whose interest is involved; and this can be called natural law by supposition: for example, according to Isidore in the passage cited above, natural law is the restitution of a thing which has been deposited, or of money which has been lent, and the repelling of force with force. For these principles are not natural laws in the first sense nor in the second, since they would not have existed in the original state of nature and would not exist among those who, living in accordance with reason, would be content with natural equity alone without any human custom or statute. For among such men nothing would be deposited or lent, nor would anyone use force against another. Therefore these principles are natural laws by supposition, because if it is supposed that goods and money are private property by the law of peoples or by any human law, it is inferred by evident reason that the thing deposited and the money lent ought to be restored, unless for some reason the contrary was ordained by the person or persons whose interests were involved. Likewise, on the supposition that anyone should in fact use force injuriously against another—which does not belong to natural law, but is contrary to it—it is inferred by evident reason that it is permitted to repel such force with force.

Therefore, on account of these three senses of natural law, they say that the Romans have from divine law the right of electing the supreme pontiff, if the concept of divine law is extended to include all kinds of natural law, and that, if it were extended only to natural law in the first sense, . . . they would not have from divine law the right of electing the supreme pontiff. . . .

PUPIL: You have explained why those who hold the opinion under discussion say that the Romans have from divine law the right of electing the supreme pontiff, if the concept of divine law is extended to cover all kinds of natural law. Now tell me why, according to this same opinion, all kinds of natural law can be called divine.

TEACHER: They say so for this reason: because every law which comes from God, the founder of nature, can be called divine law; now, every kind of natural law comes from God, the founder of nature; therefore, etc. Also: because every law which is explicitly contained in the divine Scriptures can be called divine law, since, as is said in the *Decretum*, c. 1, di. 8, divine law is contained in the divine Scriptures; now, all natural law is explicitly or implicitly contained in the divine Scriptures, since there are in the divine Scriptures certain general rules, from which, singly or in combination with others, all natural law, in the first, second, or third sense, can be inferred; thus all natural law is divine law, even though it is not found explicitly in the Scriptures.

PUPIL: You have explained, according to the opinion under discussion, two things which seemed obscure. Now tell me, in terms of the same argument, how the Romans have from divine law the right of electing the supreme pontiff.

THE IDEA OF LAW

TEACHER: On this point, it is said that the Romans have the right of electing the supreme pontiff from natural law in the third sense; for, on the supposition that someone is to be made prelate or prince or ruler over others, it is inferred by evident reason that, unless the contrary is ordained by the person or persons whose interests are involved, those who are to be ruled have the right to choose their ruler and set him over themselves, whence no ruler ought to be given them against their will. This can be proved by many examples and arguments, but I shall adduce a few. And the first is that no one should be set over a body of mortals except by their choice and consent. Further, what touches all should be done by all; now, the setting of someone over others touches all; therefore, it ought to be done by all. Again, those who can make law for themselves can, if they wish, elect their head; but any people or state can make law for themselves, which is called civil law (c. 8, di. 1); therefore, the people or state can make their own law and choose their head. And thus the election of a ruler always belongs to those who are to be ruled, unless the contrary is ordained by the person or persons whose interest is involved.

And this qualification is made for the following reason: that, in many cases at least, they can yield their right and transfer it to some other person or persons; and thus, although by natural law in the third sense the people has the right to establish laws, it has transferred that power to the emperor; and thus it was in the power of the emperor to transfer the right of election to some other person or persons. Likewise, if those who are to be ruled are in matters of this sort subject to some superior, that superior can ordain that they do not have the right of election, even though by natural law in the third sense they have the right of election; specifically, if the contrary was not ordained by themselves or by their superior. And thus it seems to those who hold this opinion that the foregoing proposition is to be regarded as evident.

Now the supreme pontiff is, in a way, especially set over the Romans, since they have no other bishop. Therefore, by natural law in the third sense (that is, by natural law by supposition—specifically, on the supposition that they ought to have a bishop) they have the right of electing him, unless the contrary is established or ordained by the Romans themselves or by someone else who is superior to the Romans and who has authority in this matter. For the Romans could yield their right, or transfer their right of electing, to some other person or persons;

83

and they could also transfer the right of constituting the electors of the supreme pontiff. And the superior of the Romans who has power in this respect can grant the right of electing to others than the Romans; but that superior is Christ and not the pope. And therefore Christ and not the pope could deprive the Romans of the right of electing the supreme pontiff; but Christ has not deprived the Romans of this right. For when Christ set the blessed Peter over all Christians, giving him authority to be, in a way, the particular bishop of whatever place he should choose as his seat, He did not deprive the people of that place of the right which, unless the contrary is ordained by them or by their superior, belongs to all those over whom some authority, whether secular or ecclesiastical, is to be set. Therefore, when the blessed Peter chose the see of Rome, it followed that the Romans had the right to elect the successor of the blessed Peter who would be set over them in spirituals. And thus the Romans have by divine law, if one extends the concept of divine law to cover every kind of natural law, the right to elect the supreme pontiff.

PUPIL: It seems that it would be better to say that, according to that opinion, the Romans have the right to elect their bishop from the law of peoples, since the principle that all those over whom someone is to be made ruler have the right to choose that ruler, unless they yield their right or a superior ordains the contrary, belongs to the law of peoples.

TEACHER: Although many things that belong to the law of peoples are natural rights in the third sense of natural law, yet, according to that opinion, it is more proper to say that the Romans have the right to elect their bishop from natural law in the third sense than from the law of peoples, for this reason: that to have a catholic bishop does not belong to the law of peoples but to divine law, although the principle that he who is to be set over others ought to be elected by those over whom he is to be set belongs to the law of peoples. It belongs no less to divine law, for this reason: that it can be inferred from those things which are in the Scriptures, putting one with another; and thus the two suppositions from which it is inferred that the Romans have the right to elect their bishop belong, though in different ways, to divine law, whereas only one of the two belongs to the law of peoples. And for this reason it is more proper to say that the Romans have the right to elect their bishop from divine law, or from natural law in the third sense, than from the law of peoples. Yet those who do not care to quibble over words say that it is enough for them that the Romans have the right to elect their bishop because they ought to have a bishop and because those over whom someone is to be set ought to elect him unless they yield their right or unless the contrary is ordained by a superior. But whether, properly speaking, it should be said that the Romans have the right of election from divine law or from natural law in the third sense, or whether from both divine law and the law of peoples, they do not much care. Yet it appears to some men that it is more proper to say that they have the right of election from both divine law and the law of peoples.

Sir John Fortescue

[Sir John Fortescue (ca. 1394–ca. 1476) was, by birth and opinions, representative of the class of English gentry which in the fifteenth century was becoming the backbone of English constitutionalism. He was educated at Oxford, studied law at Lincoln's Inn, and embarked on a legal career which culminated in his appointment as Chief Justice of the King's Bench in 1442, a post that he filled effectively. In his politics, unlike most of his legal colleagues, he was a staunch partisan of the Lancastrian cause, which was also the cause of the gentry. He followed Henry VI into exile in 1460 and spent most of the following decade on the continent with the royal family. In 1471, when the Lancastrian cause seemed hopeless, he finally made his peace with Edward IV.

The *De Laudibus Legum Angliae* was written in exile for the instruction of the young Prince Edward; it was first printed under Henry VIII. Here Fortescue developed the thesis, outlined in his earlier *De Natura Legis Naturae*, that the English government was 'a lordship both political and regal,' in which the royal power was limited not only by the law of nature, but also by the laws of England. The selection translated below, from chs. 15–18, illustrates the late medieval transition between the idea of the authoritative finding of customary law and the idea of authoritative legislative enactment. I have used the text edited by S. B. Chrimes (Cambridge, 1942) and checked my translation against his.]

XV. I would have you know that all human laws are either the law of nature, customs, or statutes . . . but when customs and the principles of the law of nature are put into writing and promulgated by the sufficient authority of the prince and commanded to be kept, they are changed into statutes, and, by the severity of that command, bind the subjects of the prince to observe them under a greater penalty than before. Statutes of this sort form a considerable part of the Civil Laws which are digested in great volumes by the princes of the Romans and whose observation is commanded by their authority. Whence that part has received the name of Civil Laws, like other imperial statutes. If, therefore, I prove the shining excellence of the law of England in each of these three categories, which may be called the wellsprings of all law, then I shall have proved that it is good and effectual law for the government of that kingdom. Then if I clearly show that it is as well suited to the utility of that kingdom as the Civil Laws to the good of the Empire, I shall have demonstrated not only that this law is excellent, but also that it is as excellent as the Civil Laws. . . .

XVI. The laws of England, in so far as they are deduced from the law of nature, are neither better nor worse in their judgments than the corresponding laws of all other states and kingdoms. For, as the Philosopher says in V *Ethics*, [ch. 7], 'Natural law is that which has the same force among all men'; wherefore we need debate no further on this point. But now we must examine the nature of the customs and statutes of England; and we shall first investigate the characteristics of its customs.

XVII. The realm of England was first inhabited by the Britons; then it was ruled by the Romans; then the Britons again possessed it, and next the Saxons, who changed its name from Britain to England. Then this same kingdom was dominated, for a time, by the Danes; and again by the Saxons; but, at last, by the Normans, whose descendants hold the kingdom to this day. And during all the times of those nations and their kings, this kingdom has been regulated continuously by the same customs by which it is now ruled. And if those customs had not been the best, some of those kings, inspired by justice, reason, or inclination, would have changed them or entirely abolished them—especially the Romans, who judged all the rest of the world by their own laws. Likewise others of the aforesaid kings who possessed the kingdom of England only by the sword could by the same power have destroyed its laws. Now the Civil Laws, in so far as they are Roman, were not aged by the passage of so great time; nor were the laws of the Venetians, which are said to surpass all others in antiquity; for the island of the Venetians was not inhabited when British customs began, nor was

Rome yet founded; nor have the laws of any kingdom in Christendom endured so long. Thus one cannot say or even suspect that the customs of the English are not good—nay, more, that they are not the best.

XVIII. It only remains to examine whether the statutes of England are good or not. Now they do not flow solely from the mere will of a prince, like the laws in those countries which are governed only regally, where the statutes sometimes further the single advantage of him who makes them and thus redound to the detriment and damage of his subjects. Sometimes, too, by the inadvertence of such princes and the inertia of their advisers their laws are so thoughtlessly framed that they deserve the name of seductions rather than of laws. But the statutes of England cannot be thus formed, since they are established not only by the will of the prince, but with the consent of the whole realm, so that they cannot bring about injury to the people, or fail to procure their advantage. Moreover, they must necessarily be deemed to have been shaped with wisdom and prudence, since they are produced not by the prudence of one man or of a mere hundred counsellors, but by the prudence of more than three hundred select men—such a number as once ruled the Roman Senate—as those who know the form of the Parliament of England and the order and method of its convocation can more specifically explain. And if these statutes, the product of so much solemnity and prudence, should happen not to be so efficacious as their makers hoped and intended, they can immediately be reformed with the consent of the Commons and Lords of the realm, with which they first were made.

Chapter Two

PROPERTY AND LORDSHIP

EDIEVAL ideas about the nature, basis, and limitations of the property right were an integral part of medieval thought on government and law. Feudalism tended to dissolve governmental functions themselves into forms of property; on the other hand, the restraint of the king by customary law involved a theory that jealously guarded the property of subjects from his power. The scholastic and canonist application of natural-law theory to problems of property laid a theoretical foundation for governmental intervention in economic matters; the medieval infancy of commerce was nurtured by structures and doctrines perhaps more essentially political than economic. The medieval solution of the problem of authority and liberty involved a statement of the relations of property and government more complex than that on which more recent solutions have been unsatisfactorily based. Controversies between king and subjects, between church and king, were often fought out in terms of a doctrine of 'divided lordship' which is the peculiar contribution of the Middle Ages to the problem of the structure of rights; and medieval constitutionalism is not completely intelligible unless one understands that doctrine.

Before analysing the philosophic theories of the origin and characteristics of proprietary rights, it may be well to explain the new conception of the structure of property which feudalism introduced and which was ultimately set forth in technical terms by lawyers trained in the very different Roman conception.

PROPERTY AND LORDSHIP

The conception of property which dominated Roman private law was simple and individualistic.[1] Property, according to the Roman lawyers, involved the right to use the object in question, to receive its fruits, and to dispose of it freely. Of these three, the right of disposal was the essential feature of ownership. Thus ownership was regarded as indivisible and unique, absorbing the object owned. It was a maxim that there could not be two lords over the same object. Roman private law accordingly made a sharp distinction between property-rights and rights in the property of another, such as a tenant has. In the later imperial period, however, tenancies of indefinite duration, in which the owner's contact with his property was practically little more than the receiving of fixed dues, became common. Many of these applied to lands owned by the state, and public law came to a grudging half-recognition of their peculiar status by granting to holders of such tenancies a real action in law not unlike that of a private-law owner. Ultimately private law followed suit, allowing the tenant *in superficie* certain legal actions which gave his right also a marketable value, like that of an owner. Thus Roman law came close to recognizing a sort of temporary property right for the tenant who had an indefinite use of land which continued to belong to another. Such cases were regarded as exceptional. But they are significant for medieval legal theory, for they were to serve as the opening wedge for medieval speculation on the structure of property.

The Roman view of property was in sharp contrast to that of the Germanic tribes.[2] For Germanic property belonged primarily not to the individual, but to the family or clan. Thus the individual owner could have no right to dispose of his property. Individual ownership could apply only to the use and fruits of the object in question; and from this point of view there could be no essential difference between usufruct and property, and therefore no obstacle to a concept of multiple ownership. Ownership could not absorb the object; it was simply a right in regard to the object; and such rights might be numerous and widely distributed.

The development of feudalism established as the normal form of land-holding what in the Roman empire had been exceptional—a tenure in which the original holder of the land did not relinquish his legal 'lordship' of that land, although his actual relation to the land was very slight. The use and revenue of the land passed to the vassal for an indeterminate period and gradually became hereditary; and feudal custom came to assure his unquestioned tenure and full control, subject only to the fulfilment of certain conditions. By a fixed contract, the original lord still received his regular yearly dues and certain extraordinary dues on definite occasions. Because the land remained permanently subject to these annual and extraordinary charges, the vassal's rights of alienation were at first severely limited. At his death, the land normally passed to his heir, with the payment of a 'relief' to the lord, recognizing his continuing right; if the vassal died without an heir or broke the terms of his contract, the land reverted to the immediate control of the lord. The sale of land thus burdened was, in the earlier feudal period, virtually impossible; but the vassal might by subinfeudation with the lord's consent grant the land to a third holder on similar terms. Thus land-holding became a complicated chain of two-sided contracts, and a single piece of land might be subject to the lordship of a whole series of lords above the person who actually controlled its use and received its products, and who might expect permanent tenure for himself and for his heirs provided that he regularly fulfilled the duties that he owed to the lord from whom he had immediately received it.

With the relative peace and emerging money-economy of the twelfth and thirteenth centuries, the value of the vassal's services to the lord began to be depreciated, while the value of the lord's protection likewise became obsolescent; at the same time the immediate holders of the land were growing more secure in their familiar possession and becoming economically and politically an important class. The result was a legal tendency to recognize and enforce their rights in the land, and to limit the rights of the overlord to the stipulated dues. Thus feudalism splintered land-ownership into a bundle of rights, equally recognized and protected by law, no one of which was an absorptive ownership.[3] This concept was the background for much of medieval political thought, although, like so many of the concepts with which feudalism worked, it did not receive explicit formulation till after feudalism had passed its zenith.

The revival of Roman law at first brought with it the revival of the Roman concept of indivisible property. But the Roman concept did not fit the medieval scene; and gradually, under the insistent pressure of their environment, the civilists were induced to construct a new definition of the structure of property.[4] The development of that definition was necessarily a slow and timid process, involving, step by step, a continual reinterpretation of the honoured Roman terms. The civilists were initially aided by the permission of real actions to exceptional classes of tenants in the late Roman empire, which gave them a precedent and a terminology for their thought. To meet the vassals' assertion of proprietary rights, the civilists first broke the concept of ownership in two, recognizing that a particular property might be subject both to the 'direct lordship' (*dominium directum*) of its original holder, and to the 'lordship of use' (*dominium utile*) of the vassal who held from him by feudal contract and who immediately controlled the land. Then in the early fourteenth century Bartolus placed this recognition of plural ownership on a solid theoretical footing. He broke the concept of property into its component parts, and pointed out that there could be as many lordships of use as there were uses of a thing. Thus he preserved the Roman principle that there could be only one lord for each object of ownership— but the object of ownership was, in his mind, not the corporeal thing but an incorporeal right of using that thing.[5] Besides the one direct lordship—the title held by the ultimate lord—there might be any number of lordships of use, each seizing upon one aspect of a particular body of property; and all these, from the direct lordship of the suzerain down to the merest right of use of a temporary tenant, were theoretically coordinate, distinct from each other, recognized and preserved by law as genuine property-rights. A last step remained to be taken, to meet the fact that an identical right of use might by subinfeudation be subject to several different lords at once. This problem was solved by the French lawyers of the fourteenth century, and in particular by Joannes Faber, who argued that each of these lords was lord of this right in a particular way.[6] From one point of view, the vassal who subinfeudated his holding might be considered to have alienated his lordship of use; but, from another point of view, he still retained it. In relation to his vassal, he now occupied the position of direct lordship, while, in relation to his own lord, he still appeared as a vassal—that is, as having still the lordship of use.

The development of the concept of divided lordship gave medieval minds a frame within which the problem of the relations between the rights of the king and of private individuals could be analysed. The simple classical dichotomy between property and government was as inapplicable to the medieval situation as was the classical doctrine of indivisible property. For, besides splintering ownership, feudalism tended to obliterate the distinction between lordship over things and lordship over persons. The feudal contract involved not only a disposition of land and revenue, but also a relationship of persons: a relation of leadership and protection on the one hand, of loyalty and service on the other. The lord held a court at which his vassals were bound to appear; he led them in war; he exercised rights of wardship and marriage over their children. Again, the land which was disposed of by feudalism was no bare land, but land to which were bound the servile workers who cultivated it for themselves and for its holder; thus the control of land involved a certain control of persons. Moreover, with the decay of central government in the ninth and tenth centuries, administrative and judicial offices came to be held as feudal property; their character as public services was almost lost; they appeared most obviously as sources of private income. Finally, the private attributes of the king as feudal landlord and suzerain blurred his general public quality as leader, administrator, judge. Thus the doctrine of divided lordship provided a common denominator for property and politics, and had significance far beyond mere questions of landholding.

While ecclesiastics struggled to maintain the ancient concept of the kingship as a public office, feudal thought inevitably encouraged kings to treat their rights as private property. And when the Roman concept of absorptive and indivisible ownership was first applied to the medieval situation in which lordship implied no distinction between property and government and in which the king was legally construed as ultimate landlord, the immediate result was confusion. In the search for a single owner behind the feudal chaos of divided rights, some twelfth-century students of Roman law naturally turned to the emperor, and interpreted a phrase from the *Corpus Juris*, '*Cum omnia esse principis intellegantur*,' as meaning that the emperor was the true proprietor of all the wealth of his realm and thus had the right arbitrarily to expropriate or reassign any of the possessions of his subjects.[7] But this interpretation, welcome as it was to the Hohenstaufens, had little chance of being assimilated into the medieval view of kingly right; and other civilists were quick to insist that 'all things are understood to belong to the prince' only in the sense that they are subject to his protection and jurisdiction.

Even when it tangled the king in that confused structure of proprietary and political rights which were all subsumed under the one category of lordship, feudal thought, because of the notion of divisible lordship, was able to regard the rights of the king as simply one among the many lordships which applied over the same kingdom and which were equally protected by the law of the land. It might permit the king to treat his particular rights as if they were his own, but it could not permit him to treat them as exhaustive and limitless. Rather, it saw those rights as limited by the very law in which they were rooted. They might bear upon the same ultimate object as the rights of private men, but they could not cancel or supersede those other rights. The king as landlord could have only the rights which any lord retained over an infeudated fief. The king as king could have only the rights implicit in a kingship.

Popular thought in the Middle Ages commonly assumed that the relations between the lordship of the king and the lordships of his subjects were adequately defined by the customary law. Men were willing to pay—grudgingly, no doubt, but without fundamental question—whatever aids, taxes, services could be shown to have precedent behind them. They were willing to buy with new payments whatever privileges or services the king had for sale. They endured without serious complaint a miscellany of other royal prerogatives enshrined in custom: for instance, the right of purveyance, which we should regard as extremely onerous. And they tended to think that the use and expenditure of what he received in these various ways was the king's own business. But a long series of insurrections—of which the great English revolt that led to *Magna Carta* is merely the most famous example—expressed their obstinate conviction that kingship involved no right in the property of subjects save that which custom recognized.

Such were the ideas in regard to property that grew out of the actual medieval situation, and were more or less taken for granted by the common man. But scholarly minds of the Middle Ages drew also on doctrines taken from Roman jurisprudence, patristic teachings, and Aristotelian analyses. Less willing to accept custom as the final standard by which the rights of men were measured, they gradually built from ancient and medieval sources a variety of complex doctrines of their own.

The lawyers whose opinions had been preserved in the *Corpus Juris* had in general agreed in classifying property among the institutions of the *jus gentium*,[8] a classification which, for those who made no distinction between the law of peoples and natural law, was the same thing as saying that its universal occurrence in the civilized world gave it the prestige of a natural institution. This view was in harmony with the legal situation in the Roman empire, which imposed almost no restrictions on the right of a man to do as he liked with his own. In the thought of Seneca, however, there was a distinction not reflected in the juristic writings. In the golden age of human innocence, said Seneca, all goods were common; private property is the result of human greed and a necessary, but conventional, restraint upon it.[9]

To these ideas, Christianity added a distinctive moral attitude.[10] The Christian subordination of all temporal affairs to the purposes of salvation, the sense of human dependence on the providence of a fatherly God, and the origin of Christianity among the poor and exploited classes resulted in a severe attitude toward property. Early Christian teachers emphasized the dangers of wealth and the sin of avarice; they urged the duty of charity; they spoke of private property as a trust held from God, to be received with grateful humility and applied to redressing the wants of others; they defined benevolence and mercy as a part of justice itself. This doctrine of Christian stewardship at first called forth extremes of communistic enthusiasm, but its general tendency was not toward fundamental criticism and reconstruction of social institutions. Christian thought accepted the existence of private property and of economic inequality without deep question, and only insisted that the goods of this world be utilized in a manner consistent with the ideals of a Christian life.

For the basis of their economic morality, the Fathers assimilated the Stoic history of property. They developed the thesis that before the Fall all goods were given bountifully by God to man for common ownership and common use; the fact of sin necessitated the establishment of private property to check man's avarice and to secure such order as might be. Thus private property had the dignity of a necessary, God-approved corrective of evil; yet this did not invalidate the higher truth that the fruits of the earth were created to serve the needs of all men. The rules of ownership could not override man's natural right to the satisfaction of his needs, and it was in this deep sense that benevolence became an act of justice. Private property was not an absolute right, but a right burdened with an imperative duty.

The main outlines of the patristic view of property were repeated without significant change by the ecclesiastical writers of the eleventh and twelfth centuries. The concept of Christian stewardship and the duty of charity were constantly emphasized. In the *Decretum*,[11] Gratian set forth the familiar doctrine of the origin of property in a condensed and challenging form: by natural law all things are common; private property is the creation of custom and statute. He added Augustine's letter against the Donatists, which asserted in no ambiguous terms that proprietary rights rested on the law of kings and emperors.

When, in the thirteenth century, Aristotle's discussion of property was added to the sources upon which medieval thought could draw, it provided a specific defence of the utility of private property and a suggestive distinction between common ownership and common use.[12] From Aristotle's discussion of commutative justice useful principles to guide the regulation of business could be borrowed.[13] Perhaps even more important was the influence of Aristotle's general tendency to equate social utility with right.

From these sources, medieval scholars worked out their philosophical theories of the origin, nature, and limitations of the property right. The process began with the theoretical analyses of canonists and theologians, who defined the relation of property to natural law and sketched out moral principles for economic relationships. Further thought was stimulated by two great practical controversies. Aegidius Romanus and other fourteenth-century spokesmen for the expanding claims of the church developed a theory of property which supported papal intervention in the rights of laymen, and their views were warmly attacked by John of Paris, William of Occam, and others. On the other hand, as early as the twelfth century, isolated groups like the Waldensians had pointed to the wealth of the church as a source of corruption, and sketched out the doctrine of apostolic poverty, which was later taken over by one wing of the Franciscan Order, the Spiritual Franciscans. The doctrine that Christ and the apostles had owned no property either individually or collectively and that their example should be followed by those who especially professed the religious life naturally aroused a furious discussion, which culminated in the fourteenth-century struggle between the Spiritual Franciscans, represented by Michael of Cesena and William of Occam as their principal theorists, and Pope John XXII.[14] The Spiritual Franciscans were crushed, but horror at the corrupting wealth of the church lived on in many minds and broke out again in the arguments of John Wyclif in England, which in turn were taken up by John Hus in Bohemia. Despairing of the church's self-purification through the voluntary abnegation of property, they suggested governmental expropriation of the church, using a theory which blended the doctrine of apostolic poverty with an analysis of property rights descended from the very conceptions which Aegidius Romanus and his school had developed to justify papal control over the proprietary rights of laymen.

Sometimes as part of these discussions, sometimes independently, theories of the secular ruler's relation to the property of his subjects were worked out. Canonists and theologians developed a system of business ethics and called upon secular governments to enforce it. The civilist lawyers, with some help from the theologians, produced theories to justify a royal power of expropriation and taxation for the common good; and these theories in turn met opposition from men bred in the older medieval notion that kings might take property only with the consent of its owners.

The history of the development of the medieval theories of the bases of property is thus one of extreme complexity. Yet, as in all medieval controversies, the combatants had many premises in common, and it is possible, therefore, to present a logical analysis of the various schools of thought in a more or less orderly fashion.

To begin with, it was virtually impossible for medieval minds to think of private property as bad, or as merely the result of arbitrary convention. Medieval thought in general followed the patristic tradition that justified property in terms of its usefulness to human needs —at least, to the needs of sinful men. Rufinus saw private property as one of the things that natural law neither commanded nor forbade, but indicated as expedient after the Fall.[15] 'Natural law is mutable in respect of its precepts and commands,' said Alexander of Hales. 'In the state of corrupted nature' it dictates 'that it is good that some things be private; for otherwise good men would be in want and human society would not endure, because the wicked would seize everything.' But natural law also 'dictates as obligatory that in case of necessity all things are common.'[16] The great canonist Innocent IV explained that all things 'were common from the beginning of time, until by the usages of our first parents it was introduced that some appropriated some things, others other things, for themselves. Nor was this evil, but rather good, since it is natural that things held in common should be neglected, and common ownership breeds discord.'[17]

Aquinas, whose definition of natural law allowed him to escape from the tradition that natural law had prescribed a pristine communism, classified private property among those things that human reason had added to natural law as a deduction from its general principles on the ground of its demonstrated utility to human ends. He saw in the nature of goods themselves, measured by the test of utility, a disposition to be privately owned. With Aristotle, he distinguished between property as the right to acquire and administer and property as the right to use for one's own advantage. In the former sense, private property had the natural sanction of social utility; but as a right of use it remained subordinate to and restricted by the principle that material things were created by God for the common good of men.

Thus private property appeared as blessed by reason and more or less directly by natural law. It was most often classified as an institution of the *jus gentium*, with the implication that, while its human origin was a matter of agreement, that agreement reflected a universal need. Moreover, as an institution of the law of peoples, property appeared as coordinate in origin and dignity with rulership, and this construction provided a basis for the protection of property from the arbitrary intervention of the king, even while it left the way open for the subjection of property to his control in other ways.

It was, indeed, argued—and by no less a personage than John XXII —that, if property rested on human law, as the Spiritual Franciscans asserted, that law must be, according to Augustine, the law of kings and emperors. He attempted to demonstrate that property must therefore be based on divine law, since, as the Bible stories showed, it had appeared before there were any kings. But his attempt to find so absolute a basis for the proprietary right was alien from the general medieval tradition and was vigorously refuted by Occam, who pointed out that human law also included the pre-political law of peoples, and that it was by this law that private lordships were introduced. Occam's goal in this particular argument was to show that the principles of poverty maintained by the Spiritual Franciscans were not, as John XXII would have them, contrary to divine law; but the medieval tradition which he reasserted had another significance.

For no absolute and inviolable right of property in every instance—such as the followers of Locke and Kant later deduced from their concepts of property as a necessary conclusion from individual personality —could be deduced from a doctrine that classified property under the law of peoples. A right based on social utility must vary with its social utility; it was subordinate to and could on occasion be over-ridden by the ends for which it existed. This relativity of the property right, then, supported the principle that in case of necessity all things were common; it allowed medieval moralists to treat charity as an aspect of justice; it permitted Aquinas—though here he was exceptional—to justify even theft undertaken for the relief of urgent need.

The construction of property as a secondary right subordinate to natural-law principles had also several results more directly important for political theory. In the first place, it served as the premise for the rationalization of legal limitations on the freedom of commercial and financial transactions.[18] In the second place, it provided the basis for the slowly-developing doctrine of the ruler's right to expropriate and tax the property of his subjects for the common good.

Medieval minds were unable to anticipate the *laisser-faire* economists in their happy conviction that social good could best be secured through the automatic workings of the free market. The circumstances in which medieval trade developed encouraged stringent regulation. The problem confronting medieval men was a shortage of goods which might easily mean famine or the arbitrarily high prices of an easy monopoly. Medieval capitalism could not afford to be individualistic, and guild and town testified alike to the need of common protection which drew traders together in local associations and induced them to submit to rigid regulation to protect them both as buyers and as sellers from monopoly prices, cut-throat competition, goods of inferior quality, and so forth. As medieval trade developed, the townsmen often looked to the government of the kingdom for aid in problems too large for local control: the regulation of the currency, of weights and measures, of foreign merchants, and such matters. Thus a transition from municipal to national regulation occurred with relative ease, and late medieval developments moved not toward *laisser-faire* but toward the mercantilism of early modern times.

Another factor which furthered the growth of the ideology of regulation was the natural resentment which an originally agrarian society felt toward the rising class which lived by trade and which through its possession of ready money gradually acquired a painful financial influence over the rural areas. Agrarian thought, which typically included ecclesiastical thought, reached a grudging tolerance of the merchant only in so far as he could be considered useful to society in general, and thus was predisposed to approve a degree of political control over business enterprise which it would not have dreamed of applying to agriculture. The general agrarian resentment of the trader was directed above all at the urban money-lender who took advantage of the poverty of his fellow-men to enrich himself by usury. In a period when most debt was incurred primarily for the relief of personal need or for non-productive enterprise rather than for profitable reinvestment, condemnation of usury as immoral and unchristian was a natural attitude; and the church had early become the stern spokesman of this feeling and had lent its courts to enforce it. Its first policy was an absolute prohibition of all charges for the use of money, but, as medieval capitalism developed, ecclesiastical thought began to distinguish between legitimate and illegitimate charges.

The first elaboration of principles for the regulation of commerce and money-lending was made by Aquinas.[19] The premise of his thought was the thesis that commerce, by its very nature, existed for the common advantage of the participants rather than for individual advantage; justice therefore demanded that neither party be the loser in the transaction. This thesis was applied to specific problems of sales and of money-lending (which Aquinas classified as a sale with deferred payment).[20] Its heart was the conception of the 'just price.' The idea was apparently derived from Augustine; in a rough form, the concept was sufficiently familiar to be taken for granted in Aquinas's day. Briefly defined, the just price was the price which corresponded to the intrinsic value of the object, and thus assured equality of exchange between buyer and seller. Aquinas did not work out in detail the considerations involved in determining the just price; it was a composite of many factors, varying with the circumstances of time and place, with the rarity of the article, with the cost of production and transportation, with its usefulness to the average buyer, and with the loss occasioned to the particular seller by parting with it; it was determined by a consideration of past and present conditions only, not of the unpredictable future. The principle of the just price forbade the merchant or money-lender to take advantage of the ignorance, the exceptional need, or the subsequent gains of the buyer or borrower.

It is clear that Aquinas's idea of the just price in its application to a particular situation involved a far from individualistic conception of the rights and obligations of property. The tendency of his code was to protect the consumer—that is, the community as a whole—rather than to further the expansion of individual wealth; and, although he hesitantly justified the trader's vocation, it was only on the assumption that the trader's activity would be useful to the community or that his 'moderate gains' were intended for the maintenance of his household or the assistance of the poor.

The outlines of Aquinas's business ethics became the basis for the amplified treatment of later theologians and canonists, with no important modifications. Later writers refined yet further the concept of the just price, elaborated Aquinas's summary rules to an infinite precision of casuistry, and made some concessions to the growth of capitalism by permitting a few business practices which Aquinas had disapproved[21]; but he continued to be recognized as the ultimate authority, and later thinkers consciously worked in the light of his earlier wisdom. Aquinas had brought business dealings under the rule of natural law; it was an easy step for later thinkers to bring them explicitly under the control of the state. In this they reflected medieval practice as well as the accepted theory that the prince was charged with the application and enforcement of natural law.[22]

A second consequence from the subordination of property to natural law was the development of doctrines justifying taxation or the confiscation of private property for the common good. In his *De Regimine Judaeorum*, Aquinas asserted that taxes beyond the accustomed revenues could be levied for the common utility of the kingdom if they were moderate or justified by extreme public emergency. John of Paris insisted that 'true lordship' belonged to the individuals who had acquired goods by 'their own skill, labour, and diligence,' and that the prince had 'neither the lordship nor the administration of such goods' but only the control appropriate to his office as a judge of right. However, he visualized that judicial control as including the function of determining what proportion of the subjects' goods should be taken for the 'necessity or utility' of their country.

As the notion of several levels of lordship gained currency in political and legal theory, the doctrine of confiscation and taxation was commonly stated in terms of a superior lordship of the ruler which was superimposed on the particular lordship of the subject and carefully distinguished from it. Thus Occam maintained that the emperor was lord of all things 'in a certain way' in as much as he could rightfully take them away from the possessors and appropriate them himself or grant them to others 'for cause, or on behalf of the common utility, or on account of a crime of the possessors' but not 'arbitrarily at his pleasure.'[23] His lordship, therefore, was a real lordship, though it would come into play only when he saw that the common utility ought to be preferred to private rights; it was accordingly less complete than the type of lordship held by the immediate owner, which included an arbitrary right of use and alienation. The distinction between the lordship of a king who could use and alienate his subjects' goods at his own pleasure and the lordship of a king who could touch such goods only when the common interest demanded it was for Occam and for many other medieval theorists the distinction between despotic or seignorial and 'regal' government.

The doctrine of a royal right of expropriation was especially developed by the civilist lawyers, some of whom, like Occam, thought of the ruler's right as a kind of general lordship superimposed on the private and particular lordships of individuals. Whether they talked in terms of a hierarchy of lordships over the same object of property, or contrasted the 'jurisdiction and protection' of the ruler with the 'lordship' of the owner, they agreed in regarding the ruler's right of expropriation as limited and qualified. There could be no expropriation without just cause: forfeiture for crime was one just cause, the demand of the common utility interpreted by the ruler was another. Some argued that those who were required to sacrifice their property for the sake of the common good should be compensated, but others thought compensation unnecessary in the case of a general levy or if the expropriation was motivated by urgent public necessity. General expropriation without compensation was, of course, indistinguishable from taxation. The imposition of new taxes was usually conceived as exceptional rather than as the normal means of financing government; the king was expected to meet normal expenses from his accustomed revenues. But rising costs toward the end of the Middle Ages, coupled with the steady expansion of governmental functions, tended to make a rule out of the exceptions.

The civilists, and such publicists as were influenced by them, assured the medieval king that the right to determine extraordinary taxes at his own discretion was an integral part of his authority as guardian of the general welfare.[24] He was the appropriate judge of the demands made by the common good against his subjects' property. Such a doctrine was not easily assimilated into the common thought of the Middle Ages. Men of substance were glad to bolster the feudal tradition of the immunity of property with the scholars' defence of property as an institution of the *jus gentium* and to assume that the property law of their own countries corresponded to the *jus gentium* and was normally superior to the ruler's determinations; but, on occasion, they stubbornly resisted the implication that a still higher law might abnormally justify the ruler's infringement of customary rights. The development of estates as tax-granting bodies provided a practical *modus vivendi*. The more moderate of the civilists harmonized their doctrine with medieval tradition by urging that even though it was the final right of the king to determine when the common good required new taxes, that determination should be formalized through established processes of consultation and consent. Occasional instances of deadlock between the king's prerogative and the subjects' consent were resolved in terms of the immediate balance of force without the formulation of further principle. On the whole, constitutional practice in the later Middle Ages achieved a precarious reconciliation of the rights of property with the demands of the common utility and thus postponed to a later period the final settlement of the theoretical issue.

Some political theorists could not see that the fine distinction between a regal and a despotic control over property—a difference in the conditions rather than in the maximum range of power—was a real distinction: any government in which the ruler enjoyed a final right to take property without the consent of its holders seemed to them *ipso facto* a despotism. This attitude was illustrated by the thirteenth-century Italian Tholommeo of Lucca[25] and by the fifteenth-century English jurist Fortescue. Fortescue's treatment of the origin of property blurred the scholastic distinction between the immutable law of nature and the variable law of peoples. In fact, his outline of that origin was an anticipation of Locke's labour theory. Like the typical squire that he was, he stoutly insisted that private property, given to Adam and his descendants as a recompense for toil and sweat, rightfully had an unqualified immunity from royal seizure without consent; and he shuddered in good English horror at the unhappy condition of contemporary France, which, he believed, was being reduced to a slavish and miserable poverty through its acceptance of despotic taxation.

Civilist influence was, indeed, stronger at the fifteenth-century French court than in England. Yet Frenchmen in general had not accepted the extreme civilist teaching so slavishly as Fortescue supposed. Comines, insisting that neither the king of France nor any other king had the privilege of taxation without the consent of his subjects, could speak with the assurance of one who knew that precedent, public opinion, and one school of constitutional theory were on his side.

As we have seen, the justification of private property through its social utility allowed various qualifications of proprietary rights even for those thinkers who, like Aquinas, tended to regard social utility as a fairly solid basis for any right. But thinkers differed in the value they were willing to assign to social utility. It was possible to combine the Christian doctrine of the divine origin of all temporal lordship with the general medieval theory that private property originated in human agreement after the Fall, and to argue thence to the thesis that proprietary rights must be tested by religious as well as social criteria, and that accordingly the right of any individual owner must vary with his relation to God, from Whom all rights were ultimately held. This doctrine of lordship[26] contingent on grace was first developed to serve the ambitions of the church; and precisely as some theorists used the feudal notion of divided lordship to introduce a superior lordship of the prince as guardian of the common good, so Aegidius Romanus and others used it to introduce a superior lordship of the church as agent of God's will above the lordship of the individual.

Accepting the familiar doctrine that the partition of ownership among individuals had a partial basis in natural utility, Aegidius Romanus insisted that this quasi-natural right gave only a presumptive title, and that rights of lordship, whether governmental or proprietary, were finally determined by the individual's relation to God. To Aegidius Romanus, any disposition of lordship made by earthly law was valid only if the person enjoying it was duly subordinated to God his Lord and was in receipt of His grace. Thus infidels and excommunicates could have no valid title to property. Moreover, Aegidius argued, without the approval of the church no man could justly be considered lord of anything; the church had accordingly a general lordship over all earthly goods, which was recognized in the payment of tithes; and while the lordship of the church did not destroy or diminish the particular lordships of those who duly fulfilled their obligations, it was able to abrogate their rights when they were forfeited by breach of the terms on which all valid lordship depended.

Aegidius's theory, soon adopted by other advocates of papal supremacy,[27] was immediately attacked by John of Paris and later by William of Occam. John of Paris stoutly asserted that the pope had neither lordship nor administration in the private goods of men: while he could decree tithes for the regular support of the church or special contributions in an emergency, he acted on such occasions simply as the definer of right, not as the holder of any lordship over the goods themselves. Occam's attack on Aegidius's position was in harmony with his doctrine that social utility gave property rights their quasi-natural claim to be respected and that only the imperative necessities of human society could abrogate that claim. The church was not—unless all other authorities failed—the agent of social utility. Its mission was spiritual and it had only such lordship as that mission demanded. The spiritual lordship of the church was not an all-inclusive despotism; it supplemented but did not weaken the rights that rested on the needs of human nature itself. Thus the right to property was independent of religious status, common to Christians and infidels alike, and in no way subject to the determinations of the church.[28] The fundamental issue between the point of view represented by Aegidius Romanus and that represented by his opponents was obviously their whole conception of the relations between institutions devoted to spiritual and to secular purposes.

The doctrine of lordship founded in grace was greeted with papal favour so long as it was applied to the strengthening of papal claims to intervention in secular matters. The case was, of course, far different when, toward the end of the fourteenth century, Wyclif used a variant of this doctrine to threaten specific ecclesiastical titles to property. Wyclif's conclusions from his theory of lordship were radically new;

but the theory which he used as a premise was borrowed from the archbishop Richard Fitzralph, who had presented it as a preliminary to highly technical attacks on the Fraticelli. With Fitzralph's applications of his analysis of the property right we are not here concerned; but the analysis itself is interesting. In his theory, the patristic notion of the cleavage between natural communism and the private ownership created by positive law was pushed to an antithesis much more sharp than that which Aegidius had outlined. He also modified Aegidius's conception by his assertion that men held directly from God; in his system, there was no need of the church as mediate lord between God and man.

Fitzralph sharply distinguished between natural and civil lordship. Natural lordship was the lordship enjoyed by man before the Fall, and restored to him thereafter through grace. By natural lordship all things were common to all men in a condition of grace; the division of ownership into separate hands was the creation of civil law alone. Fitzralph's terminology distinguished ownership from lordship: ownership was that kind of lordship which excluded others and which had only a positive basis. Legal principles marking off a system of private rights were simply a guarantee that the force of positive law would be used to protect the claims of the holder: positive law could neither give nor imply any right beyond the promise of its own enforcement. Fitzralph refused to accept the doctrine that natural law was superseded as a result of the Fall. The right to lordship, in his thought, always rested and still rests upon grace, and a stranger might have through grace a better title to any object than a sinner with a flawless positive-law title. Positive law, however, should seek to establish an order of lordship corresponding to that which rested upon grace— though how this was to be accomplished Fitzralph did not say.[29]

Wyclif emphasized the doctrines derived from Fitzralph that men held directly from God without intermediary,[30] that lordship was contingent on service to God, and that no positive-law title was valid unless it conformed to the conditions of God's grant of lordship;[31] and he turned the whole into the argument that it could be the duty of the secular power to take from the clergy the property of which they were making evil use and to which, accordingly, they would have no right.[32] The right of the king to expropriate the clergy within his kingdom was based on the general function of the king as the wielder of coercive power, responsible to God, by the terms on which his own lordship was granted him, for the maintenance of justice in the kingdom and for the protection of the church in its proper mission. Other applications of his principles Wyclif was not concerned to make. Otherworldly in his whole scheme of values, convinced of the transitory and sin-corrupted nature of this world and of the duty of obedience to the powers that be, he could dogmatically assert that a Christian man was by right lord of all things, and that 'according to law it were better that all things be had in common,'[33] but nothing was further from his thought than that such communal lordship should be attempted in this life.[34]

Wyclif's thesis that 'no one is civil lord, no one is prelate, no one is bishop, while he is in mortal sin' and Hus's statement of the same doctrine were condemned as heretical by the Council of Constance; and thus, in effect, the pivot of Aegidius Romanus's system was also condemned. The Lollards in England, the Hussites in Bohemia carried on in spite of persecution the notion that clerical titles to property were unsound, and thus helped pave the way for the expropriations which characterized the Protestant Reformation. Meanwhile, papal spokesmen, sensitive to the new atmosphere of collaboration with the secular powers which the Conciliar period ushered in, dropped the church's claim to temporal suzerainty and the doctrine of lordship contingent on grace on which it was partly founded. Orthodox ecclesiastical theory thenceforth agreed on the proposition that proprietary rights were firmly grounded on the social utility of property.

The medieval centuries did not see the final decision of the question of the ruler's rights over the property of his subjects. As the costs of government expanded, the old medieval notion that the king should 'live of his own' became hopelessly inapplicable, but so long as king and estates could agree on the desirability of increased revenues, the choice of alternative solutions was happily postponed. When that harmony disappeared in seventeenth-century England, the question of the king's right to tax became an issue in a bloody civil war, in which both sides could draw on medieval theory and precedent for their justification. In the course of that struggle, the medieval concepts of property were themselves transformed—grafted on to new philosophies, pruned of their old corollaries, and taught to shelter institutions of which the medieval thinkers had not dreamed.

It was the obstinacy of property that blocked the way of early modern absolutism and in the fury of civil war befriended parliamentary government and civil liberties and the rule of law. The medieval theory which protected property by law and made it independent of the king was victorious over the theory that the king could tax at his discretion for the common good. The power to tax was transferred to the assembly that represented the property owners; and that assembly itself came with time to be thought of as the supreme governing body, taxing by virtue of its governmental authority rather than as the agent of the owners' consent. It thus ultimately inherited the arguments by which one school of medieval thought had justified governmental expropriation on behalf of the common good. Meanwhile the concept of the property right had been so transformed that the medieval basis for governmental regulation had virtually disappeared. The seventeenth and eighteenth centuries, in their reinterpretation of natural law, moved far from the medieval conception of private property as justified and ruled by social utility when they discovered it to be a natural right of the individual, irrelevant to considerations of social effect, and in their thought obliterated the fine medieval distinction between ownership and use. Certain fragments of the medieval theory have lingered in juristic thought and have been recently refurbished as weapons in the struggle against the consequences of the individualistic natural-rights theory. Such concepts as 'fair competition' and 'fair return' on investments echo the medieval theory of the regulation of property by the criteria of a higher natural law. More significant in recent thought has been the revival of the view of property rights as based upon and qualified by their utility to human ends.

The medieval view of property as a group of distinct and separable rights in regard to an object easily gave place to a revived Roman conception of indivisible and absorptive ownership with the passage of the peculiar feudal circumstances which had given it birth. Traces of it remain—most conspicuously in the concept of the 'eminent domain' of the state—but these are mere traces. It is idle to speculate what might have been the effects on modern thought if the notion of the divisibility of ownership had been retained: whether it might have provided a framework within which the interests of capital, of labour, of the consumer in regard to any industry might have been considered on a common ground as property rights of coordinate validity. The theory of divided lordship is a way of thinking of rights that actually assert themselves; it cannot of itself create rights out of empty air, nor redistribute rights that have in practice cohered in a single hand. Yet, as a tool of thought, it may be useful again; for if, as appears not unlikely, the coming years will see great and deliberate changes in the disposition of property, it will be well to remember that the powers which seem inseparable are not necessarily so.

Thomas Aquinas

[Aquinas's theory of the basis of property is most fully stated in his *Summa Theologiae*, 2a 2ae, qs. 57 and 66.]

QUESTION LVII

Article 3. Whether the right of peoples is the same as natural right

.... The natural right or just is that which by its own nature is equal or commensurate with another. Now this can happen in two ways: first, according as it is considered absolutely: thus a male by his very nature is commensurate with a female to beget offspring by her, and a parent is commensurate with the offspring to nourish it. In a second way, something is naturally commensurate with another not in accordance with its inherent nature, but in accordance with something resulting from it: for instance, the ownership of possessions. For if a particular field is considered in itself, there is no reason why it should belong to one man more than to another; but if it be considered in relation to the opportunity for cultivation and the peaceful, unmolested use of the land, it has a certain commensuration to belong to one man and not to another, as the Philosopher shows in II *Politics*, [ch. 2].

Now to apprehend a thing as it is in itself belongs not only to man but also to other animals; therefore natural right (that is, right in accordance with the first kind of commensuration) is common to us and other animals. 'But the law of peoples,' as the Jurist says [*Digest*, 1, 1, 1], 'falls short of natural right in this sense,' because 'the latter is common to all animals, while the former is common to men only.' However, to consider a thing in relation to its result is proper to reason, and therefore this is natural to man in accordance with natural reason, which dictates it. Hence the lawyer Gaius says [*Digest*, 1, 1, 9]: 'Whatever natural reason decrees among all men is observed by all peoples and is called the law of peoples.'

Article 1. Whether it is natural for man to possess external things

. . . . External things can be considered in two ways. First, as regards their nature, which is not subject to the power of man, but only to the power of God, Whose nod all things obey. Secondly, as regards their use; and in this way man has a natural lordship over external things, because, by his reason and will, he is able to use them for his own advantage, as having been made for his sake: for the more imperfect things always exist for the sake of the more perfect. . . . And by this argument the Philosopher proves in I *Politics*, [ch. 3], that the possession of external things is natural to man. Moreover, this natural lordship of man over other creatures, a lordship which properly belongs to man because of his reason, in which consists his likeness to God, was shown forth in man's creation, as we learn from the words of Genesis 1:[26]: 'Let us make man in our own image and likeness, and let him have lordship over the fish of the sea,' etc.

Article 2. Whether it is lawful for man to possess something as his own

. . . . Two things are within man's competence in regard to external things. One is the power to procure and administer them, and in this respect it is lawful for man to possess property. And this is also necessary to human life for three reasons. First, because a man is more careful to procure what will belong to himself alone than what would be common to many or to all: since each one would avoid labour and leave it to another to procure what would belong to the community, as happens where there are a multitude of servants. Secondly, because human affairs are conducted in a more orderly way when each man has his own responsibility for procuring particular things, whereas there would be confusion if everyone indeterminately had to look after everything. Thirdly, because a more peaceful state is insured to man when each one is satisfied with his own. Thus we see that quarrels arise more frequently among those who possess things in common without partition.

The second thing that is in the competence of man in regard to external things is their use. In this respect man ought to possess external things not as his own but as common: that is, so that he may readily share them with others in their need. Whence the Apostle says in I Timothy 6:[17, 18], 'Charge them that are rich in the world to give readily, to share,' etc.

. . . . Community of goods is ascribed to natural law, not because natural law dictates that all things should be possessed in common and that nothing should be possessed as one's own, but because the division of possessions is not part of natural law, but rather arose from human agreement, which belongs to positive law. . . . Thus the ownership of possessions is not contrary to natural law, but is an addition to natural law devised by human reason.

Article 7. Whether it is lawful to steal on account of necessity

. . . . Things established by human law cannot derogate from natural right or divine right. Now, according to the natural order established by divine providence, inferior things are ordained to the purpose of succouring man's needs. And therefore the division and appropriation of things, based on human law, can not overrule the principle than man's needs are to be succoured by such things. Thus whatever one has in superabundance is due, by natural law, to the sustenance of the poor. Therefore Ambrose says, as we find in the *Decretum*, [c. 11], di. 47: 'It is the hungry man's bread that you withhold, the naked man's cloak that you store away; the money that you bury in the ground is the price of the needy man's redemption and freedom.' But, because there are many who suffer need and cannot all be succoured by means of the same thing, each man is entrusted with the administration of his own property, so that from it he may give aid to the needy. If, however, the need is so manifest and so urgent that it is evident that the immediate need must be remedied by whatever means are available, as when a person is in imminent danger and no other remedy is possible, then it is lawful for a man to succour his own need by means of another's property, by taking it either openly or secretly. And this is not, properly speaking, theft or robbery.

[In answer to a series of practical questions from the Duchess of Brabant, Aquinas wrote in 1261 or 1270 a little treatise which goes by the name of *De*

PROPERTY AND LORDSHIP

Regimine Judaeorum (*Opusculum* 21 in *Opera*, Venice, 1754, vol. XIX). It included his opinion on the question of taxation—a philosopher's statement of a common theory of his time.]

. . . . You asked whether it is licit for you to make exactions from your Christian subjects. In regard to this, you ought to consider that the princes of the earth were instituted by God not to seek their own gain, but to look after the common utility of the people. . . . For this reason the revenues of certain lands were established for princes, that, living on them, they might abstain from the despoiling of their subjects. . . .

Yet it sometimes happens that princes do not have revenues sufficient for the custody of the land and for other duties which reasonably fall upon them; and in such a case it is just that the subjects render payments from which their common utility can be cared for. And thence it is that in some lands, by ancient custom, the lords impose fixed taxes on their subjects, which, if they are not immoderate, can be exacted without sin; for, according to the Apostle [I Cor. 9:7], no one serves at his own expense. Wherefore the prince, who serves the common utility, can live on common property, and can look after the common affairs either from his assigned revenues or, if they are lacking or insufficient, from those which are collected from individuals. And the same reason seems to apply if some new situation arises in which it is necessary to spend more for the common utility or in order to maintain the honourable status of the prince, to which his own revenues or the accustomed exactions are insufficient: for instance, if enemies invade the land or some such situation arises. For then, in addition to the accustomed exactions, the princes of the lands can licitly exact from their subjects some payments on behalf of the common utility. But if they wish to exact more than has been instituted, for the sake of having their own desire or on account of inordinate or immoderate expenses, this is not at all licit for them. Whence John the Baptist said to the soldiers who came to him [Luke 3:14], 'Do violence to no man, neither accuse any falsely; and be content with your wages.' For their revenues are, as it were, the wages of princes, with which they ought to be content, that they may not exact more unless because of the aforesaid reason and if the utility is common.

III

Aegidius Romanus

[Widely different in tone from his earlier *De Regimine Principum*, the *De Ecclesiastica Potestate* written by Aegidius Romanus in 1302 was an extreme and original development of the thesis of the illimitable direct power of the pope in temporals as well as in spirituals. An important part of his argument was his development of the theory of lordship contingent on grace, with its sweeping implications. Weaving together Augustine's definition of justice and the concepts of feudalism, the commonly stated interpretation of the historic beginnings of property and the ecclesiastical doctrine of the meaning of excommunication, the chapters translated below are a *tour de force* of brilliant, radical, and quite unrealistic speculation: *De Ecclesiastica Potestate*, ed. Richard Scholz (Weimar, 1929), bk. 2, chs. 7 and 12.]

CHAPTER VII

We intend . . . to show that there is no lordship with justice, either of temporal things or of lay persons or of anything whatever, except under the church and through the church: for example, a man cannot have with justice, unless he has it under and through the church, his field or his vineyard or anything else that he has.

For we say with Augustine in his *De Civitate Dei*, bk. 2, ch. 22, that true justice does not exist except in that commonwealth whose founder and ruler is Christ. For the Roman gentiles seemed to talk much of justice and to make much ado over their commonwealth. But that commonwealth, as Augustine says in the above-mentioned chapter, was not a living fact, but a painted picture. For . . . true justice could not exist in their commonwealth, where the true God was not worshipped; and since the passion of Christ no commonwealth can be a true commonwealth unless the holy mother church is cherished there and Christ is its founder and ruler. For this reason Augustine, *De Civitate Dei*, bk. 29, ch. 21, thinks that the commonwealth of the Romans was not a true commonwealth because true justice was never there.

And in case someone may not be satisfied with the citing of authorities, we wish to add arguments to show that no one can with justice hold lordship of anything unless he has been reborn through the church. For, as Augustine says in the aforesaid book and chapter, justice is the virtue which distributes to each his own. Therefore, there is no true justice unless to everyone is rendered what is his. Therefore, since you ought to be under God and under Christ, you are not just unless you are under Him; and because you are unjustly withdrawn from your Lord Christ, everything is justly withdrawn from your lordship. For he who is unwilling to be under His lordship cannot with justice have lordship of anything. For if a knight were unwilling to be under the king, it would be fitting that the subjects of the knight should not be under him. If, therefore, a knight unjustly withdraws himself from his lord, he is justly deprived of all his own lordship. But whoever is not reborn through the church is not under Christ his lord; fittingly, there-fore, is he derived of all his own lordship, so that he cannot justly be lord of anything.

You see, therefore, that for a just and worthy possession of things spiritual regeneration through the church is more important than carnal generation through a father. . . . Carnally born, we are by nature sons of wrath, we were conceived in iniquities, and as a result we are not under our Lord, as we have said. It is fitting that he who was carnally born of a father should be deprived of all his lordship, nor can he justly succeed into the lordship of the paternal heritage unless he be reborn through the church; for by this regeneration he is brought under Christ his Lord, and thus he is not deprived of his lordship, but the lordship of his heritage is justly due him. . . .

It follows that you ought to recognize that your heritage, and all your lordship and all your possession, are yours from the church and through the church and because you are the son of the church, more than from your carnal father, or through him, or because you are his son. It follows also that if your father, in his lifetime, is more lord of the heritage than you, the church, which does not die, is more lord of your possessions than you.

Yet it should be noticed that, although we say that the church is mother and mistress of all possessions and all temporal things, yet we do not thereby deprive the faithful of their lordships and possessions, because . . . both the church and the faithful have lordship of a kind: but the church has universal and superior lordship, while the faithful have particular and inferior lordship. We therefore render unto Caesar the things that are Caesar's and unto God the things that are God's, because we assign the universal and superior lordship of temporal things to the church, distributing particular and inferior lordships among the faithful.

CHAPTER XII

We wish, moreover, to show clearly that whoever is bound by the church, or excommunicated by her, can call nothing his own—or, if he can, it will be only by the indulgence of the church. And when this has been shown, it will be plainly revealed that the church has the superior lordship over all temporal things and over all possessions in such a way that nothing will remain as his own to him whom she binds, unless through her indulgence.

Therefore, it should be known that originally the possession of one thing or another, so that a man could say, 'This is mine,' was rightful only through an agreement or compact maintained among men. And this agreement or compact for the partition and division of the earth at first amounted only to this: that the sons of Adam had in this way appropriated certain possessions, and in this way they had held them as their own in proportion as they had divided the lands, and by this agreement and compact they had conceded that one thing should belong to one man, another to another. . . . But later, . . . when men had become more numerous, such agreements and compacts were necessarily multiplied, so that there came to be possession of lands and fields, not only in accordance with such partition as occurs among the sons of one father, but also in accordance with sales, grants, transfers, and other methods which depend upon an agreement or consensus of minds: because neither buying nor sharing nor granting could occur if the consensus of minds did not accompany them.

Moreover, after men began to dominate the earth and became kings, there followed laws which contained these agreements and also added other matters. Now the intention of the laws is that legal compacts and legal agreements and legal contracts should be observed, so that on the basis of these legal compacts one can say, 'This is mine, that is yours.' Moreover, the laws added other things besides agreements, contracts, and compacts: as, for instance, the rule that if for a certain period of time a man is the peaceful possessor of a certain thing, or if he meets other conditions set by the laws, he becomes the owner of that thing. Statutes and laws, therefore, contain all those conditions by virtue of which a man can say, 'This is mine,' because they contain legal contracts, agreements, and compacts, and other conditions through which one is judged the just possessor of things; and thence, perhaps, came the saying [cf. Augustine in c. 1, di. 8] that if the laws were

114

abolished it would be impossible for anyone to say, 'This is mine, that is yours.'

Therefore let us begin with the foundation, and let us say that when the foundation is abolished the whole structure falls into ruins. . . . Now the foundation of all these things is the communication of men with one another; for thence have arisen partitions, grants, transfers, and sales. Wisely, also, laws are collective, because, as the Philosopher says in the *Ethics* [bk. 5, ch. 6], no man can do injustice to himself. If, therefore, men should in no way communicate with one another, but each lived to himself alone, the laws, whose function it is to discern what is just and what is unjust, would in no way be necessary. . . . If, therefore, the church can bring it about that someone is deprived of the communion of men or the communion of the faithful, she can bring it about that he is deprived of that foundation upon which all these things are built. Therefore, to a man so deprived, partitions, sales, grants, transfers, and laws of every kind avail nothing. Therefore, he cannot say that anything is his, since all the aforesaid conditions on the basis of which a man can call a thing his own are founded on the fact of communication.

John of Paris

[Jean Quidort, or Jean Le Sourd, was born no later than 1269, probably in Paris. In 1290 he is mentioned in the records of the University of Paris as a bachelor of arts. Shortly thereafter he entered the Dominican Order and devoted himself to theological studies, in which his capable support of Thomistic doctrines won him some celebrity. In 1300, he produced a treatise *De Antichristo* against Arnold of Villanova, whose somewhat heretical doctrines were shielded by the protection of Boniface VIII. In 1302 he wrote his *De Potestate Regia et Papali*, obviously in answer to the treatises of Aegidius Romanus and James of Viterbo, which appeared in the same year. In 1303, he appears as one of the members of the Dominican convent who with the University of Paris were demanding a general council. In 1305, his treatise on transsubstantiation was condemned by a bishops' court at Paris, in which Aegidius Romanus was one of the judges, and the theological faculty denied John the right to lecture and dispute in the university. He appealed to Clement V, but died at Bordeaux in 1306 before the case was settled.

The *De Potestate Regia et Papali* was a keen and balanced criticism of the doctrine of direct papal control in seculars, showing that John had thoroughly assimilated the spirit of his masters Aristotle and Aquinas and had, in addition, the gifts of clarity in formulating his own position and remarkable neatness in pointing out the weak points in the logic of his opponents. His treatise had considerable prestige among later thinkers who sought a moderate view of the relations between state and church; it was used by Occam, but particularly valued by Gerson and other Gallicans of the period of the Great Schism.

In his seventh chapter John of Paris briefly presents his theory of property, which he took in part from Godefroid de Fontaines, master of theology at the University of Paris. The following translation is based on the text in Jean Leclercq, *Jean de Paris et l'ecclésiologie du xiiie siècle* (Paris, 1942), Appendix.]

CHAPTER VII. *How the pope is concerned with the goods of laymen*

. . . . The pope has a weaker lordship in the external goods of laymen [than in those of clerics], since in regard to these he is not an administrator, unless perhaps in the ultimate necessity of the church, and even in that case he is not an administrator but simply the declarer of right. To prove this, it should be considered that the external goods of men are not granted to the community as are the goods of the church but are acquired by individual persons, by their own skill, labour, and industry. And individuals, as individuals, have right and power in them, and true lordship; and each can ordain concerning his own, dispose, administer, retain or alienate them at his pleasure, without injury of another, since he is the lord; and therefore such goods have no relation or connection with each other, or with any one common head who might have a right to administer or dispose them, since each man at his pleasure is the ordainer of his own property. And therefore neither prince nor pope has lordship or administration in such goods.

But because it sometimes happens that on account of such external goods the common peace is disturbed, when someone usurps what belongs to another; and also because men who love their possessions too much sometimes do not share them as befits the necessity or utility of their fatherland; therefore the prince has been set up by the people to preside as judge in such cases, defining the just and the unjust, and as the punisher of injustices, and as the measurer who takes goods from individuals, in accordance with due proportion, for the common necessity or utility. But because the pope is the supreme head, not only of the clergy, but of all the faithful in general as such, he has the right, as the general formulator of faith and morals, in the case of the supreme necessity of the faith and of morals—in which case all the goods of the faithful are common and to be shared, even the chalices of the churches —to dispense the goods of the faithful and to define what ought to be given up, as befits the common necessity of the faith, which otherwise might be overturned through an invasion of pagans or something of the sort. And the necessity might be so great and so evident that he could exact tithes or definite portions from the individual believers— in accordance with due proportion, however, lest some should without reason be more burdened than others in succouring the common necessity of the faith; and the ordaining of this by the pope is nothing except a declaration of right. And he could also compel those who were rebellious or refractory, through the censure of the church. And if the believers of some parish were recently multiplied to such an extent that the ancient returns of the parish were inadequate to the care of the parish because for the care of the parish the priest would need many new coadjutor chaplains, the pope could by similar means ordain that the believers of the parish should add more from their own goods, up to the sufficient amount: in which case, such an ordaining would be a declaration of right. But except in such cases of necessity, for the sake of the common spiritual good, the pope does not have the disposition of the goods of laymen, but each man disposes of his own in accordance with his will, and the prince, in case of necessity, disposes them for the sake of the common temporal good. In cases not of necessity, however, but of some spiritual utility, or where it is clear that the external goods of the laymen are not due for such utility or necessity, the pope does not have the right to compel anyone; but in this case he could give indulgences for aid brought by the faithful, and nothing else, I think, is allowed him.

William of Occam

[The *Opus Nonaginta Dierum contra Errores Johannis XXII Papae* (Goldast, *Monarchia.* . . , vol. II, pp. 993–1238) was written in 1333 or 1334, defending the Franciscan position on the doctrine of apostolic poverty and attacking what Occam considered the errors and heresies of John XXII. In the chapter translated below—pt. 2, ch. 88—Occam quotes and attacks passages from

Quia vir reprobus, in which, in 1329, the pope had presented his reasons for regarding Cesena's position as heretical. John XXII had argued against the doctrine of apostolic poverty on the ground that the property right must have been introduced by divine law, since, according to Augustine, it could otherwise have been introduced only by the laws of kings. Occam's criticism of John XXII's alternative introduces his characteristic concept of a type of human law antecedent to the laws of kings.]

'*But by divine law*': This can be granted in one sense: that all lordship has been introduced by divine law in the sense in which the Apostle says in Romans 13: [1,] 'There is no power but of God.' Thus there is no lordship which is not in some way based on divine right: because all lordship is from God. But he who distinguishes between the lordships which are based on divine right and the lordships which are based on human right does not speak in this sense. And therefore . . . it is said that that lordship which is possessed by virtue of a gift of God through a special and manifestly divine revelation is lordship by divine right. And thus not all lordships are lordships by divine right.

'*Not by human law, lordship was first introduced*.' That negative is false in every sense . . . because private lordship was first introduced by human law. Therefore let him who holds the doctrine of Thomas notice what he himself says. For he says, in [*Summa Theologiae*], 2a 2ae, q. 66, art. 2, 'According to natural law there is no distinction of possessions, but according to human law, which belongs to positive law, as was said above, it was established. Whence ownership of possessions is not contrary to natural law, but is added to natural law by the invention of human reason.' Therefore, according to that statement, the ownership of lordships was introduced by the invention of human reason.

'*For divine law is that which we find in the divine Scriptures, as we read in* [*the Decretum*], *c. 1, di. 8.*' [Occam comments that not everything in the Scriptures is divine law.]

'*And human law is that which we find in the laws of kings.*' That was true for the time of Augustine, for which he spoke against the heretics of his time, since at that time all nations were subject to kings, if we include emperors under the term kings. And therefore at that time all temporal lordships were possessed by virtue of the laws of emperors or kings; but at many other times this was not true, unless we extend the term kings to all who have some authority over others. And perhaps in the first division of things even this was not true, because perhaps Cain and Abel, without the authority of any superior, divided things between themselves by their own authority, even as Abraham and Lot, as we read in Genesis 13:[8–11], seem to have divided territories between themselves by their own authority. But that, if we use the term kings in the strict sense, human law was not always found in the laws of kings is obvious, because, as we read in the *Decretum*, c. 8, di. 1, any people and state can constitute its own law for itself. And peoples and states and other communities can, without kings, constitute human laws for themselves; and it is certain that many peoples and states have done this. Whence also the Romans at one time lacked kings, and yet they used human laws, and also made human laws, and things were possessed by virtue of their laws at that time.

'*Moreover, we find in the divine Scriptures that before there were laws of kings, nay, before there were any kings, certain things belonged to certain persons.*' This is true, since before the times of kings certain things were possessed by divine right and some by virtue of human law, although not by virtue of the law of kings.

'*By divine right, someone could say that something belonged to him.*' This is to be granted, although it does not follow from its antecedent, precisely taken. But one cannot proceed from this affirmative to the negative: that nothing was then possessed by virtue of human law.

. . . . In the state of innocence Adam could say, without law of kings, that something was his in regard to the power of using it and in regard to lordship. But after the sin of our first parents—namely, Adam and Eve—someone could say, without law of kings, that something was his in regard to use and in regard to lordship that was in a way common. But someone else could say, without law of kings, that something was his in regard to private lordship introduced by human law. After the Deluge, some persons could say, without law of kings, that some things were theirs by divine right, and some could say that some things were theirs by virtue of human law, and yet without law of kings.

[Occam asserted the same thesis briefly and positively in bk. 3, ch. 14 of his *Breviloquium de Principatu Tyrannico*, ed. R. Scholz, *Wilhelm von Ockham als politischer Denker und sein Breviloquium de principatu tyrannico* (Leipzig, 1944). This controversial tract, of which we have only fragments, was written in 1341 or 1342.]

.... The authority to establish laws and human rights was first and
principally in the people. Whence also the people transferred to the
emperor the authority to establish laws. Thus also the people, namely,
both Romans and others, have transferred the authority of making
laws to others: sometimes to kings, sometimes to others of less and
inferior dignity and authority. These facts can be shown not only
by histories and chronicles, but also partly by divine Scripture; but
for the sake of brevity I pass on.

From this, moreover, it is evidently inferred that human laws were
not only the laws of emperors and kings, but also the laws of peoples
and of others who received from the peoples the authority to make and
constitute laws, and also laudable and useful customs introduced by
the peoples. And therefore, because the power of appropriating things
was given by God to the human race, the temporals which were possessed by human law could be possessed not only by the laws of
emperors and kings, but also by the laudable and reasonable customs
and laws and human ordinances introduced by peoples and by others
who had the power and authority from the peoples; and in fact before
there were emperors and kings many private lordships were possessed
by such human law. And therefore what Augustine says [*Decretum*,
c. 1, di. 8], 'We have human law in the laws of kings,' ought to be
understood as applying to his own time and to the regions where he
and the heretics whom he wished to refute lived; but it should not be
understood as applying to the human law which preceded the laws of
emperors and kings, and which, in the time of Augustine, was, at least
in great part, abrogated or changed.

Richard Fitzralph

[Richard Fitzralph was born in the late thirteenth century and died in
1360; he was educated at Oxford, attained a doctorate in theology, and
became vice-chancellor or chancellor of the university ca. 1333. After holding important offices in various English dioceses, he was given the provision
of the archbishopric of Armagh by Clement VI and was consecrated in 1347.
His ecclesiastical career obviously owed much to the favour of the papacy,
and there is evidence that he may have been at Avignon continuously from
1335 to 1345. In 1349 he was one of a group who were examining on behalf
of the Pope the doctrines of the schismatic Armenian Church, which had

asked for papal aid against the Turks. In 1350, Clement appointed him to a three-man commission to study the problem of apostolic poverty, still a vexed question among the friars. The commission accomplished little, but Fitzralph, at the suggestion of some of the cardinals, began the writing of *De Pauperie Salvatoris*, which is an elaborate analysis of the whole question. In 1356, he preached against apostolic poverty in London and stirred up hot opposition. He was summoned to defend his opinions before Innocent VI and probably completed and published his treatise at this time. No condemnation is on record; presumably he died at Avignon before judgment was pronounced or perhaps even contemplated.

The *De Pauperie Salvatoris* (ed. Reginald Lane Poole as an appendix to his edition of John Wyclif, *De Dominio Divino*, London, 1890) concludes with an emphatic assertion of the natural and indefeasible lordship of Christ as man over earthly goods. Its chief interest to us, however, lies in the general analysis of property and lordship which is the basis of this conclusion, and which was turned to a radically different application by Wyclif. The translation is taken from bk. 1, ch. 2, and bk. 4, chs. 1–6, *passim*.]

RICHARD: Tell me first what is the difference between ownership and lordship.

JOHN: These two are related as narrower and broader categories; for all ownership is lordship, but the contrary is not true. Therefore, I do not use the term 'ownership' except in regard to private lordship over something: that is, the right which belongs to one lord alone.

RICHARD: Since, therefore, there exist several rights of lordship over one thing, each of which belongs to one man alone—as, in the case of a barony, the baron has his own lordship, his lord the earl has his own lordship over this same barony, his duke has his own lordship over this very same barony, and even the king has his own royal lordship over it—it follows that each of these has the ownership of the barony in question. Yet no one, I think, would doubt that he who has the ownership of anything whatever may use that thing without wrong to anyone else; and thus it follows that each of these can use the barony without wronging any of the others; and thus, apparently, any of the superior lords just mentioned can take the revenues of the barony without wronging the baron, and use them as he pleases—which is not true.

JOHN: This would seeem to follow, although I do not see how it can be, because the baron can and should freely use the revenues of the barony, but not so his superior lords, except with his consent.

RICHARD: Your last point is not correct, because if the baron tries to prevent his king, his duke, or his earl from exercising the use appropriate to his lordship in regard to the revenues of the barony, then the baron would be inflicting a wrong upon his lord, since it is just and right that his lord should have the use of those things that are subjected to his lordship. For instance, if the earl, duke, or king should summon the baron to his parliament, or to a just war which concerned them in common, and should decree reasonable stipends for a definite number of knights to be paid out of the baron's revenue, for carrying on the war, he would be acting justly, nor could the baron resist him without wrong. And so it is in many other instances; and thus the king, duke, or earl can, in his own cause, freely use the revenues of the barony and the very person of the baron; yet they do not own the revenues of the barony nor the body of the baron, although each has his own lordship over the barony. And thus it follows that not every right of lordship belonging to one person alone is, or can be called, ownership.

JOHN: So I see, because the lordship of the aforesaid superiors, although it is a lordship belonging to them individually, is not a full and complete lordship in regard to the barony; since none of these greater lords can give or sell the barony, nor exercise any complete or general act of lordship in the barony itself, as the baron can. Thus it seems to me that the lordship of the baron in the barony itself—that lordship through which the baron can, completely and generally, exercise every kind of use of the barony—should be called ownership; but the lordship of the others should not.

RICHARD: To everything that belongs to someone there corresponds a right of ownership; therefore, as each of these has a lordship belonging to him, so in each of them there exists a right of ownership. But perhaps you do not notice the distinction between ownership of a lordship, and ownership of the thing dominated. For each of these lords owns, individually and exclusively, a right of lordship, and so also does the baron; but besides owning this the baron also owns, individually and exclusively, the barony itself, because it is he that can freely exercise every kind of use in it which his reasonable desires suggest. . . .

JOHN: Tell me how the right of using is distinguished from lordship; for it seems to me that every lordship is a right of using the thing dominated, and, equally, every right of using seems to be lordship.

RICHARD: I think it would be well for you first to distinguish between the different kinds of lordship, so that the answer to your question may become more clear.

JOHN: It seems to me that there are three kinds of lordship: divine, angelic, and human.

RICHARD: You are right; but human lordship seems to include various kinds of lordship: namely, the natural or original, and the adventitious or political. . . . And this second kind of human lordship, the political, is divided by philosophers into three classes: domestic lordship, civil lordship, and the lordship of a realm. And these three you should distinguish as follows: domestic lordship concerns the goods of one family, of one immediate lord; civil lordship concerns the goods of a city or of a community of many immediate lords; and regal lordship concerns the goods of one kingdom or the rule of one lord over one or many lesser lords; so that regal lordship in this philosophic sense is common to a dukedom, a marchionate, an earldom, a principality, a barony, a knighthood, and to every lordship which contains under itself lesser lordships and lesser lords; because the word regal is derived from the verb *rego*: yet regal lords in this sense have more than the word itself implies: namely, lordship in the realm itself in respect of everything which supports the dignity of their rule; but the word *regere* does not imply lordship.

JOHN: How the king can be called the lord of a barony, as you have suggested, I do not see, since he can neither sell the barony nor give it away nor freely use its products.

RICHARD: I told you before that such lordship is not complete and entire; but because some acts of lordship are in his competence as appropriate to his lordship, therefore, in his own way, he is called, and appears to be, its lord. For no one except a lord can of his own authority compel a lesser lord, subjected to him, to make certain expenditures, and, upon occasion, himself expend the goods of another, as we have said that the king can do with the goods of the baron. Therefore lordships of this kind, in so far as they have more or less authority proper to them in regard to the acts proper to lordships, are called more remote and more excellent lordships. From this you can, if you wish, discover how the right of use differs from lordship; because every lordship is truly a right of use, even as all ownership is lordship, but not vice versa; because the right of use is not always lordship, since one man can grant to another the right of using his goods while the lordship remains in the hands of the grantor; for lessees and commendatories and licensees have the right of using the things leased and entrusted to them by others, and yet they have not lordship over these things.

JOHN: I follow that well enough, and am glad to use the terms with these meanings.

BOOK IV, CHAPTER I

JOHN: Now I wish that you would discuss the ownership of things, because ownership appears to be a kind of lordship; for, behold, when things are occupied from original lordship, it seems to me that, in such occupation, ownership is acquired, because things so occupied seem to me to be so appropriated by him who occupies them that through that occupation the use of those things by others is excluded. I should therefore wish to be shown what ownership, in this case, may be.

RICHARD: You have already declared the contrary in our previous discussion [in bk. 3]: namely, that no just man possessed of original lordship can, simply because something has been occupied, be justly excluded from the right of using that thing. But if some just man is excluded from the use or the right of using that thing, it is not because of lordship or possession of the thing thus possessed, but because of positive law which excludes others than the possessor from use. . . . Since it is fitting that all the just hold equally the original lordship of all things possessed by all men, nothing is, through such lordship, removed from anyone nor drawn closer to anyone. But through ownership, which makes a thing the property of a single man, that thing is drawn close to the will of that man, and removed from others. Therefore ownership is not original lordship. . . .

CHAPTER II

JOHN: From these considerations it seems to follow that no one having natural rights alone has true ownership of anything whatever.

RICHARD: That is a rational inference. And therefore, ownership of a thing, in the original sense of the word, is nothing but the acquired lordship of one or several, which is called civil or political lordship. . .

CHAPTER III

JOHN: Now I wish that you would describe to me the nature of this positive lordship. . . .

RICHARD: The general description of all adventitious lordship is, evidently, the civilly-acquired right or fundamental authority of a rational mortal creature to possess things subjected to him by positive law, and to use them freely in conformance with reason. . . .

JOHN: . . . . I do not see why you use the word 'acquired'—since this word is customarily used only for what is received through labour, and many are lords without labour, by hereditary right, at the moment of their conception. . . .

RICHARD: . . . . It is not as you think, because in the pure sense of this word 'lord' no one is lord of anything, except he be righteous through justifying grace. . . .

JOHN: Please explain this more clearly.

RICHARD: Would you say that some just man in India, called John, for example, might have a better and clearer right to some heritage than its lord, whom we may call Robert?

JOHN: I am not so insane as to prefer a stranger to the legal lord of these things.

RICHARD: In these things as in others, original lordship is a better and clearer right than any civil lordship. . . . Now John in India, who has obtained grace, has original lordship of these things, while your Robert has only what you call civil lordship in these things. Therefore, the righteous John living in India has a better and clearer right than your fictitious impious lord Robert living in this country; and if each of them equally wanted the use of these things, John, having the better title to that use, ought to be preferred to your Robert.

JOHN: I affirm the contrary, because any just judge, doing justice between them, would prefer Robert.

RICHARD: God, who is the most just judge, would in no way do so, nor would any just man who knew these facts; otherwise he would judge against his own conscience. . . .

JOHN: Please explain where your argument is tending.

RICHARD: Civil lordship, like original lordship . . . is given by God to men in consideration of their maintaining the service due to God who gives it to them; therefore, when anyone sins mortally, losing and forfeiting his original lordship thereby, he equally and with equal reason forfeits his civil lordship. . . .

CHAPTER VI

JOHN: It seems to me that, if this is a true description of lordship, all human laws concerning the lordship of things, which are made indiscriminately for the good and the bad, would be overturned. . . .

RICHARD: You do not rightly infer that human laws are thus overturned, because no just law is overturned thereby, but only those laws which make no distinction between the righteous and the wicked; because a law adjudging to a legatee his bequest, to a son his paternal inheritance, to wage-earners their promised or contracted wages, or to the receivers of gifts their gifts, without regard to whether these men are good or bad, does not confer on them the lordship of these things, or any right whatever. . . . But the law or the judge merely adjudges such things to those men in such a way that if they wish they may hold them without molestation from human law; and it does not thereby make them lords, or establish any right whatever for them. . . .

John Wyclif

[Wyclif was born ca. 1320, of good English family; he studied arts and theology at Balliol College in Oxford and was Master of Balliol for a short period sometime between 1356 and 1361. In 1372, he became a doctor of theology. At Oxford he was regarded as outstanding in disputations and lectures. During this period his opinions seem to have been orthodox; he was given several benefices and was considered a loyal supporter of the pope.

His academic distinction, and perhaps some suggestive tendency toward his later opinions, attracted royal favour, at a time when the party led by John of Gaunt was attempting to curtail papal influence in England. In 1374 Wyclif was presented by the crown to the rectory of Lutterworth; in the same year he was appointed a member of a commission to negotiate with papal envoys the vexed question of provisions. This experience opened a period in which his thought developed rapidly in harmony with the trend of English resistance to ecclesiastical abuses. In lectures at Oxford and in popular sermons in London, he criticized clerical corruption and moved on to the thesis developed particularly in his *De Civili Dominio* (1376), which justified royal expropriation of the clergy on the basis of a general doctrine of apostolic poverty and of his own version of the doctrine of lordship contingent on grace. In 1377 Gregory XI condemned eighteen of his opinions as heretical and called for his imprisonment and an examination of his guilt. But the government and the university were disposed to protect him; he remained at liberty and continued to defend his position.

In fact, he now opened a wider campaign of propaganda for his opinions, which steadily grew more revolutionary as he moved from criticism of ecclesiastical abuses to an examination of the fundamentals of Christian doctrine.

Appealing to the Bible as the only authority for religious truth, he began to translate it into English. His organization of the 'poor preachers' aimed to bring religious instruction in the vernacular to the common people. The scandals of the Great Schism helped to convince him that the pope, as such, was Antichrist. His predestinarian conception of grace, his idea of religious experience as a direct relationship between God and the individual, his view of the sacraments as desirable but not essential to salvation, and finally his denial of transsubstantiation were basic attacks on the institutional idea of the church and the theological counterpart to his interpretation of the church as a spiritual community of the elect in which all priests were intrinsically equal in power, and to his interpretation of all clerical jurisdiction as derived only from the king.

Wyclif's attack on the doctrine of transsubstantiation alarmed his patrons; the outbreak of the Peasant's Revolt in 1381 led to a conservative reaction in England. An ecclesiastical court condemned a number of Wyclif's theses as heretical or erroneous; his more prominent adherents were forced to recant; and Wyclif himself went into retirement, but continued to write. He died in 1384.

Wyclif's *De Civili Dominio* has been edited by R. L. Poole and I. Loserth, four vols. (London, 1885–1904); the following passage is from bk. 1, ch. 37 (vol. I, pp. 265–272).]

From these things it seems to follow plainly as a corollary that kings, princes, or temporal lords can legitimately and meritoriously take riches away from any ecclesiastical community or person that habitually misuses them, even though such riches were confirmed to them by human grants. And although that conclusion is demonstrably and unquestionably true . . . yet it is necessary to prove it step by step.

For if God exists, the clerical part of the church can misuse riches; and if so, temporal lords can meritoriously take those riches away from them; therefore the conclusion is based on the existence of God, for God could not allow such evil if he could not command his servants to punish it by despoiling them and to regulate them in the worthy execution of his pleasure; therefore, undoubtedly, if God exists, temporal lords can legitimately and meritoriously take away the goods of fortune from a delinquent church.

Again, every Christian has the right and duty of helping his neighbour, especially in such matters as concern the public good; but the taking away of riches from an ecclesiastic would be a great help, if they impeded him in the service due to God; therefore, by the law of Christ he has a greater right and duty to take away the goods of fortune in such a case. But kings and temporal lords have the greatest right to do this . . . and undoubtedly this would especially concern the public good, since by such unloading of the goods of fortune, which are a natural burden, . . . ecclesiastics would become more capable of instilling in the people that spiritual life by whose lack churches are most perilously injured.

Again, whatever, by the law of Christ, an ecclesiastic ought to exact from the secular arm, the secular arm ought, by the same law, to perform; but the ecclesiastic, fettered by riches, ought to exact from the secular arm assistance in administering those riches; therefore, by the law of Christ, the secular arm in such a case ought to undertake the service of acquiring, protecting, and removing that wealth. The major [minor(?)] premise is drawn from this principle: that no one ought to have riches except in so far as they are aids to the performance of the office assigned to him by the Bridegroom; therefore when civil possession hinders him in that service he ought to refuse it. . . . Therefore, undoubtedly, if civil possession or an alleged lordship in temporals impedes the clerical part of the church from carrying out the law of Christ, they ought to renounce such goods; and if they are obstinate and unwilling to do so, the secular part ought to snatch such goods away. . . .

Now whether the church is in that situation today is not for me to discuss, but for the statesmen who attend to the affairs and condition of kingdoms. I protest that I am setting forth conditional truths about possibilities, leaving to others the judgment of fact. I know that it is the province of temporal lords to examine such facts; and when a defect exists they ought, according to the rules of charity, to amend it. . . .

And [the king's right to act] can be shown as follows. If foreign enemies invaded the kingdom, preying on the goods of nature and fortune which belong to the people, the king ought to resist them with the secular arm; but injury by fellow-countrymen to the people of his kingdom with regard to the goods of fortune and of grace would be a more dangerous invasion; therefore the king ought to resist them more particularly; for the king must intervene in all things which concern the goods of fortune or of body belonging to the inhabitants of the realm, because he has rule and wardship.

Again, the king has the most universal human coercive power of his kingdom; therefore, granted, as possible, that it is expedient for the clergy to be castigated by being deprived of their temporals against their will, this belongs in principle to the office of the king. For whose it is to supply a lack, his it is to subtract a superfluity; whose it is to defend from a foreign enemy, his it is to bring corporal aid against the madness of his liegeman. It appears, therefore, that since the church, through the greater and principal part of the clergy, can sin irremediably in love of temporals, . . . God can ordain another part of the church to bring a remedy through coercive power. Moreover, this is consonant to the law of God, since God fits the punishment to the sin: therefore a cleric who sins by usurping secular power ought to be deprived of it through the secular power; for otherwise, if secular lords could not do this, they would bear the sword in vain, which is contrary to the saying of the apostle in Romans 13:4. . . .

This is confirmed by the saying of Isidore, which appears in the *Decretum*, C. 23, [q. 5, c. 20]: 'Secular princes,' he says, 'sometimes hold the heights of power attained within the church that through this same power they may assist ecclesiastical discipline; but powers would not be necessary within the church were it not that what priests cannot accomplish through the potency of teaching the power may command through the terror of discipline.' And he continues: 'Let secular princes recognize that they must render an accounting to God for the church which they receive from Christ to be protected; for whether the peace and discipline of the church be increased through faithful princes or whether it be dissolved, He Who entrusted His church to their power exacts an accounting from them.' Behold the opinion of this saint, that kings and temporal lords are open to condemnation if they do not, by taking away the things which impede them, force those who are subject to their laws, and especially those who cannot be more efficaciously corrected otherwise, to surrender to the laws of Christ.

Again . . . God does not approve the appropriation of temporals by His church except in so far as they promote the observance of His law; therefore, if the acquisition of temporals has the opposite effect, divine approval is lacking and consequently the justice of possessing is lacking; nor can this be turned to doubt, since the unjust man unjustly acquires what he has. Therefore, since the final cause for which temporal lords endowed the church was the furthering of the Christian religion, it seems that when that cause ceases the endowment ought to cease; therefore an ecclesiastic cannot claim lordship contrary to the law of Christ by title of an endowment thus qualified. Nor is there any doubt that, since it is just to deprive such persons of lordship, God can impose on temporal lords the authority and office of carrying out this justice.

But this authority and office.they have, whatever inventions of men have blindly maintained the contrary. For to whom, I ask, would He give civil lordship if not to a secular lord? Who would coercively dispose the goods of kingdoms, if not the kings to whom their custody is entrusted?

Somnium Viridarii

[The *Somnium Viridarii* (text in Goldast, *Monarchia. . .* , vol. I, pp. 58–229) was written anonymously ca. 1376 or 1377; a French version, *Le Songe du Vergier*, appeared soon after. It was an expansion of the anonymous *Disputatio inter Clericum et Militem* written under Philip the Fair (cf. p. 468 below); it incorporated and reworked large sections of Occam's *Dialogus* and also borrowed extensively from the *Defensor Pacis* and from the *De Regimine Principum* of Aegidius Romanus. It was, in fact, a compendium of Gallican argument and was frequently cited by later Gallicans. The selection translated below, from pt. 1, chs. 140 and 141, is a good summary of late medieval theory on taxation.]

CHAPTER CXL

CLERK: Again, honoured Knight, because you seemed above to clear the present king of France from tyrannic acts, I ask by what right can the king of France levy *gabelles*, impositions, and other unendurable and impossible burdens on his subjects? . . . Is not that act tyrannical? for through this he holds the people in servitude. . . .

PROPERTY AND LORDSHIP

CHAPTER CXLI

KNIGHT: . . . . It appears that kings, especially those who recognize no superior in their lands, can introduce such exactions; and the king of France is of this sort. This Innocent expressly noted in [his decretal *Per venerabilem, Decretals*], ch. 10, bk. 3, tit. 39. For kings can impose new taxes or impositions; but they sin if they do this without cause. For they are imposed with cause, as for the defence of the commonwealth against robbers on land or pirates on sea, or for the defence of the faith and fatherland against pagans or heretics, or for some other similar cause. If the recipient does that for whose sake they were imposed, he can receive them freely and without scruple of conscience; but if they are turned to other uses, the blood and sweat of the labours of the subjects will be exacted from the hands of the lords in the day of judgment, and their cry will arise for ever. . . . Whence it should be known that the lord ought not regularly to seek anything from the subjects except those things which belonged beforehand to him and his predecessors honestly and in good faith without force or fraud; therefore all things imposed from the beginning, so long as they are not shameful or against God, can be sought and ought to be paid. . . . And those are the ordinary revenues of kings and other princes. . . . For it is to be believed that those revenues were granted to princes for a just cause, namely, for the defence of the country, for the exercise of justice among the people, and the like, but on condition that the lord fulfill that for whose sake the said revenues were instituted. For if the prince denied justice to his subjects—for instance, if he should not receive appeals or defend the country—he would have no right to such ordinary revenues, *gabelles*, impositions, hearth-money, and the like; if such ordinary revenues were introduced for a just cause, namely, for the defence of the country, and it is not defended as it can and ought to be, and the revenues are not applied to that use but to another, then such ordinary revenues could justly be denied, nay, by written law based on the dictate of right reason he should deservedly be deposed from the government as unworthy. And if he were thus negligent in the government of the whole kingdom he ought to be entirely deposed, and it would be licit for the people to choose another prince; if he neglected this in a part of the kingdom only, the people of that place would be permitted to choose themselves another prince, even when the prince was such that he recognized no superior in his lands. . . . But if the people, through love or fear, were reluctant to depose him, the said prince should at least be induced to restitution in the court of penitence. . . .

Yet I know that there are certain causes for which the prince can licitly impose new talliages on his subjects. One is for the defence of the country, when it is unjustly invaded by enemies. . . . Another is, if the lord wishes to join an army summoned by the church against schismatics, heretics, or Saracens, and cannot meet the expenses out of his own resources without serious loss. The third is, if the lord is captured by the enemy in a campaign of war which, so far as he is concerned, is just, and cannot pay his ransom out of his own resources without serious loss. Again, when a lord knights his son, or gives his daughter in marriage, or takes over new territory. For these involve an advantage to the subjects, because the lord thereby becomes more powerful or richer and thus can spare his subjects in the future. And it seems that for such purposes the lord can take contributions from the subjects, where it is so established or accustomed, provided that he takes moderately. If, however, the lord wishes to play at dice, or exceed his resources in expenditures for pleasure, clothes, guests, or building castles not necessary to the protection of the commonwealth, he ought [not] for these purposes to extort anything from his subjects; and if he does he is obligated to restitution. And likewise, if he is captured in an unjust war, he cannot exact all or part of the ransom from his subjects.

Others, however, distinguish in regard to the talliages to be imposed by lords, according to whether the subjects are slaves or free. If slaves, the lords have an absolute right of taxation and can impose taxes on them for the sake of the good of the lords, and the slaves are bound to obey the said lords, because the slave and his goods are a possession of the lord, whence the Philosopher says in I *Politics*, [ch. 2], that 'a slave is a thing possessed.' . . . If, however, they are free, so that the lord rules politically, that lord is either a king or prince or an inferior lord. If he is a king, he can on his own authority impose new talliages for the utility of the common good, the resources of the subjects having been taken into account (*Digest*, 39, 4, 10): that is, if the king or prince does not have adequate resources for the defence of the commonwealth. If, however, such talliages are not for the sake of the common good at all, neither king nor prince can impose them, and if he does the subjects are not bound to pay because he exceeds the limits of his authority. If, however, he is an inferior lord, he cannot impose talliages on his subjects; and if he imposes them, since he exceeds the limits of this authority, the subjects are not bound to obey, especially when they are imposed without the consent of the king or prince; and this is set forth in the *Decretals of Gregory IX*, ch. 10, bk. 3, tit. 39, and in the *Codex*, bk. 4, ch. 62.

Also it should be known that sometimes newly-imposed talliages are directly for the utility of the common good, as when they are for the defence of the faith or of the realm; but sometimes indirectly and not so openly, as when some injury is inflicted on the king outside his kingdom; for instance, when the brother or son of the king is held by enemies or some land which has newly devolved on the king is violently occupied by enemies; then the king can levy talliages on his subjects by means of which he can recover his brother or son or lands, for this redounds to the utility of the subjects, because when the king fights enemies vigorously he is as a result more honoured and feared by the enemies, and consequently his faithful subjects enjoy and possess their goods more securely. Whence, therefore, if in such a case the king's resources are not adequate, he can ask moderate aid from his subjects. Yet it seems that when the business has been settled, if the resources of the king are increased and some notable communities are burdened, the king ought to help them as they in his necessity helped him. For when the head suffers, the other members minister to him, and likewise *vice versa* the head to the other members. It should also be known that because the resources of kings are granted them for the promotion and defence of the common utility, if the resources of the king are adequate for the defence of the kingdom or the faith they ought not in that case to talliage their subjects. . . .

Sir John Fortescue

[Fortescue wrote his *De Natura Legis Naturae* (text in *The Works of Sir John Fortescue, Knight*, ed. Thomas Fortescue, Lord Clermont, London, 1869, vol. I) some time before his *De Laudibus Legum Angliae*. The first part of the treatise is a general discussion of natural law and of government; the second part attempts to deduce natural law principles on behalf of an antifeminist law of succession. In pt. 1, ch. 20, and pt. 2, ch. 33, he presents his case for regarding the property right and the right of inheritance as prescribed for sinful man by natural law itself.]

PART I, CHAPTER XX

And when the Lord said to Adam, 'In the sweat of thy countenance thou shalt eat thy bread,' [Genesis 3:19] was not Adam from thenceforth permitted to sell the bread which the Lord had said was his own? And when it is written in Genesis 4:[4] that Abel offered of the firstborn of his flock, were they not then his which the Holy Scripture speaks of as his? And at that time it is certain that the laws of peoples did not exist, since two brothers could not form peoples. Wherefore it is necessarily conceded that the ownership of things, especially of things acquired by sweat, first accrued to man by the law of nature alone, since there was then no other human law; and consequently buyings, sellings, lettings, hirings, and the like originated in the law of nature, which law is perpetual and, as the . . . canons say, began with the beginning of rational creatures and does not vary with time but remains immutable. Yet the status of man was changed by sin, but not the law of nature, of which also the Civil Laws say that natural rights which are preserved among all peoples everywhere, constituted by a certain divine providence, remain always firm and immutable (*Institutes*, 1, 2). For that law which now makes us say, 'This is mine and that is thine,' prohibited us to say so before the sin of man. For that law is the same when it decrees that the innocent enjoy liberty and when it deprives of liberty the same man conscious of crime, and thrusts him into fetters, and for his crime deprives him of all his goods; for in these cases the status and merit of the man, but not the law of nature, is changed. It is the same sun which condenses liquid mud into brick and melts frozen into flowing water; and the wind which kindles the lighted torch into flame is no other than that which cools the hot barley-porridge; for in these cases the qualities of the objects cause the mutations which the objects themselves undergo; but the efficient cause remains stable and is not changed. Even so the equity of natural justice which once assigned to innocent man the common ownership of all things is none other than that equity which now, because of his sin, takes away from man corrupted by guilt the good of common ownership.

PROPERTY AND LORDSHIP

.... If I am not mistaken, before the fall of man the law of nature in no way revealed that right to man. For the right of the descent of possessions was not known to our first parents while they preserved their innocence, since they then possessed all things in common and thus were entirely ignorant of property which could descend; but then, when they lost their innocence, the Lord soon said to mankind [Genesis 3 : 19], 'In the sweat of thy countenance shalt thou eat thy bread,' in which words there was granted to man property in the things which he by his own sweat could obtain. . . . For since the bread which man would acquire in sweat would be his own, and since no one could eat bread without the sweat of his own countenance, every man who did not sweat was forbidden to eat the bread which another had acquired by his sweat. And in this way ownership of the bread acquired accrued only to him who sweated, and consequently no other men continued to share in common rights. And thus the inheritable ownership of things first broke forth. For by the word *bread*, our elders teach us, we are to understand not only what is eaten and drunk but everything by which man is sustained; and by the word *sweat*, all the industry of man. And because property thus acquired comes in recompense of the sweat by which the body of the acquirer is weakened, the reason of the law of nature has united it to its acquirer, that the property gained may compensate for the loss of his lost wholeness; and thus property takes the place of the lost human wholeness and adheres like an accident to him who sweated; and consequently it thereafter accompanies his blood. Yet property is not an accident natural to man, but it happens to man by the rules of the law of nature, and is joined to man after the fashion of a natural accident—not by the bonds of the right of nature as nature was first instituted, but as nature now exists, destitute of liberty and her pristine forces, in accordance with the deserts of man.

[In ch. 36 of his *De Laudibus Legum Angliae* Fortescue described the security of private property under the ideal 'political and regal lordship,' as illustrated in England.]

CHAPTER XXXVI

In the Kingdom of England, no one takes up his abode in the house of another against the will of its lord, except in public inns, where, before he leaves, he pays in full for all his charges there. Nor does anyone with impunity take the goods of another without the consent of their owner; and no one, in this kingdom, is hindered from providing himself with salt, or whatever other wares he wishes, from whatever merchant. The king, however, through his officials can take things necessary for his household against the will of the possessors, for a reasonable price assessed at the discretion of the constables of the villages; but nevertheless he is bound by the laws to pay that price at once, or at a day fixed by the greater officials of his household; because he cannot legally take the goods of any of his subjects without paying a satisfactory price for them. Nor does the king of this country, either through himself or through his ministers, impose talliages, subsidies, or any other taxes upon his subjects, or change their laws, or establish new laws, without the express grant or consent of all his kingdom in his Parliament. Wherefore every inhabitant of his kingdom uses at his own pleasure the fruits which his land yields to him, and which his herds produce, and all the gains which accrue to him from his own labour or that of another, on land or sea; and if he suffers injury or robbery he receives the amends due to him thence; whence the inhabitants of that country are rich in land, and have abundance of gold and silver and all the necessities of life. They drink no water, except when they are abstaining for a time from other drinks on account of piety or the zeal of penance; they are plentifully fed with every kind of beast and fish, with which their country is well supplied; they wear cloth of good wool for all their garments, and they also have abundance of bedding and whatever other household furnishings are best made of wool; and they are rich in other household goods, and in the tools of husbandry, and in all things which are needed for a quiet and happy life, in accordance with their status. Nor are they led into law-suits except before the ordinary justices, where they are dealt with justly by the law of the land. Nor are they summoned or impleaded in regard to their movables or their possessions, or accused of any crime however great or enormous, except according to the laws of their land, and before the aforesaid judges. And these are the fruits which are born of a political and regal lordship. . . .

Philippe de Comines

[Comines was born in 1415 of an illustrious Flemish family. He spent his youth at the court of Philip the Good of Burgundy and became the intimate associate and adviser of Charles the Bald, who used his services in various diplomatic negotiations. As the impetuous Charles became increasingly irritated at his sage counsels, Louis XI of France was able in 1472 to detach Comines from the Burgundian court, and Comines thereafter played the same role for a more appreciative master. Louis rewarded him with estates and a rich wife and made him Seneschal of Poitou. After Louis's death, Comines was active in the intrigues of the regency period on the side of the princes, but was ultimately pardoned and employed by Charles VIII. He died in 1509.

His *Mémoires* (ed. B. de Mandrot, Paris, 1901) were written after 1495, covering the reign of Louis XI, 1464–1483. They are remarkable among medieval historical writings for their realism and cool, objective judgment of events and personalities that Comines was able to observe at close hand.

The section translated below, giving Comines's opinion on arbitrary taxation, is from bk. 5, ch. 19.]

. . . . Is there any king or lord on earth who has power, outside his domain, to raise one penny from his subjects without the grant and consent of those who are to pay it, unless by tyranny and violence? One could answer that there are occasions when it is impossible to wait for the meeting of an assembly, and that it would be too long to wait before beginning a war. But it is not necessary to hurry so much; there is enough time; and I tell you that kings and princes are strongest and most feared by their enemies when they make war with the consent of their subjects. And when it is a matter of defence, one sees the storm coming from far off, especially if foreigners are making an invasion (and in that case good subjects ought not to complain or to refuse anything); and no case could happen so suddenly that one could not call together some important persons so that one could tell them, 'It is not done without cause'; and one ought not to have recourse to fiction nor start a little war wilfully and pointlessly just to have an excuse to raise money. I know, of course, that money is necessary to defend the frontiers and to guard the environs against surprise attacks, even when there is no war; but everything should be done moderately.

And in all these questions the good sense of the wise prince is important, for if he is good, he knows what God is, and what the world is, and what he can and ought to do and to avoid. And in my opinion, among all the lordships of the world of which I have knowledge, the one where the commonwealth is best managed, where the least violence holds sway over the people, and where there are no buildings broken down or demolished by war, is England; and misfortune and misery fall on those who make war.

Of all the lords in the world, our King has the least cause to say, 'I have the privilege of raising as much as I like from my subjects.' For neither he nor any other prince has such a privilege. And those who say this to make him appear greater do him no honour, but make him hated and feared by his neighbours, who would not be at all willing to live under his lordship (and even some subjects of his realm, or those who hold from it, would gladly leave it). But if our King, or those who wish to praise and aggrandize him, would say, 'I have subjects so very good and so very loyal that they refuse me nothing that I ask of them, and I am more feared and obeyed and served by my subjects than any other prince who lives on this earth; and no one has subjects who more patiently endure all evils and severities, or who are more forgetful of past injuries,' it seems to me that that would be greater glory for him— and I tell you the truth—than to say, 'I take what I want; I have the privilege of doing so, and I intend to maintain it.' King Charles the Fifth never said such a thing; indeed, I never heard kings make such claims, but I have often heard them made by their servants under the belief that thus they did the king a service; but, in my opinion, they were mistaken about their lords, and they said it only as courtiers; and I also think that they did not know what they were saying.

And, as an instance of the goodwill of the French, I need only mention, for our time, the meeting of the Three Estates held at Tours after the death of our good master King Louis—may God forgive him —which was in the year 1483. It was possible then to regard that meeting as dangerous; and some people of low rank and little virtue said then and have often repeated since that it is the crime of *lèse-majesté* to talk of assembling the Estates and that it diminishes the authority of the King. But those who say such things are committing that very crime against God and the King and the commonwealth, but such words are and have been useful to those who enjoy authority and reputation;

without deserving them in the least, and who are accustomed to do nothing but flatter and whisper lies, and who dread the large assemblies for fear that they will be found out and their works condemned. At the time of which I speak, everyone thought that the kingdom was very weak, the great, the little, and the middle people, since they had borne and suffered great and horrible taxes for twenty years or more....

At the said assembly of the Estates some requests and remonstrances were made in great humility for the good of the kingdom, everything being always referred to the good pleasure of the King and his council. They granted him everything that he wished to ask of them and whatever one showed them in writing to be necessary for the King's expenses, without saying anything against it.... And the said Estates supplicated that at the end of two years they should be reassembled, and that if the King had not enough money they would supply him with as much as he wanted, and that, if he had a war or if someone wished to injure him, they would be ready with their persons and their fortunes, without refusing him anything of which he had need.

Is it over such subjects as these that the King should allege the privilege of being able to take at his pleasure what they so liberally give him? Would it not be more just toward God and the world to raise it by this form rather than by arbitrary will? For no prince can raise it otherwise than by grant, as I have said, if it be not by tyranny and if he be not excommunicated. But there are many foolish enough not to know what can be done and left undone in this matter, as well as people who offend against their lords and do not obey them nor succour them in their necessities, but instead of aiding them when they see them in trouble disdain them or rise in rebellion and disobedience against them, and violate the oath which they have made.

Chapter Three

THE ORIGIN AND PURPOSE OF POLITICAL
AUTHORITY

THE origin of political authority was not, for medieval publicists, primarily an historical question. It is not quite true to say that medieval minds were not aware of historical growth and change, but they had no elaborate consciousness of history. One event which they believed historic was often crucial in their thought—the Fall of Man; but on the whole their limited and shallow knowledge of the past and the apparent stability of their own environment saved them from the modern problem of attempting to construct an enduring doctrine on the shifting sands of historical instances. The question they chiefly asked was what made authority legitimate; they tried to answer it in terms of purposes assumed to be permanent and sought their premises in the nature of man and the providence of God.

The problem first appeared to them as the problem of the basis of kingship rather than of 'the state.' The notion of a politically-organized community was all but absent from the writings of the eleventh and twelfth centuries: it appeared only in fragmentary survivals of Germanic ideas and occasional echoes of the classical tradition. By the thirteenth century, under the tutelage of Roman law and of Aristotle, men had begun to recognize the complexity of the political units which were being precipitated from feudal dissolution; but the first pattern of medieval thought, and one which continued important throughout the medieval centuries, was a very simple picture: on the one hand, a king; on the other, a vague aggregate of 'those subjected to him.'

Ideas inherited from the Germanic kingship hovered about the king. He was the leader of a people, especially in war. His claim to authority was based at least partly on his people's consent, as illustrated in the still-lingering rites of election. In practice, of course, that consent was expressed mainly by an indefinite group of magnates; moreover, the idea that kingship rested on consent was fused with two other ideas: the idea that certain families had an hereditary claim to the kingship and the idea, expressed in the role of the priesthood in the coronation ceremonies, that kingship rested on divine institution. In a rather vague way, the king was felt to be a sort of trustee under the common law for the common interests of his people, who might appropriately depose him if he proved false to his task. His function might be described as the maintenance of justice and peace.[1]

But feudalism had deeply eroded the Germanic conception of the relations between king and people. It tended to transform the kingdom into a mere network of personal, contractual relations, defined and maintained by private-law principles. It tended to construe all authority as proprietary, and to treat the rights of a king as simply a particular agglomeration of property-rights, established within the framework of the same legal principles as governed the property-rights of his subjects. Feudal thought encouraged the king to regard his power as his private affair, to make no distinction between the administration of a kingdom and that of any seignory, to merge his public and his private treasury, to infeudate governmental functions, to reconstitute the national council as a council of vassals. The selection of a king was increasingly affected by feudal analogies which supported dynastic ambition. The rule of hereditary succession by primogeniture was gradually established in England, France, and other kingdoms of western Europe; in the Empire and other central-European kingdoms, less completely feudalized, elective succession survived with some difficulty. In the investiture struggle, it was possible for one publicist, Peter Crassus, to attack Gregory VII's deposition of the emperor Henry IV on the ground that Henry, having duly inherited the crown from his father, enjoyed an indefeasible property in the kingship.[2]

Other aspects of feudalism were more readily harmonized with the older view of kingship: to the extent that the king was entangled in the contractual system, his rights appeared to be limited by law like all property-rights, and his claim to obedience appeared as legally contingent on his performance of the stipulated duties which a lord owed his vassals. Feudal law consistently sanctioned the withdrawal of obedience from a king as from any lord who failed to give his vassals justice and protection.

In the scholarly theory of the early Middle Ages, Germanic and feudal attitudes were reflected, but the strongest influence was patristic thought, which had already combined Scriptural teachings with some classical ideas into systematic theory. The centre of that theory was the emphatic words of St. Paul:

'Let every soul be in subjection to the higher powers: for there is no power but of God, and the powers that be are ordained of God. Therefore he that resisteth the power withstandeth the ordinance of God: and they that withstand shall receive to themselves judgment. And wouldst thou have no fear of the power? do that which is good, and thou shalt have praise from the same: for he is a minister of God to thee for good. But if thou do that which is evil, be afraid; for he beareth not the sword in vain: for he is a minister of God, an avenger for wrath to him that doeth evil.'[3]

The Old Testament tradition of the king as 'the Lord's anointed' was in harmony with this teaching. There were, however, Old Testament stories of somewhat different implications. The first lordship recorded in the Bible, that of Nimrod, was apparently grounded simply on force: 'he began to be a mighty one in the earth.'[4] The first kingship in Israel, that of Saul, was ordained by the people in rebellion against the divine will: not planned by God, but permitted as a penalty for the sin that had brought it into being.[5]

But the dictum of St. Paul had from the beginning the greater weight. The necessity of repressing anarchic tendencies in the early church and the later cooperative relations with the Christian emperors brought the Fathers to vigorous support of the principle that the authority of rulers was derived from God and that obedience was therefore a part of Christian duty. Merging with Christian thought the Stoic concept of the relations of nature and convention, they sketched the doctrine that in the state of natural innocence before the Fall there was no coercive dominion, but with the coming of sin and the resulting social disorder coercive authority became necessary to punish evildoers and compel mankind to some degree of order and justice. Whether the ruler seized power by force or was established by some vague popular agreement or was directly instituted by God was a moot point but not an important one. Whatever the historical origin of his authority, its fundamental condition was sin, its fundamental cause the will of God, and its fundamental purpose order and justice.[6]

A more important difference of opinion appeared on the question whether the evil ruler as well as the good derived his authority from God. The idea that justice gave validity to kingship led easily to the idea that the unjust king had no valid claim to obedience. On the other hand, the wicked ruler, as many Old Testament examples showed, might well have been sent by God as a punishment for sin and thus be bulwarked by a higher justice than his own. In general, the early church accepted this possibility, which was developed by Gregory the Great into an explicit statement of the duty of passive obedience to all rulers.[7] But the tendency to measure the ruler's legitimacy by the test of justice was also vigorous and found influential expression in Isidore's *Etymologies*:

'Kings are so called from ruling (*reges a regendo*). . . . Therefore by doing righteously the name of king is retained, by wrong-doing it is lost. Wherefore this was a proverb among the ancients: "You shall be king if you rule rightly; if you do not, you shall not be." '[8]

A few other important ideas and phrases destined to later development appeared in patristic writings. In an often-cited passage, Augustine quoted Cicero's definition of a commonwealth: 'A commonwealth is an affair of a people (*res publica est res populi*): moreover a people is not any association of men brought together in any way whatever, but is an association of a multitude united by consent to law and community of interests.'[9] He developed the idea that justice was the necessary characteristic of a true commonwealth: 'Without justice, what are kingdoms, but great robber-bands?' Conceiving perfect justice to involve the rendering of worship and obedience to God, he distinguished between the imperfect commonwealths—the mere *civitates* and *regna*—of the pagans and the true Christian commonwealth.[10] Augustine's conception of justice was related to his important idea of 'peace' as 'the tranquillity of order.' Order was 'the distribution which allots all things, equal and unequal, each to its own place.' 'Civil peace' —'well-ordered concord among citizens in commanding and obeying' in conformity with the divine plan—was only one instance of the divinely-established order in whose tranquil maintenance the universe found its peace.[11] This idea was further developed by Gregory the Great, who saw a hierarchy of ranks and orders as part of God's original plan. Coercive authority was the result of sin, but non-coercive rule was proper to sinless nature, as was shown by the hierarchy of the angels.[12] In another often-quoted passage, Augustine remarked that there was 'a certain compact of men to obey their kings,'[13] but since he also argued that men must obey wicked kings, this compact did not imply a contract.

The question of the origin of political authority received considerable attention in the course of the investiture struggle, when Gregory VII's attempt to depose Henry IV split churchmen into two camps and set off a barrage of controversial pamphlets. Gregory himself, in two famous letters to the Bishop of Metz, implied that kingship originated simply in the human will to power. 'One can infer from their origins,' he wrote, 'how much the royal dignity differs from the episcopal. For human arrogance invented the one, divine piety instituted the other.'[14] 'Who does not know that kings and dukes took their origin from those who, ignorant of God, through arrogance, rapines, perfidy, murders, and in short by nearly all crimes, instigated by the devil, prince of this world, sought with blind lust and intolerable presumption to rule over their fellow-men?'[15] These angry statements, which did not reflect Gregory's calmer opinion, still less the normal thought of his period,[16] were vigorously answered by Hugh of Fleury. He marshalled authorities and arguments to show that 'there is no power but of God' and also picked up and developed further the theory outlined by Gregory the Great of the natural hierarchy of lordships in the universe.

The ultimate divine origin of royal authority was really not an issue in the investiture struggle but, in general, a premise for both sides. However, two important theories of its mediate origin appeared in the course of the controversy. Manegold of Lautenbach justified the deposition of Henry IV through an assertion of the popular basis of the kingship. He first presented a clear, if skeletal, statement of the contract theory, in which the king appeared as chosen agent of the people, who retained the right to overthrow him if he should violate the terms of the implied contract. More useful to later ecclesiastical strategy was the doctrine quaintly developed by Honorius Augustodunensis from the materials of sacred history: that secular government had been instituted by God through the mediation of the church.[17]

Honorius's view was unique in this period, but the idea that the king had been ordained by God as His minister had already suggested that he must be in some sense an officer of the church—which in this period was conceived as the *Respublica Christiana*, the whole Christian society, without the later sharp distinction between clergy and laity. Isidore had written: 'Secular princes sometimes hold heights of power within the church, that through that power they may strengthen ecclesiastical discipline. Powers would not be necessary within the church were it not that what the priest cannot accomplish through the word of his teaching, the power may command through the terror of his discipline. The heavenly kingdom is often aided by the earthly kingdom, that those members of the church who act against the faith and discipline of the church may be destroyed by the force of princes. . . . Let secular princes know that they are responsible to God for the church which Christ has given to their protection.'[18] The intimate relations that developed between the Carolingian emperors and the clergy strengthened the notion that the king was endowed with the temporal sword for the enforcement of ecclesiastical discipline and the protection of the faith as well as for the performance of justice in general. Throughout the Middle Ages a special aura of holiness clung about the king and, even more notably, about the emperor.[19] Beyond this, the consecration of kings seemed, to many tenth-century minds, to give the king a priestly character,[20] and this idea appeared in several pamphlets opposing the pope in the investiture struggle.[21] Papalist thought discouraged it, and ecclesiastical writers thereafter stressed the sharp distinction between king and priest, while still insisting that the protection of the church was particularly a royal duty.

Formal theory steadfastly opposed any suggestion that the power of kings was their private affair. Ecclesiastics repeated again and again that royal authority existed for the advantage of the subjects; lawyers incorporated their phrases in legal treatises. The king, as John of

Salisbury put it, was 'minister of the public utility and servant of equity.' '. . . . The power of all the subjects is gathered together in him that he may be strong enough to seek out and perform what is needful for the welfare of each and all, and that the condition of the human commonwealth may be best disposed. . . .'[22] 'The people,' said Manegold, 'exalts someone above itself for this purpose: that he may govern and rule them with justice.'[23] 'Moreover, the king was created and chosen for this,' said Bracton: 'that he should make justice for all, and that the Lord should sit in him.'[24] St. Paul's vision of kings as ministers of God was constantly quoted, as was Isidore's argument from etymology. The view that kingship was a public office rather than a private right was stated with increasing clarity as publicists pointed out that the authority of a king was attached to his office rather than to his person, could properly be used only in ways consistent with the purpose for which it existed, and was forfeited if it was abused. 'For *king* is not the name of a nature, but of an office, like bishop, priest, deacon. And when any man for certain causes is deposed from the office entrusted to him, he is not what he was, nor should the honour due to the office be afterwards paid him.'[25] 'The king's power is of right and not of unright. . . . Therefore, the king ought to exercise the power of right as God's vicar and minister on earth, because that power is from God above; but the power of unright is from the devil and not from God, and the king will be the minister of that one of the two whose works he does.'[26]

If the king was God's minister, he was especially God's minister 'for wrath.' The purpose of secular authority was commonly defined as the maintenance of justice and peace, and the greatest emphasis was on the coercive aspect of the royal office. The influence of the patristic doctrine that government was 'the penalty and remedy for sin' was overwhelming; and so long as human nature was conceived as primarily sinful, the primary function of government must be the repression of sin. This essentially negative and static view of government virtually monopolized ecclesiastical thought up to the time of Aquinas. It fitted well enough with the conditions of the feudal period, in which the organization of society seemed to be secured through private and customary relationships in which the king ought not to interfere. To the majority of early writers, therefore, the maintenance of justice meant simply the maintenance of the customary law—an identification which obviously facilitated the distinction between the just and the unjust king.

There was, indeed, an occasional suggestion of a deeper conception of justice, which stemmed from the more sophisticated classical and Augustinian traditions. For John of Salisbury, in particular, a kingdom was an ordered community, in which each social group had by divine appointment a necessary part to play for the well-being of the whole. It was the mission of the king to preserve the harmonies of this social order by ensuring that every individual enjoyed the rights and performed the duties implicit in his function. Yet John of Salisbury seems to have regarded the ideal order as already embodied in the institutions of his day and to have asked of the king no more than a constant vigilance to protect the status quo. Thus, although in general he used high language to describe the dignity of kings, he could also say that the royal office was lower than the priestly, 'because it deals with the punishment of criminals, and seems to resemble that of the executioner.'[27]

As medieval monarchy developed, it began to burst the boundaries of the role which had been assigned to it by ecclesiastical and feudal thought. The administration of justice and the maintenance of peace and order remained its cardinal functions but, with the development of regular machinery for these functions, their significance was quietly transformed. This transformation did not merely consist in making effective what had been all too often an empty theory; a more profound change was the gradual emergence of systematic, constructive policy. The moulding of governmental machinery was itself a triumph of creative effort. The medieval ruler could not administer justice without working out systematic norms of justice; he could not preserve order without making order. This change might easily be over-emphasized. In comparison with the rulers of the sixteenth century, medieval kings were utterly timid and conservative; but there is a line of continuous development from William the Conqueror to Elizabeth, from Louis le Gros to Henri Quatre, a line which notably contrasts with the aimless paths of earlier feudal kings.

At the same time, the subjects of the king were being organized in self-conscious units—partly through their own initiative, but as often through the organizing pressure of the king. The feudal linking of individual to individual by private contract ceased to be the sole principle of social cohesion: the feudal aristocracy slowly became an estate of the realm and showed signs of class-conscious activity, while more and more the kingship entered into direct relations with the lowest sub-vassal. The ties among the clergy were drawn closer and their position as a part of the kingdom became institutionalized. And beside these two great estates appeared the mercantile towns with their intense awareness of solidarity, complementing the kingdom with a new form of political life; and here and there agrarian regions were shaped into political units whose basis was territorial rather than feudal.

It is typical of the peculiar quality of medieval intellectual life that the reflection on political theory of these important developments in political fact came only after the minds of scholars had been sensitized by the study, first, of Roman law and, later, of Aristotle. It is equally typical that that new vision, when it came, was often classical in form and in its essence timeless.

With the twelfth-century revival of Roman law the notion of a political community corporately organized for the pursuit of its common interests began to enter medieval thought and to substitute for the earlier conception of lordship something approaching the modern conception of a state. This tendency appeared in the civilists' acceptance of the Roman distinction between public law, which dealt with the interests of the commonwealth, and private law, which dealt with the separate interests of individuals; in their attempts to analyse the relations between the two; and in their very gradual recognition that the law which concerned the transmission, use, and extent of royal powers should be classified as public law, although these powers were also in certain ways involved in the private-law system.[28] Roman law also provided material for the conception of the ruler as the officer in whom a corporate community had voluntarily focussed a governing authority. The centre of this conception was the idea of the *lex regia*, by which the people of the formerly self-governing Roman republic 'conferred upon the prince all their power and authority.'[29] Originally applying to the emperor, this account could be gradually generalized to apply to all political authority. It was a plausible expansion of Hermogenian's suggestive statement that 'by the law of peoples . . . kingdoms were founded.'[30] Roman law also provided the maxim, 'What touches all should be approved by all'[31]—in a specific private-law context, indeed, but stated in a general form that suggested its use as an axiom for political relationships. When they finally related the authority of a ruler to the constituent act of a community, the civilists took one step toward the modern idea of representative government and, at the same time, one step away from the ecclesiastical view of kings as ministers of God. But their conception of the state was not articulated with any general philosophical system, except as it assumed basic relationships between natural law, the law of peoples, and the civil law.

The philosophy of Aristotle provided materials for a theory of political organization profoundly different from the political theory which for centuries had dominated ecclesiastical thought. The Stoic-patristic view of the state of innocence had assumed the self-sufficiency of individual men and had concluded that political organization would have been unnecessary had it not been for the appearance of sin. But Aristotle had said that only a beast or a god could exist without the state. In his innate deficiencies as in his special gifts, man was distinguished as the 'political animal,' for only through the interdependence of an organized community did life become possible for him, and his unique capacity for speech made such cooperation possible. The state was intrinsic to man not only for the service of his physical needs but also for the fulfilment of his moral and rational potentialities. The full life of the state was the end toward which human nature tended. In contrast to such imperfect social forms as the household and the village, the state was the 'perfect' community, because it included all that was necessary 'not only for living, but for living well.'

Such concepts could never have exactly the same force for medieval minds as they had had for a mind nurtured in the intimate life of the Greek city state. No medieval structure—even the Italian commune which provided the closest parallel to the ancient *polis*—could possibly mean so much to its citizens as Athens meant to Aristotle. The substitution of Christianity for civic religion was an obvious difference, and medieval students of Aristotle were all obliged to modify his thought to make room for a human need that could not find fulfilment in civic life. Again, no political institution of the Middle Ages was so closely fused with the other institutions that shaped man's secular life as the ancient state had been. It is significant that where Aristotle had used the term 'political animal,' Aquinas could express his meaning only with the coupled adjectives 'political and social.' Medieval Aristotelians, even including Aquinas, often tended to think of the state primarily as a relation between ruler and subjects, superimposed upon other institutions, rather than as a whole system of community life; and to think of rulership as concerned primarily with justice and peace, although they might relate this function to the rational and moral ends of man. Many passages in Aristotle's political writings lent themselves readily enough to this narrower emphasis. Moreover, his general philosophy could be used to support and further develop the idea that hierarchic relations of lordship and subjection were, in God's plan, the principle that gave order to multiplicity throughout the universe. Thus the Aristotelian idea that the state was natural could be fitted into a tradition already deeply-rooted; and, although it was impossible for medieval minds to assimilate Aristotle's full meaning, this idea helped them to understand and express their growing sense of the positive value of government.

It was Aquinas's task to reconcile the Aristotelian approach with the essentials of the Christian view of the universe. The fact of sin and the resulting necessity for coercive control continued to loom large in his writings. But integrated with these patristic ideas was Aristotle's emphasis on the social nature of man and on the necessity of division of labour and mutual cooperation as the conditions of the fulfilment of man's needs on every natural level, and the recognition of government as the natural and necessary instrument through which the varied activities of men in a community were coordinated so that 'the good and sufficient life' might be realized for all. Thus the state, for Aquinas, was natural in origin—natural in the secondary sense which he first defined: it was one of the things invented by man in accordance with the ends defined by his nature. It was natural also in a primary sense: even in an age of innocence, a human society without diversity, coordination, and leadership was unthinkable. Thus the state was one instance of the hierarchic pattern of the universe.[32]

However, as Aquinas pointed out, the position of man in the universe was unique. He alone of earthly creatures was endowed with reason and will, through which he could grasp the fundamental principles of God's plan so far as it concerned him and could actively participate in the establishment of the means through which the destiny of his peculiar nature could be fulfilled.[33] The compelling logic of his own characteristics made man a social and political animal and inclined him to associate himself with his fellows under a coordinating government; but it was his own reason that devised the institutions that his nature sought. Thus the authority of governments was immediately based on human institution though it was ultimately based on the will of God, Who was the cause both of the need and of the reason that found the answer to the need.[34] This principle, incidentally, gave legitimacy to heathen as well as Christian states.[35] The details of the human process through which the state arose were not important for Aquinas. Apparently the consent of the subjects might be a factor in particular situations; but the general basis of the legitimacy of governments was, for Aquinas, their rationally demonstrable necessity to the natural needs of man.[36]

Hand in hand with this more penetrating analysis of the basis of the state went a new view of its purpose. 'The end of the state must be considered to be the same as the end of any one man.'[37] The natural end of any one man as a human being was the full development of the natural human potentiality for a rational and virtuous life, a development that should culminate, as Aquinas made clear elsewhere,[38] in the discovery of God to the extent that He could be grasped by reason. This view gave the state a positive moral goal, transcending the earlier view that it could be justified only negatively as the penalty and remedy for sin: 'the end of the associated multitude is to live according to virtue.' But the new moral dignity of the state in Aquinas's system brought it into a new relation with the church—not as a mere 'executioner' to make the world safe for Christianity, but as the institution whose natural ends should fittingly be crowned by the supernatural gifts administered through the church. In Aquinas's thought, two tendencies were held in quiet harmony: on the one hand, an appreciation of secular and natural values as good in themselves; on the other, an acknowledgement of the pre-eminence of spiritual goods, to which all lesser goods were finally ordained. As revelation completed the work of reason, as grace fulfilled nature, so the church must supplement and guide the state. The institutional application of this principle Aquinas left ambiguous:[39] he was concerned with ends, not means.

The Aquinist view of the state obviously implied a more positive and dynamic view of the functions of government within the state. Aquinas compared the ruler to the pilot who steered a ship toward a distant goal. He defined his task not as the maintenance of already-established relations, but as the coordination of the community in their pursuit of the virtuous life. Certainly this involved the defence of the peace and the enforcement of justice between man and man; for peace and order were good in themselves and necessary conditions of human development. It was, however, characteristic of Aquinas that even in the discussion of coercive justice he stressed a positive aspect. 'The purpose of the laws,' he said, following Aristotle, 'is to make men good,'[40] and he thought the coercive power of the king valuable not merely because it provided security for the virtuous but also because of its deterrent and educational influence on the immature and the perverse. But the steering of the community toward its common goal meant much more than the maintenance of justice and peace. It was the duty of the ruler to see to it that the community was self-sufficient in all the things that were necessary for living and for living well. The insurance of an adequate food-supply, the maintenance of the proper balance and variety of crafts and professions, and the provision of educational opportunities were part of the ruler's responsibility.[41]

Theoretically, at any rate, this richer concept of the purpose of the state would seem to justify not merely a broader scope for governmental activity, but also greater freedom in its methods. For reason, not custom, must determine what policies are appropriate for a society which is in process of development; and reason, as Aquinas well understood, is a dynamic and creative principle. It was no coincidence that the redefinition of the purpose of the state was combined in his thought with the concept of a ruler who could cautiously change the laws 'when something better offered itself,'[42] or that he defined the tyrant in Aristotle's flexible terms as the ruler who subordinated the good of the community to his private good. The doctrine that the end of the state was the good life of men gave added force to the familiar medieval doctrine that the legitimacy of authority was contingent on its use. But the distinction between king and tyrant in a state moving toward an end could not be made by application of the simple yardstick of an existing law.

Neither the suggestions of Roman law nor the Aristotelian ideas used by Aquinas won an immediate or sweeping victory in medieval thought.[43] Germanic, feudal, and patristic concepts continued to play an important part in the thought of the later Middle Ages, though most frequently in some sort of combination with the ideas more recently introduced. The combinations were various, the pattern of intellectual development by no means a simple one. Among civilists, the purpose of the state was found in the common interests of the subjects, taken simply as facts, usually without the help of either a patristic or an Aristotelian analysis of human nature. Among theologians, the old picture of government as a conventional remedy for sin continued sometimes to appear, but often in relation to Aristotelian ideas. Those who described the establishment of government as resting on human agreement usually made it clear that this agreement was itself the product of human nature or of reason. While the maintenance of justice and peace still seemed the chief function of the ruler, this function was often related to the good life as its necessary condition. A distinction between organization and leadership, necessary for innocent men, and coercive government, necessary after the Fall, was widely adopted.[44] In general, one can distinguish two main tendencies in later medieval thought: a tendency to associate authority with the natural needs of man rather than merely with the catastrophe of sin, and a tendency to find its immediate cause in the consent of subjects rather than in simple institution from above.

The fourteenth-century revival of conflict between the papacy and secular rulers focussed the attention of theologians on the definition of the purpose of secular authority, though there was no clear-cut division of opinion between the extreme papalists and their opponents. An incisive attack on the dignity of secular rule appeared in a formula that was popular among papalist writers, assigning to kings the control of corporal affairs in contrast to the spiritual sphere of the priesthood.[45] This formula was accepted by some of their opponents, hotly attacked by. others. 'It supposes,' said John of Paris, 'that the regal power is corporal and not spiritual, and has the care of bodies and not of souls; but this is false . . . since it is ordained to the common good of citizens, which is not any good whatever, but to live in accordance with virtue. . . .'[46] Dante stressed the twofold nature of man, mortal and immortal; the temporal felicity which was the goal of his mortal nature consisted in the full actuation of his rational capacities, both speculative and practical; political control—for Dante, the control of a universal monarch—was necessary for the attainment of man's natural beatitude because it alone could provide the peace which reason needed for its fulfilment.[47]

Even among the papalists, there were some who refused to degrade the state to purely corporal concerns. 'Since . . . the rational creature was ordained and produced to be capable of God, and this is its special end . . . therefore, for the attaining of this end, even if man is aided by the divine light of grace, he is especially led along by the governors of this world, through examples of the good life, through daily teachings, and through continuous correction. . . ,' said Tholommeo of Lucca.[48] James of Viterbo analysed the whole question with his typical clarity, pointing out that the term 'spiritual' was used in two senses: in so far as it referred to matters of grace as distinguished from matters of nature, the spiritual was no concern of the secular power, but in so far as it referred to matters of the soul as distinguished from matters of the body, the term was correctly applied to the sphere of the secular power, which 'has as its principal and final purpose the directing and leading of the subjects to a virtuous life.'[49]

Both the idea that political authority was a mere remedy for sin and the idea that it furthered the positive fulfilment of human nature could, as we have seen, be fitted into the general position that all authority was derived from God. Similarly, both views could be made to serve the new claim of extreme papalists that that derivation from God proceeded by way of the church, without whose sanction no instance of earthly lordship was finally legitimate. Thus, by different routes, Aegidius Romanus and James of Viterbo arrived at a philosophical demonstration of the theory of the ecclesiastical origin of political authority which Honorius Augustodunensis had once presented in terms of sacred history. In his *De Regimine Principum*, Aegidius had presented a picture of the origins and functions of authority which was permeated with Aristotelian naturalism; in his *De Ecclesiastica Potestate*, written seventeen years later, he made use of patristic concepts which depreciated secular institutions, while other aspects of Aristotelian thought contributed to his general theme of the hierarchic relation of control and subjection appropriate to institutions aiming at higher and lower ends.[50] He treated political authority as one kind of lordship, having for its object 'men, and especially wicked men'[51]; its function was justice, and he turned to Augustine to show that there could be no true justice without grace. In contrast, the *De Regimine Christiano* of James of Viterbo showed that a fully-assimilated Aristotelian analysis of the state could be the basis of a system of papal supremacy as majestic as that which Aegidius had erected on different

154

foundations. He treated the state as a developing community arising from man's nature and aiming at its moral fulfilment; but he argued that that very view led to the conclusion that a state not effectively controlled by Christianity—not 'perfected by grace'—was but a rudimentary and imperfect state. Thus they agreed that truly valid authority could not be mediated by nature alone; and the church accordingly appeared in their systems as directly supreme over a state which employed a delegated power under its general direction and subject to its intervention.[52]

The typical answer to these arguments was simply an attempt to maintain the independent purpose of political authority and, accordingly, its independent origin. Only Marsiglio met the papalist arguments with a counter-claim that the state must include the church. To his secular temper, nature seemed a completely adequate basis for all coercive authority exercised on earth: God, indeed, appeared in his system as the 'remote cause,'[53] but his interest was directed upon the immediate efficient cause. The daring originality of his thought derived partly from the fact that he alone among medieval publicists followed up some of the implications of the Aristotelian view of the state as the perfect community whose self-sufficiency was achieved through specialization of function and the coordination of specialized activities. This idea appeared in his comparison of the state to a healthy animal each of whose organs was carrying out its proper function.[54] It appeared in his analysis of the parts of the state—the agricultural producer, the craftsman, the merchant, and, in a more exact sense, the priest, the warrior, and the ruler; in his inclusion of both priests and ruler among these parts; and in his choice of the term *'pars principans'* for the ruler, a term which marks the antipodes of the earlier medieval notion of lordship. Finally, it was basic to his insistence that all power wielded on earth for whatever purpose must be finally vested in the corporate legislator.

For the self-sufficient community, in Marsiglio's thought, must not only include what was necessary for life and the good life on earth; it must also concern itself with 'the state of the life to come,' so far as authority exercised on earth was relevant to that future. On this view he based his radical conclusion that the function of the state included the provision and protection of religious opportunity through the institution, supervision, and discipline of the priesthood and, in general, through the coercive implementation of divine law wherever such implementation was appropriate to man's earthly or otherworldly needs.

But the state of Marsiglio's system was not really the perfect community in Aristotle's sense. In his account of its origins, the human need for living and for living well carry men to the formation of an inter-communicating society; but the state, in characteristic medieval fashion, is superimposed on that society primarily as the arbiter of disputes rather than as the destined conclusion of the human impetus toward rational and virtuous life. Thus Marsiglio's state tends to appear simply as an agency for the service of human needs; moreover, these needs tend to be regarded simply as facts without clear gradations of value. Living and living well seem to have had the same kind of importance for Marsiglio; and although he frequently asserted the primacy of man's spiritual over his temporal needs, his warmest sympathies seem to have been attached to the temporal area. In contrast to the normative Thomistic system, in which human values were hierarchically related to one another as levels in the self-fulfilment of man and finally articulated with the whole structure of the divine plan, Marsiglio tended to base his system on a mere aggregate of human needs related to one another only through the circumstance that they all occurred in man and through their practical, external interaction. Thus his case for the concentration of all kinds of coercive functions in the self-sufficient community had as its ethical foundation little more than the coincidence in all human beings of demands for security of subsistence, for peace and justice, and for assured access to the way of salvation.[55]

Other opponents of the extreme papalist position did not follow Marsiglio. They regarded the sphere of the state as normally determined by the boundaries of man's natural capacities and of his temporal ends; thus they disclaimed for it any regular control over the instruments of grace, while finding in its positive necessity to human nature, or in its necessary restraint of sin, or in both, sufficient evidence that it was derived from God in its own way and needed no further confirmation by the church. Intervention of the state in the organization of the church was defended only on the ground that specific powers were essential to the secular role of the state and not an infringement on the truly conceived mission of the church, or on the ground that the Christian ruler had an obligation to protect the true religion in the abnormal case that it was betrayed by its proper guardians. Papalist thought opposed these claims; but by the fifteenth century, the view that God had ordained secular power through the mediation of the church had begun to disappear from even the most extreme of papalist writings.[56] The independent origin of the state thereafter became an undisputed principle of Catholic political thought.

The fourteenth-century defenders of the independent origin of temporal authority differed widely in regard to the aspects of that origin which they emphasized. The simple statement that all power was ordained by God had, as we have seen, sufficed many thinkers of the earlier Middle Ages; and in some later writings—in Dante's, for example—the idea of the immediate grant of authority from God was still so prominent as to reduce all human agencies to the role of mere machinery. 'God alone chooses, He alone confirms that guardian who has no superior,' Dante said of the emperor. 'Thus, therefore, it appears that the authority of temporal monarchy flows into it directly, without any intermediary, from the fountain of universal authority.'[57] Later still, the heart of Wyclif's political thought was the notion that all human lordship was held directly from God by a sort of infeudation.[58] At the opposite extreme were the civilists, now developing the theme of the *lex regia* into a general principle of the origin of authority; they might, like Marsiglio, think of God as the remote cause, but their attention centred on the human process through which authority arose. Philosophical publicists of the later Middle Ages commonly reconciled these two views through the principle, which we have already seen suggested by Aquinas, that God worked through the mediation of human reason; and this principle was increasingly associated with the further idea that human reason issued in the popular consent which was the immediate basis of valid authority.

From the middle of the thirteenth century, brief sketches of the supposed historical origin of government began to appear with some frequency in political treatises. Often these were little more than literary flourishes; but they are significant in reflecting the variety of ideas derived from sacred and classical sources and in revealing a dominant emphasis on the constituent act of the community. Aegidius Romanus in his *De Regimine Principum* followed Aristotle in describing the state as necessary to human nature and as the end of a gradual evolution in which the family and the village appeared as earlier stages. To Aegidius, this seemed the most 'natural' way for a state to be formed, but he also recognized a deliberate compact between community and ruler as a natural method and thought that still other states had originated in conquest.[59] John of Paris combined Aristotelian ideas with Cicero's concept of a pristine age in which men lived in mutual isolation until led, 'by those who used more reason,' to form societies; he also spoke of authority as established 'by the act of the people under the inspiration of God.'[60] Tholommeo of Lucca saw the earliest states, like those of Cain and Nimrod, arising from conquest but legitimized by divine recognition of their usefulness.[61] Marsiglio's Aristotelian account of the evolution of society culminated in a story of the formation of the state by the deliberate act of the community, which organized itself as a corporate legislator and set up its constitution and its ruler; only in this way could valid authority be established. Very common were such stories as those told by Beaumanoir and Engelbert of Admont and Aeneas Sylvius: simple stories of men who originally lived without government and to end their strife created a government by common consent.[62] The later writers tied these stories to Aristotelian ideas by pointing out that a 'natural need' or a 'certain impetus of nature' inspired the process.[63] Particular interest attached to the question of the origin of the Roman empire, which obviously owed much of its authority to conquest; those who rejected the papalist theory that its authority was merely permitted by God, as useful pending the appearance of the Christian church, often argued that the imperial sway had been legitimized by its utility; some added, by the ultimate consent of the subject peoples.[64]

The growth of the idea that authority was based in popular consent was, of course, primarily the result of the territorial consolidation and institutional maturation of medieval kingdoms, which made it possible to conceive of a people as an organized body capable of providing for its own government; it was supported by the now familiar spectacle of corporations vesting authority in their officers. In this actual context, ideas from many sources—the Germanic tradition of elective kingship; the Roman doctrines of the *lex regia*, of the approval of all to 'what touches all,' and of the origin of kingdoms in the law of peoples; the canon-law rule that 'any people or state can establish law for itself';[65] Aristotle's contrast between the rights of free men and those of slaves; the Stoic doctrine of the original freedom and equality of men—

became significant. Particularly in imperialist circles, the formulation of the idea of the popular basis of authority was immediately stimulated by the papalist derivation of secular power from the primary authority of the papacy.

The first systematic statement of the popular basis of authority, that of Marsiglio, owed little to the legal traditions associated with the empire; so far as it was influenced by a contemporary model, that model was the Italian commune with its corporately-constructed constitution; but his argument was set forth in general terms. The crux of his theory was his concept of the community as the legislator from whose unique coercive authority all valid law must proceed. As we have noticed,[66] the arguments by which he reached this concept left something to be desired; but, granted this, no objection can be made to his further deduction that the 'ruling part' could derive its authority only from the people from whom the legal 'form' of the state had proceeded. It was not logically necessary to Marsiglio's system that the ruler continue to be elective, though for reasons of expediency he regarded elective succession as usually preferable.[67] At all events, the power which the ruler exercised was a power inherent in the corporate body of the community and focussed in the ruler by its act.

The defenders of the popular origins of imperial power typically followed a different route, a combination of legal and historical analysis which issued in the construction of the imperial electors as a corporate body, representing the corporate consent of the people, and as such completely capable of bestowing imperial authority regardless of papal approval.[68] William of Occam made particular use of the principle that any people lacking a superior could choose a head for themselves. This, he asserted, was a principle of the law of peoples, or of 'natural law in the third sense': that is, of the rational system which men had universally inferred from the facts of actual life.[69]

By the fifteenth century, the idea that the lordship of all secular rulers had originated in a grant of power by their subjects was a familiar theme in legal and theological writings, so familiar that the more radical of conciliarist thinkers could attempt to apply the same principle to the holding of authority in the church. Most important of these was Nicholas of Cusa, whose De Concordantia Catholica included a systematic attempt to demonstrate theoretically the popular basis of both secular and ecclesiastical government through the use of the old Stoic.

and patristic principle of the original freedom and equality of men. While such a papal protagonist as Turrecremata repudiated in horror any suggestion that the essence of ecclesiastical authority could possibly be mediated by popular consent, he now accepted as an established principle the idea that secular authority came from God by way of the community.[70]

There is a wide gulf between medieval doctrines of consent and such theories as those of Locke or Paine. Medieval theories could not begin with the self-sufficient individual who freely chose to give up some of his rights in order better to protect his other rights. Not the individual, but only 'the community or him to whom the care of the community has been entrusted' was conceivable as a holder of the coercive power which medieval minds now conceived as inherently public in its purposes and methods. Moreover, medieval theories were, on the whole, developed within the framework of the conviction that such authority ultimately came from God and was necessary and in some sense natural to man. Thus the consent on which authority rested could not be construed as the free choice of self-determining wills—with an open alternative, perhaps of continuing in primitive anarchy; it was a choice conditioned by the principle that authority must exist. And, accordingly, the resulting obligation of obedience could not be construed in the simple terms of a contract.

For Marsiglio, the right of the community to provide for itself the law and the government that would best serve its needs was the right of the whole community, organized within itself and differentiated in 'quality,' not a total of pre-existing, equal, individual rights. The right of the individual was simply the right to have his voice at least included in the community decision. These rights rested directly on utility. Marsiglio's arguments were logically the cousins of those by which Aquinas arrived at the authority of the king: both proceeded from ends to means, from the purpose to the best location of power.[71] Thus Marsiglio's theory was not a theory of consent in the sense in which Locke's was a theory of consent, but a tight structure of rational necessities leaving little room for the play of will. His community was not free to withhold power from its ruler: if it was to be a perfect community, containing everything necessary for the fulfilment of human needs, it had to have a *pars principans*, to whom it had to convey the authority necessary for the fulfilment of those ends.

Superficially, the doctrine of Nicholas of Cusa appears somewhat closer to modern thought. Like Locke and Rousseau, he argued that the validity of coercive government among men who by nature were equal and free depended on consent. In thus making use of the natural rights of man, Cusa would seem to have made a decisive break with the medieval tradition; but Cusa's system, if closely examined, bears the marks of its medieval origin. For that system is not one in which the individual will is the ultimate unit of authority. The framework of Cusa's universe is still the divine plan which establishes the necessary existence of a hierarchy of authority, even though this authority is mediated by the people. And, although he spoke of the freedom of the individual, Cusa's development of the practical implications of his theory shows that, as Sabine puts it, his emphasis 'was all on the natural freedom of the community.'[72] Finally, he accepted the Aristotelian doctrine that men were naturally political and civil, and that the rule of the wise over the foolish was necessary to supplement the defects of human nature. While he insisted that servitude must involve an act of will, he also insisted that 'voluntary servitude was bound to that necessity, on account of the necessity itself. And thus by a certain natural instinct, the presidency of the wise and the subjection of the foolish, brought into concord, exists through common laws, of which the wise are especially the authors, conservers, and executors.'[73]

Perhaps some aspects of Occam's thought came close to the presuppositions of the contract theorists. However, since he never articulated his arguments into a fully explicit system, his doctrine must be construed from a number of scattered statements, most of which take as their first premise the axiom that any free people can establish its own head. This principle Occam usually attributed to the law of peoples or to 'natural law in the third sense.' There is a stronger statement in his *Breviloquium*: 'All mortals hold from God and from nature the right of freely giving themselves a head, for they are born free and not subjected to anyone by human law; whence every city and every people can establish law for itself.'[74] Lagarde plausibly associates this statement with Occam's general moral philosophy: its emphasis on the freedom of human will and its limited conception of divine law and 'natural law in the first sense' as sets of specific commands bounding a comparatively large area of conduct which God left open to human determination.

Freedom would accordingly be a natural right of men as such; and God would not be even the remote cause of authority except as He was the author of man's freedom. However, Lagarde also points out that the freedom which Occam postulated was freedom to choose a specific ruler and type of government, conditioned by the consideration that authority was necessary to man; and that he attached this right to peoples rather than to individuals.[75]

The doctrine that political authority arose from the constituent consent of the people helped to strengthen and clarify the concept that a king, as Gerson reminded the king of France, 'is not a private person, but a public power, ordained for the welfare of the whole community.'[76] However, the proprietary concept of kingship which feudalism had encouraged died hard. In the later Middle Ages, it appeared in the still-frequent use of the term 'lordship' in describing the ruler's authority and in the very gradual process by which the public aspects of the ruler's power were disentangled from his private rights as a proprietor among proprietors. The distinction was sometimes stated in terms of the theory of divided lordship; sometimes in terms of the classification of rights under the headings of public and private law; sometimes in terms of a difference, suggested by Aristotle, between the king, who could use his free subjects and their possessions only for the common good, and the 'despot,' who enjoyed a proprietary right to use his servile subjects and their possessions for his own advantage. However they expressed it, all theorists agreed in insisting on a distinction between kingship and property; but the point apparently had to be made again and again, and its institutional implications were only gradually seen. At the very end of the Middle Ages, public-law and private-law concepts were still blended in Fortescue's treatment of the English kingship, as in his summary of the king's position: 'Though his Astate be the highest Astate Temporal in the Earthe, yet it ys an Office, in the whiche he mynystrith in his Realme, Defence and Justice.'[77]

This persistent feeling that royal power, however public its purpose, was set within the general structure of the law that guaranteed private rights may be associated with the continuing feeling that the heart of kingship was the preservation of rights already existent, so that the private-law system was both a justification and a boundary of royal power. No later medieval thinker went even so far as Aquinas in developing the implicit dynamism of the thesis that kingship consisted in the rational leadership of men toward a common end. Publicists of the later Middle Ages seem to have felt that reason had exhausted its creative force in establishing governments and the laws that circumscribed them and must thereafter work within that setting, striving to maintain, to adjust, but not radically to alter the structure thus produced. On the other hand, the circumstances of the later Middle Ages constantly demanded a flexible interpretation of the ruler's powers, and some recognition of this demand flickers through the political theory of the period in spite of its general assumption of a static world. It appears in the frequent choice of the common good rather than the common law as the final criterion of the legitimacy of policy and as the test of the difference between king and tyrant. It is conspicuous in Aegidius's preference of the government of man to the government of laws,[78] and in Tholommeo's grudging admission that kingship, although incompatible with full human freedom, had in its flexibility a distinct advantage over a magistracy rigidly bound by law.[79] It is reflected in the lists of royal functions given by certain writers, which are somewhat broader in their scope than lists set forth in the early Middle Ages.[80] It appears in the arguments with which the dispensing power was supported and in the arguments that pressed upon the king the regulation of commerce and industry. Above all, it appears in the recognition that in situations of emergency it became the ruler's duty to preserve the common good even at the cost of private rights.

The medieval pattern of ideas whose development we have traced was inherited by some sixteenth and seventeenth century thinkers. With various elaborations and particular emphases, but without essential change, it appeared as the groundwork of such theories as those of Buchanan and the author of the *Vindiciae*, of Suarez and Mariana, of Bodin and Grotius and Althusius. But the medieval synthesis combined pairs of ideas not easily held together. There was potential disintegration in the thought that authority was derived both from God and from the community; in the idea that its cause was both a necessity of nature and an act of will; in the idea that its scope was at the same time limited by law and yet coextensive with the demands of the common good. Thus other writers were able to select from the medieval tradition particular ideas which, in new combinations, produced new theories.

By stress on the divine origin of authority and its necessity to human ends, by the denial that it could be dependent on human consent, and by the assertion that the royal duty to promote the common good could not be limited by any human laws or measured by the judgment of the community, the doctrine of the divine right of kings was formed from fragments of the medieval synthesis. In turn this doctrine was attacked by the social contract theory, which emphasized the human and conventional origin of power, limited the ruler's function to the protection of pre-existing rights, and surrounded him once again with legal restraints. Rousseau in turn combined the idea of consent with the idea that the purpose of the state was the fulfilment of men's natural capacities and that its area was as broad as the common good.

Modern thought has attempted still other syntheses. But no theory of the origin and purpose of the state has been completely successful in fusing into a stable compound all the elements which an adequate theory must include: which will do justice to the social nature of man and the necessity of political organization while still maintaining the principle that the free man must give willing consent to the authority that directs the community of which he is a part—which will protect the rights of individual personality through the limitation of authority without reducing the role of government to the mere protection of traditional privilege.

Manegold of Lautenbach

[Manegold was born ca. 1060 and entered the convent of Lautenbach, in Alsace, when young. His writings in support of Gregory VII in the investiture struggle attracted considerable attention. When his monastery was destroyed by partisans of the emperor, he and his fellow-monks migrated to Bavaria, where he was elected dean of the monastery of Raitenbuch in 1086. Returning to Alsace in 1090, he assisted in the foundation of the new monastery of Marbach, of which he became the first prior in 1096. In 1098 he was a prisoner of the imperialists; in 1103 he was again named prior of Marbach. Nothing is known of his later life.

His most important pamphlet, from which the following extract is taken (*Ad Gebehardum Liber*, ed. K. Francke, in *Libelli de Lite, MGH*, vol. I, at p. 365), was dedicated to Archbishop Gebhard of Salzburg and directed against

ORIGIN OF AUTHORITY

the imperialist arguments of Wenrich of Trier. It was written sometime between 1080 and 1085, probably in 1085.]

Therefore even as the royal dignity and authority excels all earthly authorities, so no infamous or shameful man is appointed to administer it, but he who no less in wisdom, justice, and piety than in place and dignity is superior to others. Therefore it is necessary that he who is to bear the charge of all and govern all should shine above others in greater grace of the virtues and should strive to administer with the utmost balance of equity the authority allotted to him. For the people do not exalt him above themselves in order to grant him a free opportunity to exercise tyranny against them, but that he may defend them from the tyranny and unrighteousness of others. Yet when he who has been chosen for the coercion of the wicked and the defence of the upright has begun to foster evil against them, to destroy the good, and himself to exercise most cruelly against his subjects the tyranny which he ought to repel, is it not clear that he deservedly falls from the dignity entrusted to him and that the people stand free of his lordship and subjection, when he has been evidently the first to break the compact for whose sake he was appointed? Nor can anyone justly and rationally accuse them of faithlessness, since it is quite evident that he first broke faith. For, to draw an example from baser things, if someone should entrust his pigs to be pasture to someone for a fitting wage, and afterwards learned that the latter was not pasturing them, but was stealing, slaughtering, and losing them, would he not remove him with reproaches from the care of the pigs, retaining also the promised wage? If, I say, this principle is maintained in regard to base things, that he is not considered indeed a swineherd who seeks not to pasture the pigs, but to scatter them, so much the more fittingly, by just and probable reason, in proportion as the condition of men is distinct from the nature of pigs, is he who attempts not to rule men, but to drive them into confusion, deprived of all the authority and dignity which he has received over men. . . . It is one thing to reign, another to exercise tyranny in the kingdom. For as faith and reverence ought to be given to emperors and kings for safeguarding the administration of a kingdom, so certainly, for good reason, if they break into the exercise of tyranny, without any breach of faith or loss of piety no fidelity or reverence ought to be paid them.

Hugh of Fleury

[Hugh of Fleury (died 1117) was a member of the important Benedictine Cluniac Abbey of Fleury on the Loire. He is known only by his writings, which included several works of ecclesiastical and secular history. His *Tractatus de Regia Potestate et Sacerdotali Dignitate* (ed. Ernest Sackur, in *Libelli de Lite, MGH*, vol. II, pp. 465-494) was written soon after 1102, dedicated to Henry I of England, and directed against Hugh of Flavigny, who had upheld the ideas of Gregory VII. The following translation is from bk. 1, chs. 1-4.]

CHAPTER I. *That there is no power but of God*

I know that in our times there are some who affirm that kings had their origin not from God, but from those who, ignorant of God, at the beginning of the world through the agitation of the devil strove in blind greed and unspeakable presumption and temerity to dominate their fellow-men by pride, rapine, perfidy, murders, and nearly every kind of crime. How foolish this opinion is is evident by the teaching of the Apostle, who says, 'There is no power but of God. For the powers that be are ordained of God' [Romans 13: 4]. Therefore by this statement it is certain that the royal authority on earth was ordained or disposed on earth not by men, but by God. He indeed set the first man in the world, already furnished with the primordial dowry of wisdom, above all the creatures of the world. And thus He subtly intimated to him that there is one King and Lord of the whole creation, Whom that celestial court which is above us rightly serves and obeys. And that we may recognize this equally in the form of our body, we see that all the members of our body are subject to the head. It is apparent, I say, that all the members of the human body are subject and subordinate to the head both in position and in rank. Whence it is quite clear to us that the omnipotent God differentiated not only the various members of the human body, but also the distinct ranks and powers of the whole world, corresponding to the distinctions which we know to exist in the celestial court in which God, the Father omnipotent, alone holds the kingly dignity and in which after Him, as we know, the angels, archangels, thrones, and dominations, and other powers stand one above the other in a wonderful and seemly variety of powers. Moreover, the Father and the Son and the Holy Spirit

166

are one God. The Father alone is not from another, but the Son is born of the Father. Yet, as was just said, there is one divinity and one majesty of the Son and the Father. One, I say, is God the Father, from Whom are all things, and from Whom is the Son, through Whom are all things; that the authority of one principle may be conserved in all things, and in three Persons one Deity may be adored.

CHAPTER II. *That as the head in the body, so the king in his kingdom ought to hold the principate*

In the world, moreover, God formed one man, from whom there-after every human race drew its origin. Thence, even as from God the Father was born God the Son of God, that through Him all creation might be made, so from the man was formed the woman, through whom all the human race would be made. . . . Yet the man and the woman are of one substance, but in rank the man is greater because the woman was derived from him, as the Apostle bears witness, saying, 'The man is the head of the woman' [I Corinthians 11:3]. Likewise the Father and the Son are of one substance; but the Father is known to be greater in order, not in nature, as Paul bears witness, saying, 'God is the head of Christ' [*ibid.*]. For, as was just said, the Father is from none, but the Son is from the Father, that the essence of the supreme Trinity may be adored and reverenced in the unity of the Deity. Moreover, the principal powers by which this world is ruled are two, royal and sacerdotal; and the Lord Jesus Christ Himself determined to bear these two powers in His sole Person, by a holy mystery, for He is both King and Priest: King, because He rules us, but Priest because by the sacrifice of His body He cleansed us from the filth of our sins and reconciled us to His Father.

CHAPTER III. *That the king has the likeness of the Father, and the bishop of Christ*

Moreover, the king in the body of his kingdom seems to have the likeness of the Father, and the bishop, of Christ. Whence all the bishops of his kingdom seem to be rightly subject to the king, as the Son is perceived to be subject to the Father, not in nature but in order, that the whole kingdom may be reduced to one principle. Of which mystery God evidently set forth a sign in Exodus [7:1], where He says to Moses, 'Behold, I constitute thee a god to Pharaoh, and Aaron will be thy prophet.' . . .

CHAPTER IV. *Concerning the office of a legitimate king*

Therefore the ministry of a king is to correct the people subject to him and to recall them from error to the path of equity and justice. Wherefore in the Book of Judges you will also find that, before the children of Israel had a king, Jonathan, the grandson of Manasseh, although a Levite, presumed to make himself a priest, 'because,' it says, 'each one did what pleased him, for there was no king in Israel' [Judges 17:6]. From these words it clearly appears that where there is no king to rule the people and to draw them away from arrogance, the whole body of the kingdom totters. Whence deservedly is he called king who knows how to rule their ways fittingly and to control those subjected to him. For this reason, I say, the omnipotent God is known to have set over men a king, who lives and dies like them, that he may coerce the people subject to him by his terror and that he may subdue them with laws for right living. Whence through the earthly kingdom he often aids the heavenly, since 'what the priest cannot accomplish by verbal teaching, the royal power does or commands by the terror of its discipline' [Isidore of Seville, *Sententiae*, bk. 3, ch. 51, n. 4]. For the people is easily corrected by fear of the king. But the king is deterred from the path of injustice by nothing except only the fear of God and dread of hell. Yet he ought always to ponder in his soul that saying of a very wise man, 'In greater fortune is less license.' He ought also always to help rather than harm the people subject to him. But most rulers are assigned according to the deserts of the subjects, and thus the merits of subjects and rulers are often connected with one another, so that by the guilt of the rulers the life of the subjects becomes worse, and by the merits of the subjects the life of rulers is changed. . . . Thus a good king is given to men by a propitious God, and a bad by an angry God, as He testifies to the people of Israel through the Prophet, saying, 'I will give them a king in my wrath' [Hosea 13:11]. . . . Wherefore kings and princes are to be endured by their subjects, nor are they to be rashly resisted by anyone, lest, while their injustice is checked, humility, the teacher of righteousness, be lost. . . . Also all who are placed in power are to be honoured by those over whom they preside, although not because of themselves, but because of the order and rank which they have received from God.

John of Salisbury

[The life of John of Salisbury brought him into contact with many important intellectual and political currents of the twelfth century. He was born between 1115 and 1120. From 1136 he was an arts student at the young University of Paris, where he studied dialectics under Abelard and others, and at the Cathedral School of Chartres, which was the centre of a revival of literary and humanistic study. He taught at Chartres and at Paris; he began the study of theology and logic at Paris under Gilbert de la Porrée; he was secretary to the abbot Peter of La Celle; he travelled, went to Rome, was present at the Council of Reims. About 1150, he returned to England and became the confidential secretary of Theobald, Archbishop of Canterbury. He continued to follow his intellectual interests in disputation and friendly correspondence with other scholars, and also played a responsible and busy role in ecclesiastical politics. His support of the interests of the hierarchy aroused the antagonism of Henry II, and by 1159 he had found it necessary to go into retirement, an opportunity that he used to complete his two most important works, the *Metalogicus*, a defence of logic which incidentally included a valuable and critical account of his experiences as a student, and the *Policraticus*, which described the ideal ruler.

Theobald died in 1161; John's friend Thomas à Becket succeeded him as archbishop, with a policy of stout opposition to Henry's attempt to increase governmental control over the clergy. Although John's own position was somewhat more conciliatory, he supported Thomas loyally. From 1163 to 1170, he was an exile from England, spending the years first in secluded scholarship and later, when Thomas was also an exile, in renewed negotiations on behalf of his cause. In 1170 he returned to England with the archbishop and was present at his assassination a few months later. The rest of his life was quiet; he received various ecclesiastical preferments and died in 1178 as bishop of Chartres.

The *Policraticus*, completed in 1159, was dedicated to Thomas à Becket as chancellor of England. Somewhat rambling in its organization, rich in illustrative anecdotes and quotations from classical literature and the Scriptures, written in a graceful, cultivated style, it incorporates into its argument a good deal of the urbane and pleasant scholarship of the twelfth century renaissance. Its political ideas are eclectic and by no means always reduced to consistency or to clarity. But in scope it is the outstanding treatise on political theory before the work of Aquinas: a rich storehouse of the opinions which were current in the minds of scholarly churchmen before the discovery of the *Politics* of Aristotle.

ORIGIN OF AUTHORITY

The following translation is taken from the text edited by C. J. C. Webb (Oxford, 1909), bk. 4, chs. 1, 2.]

CHAPTER I. *Of the difference between a prince and a tyrant, and what a prince is*

Therefore this is the only or greatest difference between a tyrant and a prince: that the latter follows the law, and by its decision rules the people whose servant he deems himself, and by virtue of the law claims for himself the first place in managing the affairs of the commonwealth and in bearing its burdens; and he is elevated above others in this respect: that, whereas private men have their individual responsibilities, the responsibility for the whole community falls on the prince. Whence deservedly is the power of all the subjects gathered together in him, that he may be strong enough to seek out and perform what is needful for the welfare of each and all, and that the condition of the human commonwealth may be best disposed, when all are members of one another. In this, indeed, we follow nature, the best guide of life, which has located all the senses together in the head of man, that microcosm or little world, and has subjected all the members to it so that all may be rightly moved so long as they follow the decision of the wise head. Therefore, the pinnacle on which the prince stands is exalted and made splendid with the many great privileges which he has judged necessary for himself. And rightly so, because nothing is more useful to a people than to fulfil the needs of their prince, since his will is never contrary to justice. Therefore, as the usual definition has it, a prince is a public power and a certain image of the divine majesty on earth. A great share of divine power is clearly shown to inhere in princes by the fact that men bow their necks to his will and often offer their heads to be struck off by the axe, and that, by a divine impulse, everyone who should fear him feels that fear. And I think this would not be possible were it not that the divine will makes it so. For all power is from the Lord God, and has been with Him always, and is from eternity. Therefore, what a prince can do is derived from God in such a way that the power is never withdrawn from God, but He exercises it through a subordinate hand, making all things teach His mercy or His justice. Therefore, 'he who resists the power, resists the ordination of God' [Romans 13:2], in Whom is the authority to grant power and, when He wills, to withdraw or diminish it. For when the ruler becomes cruel to His subjects it is not his own power that acts, but rather the dispensation of God, Who at His own good pleasure punishes or chastens His subjects. Thus, in the course of the Hunnish persecution, Attila, on being asked by the pious bishop of a certain city who he was, replied, 'I am Attila the scourge of God'; and, as it is written, the bishop venerated the divine majesty in him, saying, 'Welcome to the minister of God,' and 'Blessed is he that cometh in the name of the Lord,' and, groaning deeply, opened the barred doors of the church to admit the persecutor, from whom he also attained the palm of martyrdom. For he dared not shut out the scourge of God, knowing that His beloved Son was scourged, and that this scourge had no power except from God. If, therefore, good men so venerate the power which comes as a plague upon the elect, who would not venerate that which has been instituted by God for the punishment of the wicked and the reward of the good, and which serves the laws with a most prompt devotion? 'It is indeed a saying worthy of the majesty of rulers,' as the Emperor says [*Codex*, 1, 14, 1], 'that a prince should acknowledge himself to be bound by the laws.' Because the authority of a prince depends on the authority of law; and truly it is a thing greater than empire for a prince to submit his principate to the laws, that he may think nothing permitted to himself which is not in keeping with the equity of justice.

CHAPTER II. *What law is; and that the prince, although he is loosed from the bonds of law, yet is the servant of law and equity and bears the public person and sheds blood without blame*

Nor should princes think that this detracts from their dignity, unless they think that the enactments of their own justice ought to be preferred to the justice of God, Whose justice is justice for ever and Whose law is equity. Now equity, as the jurists say, is that fitness of things which balances all things rationally and seeks equal laws for unequal things, impartial to all men, assigning to each that which is his own. But law is the interpreter of equity, as in it the will of justice and equity manifests itself. Whence also Crisippus has asserted that its power extends over all things divine and human, and that it therefore presides over all good and all evil and is the prince and guide both of things and of men. To which Papinian, a man most learned in the law, and Demosthenes, that distinguished orator, seem to agree and to make all men subject to obedience to the laws, on the ground that every law is a kind of discovery and a gift of God, the precept of the wise, the corrector of excesses of the will, the bond of the state, and the banisher of all crime [*Digest*, 1, 3, 1–2], in accordance with which all men who share in the corporate life of the commonwealth should live. Therefore all men are held to be bound by the necessity of keeping the law; otherwise someone might seem to be endowed with a licence to do wrong. Yet the prince is said to be loosed from the bonds of the law, not because unjust things are permitted him, but because he ought to be one who cultivates equity not from fear of punishment but from love of justice, who seeks the advantage of the commonwealth, and in all things prefers the welfare of others to his private will. But who speaks of the will of the prince in public affairs, since in these affairs it is not licit for him to will anything except what law or equity persuades or the consideration of the common utility requires? For in these affairs his will ought to have the force of judgment; and most rightly in such matters does his pleasure have the force of law, since his decision is not discordant from the intention of equity. 'From thy countenance,' says the Lord, 'let My judgment go forth, and let thine eyes see equity' [Psalms 17:2], for the uncorrupted judge is he whose decision, from the assiduous contemplation of equity, is its very image. Therefore the prince is the minister of the public utility and the servant of equity, and he bears the public person in that he punishes the wrongs and injustices of all, and all crimes, with balanced equity. His rod and staff also, administered with the moderation of wisdom, bring back the irregularities and errors of all men to the path of equity, that deservedly the Spirit may rejoice in his power, saying, 'Thy rod and thy staff, they comfort me' [Psalms 23:4]. And his shield is strong, for it is the shield of the meek and powerfully wards off from the innocent the darts of the wicked. His office is to give the greatest aid to those who are most weak, and the greatest opposition to those who desire to do harm. Therefore not without cause does he bear the sword, with which he sheds blood without blame and without becoming a man of blood, and with which he often kills men without incurring the name or the guilt of a murderer. . . .

Thomas Aquinas

[*Summa Theologiae*, 1, q.96, articles 3 and 4.]

Article 3. Whether men in the state of innocence would have been equal

. . . . I answer that it is necessary to say that there would have been some disparity in the first state, at least in regard to sex: because without diversity of sex, there would not have been generation. Likewise also in regard to age; for thus some are born of others, nor were they who were united sterile.

But also there would have been diversity in regard to the soul, both in regard to justice and in regard to knowledge. For man did not act from necessity, but through free will; from which man had the choice of applying his mind more or less to the doing or the willing or the knowing of something. Whence some would have been more proficient in justice and knowledge than others.

In regard to the body, also, there could have been disparity. For the human body was not totally exempted from the laws of nature, that it should not more or less receive some advantage or assistance from external agents: since their life also was sustained by food. And thus nothing prohibits one from saying that according to the diverse disposition of the sky and the diverse location of the stars some would be born more robust in body than others, and larger and more beautiful and of better complexion. Yet in such a way that in those who were exceeded there would be no defect or sin, either in soul or body. . . .

Article 4. Whether, in the state of innocence, man dominated man

1. The fourth article is approached as follows. It seems that man did not dominate man in the state of innocence. For Augustine says in Book XIX of *The City of God*, [ch. 15]: 'God did not wish that rational man, made in his image, should dominate any but the irrational; not that man should dominate man, but that man should dominate the beasts.'

2. Besides, that which was introduced as penalty for sin would not have existed in the state of innocence. But the subjection of man to man was introduced as penalty for sin: for it was said to the woman after sin: 'Thou shalt be under the power of the man,' as we are told in Genesis 3:[16]. Therefore in the state of innocence man was not subject to man.

173

3. Besides, subjection is the opposite of liberty. But liberty is one of the especial goods, which would not have been lacking in the state of innocence, when 'nothing was lacking that a good will could desire,' as Augustine says in Book XIV of *The City of God*, [ch. 10]. Therefore, man did not dominate man in the state of innocence.

But, on the contrary, the condition of man in the state of innocence was not higher than the condition of the angels. But among angels some dominate others: whence also one order is called Dominations. Therefore it is not contrary to the dignity of the state of innocence that man should dominate man.

I answer, saying that there are two senses of the word 'lordship.' In one sense, it is the reverse of slavery, and he to whom someone is subjected as a slave is called a lord. In the other sense, lordship is commonly used to refer to any kind of subjection, and in this sense he who has the office of governing and directing free men can be called a lord. Therefore, taking lordship in the first sense, in the state of innocence no man was lord of another; but if lordship is understood in the second sense, man could have dominated man in the state of innocence.

The reason of this is that a slave differs from a free man in this respect, that 'the free man is his own cause,' as is said in the beginning of the *Metaphysics*, [ch. 2, n. 9]; a slave, however, is ordained to another. Thus one dominates another as a slave when he relates him whom he dominates to his own utility, namely, to that of the dominator. And because everyone desires his own good and in consequence suffers if he yields to another the good which ought to be his own, such lordship cannot exist without the pain of those who are subjected. For this reason, in the state of innocence there would not have been this kind of lordship of man over man.

But one dominates another as a free man when he directs him to the proper good of him who is directed, or to the common good. And this kind of lordship of man over man would have existed in the state of innocence, for two reasons. First, because man is naturally a social animal: thus men in the state of innocence would have lived socially. However, the social life of men would be impossible if someone should not preside to direct them to the common good: for many, through themselves, direct themselves to many goods, but one man, to one good. And for this reason the Philosopher says in the beginning of the *Politics* [bk. 1, ch. 2] that whenever many things are ordained to one end, one is

174

always found as principal and director. Secondly, because if one man should have had supereminence of knowledge and justice above another, it would have been unsuitable that this should not serve for the utility of others; according to what is said in I Peter, 4:[10]: 'Each one administering to others that grace which he has received.' Thus Augustine says in Book XIX of *The City of God*, [chs. 14, 15], that the just rule, not by cupidity of dominating, but by the office of counselling: this natural order prescribes; thus God established man.

And through this appears the answer to all the objections, which proceed from the first sense of lordship.

[*De Regimine Principum*, ed. Mathis (Turin, 1924), bk. 1, chs. 1, 14, 15.]

CHAPTER I

. . . . Now in all those things which are ordained to some one end, and in which a choice of procedures is possible, the work is under the direction of something, through whose direction it may duly attain its end. For a ship, which can be moved in diverse directions by the impulse of diverse winds, would not come to its destined end were it not directed to the port by the diligence of its helmsman. Now there is a certain end of man to which all his life and action is ordained, since he acts through the understanding, whose it is, manifestly, to operate for the sake of an end. Now it is possible for men to proceed to the intended end by diverse methods, as is shown by the diversity of human desires and actions. Therefore man needs something to direct him to his end. Now the light of reason has been naturally instilled into each man, by which in his acts he may be directed to the end. And indeed, if it were expedient for man to live alone like many animals, he would need no one else to direct him to his end, but each man would be his own king, under God the highest King, inasmuch as through the light of reason divinely given him he might direct himself in his acts. However, it is natural to man that he should be a social and political animal, living in a group, more even than all other animals. And this fact is shown by natural necessity. For nature has prepared for other animals food, a covering of hair, and such defensive weapons as teeth, horns, claws, or at least speed for flight. Now man was instituted with none of these prepared for him by nature; but in the place of all these reason was given him, through which he can provide all these things for himself by the industry of his hands. But one man alone is not sufficient to provide all these things; for one man's life does not last long enough. It is therefore natural to man that he should live in the society of many.

Moreover, in other animals there is instilled a natural tendency toward all those things which are useful to them or injurious; even as the ewe naturally regards the wolf as her foe. Also certain animals by natural skill recognize certain medicinal herbs and other necessaries of their life. Now man has natural cognition of those things which are necessaries of his life only in general, as it were, and can attain only through reason, by proceeding from universal principles to the cognition of single instances, those things which are necessary to human life. Now it is not possible for one man through his reason to arrive at all things of this sort. Therefore it is necessary for man that he live in a multitude, that one may be aided by another, and different men may be occupied in finding out different things by reason: for instance, one in medicine, another in something else, and yet another in something else. This, moreover, is revealed most evidently through this fact: that it is proper to man to use speech, through which one man can totally express his conception to others. Other animals, indeed, express their passions in a general way, as dogs express anger by barking, and other animals express their passions by various means. Therefore men are more communicative to one another than any other animals which seem gregarious, such as the crane, the ant, and the bee. Considering this, therefore, Solomon says in Ecclesiastes [4:9], 'Two are better than one.' For they have the advantage of mutual society.

If, therefore, it is natural to man that he live in the society of many, it is necessary that there be among men something through which that multitude may be ruled. For when there exist many men, and each looks out for what is suitable for himself, the multitude would be dispersed in diverse directions, if there were not also someone who has the care of that which pertains to the good of the multitude, even as also the body of man, and of any animal, would dissolve if there were not some common ruling force in the body to tend toward the common good of all the members. Considering this, Solomon said [Proverbs 11:14], 'Where there is no ruler, the people will be scattered.' Moreover, this is based on reason, for there is a difference between that which is one's own and that which is common. In private ends, indeed, men differ, but in a common end they are united; now diverse ends have diverse causes. Therefore, besides that which moves toward the proper good of each individual, it is fitting that there be something which moves toward the common good of the multitude. And therefore, in all things which are ordained to one end there is found something which controls the others. For in the universe of bodies, through the first body, namely the celestial, other bodies are ruled in a certain order of divine providence, and all bodies through the rational part of creation. Also in one man the soul rules the body, and, among the parts of the soul, the irascible and the concupiscible are ruled by reason. And again, among the members of the body, one is principal, which moves all: either the heart, or the head. Therefore it is fitting that there be in every multitude something that rules.

Moreover, in things which are ordained to an end, it is often possible to proceed either rightly or wrongly. Wherefore also in the governing of a multitude both right and wrong are found. Now anything is' directed rightly when it is directed to a fitting end; wrongly, when it is directed to an end not fitting. Moreover, the end befitting a multitude of free men is different from that of slaves. For he is free who is his own cause; moreover he is a slave who, in that which he is, belongs to another. If, therefore, a multitude of free men is ordained by a ruler to the common good of the multitude, it will be a right rule, and just, such as befits free men. If, however, the rule is ordained not to the common good of a multitude but to the private good of the ruler, it will be unjust and perverse. Whence also the Lord condemns such rulers through Ezekiel [34:2], saying, 'Woe to the shepherds who feed themselves,' as if seeking their own advantage. 'Should not the shepherds feed the flocks?' The shepherds ought indeed to seek the good of the flock, and rulers the good of the multitude subjected to them. . . .

CHAPTER XIV

Now, even as the establishment of a city or kingdom is conveniently understood through the analogy of the establishment of the world, so also the nature of governing can be understood through the governing of the world. But, first, it must be noticed that to govern is to bring that which is governed suitably to its proper end. Thus, also, the helmsman is said to govern a ship when through his skill it is brought safely to its harbour by the right route. If, therefore, something is ordained to an end beyond itself, as the ship to the harbour, it will belong to the function of the governor not only to preserve it unharmed but, further, to bring it to its end. . . .

Now there is a certain good, extraneous to man as long as he is in this mortal life: namely, the ultimate beatitude which he hopes for after death in the enjoyment of God. . . . Whence the Christian man, for whom that beatitude has been won by the blood of Christ, and who to seek it has received the Holy Spirit as pledge, needs another, spiritual office by which he may be guided to the harbour of eternal salvation, and this office is performed for the faithful by the ministers of the Church of Christ.

Moreover, the end of a multitude and the end of one man must be judged to be the same. If, therefore, the end of one man were some good existing in himself, the ultimate end of ruling a multitude would also likewise be that the multitude should attain such a good and remain in it. And if, indeed, such an ultimate end of one man or of a multitude were corporeal, the life and health of the body, the office of the king would be that of a physician. If, however, the ultimate end were affluence of riches, the king would be a sort of household manager for the multitude. If, however, the ultimate end were the good of knowing such truth as the multitude could attain, the king would have the office of a teacher. But it seems that the ultimate end of an associated multitude is to live according to virtue; for this is the purpose for which men congregate: that they may live well together, an end whose attainment would not be possible to anyone who lived alone; now the good life is life according to virtue; therefore, a virtuous life is the end of human congregation. Moreover, the evidence of this is the fact that only those who communicate with one another in living well are parts of the associated multitude. For if men came together for the sake of life only, animals and slaves would be a part of the civil congregation. Or, if for the acquiring of wealth, all who do business together in one city would belong. But we see that only those who are directed to the good life under the same laws and the same government are counted as one multitude. But because man, in living according to virtue, is ordained to an ulterior end, which consists in the enjoyment of God, as we said above, there must be the same end for the human multitude as there is of one man. The ultimate end of a congregated multitude is not, therefore, to live according to virtue, but through the virtuous life to attain to the enjoyment of God.

But if, indeed, they could attain this end by the virtue of human nature, it would necessarily belong to the office of the king to direct men to this end. For we suppose him to be the king, to whom the height of rule in human things is committed. . . . But because man does not attain the end of enjoyment of God through human virtue but by divine virtue, as the Apostle says in Romans 6: [23], 'The gift of God is eternal life,' therefore to guide men to that end will not belong to human government, but to divine. . . . Therefore, in order that spiritual things might be distinct from earthly things, the ministry of that government was not committed to earthly kings but to priests, and especially to the highest priest, the successor of Peter, the Roman Pontiff, Vicar of Christ, to whom all the kings of the Christian people ought to be subject, as they are to our Lord Jesus Christ. For thus those to whom belongs the care of antecedent ends ought to be subject to him to whom the care of the ultimate end belongs, and to be directed by his command.

CHAPTER XV

Now, even as the good life of men here on earth is ordained, as to its end, to the blessed life in heaven which we hope for, so to the good of the multitude are ordained, as to their end, whatever particular goods are procurable by man: whether riches, or gold, or health, or eloquence, or learning. If, therefore, it is said that he who has the care of an ultimate end ought to control those who have the care of the things ordained to that end, and to direct them by his command, it is made manifest by these sayings that even as the king ought to be subject to the lordship and government which is administered by the office of the priesthood, so he ought to be above all human offices, and to ordain them by the command of his government. Moreover, anyone whose lot it is to perform something which is ordained to something else as its end ought to see to it that his work be congruous to its end, even as a smith makes a sword in such a way that it may be suitable for fighting, and a builder ought to dispose a house in such a way that it may be fit for habitation. Therefore, since the end of the good life that we now lead is celestial beatitude, it belongs, by this reasoning, to the office of the king to procure the good life of the multitude in such a way that it may be congruous to the attainment of celestial beatitude: namely, to prescribe those things that lead to celestial beatitude and forbid the opposite, so far as may be possible. Moreover, what is the way to true beatitude and what are its impediments is known from divine law, the teaching of which belongs to the priestly office, according to the saying in Malachi 2:[7], 'The lips of the priest guard wisdom; seek the law from his mouth.' Therefore in Deuteronomy 17:[18, 19], the Lord prescribed: 'After the king shall have sat on the throne of his kingdom, he shall write for himself a book of this law of the Deuteronomy, taking a copy from a priest of the tribe of Levi, and he shall keep it with him, and shall read it all the days of his life, that he may learn to fear the Lord his God, and to keep His words and His ceremonies, which are prescribed in the law.' Taught, therefore, by divine law, the king ought to pursue this special study: how the multitude subject to him may live well.

And this study is divided into three parts: first, to institute a good life for the multitude subject to him; second, to preserve what has been instituted; third, to improve what has been preserved. Moreover, for the good life of one man two things are needed. One, which is principal, is to act in accordance with virtue; for it is by virtue that one lives well. The other, which is secondary and, as it were, instrumental, is a sufficiency of corporal goods, whose use is necessary to the act of virtue. Now nature causes the unity of a man, but the unity of a multitude, which is called peace, must be procured through the diligence of the ruler. Thus, therefore, to institute a good life for the multitude three things are needed. The first is that the multitude be constituted in the unity of peace. The second, that the multitude, united by the bond of peace, may be directed to well-doing. For, even as a man can do nothing well unless the unity of his parts is presupposed, so a multitude of men, lacking the unity of peace, when it is at war with itself, is hindered from well-doing. And thirdly, it is requisite that through the diligence of the ruler there be at hand a sufficient supply of the things that are necessary for living well.

Thus, therefore, when the good life has been instituted in a multitude by the office of the king, it follows that he should seek to preserve it. Now there are three things which do not allow the public good to endure. And of these one proceeds from nature. For the good of the multitude ought not to be instituted at one time only, but that it may be, in a way, perpetual. Now since men are mortal they cannot live for ever; and even while they live they are not always equally vigorous, since human life is subject to many variations. And thus men are not equally fit to perform the same functions throughout their lives. Moreover, another impediment to the preservation of the public good, proceeding from within, consists in the perversity of wills, which either are slothful in performing those things which the common good requires or, worse than this, are noxious to the peace of the multitude, when by transgressing justice they disturb the peace of others. Moreover, the third impediment to the preservation of the common good is caused from without, when peace is broken by the attack of enemies and sometimes the kingdom or city is completely destroyed. Therefore a triple responsibility rests on the king in regard to these three impediments. First, with regard to the succession of men and the replacement of those who have charge of various offices: that, even as in corruptible things, since they cannot always remain the same, it is provided by divine governance that through the process of generation some succeed to the place of others, and thus the wholeness of the world is preserved, so through the efforts of the king the good of the multitude subject to him may be preserved, when he solicitously sees to it that others succeed to the places of those who are lacking. And second, that by his laws and commands, penalties and rewards, he may coerce from iniquity the men subject to him and lead them to virtuous deeds, taking his example from God, Who gave the law to men, allotting rewards to those who observe it and punishments to transgressors. Thirdly, this charge rests on the king: that the multitude subject to him be kept safe against enemies. For there would be no profit in avoiding internal dangers if the multitude could not be defended from external dangers.

Finally, there remains the third part of the office of the king, for the institution of the good of the multitude, that he be solicitous to improve what has been done in the particular matters that have been set forth: if anything is unordained, to correct it; if anything is lacking, to supply it; if anything can be done better, to strive to perfect it. Whence also the Apostle in I Corinthians, 12:[31] admonishes the faithful to be always covetous of better gifts. These, therefore, are the things that belong to the office of the king. . . .

James of Viterbo

[James Cappocci was born in Viterbo of noble parents. He entered the Order of the Hermits of St. Augustine and studied at the University of Paris, possibly under Aegidius Romanus. He became a master of theology in 1293 and began teaching with great success. His chapter gave him an annual pension for his studies, which was renewed up to 1296. In 1300 he went to Naples on business of his order and won the friendship of Charles II.

His *De Regimine Christiano*, written 1301–1302, adapted a Thomistic Aristotelianism to serve the papal claims to direct power over the secular state. It was the first book to treat the church consistently as a *regnum*. In its originality, in its subtlety and depth of thought, and in the lucidity with which its thesis is developed, it is one of the most impressive writings of the Middle Ages. Few manuscript copies survive; but since much of the text was embodied almost verbatim in the widely-circulated *De Planctu Ecclesiae* (1332) of Alvarus Pelagius, it must be considered an influential work. James dedicated it to Boniface VIII, who rewarded him by naming him Archbishop of Benevento in September, 1302; in December, at the request of Charles II, he was named Archbishop of Naples. He died in 1308.

The following analysis of the components of regal authority is preliminary to James's demonstration that power of this type properly appears in the papacy; it is translated from the text ed. H. X. Arquillière (Paris, 1926), pt. 2, ch. 4.]

.... We should next look at the things that pertain to kingship. Now the principal and special act of royal authority is to judge. Whence it is said of Solomon in the Third [First] Book of Kings, 10:[9], 'Therefore He made thee king, to do judgment and justice,' that is, to judge according to justice; and in the Psalms [99:4], 'The honour of the king loveth judgment'; and in the Book of Wisdom 6:[2], it is said, 'Hear, O kings, and understand; learn, O judges of the ends of the earth.' Moreover, judgment is the right determination of that which is just. Whence to judge is to declare the law (*ius dicere*). The word 'just,' moreover, is derived from *ius*, and thence the authority to judge is called jurisdiction, and because judgment is the right determination of the law or of that which is just, this word is applied to the determination and decision of these matters—according to the saying in Proverbs 16:[10], 'Judgment determines cases,'—and to the giving of sentences and to judging. And because inquiry is necessary as a step toward judgment, therefore the investigation and discussion of those things on which the case turns and judgment is to be given are included in the process of judging. And because the determination of what is just frequently involves correction and punishment, therefore the punishment and correction of the wicked and, on the other hand, the rewarding of the good belong to judgment. Whence Augustine says in the Thirteenth Book of the *Confessions*, [ch. 23], 'One is said to judge in regard to matters in which one has the power of correcting.' And because banishment from the fellowship of the kingdom is a kind of penalty, therefore exclusion from the kingdom and admission to the kingdom belong to judgment. And because judgment ought to be rendered in accordance with laws already determined, therefore to kings, whose it is to judge, belongs the making of laws or the acceptance and promulgation of laws made by others, and kings have the function of inducing men to observe them, both by verbal admonition and by the fear of punishment and the promise of reward. Whence kings are called lawgivers, as it is said in Isaiah concerning our highest King, 'O Lord our Judge, O Lord our Lawgiver, O Lord our King' [Isaiah 33:22]. Moreover, laws ought to be such that through them men may be made good and virtuous; otherwise they are not laws but corruptions of laws. Whence the end of the king, of the judge and lawgiver, ought to be that his subjects may live in accordance with virtue. But teaching and instruction are of great value for this purpose, and therefore it pertains to kings to teach, even as it is said concerning Solomon in the last chapter of Ecclesiastes [12:9], 'Because he was the wisest preacher he taught the people.' And because one teaches effectively when he himself performs what he teaches, therefore kings ought to observe the laws, that they may effectively induce their subjects to observe them, even as it is said concerning Christ the King of Kings that 'He began both to do and to teach' [Acts 1:1].

But because external goods are organically serviceable to the virtuous life, therefore it belongs to the king to procure and provide for the people a sufficiency of such goods as are necessary to life. Whence to feed and nourish is a function of the king, as it is said of David in the Psalms [78:70–72], 'He chose His servant David to feed Jacob His people and Israel His inheritance, and he fed them by his integrity and guided them by the skilfulness of his hands.' To the king also it pertains to administer such goods prudently and justly, and to distribute them proportionally according to the condition of each man. Whence it is said in the Psalms [48:13], 'Distribute His houses.' Moreover distribution seems truly to pertain to those things, whether external goods, as riches and honours, or labours and tasks, or offices, which are required for the order and perfection of the commonwealth.

Whence it belongs to the king to dispose and ordain through all things the multitude over which he is.

But because a community is preserved through unity and peace, therefore it belongs to the king to procure and foster the unity of peace in the multitude subjected to him. Moreover, the peace of a multitude is indeed sometimes disturbed from within through mutual injury or unjust hurt and sometimes from without through violent attack; and therefore it belongs to the king both to eliminate the internal injustices of his subjects and to protect and defend the community of the kingdom against external foes.

And because wisdom or prudence is required in all the aforesaid duties, therefore in the Holy Scriptures kings are especially urged to desire and seek after wisdom. Hence it is that Solomon asked from God not riches or external goods, but wisdom to rule the people [I Kings 3:9; II Chronicles 1:10]. Hence also Boethius in the First Book of the *De Consolatione* [*Philosophiae*] says speaking to Prophecy [Philosophy (?)], 'You have confirmed the saying of Plato that republics would be blessed if either those studious of wisdom should rule them or if their rulers happened to study wisdom.'

These things therefore are, in brief, those which belong to the authority of the kingship.

Marsiglio of Padua

[*Defensor Pacis*, dictio 1, chs. 4, 5, 15.]

CHAPTER IV. *Of the final cause of the state and of its knowable needs, and of the distinction of its parts in general*

1. Moreover, according to Aristotle, I *Politics*, ch. 1, a state is 'a perfect community, which has attained the limit of self-sufficiency, which thus, although it was made for the sake of living, exists for the sake of living well.' Moreover, these words of Aristotle, 'made for the sake of living, but existing for the sake of living well,' denote the final perfect cause of the state, because those who live as citizens of a state do not merely live, as do beasts and slaves, but live well, having leisure for liberal activities, that is, for the practice of the virtues both of the practical and of the speculative mind.

2. Now, since we have determined that the state exists for the sake of life and the good life as its end, we must next discuss that life and its modes. . . . Therefore we shall set forth, as a premise for all future arguments, a principle naturally held, believed, and willingly conceded by all men: namely, that all men not bereft of sense or otherwise impeded naturally seek a sufficient life, and hence also flee and avoid things that are harmful. . . .

3. Moreover, to live and to live well is appropriate to men in a twofold way: the one is usually called temporal or earthly; the other, eternal or celestial. And whatever that second kind of living, namely, the eternal, may be, a university of philosophers could not prove by logic, nor was it a self-evident matter, and therefore they were not concerned to teach in regard to those things that exist for its sake. But in regard to living and living well, or the good life, in the first sense, namely, the earthly, and in regard to those things which are necessary for its sake, renowned philosophers have attained understanding through almost complete logical proof. Whence they have concluded that the civil community, without which this sufficient life cannot be secured, is necessary to attain the good life. And the most distinguished of these philosophers, Aristotle, has said in I *Politics*, ch. 1: 'All men are moved to the state by a natural impulse toward it.' And although empirical observation may have shown this, yet we wish to point out its cause more specifically, saying that since man is innately composed of contrary elements, on account of the contrary actions and passions by which, as it were, some of his substance is continually being corrupted, and also, since he is born naked and without defence against the extremes of the air that surrounds him and of the other elements, capable of suffering and of corruption, as is said in the science of natural things, he needs arts of various kinds with which to ward off these dangers. And since these arts cannot be exercised except by a large number of men, and cannot be maintained except through the communication of men with one another, it has been necessary for men to congregate together in order both to attain what is useful and to avoid what is harmful.

4. Now, since among men so assembled there arise quarrels and disagreements, which, if not regulated by the norm of justice, would lead to strife and division and ultimately to the destruction of the state, it has been necessary to establish in this community a rule of just things

and a guardian or protector. And since the guardian has to prevent the excesses of dangerous men, and others, both internal and external, who disturb or seek to oppress the community, the state must have in itself a means of resisting these dangers. And also, since the community needs some resources and refuges and safe places for certain common possessions, some for the time of peace and others for the time of war, there must be in the state some men to provide such things, that the common necessity may be succoured when this may be expedient or necessary. Moreover, in addition to those things that have been mentioned, which merely succour the needs of the present life, there is something else which those who enjoy civil communication need for the sake of their condition in the future life promised to mankind through the supernatural revelation of God, and which is also useful to their condition in the present life: namely, the worship and honour of God and the giving of thanks to Him for benefits received in this world and those to be received in the future; and that these things should be taught and that men should be guided in them, the state must provide teachers. . . .

5. Therefore, men have congregated for the sake of the sufficient life, in order to be able to seek out for themselves the necessities we have mentioned and to communicate them to one another. And this congregation, thus perfected and sufficient to itself, is called a state; and its final cause, and the final cause of the plurality of its parts, has now been to some extent explained, and will be more specifically described in the following chapters. For, since various things are necessary to those who desire a sufficient life, which cannot all be procured by men of a single order or office, it was needful that there should be in the community various orders or offices of men to perform or procure the various things which men need for a sufficient life. Moreover, these various orders or offices of men are nothing else than the plurality and distinction of the parts of the state.

CHAPTER V. *Of the distinction and definition of the parts of the state, and of the necessity of the existence of each in the state in relation to the end that can be known by human discovery*

1. Let us say in summary that the parts or offices of the state are, as Aristotle says in IV *Politics*, ch. 3, of six kinds: agriculture, the arts and crafts, finance, the army, the priesthood, and the judicial or deliberative part. Three of these—the priesthood, the army, and the judiciary—are

parts of the state in the strict sense; and in civil communities these three are customarily considered honourable. The other three offices are parts of the state in a looser sense, since they are offices necessary to the state, according to the opinion of Aristotle in IV *Politics*, ch. 3; and the many who perform these offices are commonly considered plebeian. These, therefore, are the more notable parts of a city or kingdom, and all others can appropriately be brought under these categories.

[There follows a discussion of the necessity of each of the six in turn.]

10. Finally, we must discuss the necessity of the priestly part, about which men do not agree so unanimously as about the necessity of the other parts of the state. And this lack of unanimity is due to the fact that the true and prime necessity of the priesthood cannot be logically demonstrated and is not self-evident. However, all peoples have agreed that it is desirable to establish a priesthood for the sake of the worship and honour of God, and consequently for the betterment of life both now and hereafter. For most kinds of laws and doctrines promise that in the future life God will reward the good and punish evildoers.

11. But, aside from such causes of such legislation as are believed without proof, philosophers—including Hesiod, Pythagoras, and many others of ancient time—have very properly noticed another cause, which makes the teaching of the divine laws and doctrines virtually a necessity in relation to the well-being of this present life. And this is the goodness of human actions, both private and civil, on which the quiet or tranquillity of the community, and thus the sufficiency of this earthly life, in effect ultimately depends. For although some of the philosophers who invented these laws or doctrines did not themselves believe in the resurrection of man and in that life which we call eternal, yet they imagined it and persuaded men to believe in it, and to believe that its delights and miseries would be proportional to the qualities of human deeds in this mortal life, that they might thus induce reverence and fear of God and a desire to avoid evil and cultivate virtues. . . . Thus the peace of the citizens and the sufficient life of men in this present age was preserved more easily, and this was the result that those wise men had intended to follow the promulgation of such laws or doctrines.

12. Therefore precepts of this sort were handed down by the priests of the gentiles, and for their teaching of these precepts the gentiles

established temples in which their gods were worshipped and instituted men to teach these laws or traditions, whom they called priests. . . .

13. . . . . But the laws and doctrines of the gentiles and of all others that are or have been outside the Christian Catholic faith, or that, earlier, were outside the Mosaic Law, or that, still earlier, were outside the beliefs of the holy patriarchs, and, in general, outside the tradition of those things that are contained in the sacred canon called the Bible, did not have a right opinion concerning God; and therefore they did not have a right opinion of the future life and its felicity or misery, nor of the true priesthood instituted for its sake. But we have discussed their religions in order that their difference from the true priesthood, namely, the Christian, and the necessity of the priestly part of the community may more manifestly appear.

[In ch. 6, Marsiglio discusses the function of the Christian priesthood, continuing to regard it as a part of the state, but defining its role only in relation to the future life and the Christian revelation. See p. 543 below. In ch. 7, he continues his discussion of the parts of the state in terms of the technical scholastic classification of causes, and makes an important distinction between the 'material cause' of a part of the state, which is the individuals qualified by natural disposition and acquired character for the performance of a particular function, and the 'moving or efficient cause,' which makes such individuals into actual parts of the state and which, except for rare cases of divine intervention, is the authority of the legislature. This distinction is used in his explanation of the institution of the ruler (ch. 15), and is vital to the radical theory of the institution of the priesthood which he presents in *dictio* 2 (see pp. 598–601 below).

In ch. 15, Marsiglio derives the power of the ruler from the corporation citizens organized as legislator, and makes the ruler responsible for the institution of the other parts of the state. This argument of this chapter presupposes the theory of the legislator developed in ch. 12, translated above, pp. 73–78, and an analysis in ch. 14 of the personal qualifications of the perfect ruler, who is the suitable 'matter or subject' of human laws.]

CHAPTER XV. *Of the efficient cause of the preferable institution of the principate, whence appears also the effective cause of the remaining parts of the state*

1. . . . . We now show the efficient cause of the ruling part, through which cause the authority of the principate, determined through election, is conveyed to some person or persons. For a prince is actually

constituted by this authority, not through his knowledge of the laws, his prudence, or his moral virtue, though these are the qualities of the perfect ruler. For many men happen to have these qualities, who, lacking this authority, are not rulers except potentially.

2. . . . . Let us say, following the opinion of Aristotle in III *Politics*, ch. 6, that the efficient power of instituting the principate, or of choosing the ruler, belongs to the legislator or corporation of citizens. . . . The method by which agreement on this institution is reached varies from one country to another. But, however it may vary, in every case this election or instition must always be made by the authority of the legislator which, as we have often said, is the corporation of citizen, or its more weighty part. And this proposition can and should be proved by the same syllogisms through which we concluded in ch. 12 above that the making and changing of the laws, and everything else relating to the laws, belonged to the corporation of citizens, changing only the lesser term of the syllogisms by substituting for the word 'law' the word 'ruler.'

3. Moreover, its inherent truth makes this proposition very probable, if we may be permitted to call the necessary probable. For whose it is to generate a form, his it is to determine its subject, as can be seen in all the productive arts. . . . The reason for this is that the forms and their operations are the ends, the materials are the means. . . . Since, therefore, it belongs to the corporation of citizens to generate the law, which is the form according to which all civil acts ought to be regulated, it will appear that it belongs to this same body to determine the material or subject whose it is to dispose the civil acts of men in accordance with this form: namely, the ruling part. And because this is the best of the forms of the civil community, the best subject for it ought to be determined according to his inherent qualifications. . . . Whence, it seems, we can properly infer that an elected ruler, without hereditary succession, is greatly preferable for a polity to those who are not elected or those who are established with dynastic succession.

4. . . . . We must now, as we have proposed, explain the cause which effects, institutes, and determines the other offices or parts of the state. Now we say that the primary cause is the legislator, and we say that the secondary and, as it were, instrumental or executive cause is the ruler, through the authority conferred upon him by the legislator and in accordance with the form which it has established for him: namely,

the law, in accordance with which he should always, so far as possible, conduct and administer civil acts. . . . For although the legislator, as the first and proper cause, ought to determine who should fittingly fill these offices in the state, yet the ruling part, as in the case of any law, prescribes the execution or, if necessary, restrains it. For the execution of laws is more conveniently carried out by him than by the whole multitude of citizens, since for this function one ruler or a few are enough, whereas it would be superfluous to employ the whole community in it and would distract them from other necessary activities. For when the rulers do this, the whole community does it, because the rulers do it in accordance with the law, which is the determination of the community; and a few rulers, or only one, can more easily execute the laws.

8. Moreover, in accordance with the aforesaid force, namely, the law, and with the authority granted to him, the ruler ought to choose and appoint the parts and offices of the state from suitable material: from men who have the skills or qualities appropriate to those offices. For such men are the proper material of the parts of the state.

Nicholas of Cusa

[The brilliant career of Nicholas of Cusa (1400 or 1401 to 1464) was preeminently that of an ecclesiastical diplomat and statesman, but in the many-sided style of the Renaissance, for in addition to being an expert canonist he was also an enthusiastic humanist and a speculative scientist and philosopher.

Born of a modest family in a small village near Trier, he studied first at Heidelberg, then at Padua, which was at the time outstanding in humanistic studies, in science, and in canon law. Here Nicholas studied mathematics, astronomy, medicine, and Greek, as well as canon law, of which he became a doctor in 1423. In 1425, he was granted the first of a series of ecclesiastical benefices and began the study of theology at Cologne. In 1426 he became the secretary of the papal legate to Germany, a noted patron of humanists; further preferment followed.

In 1432, Nicholas came to the Council of Basel on behalf of a candidate for the archbishopric of Trier who had been unanimously elected by the chapter, but was opposed by a papal appointee. His De Concordantia Catholica, with its leading principle that all coercive authority must be mediated through the consent of the governed, was perhaps originally conceived as a plea for his candidate; it was written for the Council in 1433, while the case was still in progress, and in 1434 Cusa supported his candidate's cause with the same basic argument. At all events, he became an active leader among the more radical conciliarists, strongly opposing the influence of the papal delegates and acting as a member of the Deputation of the Faith which accused Eugenius IV of contumacy; but, soon after the Council decided against his claimant (1434), he left Basel to seek support elsewhere. Attempts to win him to the pope found him responsive; and when, in 1436, his candidate's affairs brought him again to Basel, he aligned himself on the papal side. He was a member in 1437 of the mission which succeeded, in opposition to the majority at Basel, in persuading the Greek Church to send its representatives, to discuss projected unification, to Florence rather than to Basel.

From 1438 to 1448, Nicholas was active in pro-papal diplomacy, attempting to win the neutral German princes to active support of Eugenius against the Basileans. His success as 'the Hercules of the Eugenians' was rewarded in 1448 when he was named a cardinal; in 1450, he was made Bishop of Brixen, in disregard of the fact that its chapter had already elected another candidate. In the next few years, first as papal legate to 'Germany, Bohemia, and neighbouring countries,' and later in his diocese of Brixen, he made vigorous attempts to carry through church reforms, but without great success: the problem was too great. In 1458, the newly-elected humanist pope, Aeneas Sylvius, made him vicar-general for the temporal power in Rome and the Papal States, with a programme of reform there. In 1460, he returned to Brixen, where he spent his last years in struggles with local enemies.

The question of Nicholas's motives in the brief period in which he was a leader of the extreme conciliarist faction and of the motives which lay behind his shift to the papal party is obviously open to dispute. It may be suggested that he was essentially a man of action rather than a doctrinaire; that he was genuinely interested, as his later career shows, in church reform; that, like many other reforming churchmen, he might reasonably have become disillusioned by the bickering and ineptitude of the Basileans and convinced of the superior possibilities in strong papal ·leadership. Even in the De Concordantia Catholica, he had expressed deep respect for the papal office, which he regarded as divinely ordained and essential to the unity of the church; the ideal which he set forth was one of harmony, not of a Marsiglian popular supremacy. The circumstances in which his theory of consent was developed and the fact that his later acceptance of the bishopric of Brixen disregarded it do not necessarily mean that he was insincere in expressing it in 1433. His was an adventurous, speculative mind with a rich range of interest and experience; such a mind may distinguish between the ideal and the expedient without necessarily repudiating the ideal.

ORIGIN OF AUTHORITY

In the selection translated here from the *De Concordantia Catholica* (Schard, *De Jurisdictione*. . . , pp. 465–676), bk. 2, ch. 14, Nicholas sets forth in general terms his theory of government based on consent; in the selections from bk. 2, chs. 19 and 34, translated below, pp. 418–422, he applies it specifically to the papacy.]

Every decree is rooted in natural law, and if a decree contradicts it it cannot be valid (*Decretum*, di. 9, *Dicta Gratiani*, 'cum ergo' and 'constitutiones'). Whence, since natural law is naturally in the reason, every law is known to man in its root. The wiser and more eminent are chosen rulers of others for this reason: that they, being endowed with their natural clear reason, wisdom, and foresight, may discover just laws and through them rule others and settle disputes, that peace may be preserved (c. 5, di. 2). Whence it follows that those who are vigorous in reason are naturally lords and rulers of others, but not through coercive law or judgment rendered against the unwilling. Whence, since by nature all are free, every government—whether it consists in written law or in a living law in the prince—through which the subjects are coerced from evil deeds and their liberty is regulated to good by fear of punishment is based on agreement alone and the consent of the subjects. For if by nature men are equally powerful and equally free, the valid and ordained authority of one man naturally equal in power with the others cannot be established except by the choice and consent of the others, even as law also is established by consent (c. 1, di. 2; c. 2, di. 8, where it is said that 'there is a general compact of human society to obey its kings'). Now, since by a general compact human society has agreed to obey its kings, it follows that in a true order of government there should be an election to choose the ruler himself, through which election he is constituted ruler and judge of those who elect him; thus ordained and righteous lordships and presidencies are constituted through election.

Chapter Four

THE INDIVIDUAL AND THE COMMUNITY

THE term 'organic' is an ambiguous one; the classification of political theories as 'individualistic' or 'organic' leaves the vast majority of systems wandering in the debatable ground between the two categories. On the one hand there are such clearly atomistic constructions as those of Locke and Paine, in which the state appears as a conventional device to protect individuals already endowed with full-blown faculties and rights. On the other hand one finds the definitely organic theories of Hegel or of modern fascism: here the group, whether State, *nazione*, or *Volk*, is conceived as a reality in itself; the individual finds value only through absorption in the group purpose; his rights, his functions, his objectives are defined only by the needs and purposes of the whole. So long as one considers only the pure forms of each type of theory, individualism and organicism seem sharply antithetical; but elements of the theory we call organic can form, and have formed, stable compounds with elements from individualistic theory.

Medieval political thought was such a compound. Into the making of medieval conceptions of the ethical relations between individual and group there entered a variety of influences: the feudal background; Christian and ecclesiastical tradition, with its freight of classical ideas; the experience of emerging corporate organization, illuminated by Roman law; the fundamental speculations of Aristotle. None of these influences was purely individualistic or purely organic.

The political theory implied in feudalism had many individualistic elements. The tendency of feudalism was, in fact, to reduce all social and political organization to a network of contractual bonds between pairs of individuals, to assimilate public power to private property, to regard the ruler as a part of this contractual system, and to limit the role of government to the minimum which was compatible with the unimpaired maintenance of feudal property rights. A theory in which the purpose of government is simply to apply and enforce justice in terms of a pre-existing system of legal rights, and in which the right of revolt may be called into play if the government steps beyond this narrow and negative sphere, is usually called individualistic. But if we apply this term to feudal thought, it must be with the proviso that it had no general concept of the individual: that the individual whom feudalism aimed to protect was not the essential human being as such, but the holder of a definite status in a stratified society—an animated bundle of specific custom-law rights.

Feudal law codes do not, of course, tell the whole story of feudal individualism. An agrarian economy with a wide distribution of rights in land tends to breed a sense of individual security which stubbornly resists governmental encroachment. The isolated life of the typical feudal noble, the individualistic military techniques of feudalism, and the rough-and-ready struggle for power in which self-help was the order of the day must also have contributed to the development of a consciousness of individual independence and self-reliance. Finally, the idealization of the feudal contract meant a focusing of emotional loyalty on what was essentially a man-to-man relationship. A rough measure of the strength of the individualistic spirit thus brought into western civilization may be derived from consideration of the long struggle between monarchy and aristocracy; some indication of the forms and qualities of that spirit in the Middle Ages may be found in the *chansons de geste*.[1]

As feudalism had no clear concept of the individual, so also it permitted no clear concept of the community. When political rights were attached to personal status and diffused by subinfeudation, when the king supreme in England was a vassal in France, when nobles simultaneously owed homage to different kings for widely scattered holdings, when all kinds of immunities were dotted like islands in the sea of royal jurisdiction, the geographic definition of political communities was all but unthinkable, and impossible in practice. A political community, then, could have been defined only as the vague total of those who owed allegiance to a particular king; and the absence of a clear-cut territorial basis was only one of the many factors in the early medieval situation which made it virtually impossible for such collections of subjects to develop or maintain any cohesive institutions of their own. Here and there might linger remnants of public organization on a territorial basis; but in practice what unity the early medieval kingdoms possessed was such unity as their kings might be able to impose upon them.

Several consequences of this situation appeared in early medieval political thought. One natural consequence was to think of the king as the only conceivable representative of the kingdom—and to mean by representation simply that he had authority to act on behalf of the whole. The early medieval notion of representation construed the representative as a trustee for the interests of a group rather than as the agent of their will. Secondly, if the unity of the kingdom was focused in the king, it would logically follow that the community could have no means of action against the king: resistance to him must be construed as the resistance of private individuals. Finally, even bodies that might have been construed as acting for the community through delegated power—for instance, the king's great council, or the electors of the Holy Roman Empire—tended also to appear as groups of private individuals whose right to advise, to decide, to elect was attached to each one as an incident of his individual status rather than to the whole group as a corporate body representing a larger corporation. From this conception followed the typical requirement of unanimity for the decisions of such groups.

A second major influence on medieval thought about the relation of individual and community was that of the Christian church. Like the feudal environment, ecclesiastical teaching offered medieval minds materials for both individualistic and organic conclusions. On the one hand, the Christian faith itself asserted the value of every individual soul in the eyes of God, insisted on the moral freedom and responsibility of man, and pointed to a goal of personal immortality and personal salvation. Moreover, the church transmitted to medieval consciousness the main features of the Stoic idea of man: the idea of man as a rational being, capable of shaping his life in accordance with the principles of a natural law indelibly imprinted on his mind; and the idea of the original freedom and equality of men in the primitive state of innocence. These two sets of ideas, the Christian and the Stoic, were to become the chief bases of that sense of human dignity in which every individualistic trend in western political thought is finally rooted. Thus the teachings of the church established the deepest possible foundations for individualism; moreover, by its mere presence as an institution separate from the state, competing with the state for the loyalty of men, and asserting its own claims to final control over large areas of human thought and action, the church blocked the development of those totalitarian tendencies in the state which had characterized ancient cultures and which then characterized the medieval Byzantine Empire. The significance of this fact for modern thought and history is of course tremendous; but even in the early Middle Ages its effects appeared. For the church was not always to be found on the side of the secular government; and when the two powers clashed, as in the investiture struggle, the ecclesiastical party proclaimed the dissolution of the bond of authority in the name of values far beyond the competence of the state.

We have said that the church laid the deep theoretical foundations of individualism; but perhaps it may also be said that those foundations were laid so deep that all their implications for the structure of human society were not easily understood. At all events, ecclesiastical thought also conveyed ideas which may seem to us incompatible with its profound ideas of the equality and freedom of human souls. The early church had made peace with Roman absolutism and with the great inequalities and injustices of Roman society; it was prepared to accept the stratification of the feudal age and the irresponsibility of medieval kings. For Christ's kingdom was not of this world.

St. Paul had stressed the duty of obedience to the powers that were, on the simple premise that they had been ordained by God; and he had laid emphasis on the diversity of gifts within the church and the corresponding diversity of offices. 'They are many members, but one body.'[2] Thus the Christian community was seen as a mutually interdependent fellowship of members with unequal functions and ranks; and as the Christian church made its way in the world, it expanded this conception into a general social theory. Far from preaching a revolutionary equalitarianism, it contented itself with stressing the duties that corresponded to each social station. To this attitude, the influence of neo-Platonist cosmology added new justification. The whole universe appeared as planned by God in a wonderful hierarchy of ranks and orders, in which each member had its appropriate niche, contributing in its own special way to the beauty and order of the whole. This concept was developed elaborately in patristic thought, and above all by Augustine. He found his ideal of justice in the concept of a world at peace with itself and with God, in the tranquil maintenance of the divinely-established order of diversity.[3]

Ecclesiastics also kept alive through the feudal era something of the classical notion of the state as an institution with special claims on the loyalty and obedience of men. Their scholarship brought them into some contact with classical ideas and, at least up to the time of the investiture struggle, it was usually to the interest of the church to strengthen all ideological forces making for public order and the prestige of kingship. Ecclesiastical discussions of government, it is true, often betrayed no more complex notion of political organization than that of the mere ruler-subject relationship; but here and there one finds expressions and ideas that derived from old experience of a coherent and inclusive political society.

It is possible to study in John of Salisbury's *Policraticus* an impressive presentation of some of these ecclesiastical traditions by an intelligent churchman, steeped in the scholarship of his day and also, of course, affected by the medieval environment itself. The *Policraticus* is the most systematic treatment of the relations of individual and community before the discovery of Aristotle; but it is not very systematic. John of Salisbury regarded the kingdom as an organized community: a community, moreover, characterized by the differentiation of its members for the performance of special services in the common interest. In a quaint chapter, ostensibly based on a 'little book' by Plutarch called *Institutio Trajani*, but for which no source is known,[4] he set forth a detailed comparison of each social group to a part of the human body. Organic analogies were destined to a long career in later medieval thought. Some modern readers have jumped to the conclusion that the crude anthropomorphism of the analogy drawn in the *Policraticus* implied a thoroughgoing acceptance of an organic creed.[5] Such a conclusion is dangerous, particularly in view of John's general taste for literary adornment. It is evident from this chapter and from related passages that for him the interdependence and mutual cooperation of specialized social groups was an essential feature of the political bond, and that his notion of justice was related to the Augustinian idea of order in diversity. 'Then the welfare of the whole commonwealth will be secure and glorious if the superior members take care of the inferior, and the inferior members likewise make due response to the demands of their superiors, that all may be, as it were, members one of another, and that each may deem himself best served by what he knows to be more advantageous for the others.' Like the bees described by Virgil 'so the citizens are held to their various tasks, and as long as the offices of each are so performed as to further the welfare of the whole, as long, that is, as justice is maintained, the sweetness of honey pervades the spheres of all.'[6] But it is not at all evident that he had passed beyond the patristic idea to a complete organic conception.

Feudal relationships have little direct reflection in his treaties, but the results of the feudal situation are clearly apparent. It is significant that when he had to find a word for his commonwealth he regularly used the term *provincia*—a vague term in this period; John applied it indifferently to England and to Brittany. At times he treated the king as the representative of the commonwealth, the servant of the people, the bearer of 'the public person'; at other times, and more often, he saw him as the divinely ordained guardian of the people's interests.[7] Although he occasionally called the commonwealth a corporation (*universitas*),[8] he was unable to conceive of its personality as located anywhere except in the king, or to regard it as having any possible means of action apart from or against the king. His commonwealth, then, was scarcely a state in the modern sense; nor was it, in the modern sense, composed of individuals: it was a society of ranks and orders, ordained by God; the basis of its unity was a pattern of interdependence; and the guardian of its unity was the prince who worked constantly to keep the pattern from dissolving.

A third factor in medieval thought on individual and group was the influence of Aristotelian philosophy, which was fundamental to all scholarly discussion of the problem from the time of Aquinas. Aristotle's treatment of group relationships was not, of course, accepted *en bloc*. Medieval thinkers took from Aristotle what they could understand and reshaped this in the light of their faith and their experience. But Aristotle focused their attention on the problem and gave them concepts and terminology and arguments.

Aristotelian metaphysics supported Christian faith in presenting the individual as the unit of existence. Scholastic thought saw the universe in terms of the universal forms which organized all reality into *genera* and *species*. These universals were the proper objects of thought, the aspect under which multiple reality could be grasped and dealt with by the human mind. Whether these universals had any kind of reality apart from the minds that used them, and if so how they were tied into the structure of actual things, was a problem for grave and delicate debate, in which the chief alternatives were moderate realism, like that of Aquinas, which claimed the reality of universals in individual phenomena, and the nominalism of Occam, which regarded universals merely as mental constructs. But it is important to notice that no influential school of medieval thought took an extreme realist position. All agreed with Aristotle that the real universe was a universe of individuals. Many individuals might be actuated by one form, but in uniting itself with matter, the principle of multiplicity, the form itself was multiplied. Thus real existence in the realm of phenomena was the existence of individuals and nothing existed except individuals: *'nihil est praeter individuum.'*

In the case of man, Aristotle's notion of individuation through union with matter did not satisfy medieval Christian philosophers, concerned to safeguard personal immortality. Solutions of the metaphysical problem were various and controversial, but only the Averroists clung to the notion of a universal soul for mankind. Except as it may have influenced Dante, this idea had no significance for political theory.

This general approach decisively excluded from medieval political thought the cardinal tenet of a pure organic political theory: the real, integral unity of a group. For medieval thought, the social group, no matter how intricately interdependent or closely organized, could have no existence except as a 'multitude of men.' It followed that the concept of real personality could be applied only to individuals: there was no room in the philosophy of the Middle Ages for a group mind or a group will or a *Volksgeist*.

This metaphysical individualism was not the only debt which medieval thought on the relation of individual and group owed to Aristotle. His interpretation of the origin and purpose of the state brought the state into a much more intimate relationship with the individual than was claimed by the government of medieval experience or the government of patristic tradition. The Aristotelian state was not a device for preserving an already established order and for meting out justice to men already equipped with status and rights and functions in society. It was the matured form of social order; it was the self-sufficient community of men organized for life and for the good life; and a man without the state was either a beast or a god. The state, then, obviously existed for the most fundamental service to the men who composed it; but there was also a sense in which the state was the end of man, for the complete fulfilment of human nature must lead to the development of the state and to the development of individuals as members of the state. In line with this conception, there were phrases in Aristotle which might suggest the sacrifice of individual values to group values. But Aristotle's thought implied no sacrifice, rather a natural harmony; the group values were values shared by the group; and the group was a group of real men.[9] Medieval students of Aristotle, even when they borrowed the Aristotelian phrases, were at least as far as he from any notion of the state as a mystic entity floating haughtily above the sum of its parts.

The influence of Aristotle on medieval publicists strengthened their individualism by making it more precise and giving it a reasoned foundation. But the individualism which resulted from the merging of Aristotelian doctrines with the rest of the medieval stock of ideas was an individualism of a special kind, not to be confused with other kinds of individualism the world had known and was to know. It must be distinguished from the individualism of Stoicism, of feudalism, and of the contract-theorists in its grasp of the fact that man is a social and political animal and needs the state in order to fulfil himself. It must also be distinguished from recent types of liberal individualism in its comparative indifference to what we think of as individuality.

For, as we have already suggested, a major emphasis in Aristotelian and hence in scholastic philosophy was on the characteristics common to men. The characteristics which distinguished one member of the species from another were not important in Aristotelianism or in scholasticism, and medieval minds had little technique for dealing constructively with them. Thus when medieval writers, following Aristotle, spoke of the full actuation of human potentialities as the end of man and therefore of the state, they were thinking of the fulfilment of the common human potentialities, fixed by the nature of man, perceptible by reason, capable of logical discussion. They were not thinking of men as unique bundles of special interests and desires and capacities, each with a claim to its own special kind of fulfilment as an essential part of an individual personality. They recognized variety of purposes as a fact, but the chief conclusion that they drew from it was the need of a government to take care of the much more important and thinkable fact: that certain purposes are characteristic of all men. They recognized variety of opinions and desires as a fact, but assumed that it could be explained as the result of ignorance or the corrupting influence of sin. They recognized variety of talents as a fact, but thought —in good Hellenic fashion—that it could be adequately treated under the heading of division of labour for the common end or as a basis for the natural grouping of men into rulers and subjects.

A fourth influence on the medieval theory of group-relationships was the development of corporate forms of social organization, which became increasingly important from the twelfth century on. At first corporate structures appeared side by side with the older hierarchic forms. In the church the college of canons, the monastery, the cardinal-ate, presented examples of cohesive groups which discovered techniques for joint action; in the secular world, the guild of merchants or craftsmen and the town followed similar patterns. As the Middle Ages wore on, the corporate idea seemed more and more applicable to the large structures of church and kingdom; and it may be said that the central political problem of the later Middle Ages was the thrashing out of all the implications involved in conceiving the kingdom and the church as corporate communities. At the same time, the smaller corporations grew and flourished; the corporate form was used for an increasing variety of associations; so that some thinkers, notably Gierke, have thought of the later Middle Ages as the golden age of corporate life.

It is sometimes suggested that the rich medieval development of corporations tended to submerge the individual and to make him a mere part of a larger whole. Certainly the medieval members of guild and town acquired a sense of intimately belonging to communities from which they accepted a degree of regulation which may seem drastic to us and whose success and glory became for them a vital source of self-respect. Yet these organizations served as the instruments through which the members advanced their own purposes in a dis-ordered world. And, if the corporation originated in the individual's awareness of his own weakness, it served to nurture an ultimate self-confidence. When the protection of the guild was no longer useful, individualistic capitalism hatched out of its shell; and the very towns which aroused the most fervent patriotism in their citizens produced that carnival of self-conscious individualism, the Italian Renaissance.

For political theory, the development of the corporation meant the discovery of techniques by which the common purposes of a group of individuals could be advanced without recourse to a benevolent guardian, through the joint action of the group itself. In the corporation, medieval men learnt to combine their separate wishes and opinions and to arrive at a single voted decision which could be accepted as the decision of the whole. They learnt to elect officers who acted as agents of the corporation, enforcing the rules which the corporation itself had established. Here and there corporations began also to develop techniques for controlling their officers: through short terms, through the requirement of a periodic accounting, or through the establishment of a special agency to watch and check the actions of the regular officers. In the federated monastic orders there appeared a technique for producing unity of decision among geographically separated groups—the assembly of representatives. And the corporation, outliving its individual members, exemplified the triumph of human purposes over time as well as over space.

In short, the development of corporations meant the discovery of ways in which a number of men could arrive at the unity of decision and consistency of action which characterize the human individual. It thus made the theoretical problem of the relation of individual and group a problem of practical importance, forcing the canonist and civilist lawyers who worked out the law of the corporation to deal with fundamental speculations. On the other hand, corporation law reacted on political theory, and abstract discussions of group relationships were frequently coloured by awareness of the specific and sometimes arbitrary rules which corporations had developed in practice. Above all, experience of corporate achievement began to undermine the principle of hierarchy and to substitute for the dichotomy of ruler and ruled the revolutionary idea of community.

One aspect of corporation law is particularly significant in illuminating the medieval remoteness from modern equalitarian individualism: the development of the principle of majority rule.[10] The right of a numerical majority to enforce its will over a minority seems to modern eyes an inevitable, if clumsy, deduction from the premise of equality. But in its medieval development it had no such premise.

Decision by majorities appeared in the medieval scene as the alternative to the older rule of unanimity, a rule which reflected the feudal disintegration of the sense of community. The rule of unanimity assumed that each member entered the decision fully-armed with his private, original rights, and that the rights of each member of the deciding group could be affected only with his own specific consent. In the looseness of feudal society, the rule of unanimity was more or less effectively enforced by the sheer fact that anyone who did not consent to a decision could not very easily be forced to support it. Thus while it was believed that 'the minority should follow the majority,' there was no possibility of a valid decision if it did not. The rule of unanimity resulted in a formal equality of voters; but its premise was not their theoretical equality but rather their very real independence.

The law of corporations cut into this conception by making a distinction between its members as private individuals and its members as its members, and by affirming that, on matters in the sphere of corporation affairs, a legally-defined group of members could make a decision for the whole corporation. For the civilists, the decisive power was that of a simple numerical majority, but this was simply a rule taken over from the Roman law of corporations. Characteristic medieval thinking is illuminated by the canon-law principle which gave the decisive power to the 'greater and wiser part' (*maior et sanior pars*). What was wanted, in fact, was literally 'the sense of the meeting,' and it is obvious that to the sense of the meeting some individuals will contribute much more than others. In recognition of this empirical inequality of men, votes must be weighed as well as counted, and canon law developed an elaborate system of rules for the weighing of votes; it was assumed that in the case of a disputed election, for example, the judge would apply these rules in determining which candidate was really supported by the 'greater and wiser part.' In the course of time, it came to be established that a numerical minority could not be considered to be the 'greater and wiser part,' and it came to be felt also that a two-thirds majority might be presumed to embody the preponderant wisdom. Thus ultimately a simple counting of votes came to be the practical expedient for locating the wisdom of the corporate group; but there had never been in canonist thought the premise that numerical preponderance was in itself a claim to right.

Deeply committed to the acceptance of a stratified society, medieval thought also found it appropriate that status should be recognized in the weighting of opinion. This appeared in the organization of representative bodies by estates: the slogan of 1789, 'vote by head,' would have seemed fantastic to medieval lawyers. The idea of a national assembly based on universal suffrage was, of course, beyond imagination. Communal constitutions, even where they made provision for the concurrence of the masses in elections or in the ratification of law, took it as a matter of course that the greatest political power should be concentrated in the upper classes. In Marsiglio's rather ambiguous concept of the 'more weighty part' of the community, 'computed . . . with due regard to both quantity and quality,' 'quality' seems to have implied a fusion of both status and personal characteristics. In the legislative process, quality was recognized in the principle that 'prudent and expert men,' who also would be men of rank and leisure, should be entrusted with the formulation of laws, and quantity was given its due regard in the principle that a final discussion and ratification of laws should occur in a mass assembly. Marsiglio apparently expected that the 'more weighty part' which would emerge from this process would actually be an overwhelming majority; but it never occurred to him to begin with the premise that even an overwhelming majority had an automatic claim to power.[11]

It should be evident from the foregoing summary of the influences which went to shape the medieval theory of groups that that theory could be neither purely organic nor purely individualistic. An analysis of mature medieval thought on the subject reveals a body of theory which is, on the whole, consistent within itself, a fairly stable compound of individualistic and organic elements: by no means clearly explicit in all political writings, but sometimes expressed with the utmost precision and delicacy.

In spite of a frequent use of analogies between the organized community and the human body, no medieval writer seriously defined the community as an organism or maintained that its unity was of the same kind as the unity of the human individual. That a kind of effective unity appeared in organizations of men, whether of the corporate or monarchic type, was an obvious empirical fact: the attainment of such a unity was the first purpose of such organizations. But no medieval writer argued that the unity of decision and action which appeared in a kingdom or corporate town was a manifestation of the organic unity of a suprapersonal personality.

For corporate bodies in general, medieval lawyers developed the concept of fictitious personality.[12] They recognized that when men were bound together for specified purposes, the resulting corporation could act as if it were a single person. And thus it was possible to treat it as a person in law and to conceive the corporate group as a single subject of legal rights and obligations. But the personality of the corporation was clearly understood to be an artificial personality created by legal devices. The corporation had no soul, therefore no will of its own, as Baldus said of the Empire.[13] What took effect as the will of the corporation was therefore a legal construct made up of the wills of its members when they acted collectively as members of the corporation (*omnes ut universi*, in contrast to *omnes ut singuli*, the members acting as individuals). It appeared in the decisions made by the members voting in accordance with the rules of the corporation or in the decisions of its properly constituted officers acting in their allotted spheres. The real subject of the rights and duties of the corporation was its members—as such.[14]

Discussions of the precise nature of the unity of the state are rare among medieval publicists. Those who were touched by Aristotelianism agreed in conceiving the state as the self-sufficient community, characterized by differentiation and coordination for the common good. This idea was often expressed through analogies with the differentiation and coordination of the members of the human organism. What made the unity of the state possible and desirable was the common purposes of the human beings that composed it: purposes that could not be achieved by men in isolation. They were held together by mutual dependence. In this fundamental principle, medieval Aristotelians differed from those later writers who saw no closer unity in the state than could be explained as the product of a deliberate and revocable contract. For medieval thinkers, as for Aristotle, the unity of the state finally rested on the necessities of human nature itself.

But it was characteristic of medieval thought—with its background of bitter medieval experience—that the common purpose and interdependence of men were not regarded as a sufficient cause of the unity of the state. Moreover, the cohesive factors which modern thought particularly stresses—habit, language, nationality, common traditions —could not be stressed in medieval thought because they played only the most rudimentary role in the medieval world; nor could medieval men understand Aristotle's idea of integration through education. Medieval thinkers were thus brought squarely face to face with the realization that without the continual coordinating activity of a government, the multitude would be, as Aquinas said, 'dispersed in various directions.'[15] This realization, which, incidentally, gave government a greater importance in the concept of the state than it had had for Aristotle, issued in a general demand for kingship—not, as Gierke supposed,[16] as the expressive symbol of a unity already characteristic of the group, but as the indispensable efficient cause of the unity required by the needs of its members. The personal unity that characterized the real human individual made the office of kingship peculiarly appropriate to the pursuit of the common good; and, in the sense that the king 'formed' the unity of the group and acted on its behalf, he might be described in legal language as the bearer of its 'personality.' Those who, like Marsiglio, felt that a group of magistrates might serve the same purpose as the single king, fell back on the experience of corporations to demonstrate that a group could attain an adequate unity of decision and action. But all were agreed that the unity of the state was vitally dependent on the unity, natural or factitious, of its governing head.

Lawyers and philosophical publicists, then, in spite of somewhat different vocabularies, were in essential agreement in their solution of the problem of the unity of the state. Both alike saw it as an external and functional unity, a pattern of relationships among individuals. It rested on common human needs, but it came into being only through the establishment of a definite legal organization and a ruler—what we should call a constitution and a government.

The unity of a group was defined, in Aristotelian terms, as a 'unity of order' in distinction from the absolute unity of a single person. Aquinas conceived it as a formal unity: the actuation of its members by the 'form of an ordained multitude.'[17] His concept was that of a moderate realist: the form had reality for him as an idea in the divine plan, as a final cause actuating human personality, and as a proper object of rational thought. But a form of this sort created no new substance which could be a locus of action or value. The group existed only in its parts, who still remained a 'multitude of men.' For the unity which this kind of form imposed on the multitude differed from the unity of the human person: it left its parts still capable of private, self-motivated action, unlike the action of human hand or foot. On the other hand, an ordained multitude had actions which could be described only as the actions of the entire group in cooperation or of the entire group as represented by the officer who acted in its behalf. The whole was not a simple sum of its parts, but the sum of its parts organized. The parts which formed the whole were individuals whose individuality itself included a potentiality for values that could be fulfilled only in a life of mutual communication and cooperation—an intrinsic potentiality, therefore, to become the parts of such a whole; yet they remained a multitude of individuals, each with his own moral destiny, each capable of values that would attach to him alone, as well as of values that attached to him together with his fellows.[18]

As nominalistic tendencies gained ground in medieval philosophy, other thinkers imputed even less metaphysical reality to the 'unity of order.' Marsiglio insisted that the unity of a state was not a unity of form; it consisted simply in common acceptance of a single government. Occam in his logical works emphasized that 'every whole is nothing other than its parts taken together: that is, joined and united.' The order which united a number of individuals into a whole added no new substance: 'If a house is constructed of lumber and stone, nothing new is added to the lumber and stone.' Occam rejected even the legal notion of fictitious personality: in his defence of the Spiritual Franciscan view of collective poverty, he insisted that the Franciscan Order—and every other social group—was simply the sum of its members.[19]

When we turn to the question of the unity of the church, we find much the same sort of thought. The question can receive only the most brief and tentative handling here,[20] for the church in medieval thought had many aspects which can scarcely be treated in the language of political theory. Early medieval writings in particular were full of poetic phrases suggesting a quite supernatural sort of unity for the church; later writings were also often touched with mysticism. But a few points may be made. As the Middle Ages progressed, there was a steadily-growing tendency to define the church in rational terms.

Theologians seeking to define the sense in which the church was properly spoken of as a unity worked in the general framework of an Aristotelian metaphysics and with full attention to the age-old Christian insistence on the individual human soul as, under God, the ultimate reference-point of spiritual values. Accordingly, they took the traditional phrases and safeguarded them by careful explanation. Hugh of St. Victor, in the twelfth century, could write: 'The holy church is the body of Christ, vivified by one Spirit, united by one faith, and sanctified. The members of this body are individual believers; all are one body, on account of the one Spirit and one faith.'[21] Later thought demanded sharper definition. Aquinas said that the unity of the church, Christ's mystic body, must, in spite of analogies, be distinguished from the unity of man's natural body. The unity of the church was the unity of the forms which actuated all the members: '.... Through faith in and love of the numerically-one thing believed and loved, they are united; likewise the Holy Spirit, one in number, fills all'; but faith and hope and love were 'diverse in number in the diverse men.'[22] An extremely interesting chapter by the fourteenth-century papalist, James of Viterbo, pointed out that in strict accuracy the church should be called 'united' rather than 'one.' Its unity was a unity of common forms, and a unity of order. A number of passages in the fifteenth-century *Summa* of the anti-conciliarist Turrecremata restated and elaborated Aquinas's distinction between the unity of the individual and the kind of unity that characterized the church.[23] These definitions were stated in terms of the moderate realism that asserted the reality of the unifying form in the individuals; in contrast, nominalists defined the church in simple collective terms: for Occam, it was the totality of true believers; for Gerson, the totality of the clergy.[24]

To sum up, all explicit medieval thought on the unity of groups seems to have been consistently true to the premises with which it started. The unit of will, thought, and experience was the human individual; groups were multitudes of individuals. The kind of unity they could have was the unity produced by their common needs and interdependence and by the concurrent influence on a multitude of individuals of some uniting factor, whether that factor was defined as an actuating form or merely as a coincident experience. This consistency between premises and conclusions seems, to the present writer, the most effective answer to those who see in the history of medieval political thought the history of a tendency, which only narrowly failed of success, toward an organic conception of the real personality of a group. For this view I know of no evidence except the frequency of the medieval use of physiological analogies. Medieval writers were fond of analogies, no doubt, but there seems to be no reason why we should assume that they meant more by their analogies than they said they did.

If the group was a multitude of men, its good must be in some sense a common good. Whether the purpose of the state was merely the meting out of justice and the maintenance of peace, or making it possible for men to live 'and not only to live, but to live well,' or the furtherance of a moral development of men finally ordained to their spiritual beatitude, there was no notion in the medieval mind that it could have an end aloof from the ends of its components, or that their ends could be deduced from the end of the state. 'The corporate whole —that is, the people—has this function,' said the twelfth-century civilist Irnerius, 'namely, to care for the common interests of individual men as its members.'[25] And Aquinas, although he saw with Aristotle that in a sense the state was prior to individual men and recognized that its immediate goals attached to the whole multitude rather than to its parts as individuals, still insisted that in the long run the end of the whole must be of the same stuff as the ends of individual men: 'the end of the human multitude must be the same as the end of any one man.[26] There could be no raison d'état that was not also the reason of private minds; no Hobbesian derivation of morality from the determinations of Leviathan; no Machiavellian divorce between the moral standards applicable to the Prince and those of ordinary men.

But no realistic political theory can assume that the interests of the group as a whole will always coincide with all the interests of all the members. This fact became conspicuous to medieval minds as it became apparent that contractual feudal dues were inadequate means for the maintenance of peace and order: that, in emergency situations, the welfare of the whole must require the sacrifice of individual property, perhaps also the risk of individual life. Medieval minds thus came to grips with the fundamental legal and moral problem of the nature of political obligation; they found their solution, variously expressed, in the notion of a final reciprocity between individual good and common good—between the interests of the part and the interests of the whole.

The language in which medieval writers defended sacrifice for the common good was often so vigorous as to suggest the complete submergence of men in an organically-conceived state.[27] Augustine's phrase, 'Shameful is the part that is not congruous to its whole,'[28] was frequently quoted; 'The part ought to expose itself for the sake of the whole' was a popular maxim; Aquinas himself cited Aristotle's dictum that 'to further the common good is greater and more divine than to further the good of one man' at least sixty times[29]; there appeared in medieval writings countless allusions to the desirability of amputating legs or arms to preserve the health of the body politic. But the relation implied in such phrases was always that of the part to the whole, not of the means to the ends of a superior entity. Moreover, the kind of sacrifice defended in such glowing language was only such sacrifice as the modern liberal state also thinks it appropriate to ask. And, while feudal individualism, tenacious of its contractual rights, required emphatic reassertion of the greater claims of the common good, no philosophic thinker of the Middle Ages could regard the sacrifice of property, even the sacrifice of life itself, as the sacrifice of the highest values of personality. It was not suggested that the state could require the sacrifice of human reason or human morality to its purposes; still less, of course, man's spiritual goal.[30]

When the early civilists glossed Ulpian's distinction between 'public law,' which 'pertains to the *status rei Romanae*,' and 'private law,' which 'pertains to the utility of individuals,'[31] they recognized a relationship between the two: private law pertained secondarily to the public utility, since it was of interest to the state that no one misuse his property; similarly, public law pertained to the utility of individuals, since the preservation of the republic was for their welfare.[32] This reciprocity, they seem to have felt, explained why the normal role of government was the maintenance of private rights and also why in time of emergency private rights must yield to a superior claim. That higher claim was sometimes spoken of as the claim of the 'common utility,' sometimes as the claim of the '*status rei publicae*'—a tautological phrase which may perhaps be best translated as 'the welfare of the commonwealth.' It did not imply a personification of the state or any conception that the state could have a welfare which was not inextricably linked with the welfare of its members. Many civilists believed that the king's finding of an emergency justifying extraordinary measures should be coupled with the consent of property-holders through their representatives; such a belief seems to testify to an assumption that, though private rights and public interest might clash, private men could recognize that public interest was, in the long run, their interest too.

The assimilation of Aristotelian thought allowed a more penetrating, more abstract, and more generalized analysis of the relation between the ends of individual and group than that made by the early civilists. Whereas civilists saw the issue in terms of public law and private law, theologians followed Aristotle in speaking of the relation between the common good and the good of single individuals. Aquinas dealt with the problem in a number of scattered passages; some other Aristotelians reproduced his general solution with minor variations[33]; Aristotle's significant dicta soon passed into the general stock of medieval ideas, to be used by lawyers and publicists, without further analysis, as self-evident premises for specific arguments. We cannot always say with certainty what meaning was attached to sentences thus used; but we can say that, with one or two possible exceptions, no medieval writer developed an explicit theory which involved a greater subordination of the individual to the group than did Aquinas's theory. His theory should therefore be examined in detail.

When Aquinas asserted that the end of a multitude must be the same as the end of any one man, he was not, of course, suggesting that the state need pursue the innumerable individual interests of its members— the 'private ends' in which 'men differ.'[34] The state aimed at an end common to all its members; and this end was conceived as divinely ordained, rooted in human nature itself. The assumption of a fixed common end independent of human will and knowable with certainty by human reason simplified the problem and avoided the worst of the modern liberal dilemma.

The problem of the adjustment of private-law rights with the common good was not so disturbing to Aquinas as it was to naive feudal minds or to the early lawyers. Aquinas's conception that the property-right was itself founded in and limited by its social utility clearly subordinated it to the common good. Moreover, with all his respect for the claims of man to the satisfaction of his animal needs, Aquinas regarded those needs as on a lower plane than the claims of man to the fulfilment of his rational and moral and spiritual potentialities. The common good, he insisted, took precedence over the good of single individuals only when the values at stake were of the same sort. When values of different kinds clashed, the intrinsically higher value took precedence.[35]

Finally, by starting with Aristotle's notion of man as a political animal, incapable of self-fulfilment except in the interacting life of the community, Aquinas could argue that the welfare of the community was itself one of the ends implicit in each individual: 'the common good is the end of the individual persons existing in the community.'[36] And this Aristotelian notion could in turn be fitted into the patristic Christian idea of the universe as a harmonious structure in which no single part could find its peace and purpose save in relation to the order of the whole. 'The good of the universe is the reason why God wills each particular good in the universe.'[37] And, similarly, the good of each individual man must be 'ordained to' the good of all mankind and to the good of the narrower community of which he was a member. This doctrine did not imply a clash between the ends of the individual and the community, in which the ends of the community took precedence; it rather implied the final identity of those ends in the divine plan. 'Those things without which human society can not be preserved are naturally suitable to man.' 'He who seeks the common good of the multitude consequently seeks his own good . . . because one's own good can not exist without the common good, whether of a family, of a city, or of a kingdom.' But 'private good is prior in the order of generation to common good, which rises out of individual goods.'[38]

The end of the group as such and of the individual as such were of course not immediately identical: there was a qualitative difference, which Aquinas saw as a difference of 'form.' 'The common good of the state and the good of one single person do not differ merely quantitatively, but in accordance with a formal difference. For there is one *ratio* of the whole, another of the part.'[39] The meaning of this statement is illuminated by specific descriptions of the good of the community as such, descriptions which resolve it into an aspect or a condition of the good of individuals. 'The good and welfare of an associated multitude is the preservation of its unity, which is called peace, without which the utility of social life is destroyed—nay more, the discordant multitude becomes a burden to itself.'[40] Notions of peace, order, justice have reference to group relationships and have no meaning for individuals considered in isolation; but the social individual can recognize their close relationship to his own specific ends. Aquinas's idea of the common good necessarily involved, as Linhardt puts it, a selection from and a special organization of the ends of individuals, and the introduction of 'elements which are only indirectly serviceable to, or at any rate not immediately identical with, the goals of individuals.'[41] In relation to this kind of good, the individual is of course a part of the whole, even a means to its end. But the end is a common end; and the relation is a circular one, for the good of the whole is also a means to the ends of each of its parts.[42]

Did Dante deliberately depart from this view of the relation of individual and group? Arguing for the necessity of universal empire to secure the conditions under which 'the civil society of the human race' (*humana civilitas*) might attain its end, he wrote:

'. . . . Even as there is one end for which nature produces the thumb, and another different end for which she produces the whole hand, and again another, differing from both, for the arm, and another, different from all these, for the entire man; so there is one end for which God made the individual man; and for another end He ordained the household community; for another, the village; for another, the city; and for another, the kingdom; and, finally, there is a last end for which the eternal God . . . brings into being universally the human race. . . .'[43]

Gierke regarded this sentence as illustrating a current of typically medieval organic thought; some later students have seen in it a departure from the typically medieval concern to safeguard the final reference of values to the individual.[44] The whole passage is markedly lacking in technical precision. The ends that Dante later specified for household, village, city, and kingdom were not sharply differentiated: the household prepared its members for the good life, the end of the village was 'the suitable protection of persons and property,' the end of the city was 'the good and sufficient life,' and this was also, 'with greater security of tranquillity,' the end of the kingdom.[45] In spite of the anatomical analogy, these organizations seem clearly to serve the ends common to their members. But the universal society, whose end is defined as the full actuation of human reason, is not a logical parallel to the other terms in the series. Did Dante, in orthodox intention but loose language, conceive this end as the common end of a totality of individuals in collaboration, achieving through their interaction a goal to which the isolated individual and the smaller groups were insufficient, but whose values were nevertheless finally the values of individuated human personality? Or was he asserting that the end of mankind was an end which had relevance only to a transcendent universal entity? The implication, whether deliberate or not, did not go unchallenged. In a very interesting passage, Guido Vernani pointed out that 'there is no difference between the ultimate ends of the individual and of all mankind'; mankind was not like the human body, composed of parts of different species, but was a totality of subjects alike in species and in destiny. Dante, he thought, had fallen into the Averroist heresy of asserting a separated, universal soul for mankind. Modern scholars continue to speculate over Dante's exact meaning and the possible influence of Averroism on his thought; but the evidence seems too slight to warrant a certain conclusion that Dante consciously departed from the Thomistic view.

The emphasis which medieval writers placed on the superiority of common good to private good was a response to the real medieval problem of persuading arrogant individualism to give way to community consciousness. The relationship between the state and the social animal which Aristotle had described as a simple empirical fact was an unattained ideal in the later age in which many men attempted to live in disregard of the state—and if they were not beasts, they were certainly not gods. It was also an ideal which did not quite fit the medieval scene, in which the state was simply one of many institutions related to the social life of man. It was comparatively easy for medieval ·minds to grant that human nature required society for its fulfilment; it was not difficult for them to see that the state was necessary to social life in its provision of justice and security; but it was impossible for them to hold fast to a concept which embraced society within the state. Even Aquinas, although in his more abstract writing he came close to expressing Aristotle's meaning, could not, in the more concrete *De Regimine Principum*, portray the sort of interacting community that Aristotle took for granted. His attention inevitably shifted to rulership and its purposes; and this approach was often conspicuous in later writers. But when the state was conceived as a relation between ruler and subjects, aiming at specific goals, the idea that it *was* a common end of man tended to be narrowed to the idea that, in its own special way, it *served* the common ends of man. This tendency was supported by the growth of the idea that rulership was established by a corporate people as a particular instrument of their interests, and by the growth of nominalistic empiricism, which dissolved the notion of the reality of forms as final causes. Thus later medieval thinkers—for instance, Marsiglio and Occam—were led to conceive 'the common benefit' or 'the common utility' in mere collective terms. They retained, however, the idea that the organization of a governing state was so necessary to man that its preservation was an essential aspect of the common good; they also retained the general assumption that human nature was of such homogeneous stuff that there could be no fundamental cleavage among individuals in regard to their good; and finally, in spite of some voluntaristic tendencies, they still thought of the common good primarily as something to be discovered objectively by the use of reason rather than as something to be constructed through the integration of subjective wills.

Another result of the difference between Aristotle's inclusive idea of the state and the more specific medieval view was a greater emphasis in medieval thought on the principle that the authority of the state must be a limited authority. Aristotle, indeed, had said that the state should not be so closely integrated as to turn harmony into unison; he had acutely criticized Plato on this very point.[46] But medieval minds, incorporating Aristotelian ideas with other, more deeply-rooted ideologies, put greater stress on the bounding of the state, added restrictions not present in Aristotle's thought, and tended to define the proper limits of state authority in terms of their concepts of fundamental law. Their complex and various institutional applications of these limiting principles are discussed elsewhere[47]; we are here concerned simply with a brief analysis of the principles themselves.

One limit to the rightful authority of the state was implied by Aquinas's distinction between the common good which was its proper object and the private ends in which men differ, which were properly left to private judgment and initiative. Even the pursuit of common goods required diversity and a degree of autonomy for individuals and specialized groups. 'Many things are necessary to the good of human society. But diverse things are better and more expediently carried on by diverse persons than by one.' 'The multitude would not be ordained, but confused, if there were not diverse orders within the multitude ..., a diversity of orders in accordance with the diversity of functions and acts.'[48] Marsiglio used an organic analogy for the precise purpose of stressing the necessary balance between the coordinating function of the ruler and the autonomy of other parts of society; he also remarked that unity of action was desirable for no part of the state except the *pars principans*. The principle that order required diversity was basic to all medieval thinking. Here medieval fact and the Augustinian idea of peace merged easily with Aristotle's concept of harmony. But this principle was so familiar to medieval publicists that they often failed to emphasize it. The danger that they saw was the danger of an unbridled spontaneity, of a social atomism in which the claims of the common good would be forgotten. Therefore they emphasized order and control; but by order they did not mean *Gleichschaltung*, and by control they did not mean dictatorship.

The idea that the state was subject to divine and natural law implied several fairly specific limitations upon it, aside from the general principles that it could not violate divine commands or approach its ends by means that were intrinsically evil or not rationally appropriate to the ends pursued. For medieval publicists generally believed that certain rights of individuals were based in natural law or in the quasi-natural law of peoples, although this concept was not entirely developed, or stated in the absolute terms of the later natural-rights theorists. Property-rights, as we have seen,[50] were generally regarded as based in the law of peoples. Rights to self-preservation and security of family relationships were based in natural law.[51] The right to personal freedom had a more ambiguous status. Augustine's belief that slavery was an appropriate consequence of sin and Aristotle's argument that certain people were naturally slaves, together with the fact that serfdom was part of the medieval structure of property, inhibited medieval thinkers from an unqualified assertion of a universal right to personal freedom; on the other hand, the Stoic-patristic concept of the original freedom of men and certain statements in the *Corpus Juris Civilis* tended to support the idea that freedom was a natural right. With some qualifications and some uncertainty, the political theory of the Middle Ages generally treated lordship over slaves, or serfs (the same Latin word was used for both), as part of the legitimate structure of property; the reconciliation of serfdom with natural and divine law was a matter for legal rather than publicistic determination. On the other hand, political theory sharply distinguished lordship over slaves from the authority of a ruler, which was an authority over free men. The freedom of those who were free was, accordingly, a premise in political discussion and, like the right to life, to family relationships, and to property, a normal boundary to the authority of the state. Its implications were variously drawn: Occam's conclusion, which derived from Aristotle's definition of freedom, was that free men could not be treated as a means to any end except the common good.[52]

These 'rights of man,' however, were only normal limits to state authority: all could on occasion be subordinated to the common good. This doctrine may seem to have opened a back door to the whole onrush of totalitarianism. When the ruler was deemed the proper judge of the requirements of an emergency, was not the whole structure of limitations a mere delusive façade of pious hopes?—One might suggest that any political theory which attempts to set permanent and impermeable walls around the authority of the state is at least equally deluded by vain dreams and is merely sacrificing good sense to architectural dignity. However that may be, the medieval doctrine was theoretically quite distinct from organic totalitarianism. For, in the medieval view, the boundaries of the state were assumed to be determined by the objective common good at which the state aimed—a good construed in terms of personal values—and by the rational natural-law principles to which it was subjected; and, similarly, it was assumed, objective, rational criteria would determine the occasions on which those boundaries could be violated. Moreover, for many medieval thinkers, the ruler was not the sole judge of his abnormal actions, which might require the consent of his subjects through their representatives or might be nullified by subordinate officers. For many medieval thinkers, private individuals were morally and legally justified in defending themselves against a ruler who infringed without just cause on human rights.[53] And even those whose theories made no provision for practical checks on the ruler still asserted the existence of objective norms to which his actions should conform.[54]

Marsiglio has seemed to some modern scholars[55] to be a conspicuous exception to these generalizations. He specifically denied that principles of right which did not carry with them an authoritative coercive sanction were, in the most proper sense, laws. On the other hand, his definition of law in the most proper sense included both the coercive command and a 'true concept of justice and civil good'; and it seems to me that there is no evidence in the *Defensor Pacis* that he did not intend this second qualification at its face value. On the contrary, he showed considerable concern for it in his recognition of the importance of the special role of the 'expert and prudent' in the 'discovery and examination' of law and also in the kind of argument he used to defend the final location of legislative authority in the 'more weighty part' of the community.[56] His whole argument purported to show that 'common benefit and civil justice' would be at least closely approximated through the pooling of the expert wisdom of the few with the reason and wills of the many. Unanimity he did not require, for human perversity must be a distorting factor; but since in the aggregate nature must have provided what was necessary for the fulfilment of the natural impetus to civil life, this distortion could not affect the properly computed 'weightier part' of the community. His confidence in this process was so complete that it did not occur to him to investigate the problem of the obligation of obedience to laws that might lack a true concept of justice and civil good.[57] Thus his theory, in spite of the individualism of his approach, resulted in a practical subordination of the part to the whole, apparently more complete than emerged in theories which combined a stronger emphasis on the objective character of justice and the common good with a weaker faith in the human means through which it must be pursued. Marsiglio foresaw and guarded against the possible tyranny of the single ruler; he did not foresee the possible tyranny of the corporate Leviathan. But we need not therefore assume that he intended to justify it. His intention was rather to defend the rights of individuals in the end of law through defending their rights in the process by which it was made; we know that the safeguard he envisaged would have been inadequate, but the most that we can fairly charge against Marsiglio is an error in practical judgment.

Finally, all theorists except Marsiglio agreed that the state was concerned only with the temporal ends of man, and all agreed that his supernatural good was not to be subordinated to its purposes. 'Man is not ordained to the political community in all that he is and all that he has,' said Aquinas, 'and therefore it is not necessary that every one of his actions be praiseworthy or blameworthy in relation to the political community; but all that a man is, and all that he can do, and all that he has, is ordained to God.'[58] Even Marsiglio's theory did not absorb the spiritual life of man in the state or assign all spiritual functions to its control. He recognized the duality of human ends; he asserted that it was better to obey God than man[59]; he entrusted the interpretation of divine law to the divinely-inspired priesthood, although he entrusted its coercive implementation to the Christian state. Other theorists—for instance, John of Paris and William of Occam—who visualized a possible specific and abnormal intervention of the secular ruler in the spiritual area were careful to base that intervention on the ruler's duties as a Christian king rather than on the rights of the state as such.[60]

In the area of man's spiritual life, another great institution asserted itself; and it is sometimes suggested that modern totalitarianism had a notable precedent in the claims of the medieval church. We cannot here enter into a detailed study of this complex question.[61] But a few points can be made. Through the time of Innocent III, the theory of the church specifically disavowed any direct authority over the realm of secular affairs, claiming only the right of abnormal intervention when spiritual values were at stake. The theory of direct ecclesiastical power over secular affairs was dominant in pro-papal circles in the late thirteenth and fourteenth centuries, but was questioned by a number of prominent theologians and influential ecclesiastics. It was never officially asserted as Christian doctrine. In the fifteenth century, the most ardent papalists began to return to the earlier theory.

Even the most extreme theory did not visualize a normal interference in secular relationships. It did, however, deny that secular rights could be considered rights independent of the church; it based the supposedly exceptional intervention of the church on an assumption of its ultimate all-embracing lordship. However limited an application of this doctrine was expected by its proponents, we cannot deny that it was in tendency totalitarian. If we do not call it completely totalitarian, it must be because the theory assumed that intervention would be rational and not arbitrary; yet its assertion that no man could presume to question the rightfulness of papal action left the papacy in effect untrammelled or bound only by the fear of divine disapproval. As so often occurs in the study of medieval thought, we find here principles conceived as binding upon authority yet totally lacking in earthly sanctions.

Even within the spiritual area where the church held sole authority, its claims fell short of complete totalitarianism. For ecclesiastical authority was set within a framework of revealed religious precept, which it might interpret and supplement but not fundamentally alter. The great powers of the pope were in theory based on his position as judge and interpreter rather than as sovereign lawgiver; and even the most thorough-going exponents of the *plenitudo potestatis* recognized the possibility that a pope might be a heretic and *ipso facto* deposed. Moreover, the Christian principle of the moral responsibility of the individual had its effect in the care with which the great theologians mapped out the proper limits of spiritual coercion of the individual conscience. In short, even the vast claims of the medieval church were meshed in a web of objective principles fine-spun from the very substance of medieval faith and reason. Whether or not the conception could be enforced, the rightful authority of the church, like that of the state, was conceived as limited. And the purpose of the church, like that of the state, was finally defined in individualistic terms. It existed for the sake of the salvation of souls.[62]

In its general conception of political institutions as related to human ends and in the objective limitations it placed on authority, medieval thought laid foundations for modern individualism. But the structure which medieval thinkers erected on these foundations had significant differences from modern doctrines.

One conspicuous difference was the failure of medieval philosophy to draw out of the potential equalitarianism of its premises any insistence that political institutions should aim to secure for every individual an equal opportunity to participate in the supreme values for which those institutions existed. In their claims to self-preservation, in their claims to security of property, and in their claims to adequate sustenance as a basis for individual and family life, the equality of individuals was indeed recognized by medieval philosophy at its best —though even here the attitude might well be summed up in Burke's phrase, 'All men have equal rights, but not to equal things.'[63] In so far as the state was made 'not only for living, but for living well,' medieval thought resigned itself to a more serious inequality. If recognition of a common human substance defined the common end of men as the full actuation of their potentialities for a life of reason and virtue, recognition of actual human differences in status and capacity inhibited any serious attempt to insure an equal sharing in the common end. Thus medieval thought at its best fell back on the Aristotelian conception of division of labour for the common good and on the Augustinian notion of a hierarchy of order in which the role of each individual was glorified through its place in the divine plan. Those destined by providence to realize themselves below the highest plane must find their felicity in the fact that their menial services were also good and in the fact that, indirectly, they would themselves be the beneficiaries of values realized through the mutual intercourse of the cooperative whole.[64]

When one turns to the question of the rights of man in regard to the political means through which his ends were to be attained, one finds an even wider discrepancy between medieval thought and modern individualism. Medieval thinkers saw no reason why the existence of a common human end should be paralleled by an equality of men in political rights. They saw no reason why the organization that existed to serve all its members should be governed by all its members. Their concern for the moral freedom and responsibility of men did not carry them to the modern democratic conclusion that man can be free only in subjection to an authority in which he himself actively participates. Their individualistic premises led them rather to a general acceptance of structural principles which we usually call organic: social stratification, inequality of political rights, and the concentration of an irresponsible and paternalistic authority in the hands of the few.

Logically, this conclusion was possible because of several characteristic medieval ideas. When the common end was conceived as fixed by nature and perceptible by reason, the will of the individuals concerned became irrelevant and the strongest modern argument for democracy had no force. When the choice of policies appropriate to the common end was conceived primarily as a process of ratiocination, it could easily appear that that process might most expediently be carried on by a specialist acting in the common interest, precisely as other arts and sciences were best carried on by specialists acting in the common interest. And finally, when natural law was conceived as a doctrine of ultimate ends, the whole structure of institutional rights became a secondary structure, not immediately inherent in the nature of man but deriving its validity from its demonstrable usefulness to his ends. Thus the way was clear for the application of the test of utility to all political institutions; and if one thought that an organically-constructed and monarchically-integrated society would best serve the ends of man, such a conclusion would be in logical harmony with an individualistic conception of those ends.

There were, indeed, routes through which the rudiments of democratic ideas could be introduced into the medieval pattern of authority. The doctrine of the original freedom and equality of men could be used, as Nicholas of Cusa used it, to support the idea that coercive government must rest on popular consent. The test of utility could be turned, as Marsiglio turned it, into an argument that good government was best achieved through the inclusion of all citizens in the base of authority. And the idea that 'what touches all must be approved by all' appealed to many publicists and lawyers as an axiomatic premise for an insistence that when public good demanded the infringement of private rights the ruler's action required the concurrence of private men.

The historical conclusion of these ideas was, of course, the theory and practice of the equalitarian representative democracy of modern times. But their medieval effects were blocked by the obstinate fact and almost equally obstinate theory of social stratification and by the sheer impossibility of imagining the complex pattern of institutions that could achieve a genuine participation of individuals in the course of government. Thus medieval thinkers were able to arrive at the doctrine that all secular power was derived from the people without holding either of its modern corollaries: either the doctrine that the people should intimately control the ways in which delegated power was used, or the doctrine that in that control 'each man should count as one.' Cusa's doctrine of consent turned into a rationalization of the absorptive rights of those who might be construed to represent their constituencies. Marsiglio demanded no further rights for the bulk of citizens than those that could be exercised in a mass assemblage. And legal opinion, confronted with occasional deadlock between king and estates, could find no clear solution other than to assert that the king's prerogative must have the greater weight.

The medieval applications of the theory of consent were little more than the rationalization of a hierarchic construction of power and some check against its abuse; its revolutionary effect had to wait for a later era in which the structure was itself undermined by the profounder revolutions of social and economic change. The political theorists who presided over the early stages of that revolution rejected the organic elements in medieval thought and attempted to construct the political community solely on the basis of the continuing consent of naturally free and equal individuals. But their individualism went too far. By postulating as the units of the political community men for whom the atomistic life of the state of nature was a possible alternative—abstractions fully-grown without the benefit of civil life, clothed in rights and faculties spun like cocoons from their own substance—they not only ignored the actual quality of individuality and the actual complex of interrelations between the individual and social institutions but also gave themselves no chance of satisfactorily accounting for the political community itself: for of such parts the whole is obviously more than the sum. Similarly, in tracing the bond of political obligation merely to a deliberate and conditional contract, they distorted the realities of political behaviour without solving their theoretical moral problem: for if there are no bonds among men stronger than a contract, why should a contract be sacred?

Utilitarian thought, while aptly criticizing many of the details of the contract theory and giving proper weight to the importance of habit in cementing political solidarity, was no more successful in its concept of the ultimate bond between the individual and the state: its picture of a series of rationally self-interested individuals, studiously calculating whether the probable consequences of disobedience would be more pleasurable than the probable consequences of obedience, is no closer to reality than the Arcadian fancies of Locke or Paine, no more satisfactory logically, and rather less attractive.

Rousseau attempted to restore the classical and medieval concept of the fulfilment of nature in society, together with the principle that a free man could not be subordinated to any but a common end; but, since he could not work with the assumption that the ends of man were clearly defined by reason, his synthesis broke down on the question of the integration of the will of all with the general will. Nineteenth century thought, reacting against the individualism of the Enlightenment and developing a part of Rousseau's thought, moved on to the construction of various types of organic theory, correctly emphasizing the natural growth of the state, the meaninglessness of the individual apart from the state, and the necessity of defining the bond between individual and community in terms of the positive values that are achieved by differentiated and coordinated action. But in their hypostatization of the state as the locus of those values and in their failure to do justice to the real demands of individuals, the extreme organic theories were, in their way, as unsatisfactory as the theories of extreme individualism.

Other thinkers have sought, and continue to seek, a middle ground between the two extremes, attempting to protect the individual personality as the centre of all values while recognizing the complexity of social interrelations without which individuality is meaningless and its values unattainable. For this search, the medieval system can certainly not be adopted bodily. To the extent that it assumed the rigid medieval social order, it is irrelevant and undesirable. To the extent that it assumed an Aristotelian metaphysics, it is obviously unusable. To the extent that it assumed a natural harmony of human ends in the divine plan, it requires a faith that many of us cannot provide.

The medieval view of the relation between individual and community has profound historical importance. Without understanding it, it is impossible accurately to understand the terms in which more concrete problems of political organization presented themselves to medieval minds; the influence of its leading principles has never ceased to colour the thought of the western world. But, aside from its usefulness to those who wish to understand the origins of their own intellectual tradition, it is worthy of study in itself. Incompletely stated though it was, and involved in concepts which no longer have meaning or usefulness to us, it nevertheless blocked out a system of principles which must be included in any satisfactory theory of the individual and the community: in its recognition of the fact that man is a social and political animal; in its acceptance of the state as a positive means toward the realization of personal values; in its emphasis on differentiation of human activities for the common good; in its clear distinction between institutional means and moral ends; in its justification of the demands of the state on the individual in terms of the individual's own values; in its awareness that there are limits to the rightful power of the state; and, above all, in its insistence that the values of rational and moral personality must be the criterion for the measurement of political good.

John of Salisbury

[The following passage from the *Policraticus*, bk. 5, ch. 1, is one of the most famous and most extensive uses of an organic analogy in medieval political writings.]

CHAPTER I. *What a commonwealth is . . . and what, in this commonwealth, corresponds to the soul and the members*

. . . . The prince should take stock of himself thoroughly and diligently study the condition of the whole body of the commonwealth which he represents. Now a commonwealth . . . is a certain body which is given life by benefit of divine favour, and is moved by the highest equity, and is ruled by a certain moderating reason. And those things that establish the rites of religion in us and teach us the worship of God . . . take the place of the soul in the body of the commonwealth. And those men who preside over the rites of religion should be honoured and reverenced as the soul of the body. For who doubts that the ministers of God's holiness are vicars of God? Further, as the soul rules over the whole body, so they . . . preside over the whole body. . . . In the commonwealth, the prince takes the place of the head, subject to God alone and to those who act as His representatives on earth, even as in the human body the head is animated and ruled by the soul. The senate corresponds to the heart, from which proceed the beginnings of good and evil deeds. The offices of eyes, ears, and tongue are claimed by the judges and governors of the provinces. Officials and soldiers correspond to the hands. Those who are always about the prince are likened to the sides. Treasurers and wardens (I am not speaking of those who are in charge of prisons, but of the keepers of the privy chest) are like the belly and intestines, which, if they become congested with excessive greed and too tenaciously keep what they collect, generate innumerable incurable diseases, so that ruin threatens the whole body when they are defective. Tillers of the soil correspond to the feet, which particularly need the providence of the head because they stumble against many obstacles when they walk upon the ground doing bodily service; and they have a special right to the protection of clothing, since they must raise, sustain, and carry forward the weight of the whole body. . . .

THE INDIVIDUAL AND THE COMMUNITY

Thomas Aquinas

[The following selection is from Aquinas's commentary on the *Nico-machean Ethics*, written 1261–1264: *In Aristotelis Stagiritae Nonnullos Libros Commentaria in X Libros Ethicorum ad Nicomachum*, book 1, *lectio* 1 (*Opera*, Parma edition, vol. XXI, at p. 2).]

.... Moreover, it should be known that, because man is naturally a social animal, since he needs many things for his life which he cannot provide for himself alone, the consequence is that man is naturally a part of some group, through which assistance toward the good life is furnished him. This assistance he needs for two purposes. First, for those things that are necessary to life, without which the present life cannot be maintained; and in this respect the domestic group of which he is a part may be an aid to man, for each man receives generation and nourishment and training from his parents, and the individuals who are members of a domestic family assist one another to the necessaries of life. In another way man is assisted towards the perfect sufficiency of life by the civil group of which he is a part: namely, that he may not only live, but live well, having all the things which suffice him for life; and the civil group of which he is a part may be an aid to man in this respect, not only in regard to corporals, since there are many crafts in the state, to which a single household is not adequate, but also in regard to morals, inasmuch as insolent youths, whom paternal admonition cannot correct, may be coerced through public power by the fear of punishment. Moreover, it should be known that this whole—a civil multitude or a domestic family—has only the unity of order, according to which it is not one thing in the strict sense of the term. Therefore, a part of this whole can have an operation which is not the operation of the whole, even as a soldier in an army has an operation which is not that of the whole army. Nevertheless, the whole itself also has an operation which does not belong to any of the parts, but to the whole, as a battle belongs to the whole army, and as the rowing of a ship is an operation of the multitude of the oarsmen. Now there is a kind of whole which has unity not only by order but by composition or connection, or even by continuity, according to which unity it is, in the strict sense of the term, one thing; and in this kind of whole there is no operation of the part which is not that of the whole. For in continuous things, the movement of the whole and of the part is the same; and likewise in things composed or connected the operation of the part is, in principle, that of the whole; and therefore it is fitting that consideration of such wholes and consideration of their parts should belong to the same science. However, it does not belong to the same science to consider the whole which has only the unity of order and to consider its parts. Thence it follows that moral philosophy has three subdivisions. . . .

James of Viterbo

[The following selection is from the *De Regimine Christiano*, pt. 1, ch. 3.]

CHAPTER III. *That the kingdom of the church is one, and in what way, and through what*

Now it ought first to be shown that the kingdom of the church is one. And this is evident from the fact that every multitude participates, in some way, in a unity; otherwise, as the philosophers prove, the multitude itself would be confused and distracted. Thus the blessed Dionysius [Pseudo-Dionysius], in the last chapter of his *Concerning the Divine Names*, says that there is no multitude that does not, in some way, participate in unity; but what are many in parts are one in the whole; what are many in accidents are one in substance; what are many in species are one in genus; what are many in processes are one in principle. The church, in truth, is a certain multitude of many persons: therefore it necessarily must in some way be one, as the very word *ecclesia* implies. For *ecclesia* means 'a convocation': that is, a calling of many to one and into one. Also, the church is a community, as was said above. Now unity is of the essence of any community, otherwise it would not be a community. Further, there is greater agreement among creatures possessed of intellect than among the parts of the universe, which includes both corporal and spiritual things; yet the whole universe, which comprehends so many diverse things in one, is one kingdom of one prince, God. Thus even more will the church, which contains only rational or intellectual beings, be one.

Now, we should further consider through what and in what way the church is said to be one. And on this point we must first notice the difference between 'unity' and 'union,' and, likewise, between 'one' and 'united.' For unity excludes multiplicity; union, however, is found in a multitude. Thus the term 'one' is properly applied to that in which there is no multiplicity, and that which comprehends many things is said to be 'united.' Therefore, since the church is a multitude, it is more properly called 'united' than 'one,' and its connection is more properly called 'union' than 'unity'; yet in the common usage of speech and in the Scripture the one term is indifferently used for the other, and thus they are to be used indifferently. In this treatise, therefore, whether we use the term 'one' or the term 'united,' we must see through what the ecclesiastical multitude has its unity or union.

And if we inquire what is the formal cause of its unity, the answer is that the church is one through the three virtues, faith, hope, and charity, as will appear below. If, however, we ask what is the efficient cause, the answer is that the unity of the church is derived from the whole Trinity together as its efficient principle: that is, from the Father, the Son, and the Holy Spirit. But sometimes this unity is attributed to diverse Persons, for diverse reasons. For it is sometimes attributed to the Father, for the reason that He is the principle of the whole Godhead, and unity has the nature of a principle. . . . Sometimes, however, it is attributed to the Son on account of the nature which He assumed, in accordance with which it is particularly suitable for Him to be the Head of the church as a community of men: specifically, because of conformity of nature; for from the head is derived the unity of the members. . . . Sometimes, moreover, it is attributed to the Holy Spirit, Who is love; for union is especially appropriate to love. . . .

Having seen what causes the union of the church, we must next discover the mode of its union or unity. Now the church cannot be called one as a man is called one, by unity of subject and of person, unless perhaps by analogy, because, even as the many members of a body are one body, so the many believers are one church. Nor can it be called one in accordance with the unity of the nature of the species, because the church includes not only men but also angels, who differ from men in species—although in this work we intend to discuss the church in the narrower sense as the congregation of faithful men who are called the church militant. But the church is called one by collection, even as many men are one people.

Now, to show more fully the way in which the church is said to be one, we can ascribe to it a triple mode of unity, according to which it is called one.

For, in the first place, it is called one through the unity of wholeness. For the church is like one whole whose parts are individual believers; particular churches or special colleges are also said to be its parts. For likewise in the natural body, by analogy to which the church is called a mystic body, some members are divisible and are divided into other lesser members, as the hand into fingers and the fingers into joints; some members, however, are indivisible and are not divided into other members: for instance, the joints. Similarly, certain members of the church are divisible: the particular churches and colleges; some are indivisible: the single believers. Therefore, the church is one, as one whole constituted from many parts and one body composed of many members. However, it differs from a natural body in this respect: the members of a natural body co-exist all at the same time, but the members of the church do not all exist at the same time, but daily and successively some members are generated, while the number of the sons of the church increases.

Secondly, the church is called one through the unity of a common form, because in all the parts and members of the church there is something in respect of which they resemble and conform to one another. Now this conformity of the church is not a matter of genus or species, because that kind of conformity is found among those who are outside the church as well as in those who belong to the church. But it is found in the gifts of grace, because we find among the members of the church conformity in regard to that through which they become and are called members of the church. Moreover, one is said to be a member of the church not by reason of nature but by reason of grace, there being presupposed, however, a nature which is capable of grace, as is the rational or intellectual nature. Therefore, in respect of the gifts of grace the members of the church have a common form with one another, and by that conformity of the church they are called one. For conformity is a kind of unity. Moreover, these gifts of grace, in which the members of the church share a common form, are faith, hope, and charity, and the works that proceed therefrom. And through this fact the church is described as formally one, since these gifts of grace exist in the faithful themselves as certain spiritual perfections and forms. . . .

Thirdly, the church is said to be one through the unity of attribution. For all the faithful have attribution to one end, which is salvation and eternal beatitude, and to one Principle and Head, which is the whole Trinity in accordance with the nature of Their influence, but especially to the Man Christ, in accordance with the relationship between nature and grace. For God gave Him to be Head over all the church, which is His body. . . .

. . . . We must also consider that the diversity that appears in the church is no impediment to its unity. To elaborate this further, it should be pointed out that in the church there are three general types of diversity. One is the diversity of condition, inasmuch as some are more perfect than others and stronger in merit. To this diversity belongs the inequality of grace and of virtues in various members, which is followed by inequality of rewards, of which the Lord says, 'In My Father's house are many mansions' [John 14:2], and the apostle says that star differs from star in brightness [I Cor. 15:41]. To this diversity it belongs that some are called beginners, some proficient, and some perfected.

Another is the diversity of offices, which is seen in the fact that different persons are assigned to different offices. According to Isidore, the word 'office' is derived from 'efficiendo.' For each and every person has his own appropriate function. To this diversity belongs the diversity of gifts, through which men are qualified for particular offices. Of this diversity the apostle says in Romans 12: [6], 'Having different gifts according to the grace which is given us,' etc., and in the Psalms [48:13] it is said, 'Distribute His houses,' which the Gloss interprets to mean, 'Distribute diverse offices.'

The third is the diversity of rank, in accordance with which certain persons are superior to others in the same condition or office.

Now this threefold diversity is related to three things, as the doctors teach. First, it belongs to the perfection of the church itself. For, even as to the perfection of the universe there belongs a plurality and variety of perfections, as the goodness of God is multiply and variously manifested in things, so to the perfection of the church there belongs the diversity we have described. Wherefore the apostle says in Ephesians

[4:11], 'He gave some to be apostles, some prophets, some evangelists, others pastors and teachers, for the consummation of the saints—that is, for their perfecting,—for the work of the ministry, and for the edification of the body of Christ.'

Secondly, it belongs to the necessity of the functions that exist in the church. For it is necessary that particular men be assigned to particular functions, that they may be carried out expeditiously and without confusion; even as in the body diverse members are necessary for diverse functions. Whence the apostle says [Romans 12:14], 'Even as we have many members in one body, and all members have not the same office,' etc.

Thirdly, it belongs to the dignity and beauty of the church, which consists in a certain order, for it is order that makes beauty and loveliness and adornment. Moreover, order requires diversity. But, as has been said, the diversity which is found in the church does not impede or detract from the unity of the church; rather the unity of the church needs such diversity, since it is the unity of an ordained and perfect multitude. Moreover, order and perfection require such diversity, as appears from what has been said. Thus from these considerations we can infer another twofold mode of unity, in accordance with which the church is said to be one. For it is said to be one because of its perfection, for, according to the Philosopher, perfection is a kind of unity, inasmuch as that which is perfect is called one. For this reason, in the Canticle [6:8], after Solomon has said of the church, 'One is my dove,' he adds, 'my perfect one.' Also, the church is called one because of its order, even as the universe itself is called one in accordance with a unity of order. For order itself connects the church and conserves its unity. Whence in the Decretum, [c. 7], di. 89, it is said that no corporate body can exist unless it be preserved by a great order of difference. Whence it appears that when we say that the church is a kingdom and is called one, we imply another condition: namely, that it be ordained. For, even as the universe is called ordained, because there is in it an order of those that generate and those that are generated, of movers and movables, of causes and things caused, so the church is ordained, because there is in it an order of preachers and hearers, of those who preside and those who are subject, and so on, through the other orders of the church.

It ought also to be considered that, even as the diversity of offices, conditions, and ranks does not destroy the unity of the church, so also the diversity of customs and rituals which is found in the diverse churches does not prejudice it. For in regard to those things that are necessary for salvation the church has a common custom and ritual; in others, however, there can be diverse customs and various observances which detract in no way from the unity of the church and may even be laudable.

Therefore, the ecclesiastical community is one; and when the Lord wished to show its unity He set one man at the head of the church: namely, Peter. Outside this unity of the church neither grace, nor remission of sins, nor spiritual life can be attained. And outside the unity of the church neither the receiving of the sacraments nor any other act can avail at all for eternal salvation. For even as there can be no health and life in a member unless it move within the unity of the body, so true health and life can not extend to anyone unless he be within the unity of the church. . . . Nevertheless, even as sometimes a withered limb is joined to a body, by continuity but not by influx of virtue, so there are some who by continuity of external converse are united to the church but do not receive an influx of salvation and life from Christ the Head and from its members. . . .

Marsiglio of Padua

[In the *Defensor Pacis* one finds both frequent comparisons of the state to a living organism and an emphatic assertion that the unity of the state is merely a unity of order based on its relationship to a single ruler. The passages translated below are from *dictio* I, ch. 2, sec. 3, and ch. 17, secs. 2–12. In regard to the latter passage I may add that Marsiglio's style, clumsy at best, is particularly inadequate to the technicalities of metaphysical analysis; I have given as literal a translation as possible, attempting to convey his general meaning intelligibly while resisting the temptation to improve the structure of his sentences and the precision of his definitions.]

CHAPTER II

3. Since we should describe tranquillity and its opposite, let us agree with Aristotle in I *Politics*, ch. 5, and VI *Politics*, ch. 4, that the state is like a kind of animate or animal nature. For, even as an animal that

is well disposed in accordance with nature is composed of certain proportionate parts ordained to one another, which communicate their
actions mutually to one another and to the whole, so a state that is well
disposed and instituted in accordance with reason is constituted in a
similar way. Therefore, what health is to an animal and its parts, tranquillity, it seems, is to the city or kingdom and its parts. We can accept
this inference as correct because of what all men understand in regard
to both. For they think that health is the best disposition of the animal
in accordance with nature, and, likewise, that tranquillity is the best
disposition of a state instituted in accordance with reason. Now health,
as learned physicians define it, is that good disposition of an animal by
which each of its parts can perfectly perform the function appropriate
to its nature; and according to this analogy tranquillity will be that
good disposition of a city or kingdom by which each of its parts can
perfectly perform the functions suitable to it, in accordance with
reason and its institution. And, because in a good definition the
opposite is also defined, intranquillity will be that evil disposition of a
city or kingdom, like the sickness of an animal, in which all or some
of its parts are hindered from doing their appropriate work, either
absolutely or in relation to the others.

CHAPTER XVII

2. Moreover, I say that the supreme government will necessarily be
one in number, not plural, if the kingdom or city is to be rightly
disposed. And I say the same concerning the ruler of the principate:
not, indeed, that the ruler must be a single human being, but that the
office of the ruler must be one. For there is a kind of principate,
numerically one, supreme and well tempered, in which several men
rule as one: as in the case of the aristocracy and the polity. . . . Yet these
several men are numerically one principate in regard to their office
because of the numerical unity of every action that proceeds from
them, whether judgment, decision, or command; for such actions
cannot proceed from any one of them by himself, but from the common decision and consent of them all, or of their more weighty part,
in accordance with the laws established for these matters. And because
of the numerical unity of the action which proceeds from them, such a
principate is, and is called, numerically one, whether one man or several
rule. Such unity of action is, however, not required of any of the other

offices or parts of the state, for in them a plurality of actions, either similar or diverse in kind, can and should proceed from their various members individually. For such unity of action among them would be unbearable and injurious to the community and to individuals.

3. Having made it clear how the numerical unity of the government or the ruler should be understood, we wish next to prove that either there should be only one principate or ruler in a state or that, if there are several, the highest of all should be numerically only one and not multiple. And our first proof goes as follows: if there were more than one principate in a city or kingdom, and if these were not reduced or subordinated under some one supreme principate, the judgment, command, and execution of just and beneficial things would be defective; and thence, on account of the unpunished injustices of men, there would ultimately arise strife and the dissolution and destruction of the city or kingdom. Now such a result would be an evil utterly to be avoided, and it can be manifestly shown that this would be the result of the foregoing condition: namely, a plurality of governments.

7. Again, if there were such a plurality of governments, no kingdom or city would be one. For kingdoms and cities are, and are called, one because of the unity of the principate, to which and by which the other parts of the state are all ordained, as will appear later. And, again, there would be no order of the parts of the city or kingdom, since they would be ordained to no head, and none would be held subject . . . , and there would be confusion among the parts and in the whole state, since each would choose for himself whatever office or offices he wished, when no one regulated or defined such things. . . .

8. Further, even as in an animal composed of many parts there is one first principle that rules him and moves him from place to place, as [Aristotle says] in the book, *Concerning the Movement of Animals*, because if there were many principles commanding contrary or different things at the same time, the animal would necessarily either go in opposite directions or be completely at a standstill, and thus would be unable to obtain the necessary or useful things which are sought through movement: so it is in the well-ordered state, which, as we have said, is analogous to an animal well formed by nature. . . .

9. Further, since 'art perfects those things that nature cannot perform, but imitates others,' as is written in Book II of the *Physics* [of Aristotle, ch. 8], and since in nature the prime ruler of beings is

numerically one, not plural, because 'beings do not wish to be ill-disposed,' as we read in Book XII of the *Metaphysics* [of Aristotle, ch. 10], therefore the chief principate instituted by the reason and art of men will be numerically only one. And, aside from rational proof, common experience shows this to be expedient and necessary, since whenever unity of government has been lacking in any place or country or congregation of men it has seemed impossible for it to be well disposed. . . .

10. Now, whether it is suitable to have a single supreme principate for the whole body of those who live civilly on earth, or whether in the different regions of this earth, necessarily separate in location, and especially among those who do not share the same language and who differ in manners and customs, it is suitable to have different principates at the same time—which is perhaps the result of a celestial cause, to prevent over-population—is a question capable of rational investigation, but remote from our present interest. Perhaps it may seem to some that nature, through wars and epidemics, has checked the propagation of men and of other animals, so that the land may suffice for their rearing. . . .

11. Returning, however, to the subject under discussion, let us say that it now becomes somewhat apparent what the numerical unity of a city or kingdom is. For this unity is a unity of order: not unity in the strict sense, but a plurality of persons which is called one, or who are called one, not because they are one in number formally, through some form, but because they are ordained to something which is numerically one, namely, the principate, to which and by which they are ordained and governed. For a city or kingdom is not one through any unitary natural form, as the form of a composite or mixture, because its parts or offices, and the subjects or parts of these parts, are many entities, formally distinct from one another, separated both in place and in subject. Thus they are not a unity either through any one form inherent in them, or through any one thing permeating them or containing them like a wall. For Rome and Maguntia and the rest of the communities are numerically one kingdom or empire, but not otherwise than as they are all ordained, through their will, to a single supreme principate. In a similar way, the world also is called numerically one world, not plural, yet not because of any numerical unity formally inherent in all beings, but all beings are called one world because of

the numerical unity of the prime being, since each being is naturally inclined by and depends on the prime being. Thus the predication by which all beings are said to be one world is not because of the oneness of any numerical unity formally in them all, nor of any universal; but a plurality of things is called one because it is ordained to one and by one. So also the men of one city or country are called one city or kingdom, because they will a single principate.

12. However, the unity of any part of the state is not derived from the same cause as the unity of the city or kingdom, since, although the members of the various parts agree in willing a single principate, and therefore are called one city or one kingdom, yet they are related to this one principate by the different institutions which act upon them and which are the different commands transmitted to them by the prince, through which different men are appointed to different offices. And it is this diversity of commands that formally makes them diverse parts and offices of the state. Moreover, each office is called one office and one part of the state, regardless of the numerical plurality of the subjects within it: not indeed because of a numerical unity inhering in them, but because they are related to a single command of the ruler, which acts on them in accordance with the determination of the laws.

Guido Vernani

[The following selection is from a short treatise, *De Reprobatione Monarchiae compositae a Dante Alighiero Florentino*, written in 1327 by a Dominican friar, Guido Vernani, and dedicated to the chancellor of the commune of Bologna, who was an ardent partisan of Dante. Very little is known of its author. He was born in Rimini; he also wrote another short treatise, *De Potestate Summi Pontificis*, supporting the doctrine of papal supremacy over both spirituals and temporals; quotations in both treatises demonstrate that he was well-versed in theological studies in the Dominican tradition: in particular, he quotes frequently from Augustine, Aristotle, and Aquinas. The text below has been translated from an edition of Guido's two works printed at Cologne in 1746, pp. 9–13, and compared with the text ed. Jarro (Florence, 1906).]

. . . . That book, moreover, is principally divided into three parts, in the first of which he attempts to prove that for the well-being of the world a monarchy is required: that is, a single prince and a single principate. Now, although this has some truth, yet in proving it he introduces many errors. For he proceeds by arguing that the ends of parts differ among themselves and also differ from the end of the whole: for example, there is one end of the eye, namely, to see colours and to direct those who walk, and another end of the ear, namely to discern sounds; these ends differ from the end of the individual man, of whom these parts are natural potencies. But what the end of a man is, he does not explain. Whence he says that even as the end of a part of a man is other than the end of a whole man, so the end of one man is other than and different from the end of the whole human race, since one individual man is a part of the whole multitude.

But this is manifestly false, as is proved by authorities, arguments, and examples. For Aristotle in VII *Politics*, in the chapter beginning 'Whether, moreover' [ch. 2], plainly says that the felicity of one man and of a whole state is the same, and says that everybody agrees to this: for those who say that the individual man is happy because of riches say that the state, if it were rich, would be happy; likewise, those who say that a tyrant is happy on account of his rule say also that the state which rules several is happy; and if they say that the happiness of the individual is based on virtue, they say also that a virtuous state is happy. Therefore there is not one end of the individual man and another of the whole human race. Augustine says the same thing in *The City of God*, bk. 1, ch. 15, where he says as follows: 'The city is not blessed in any other way than the individual, since a city is nothing else than a concordant multitude of men.' From which it appears, since beatitude is the last end, that there is no difference between the ultimate ends of the individual and of all mankind. And this may be proved by pointing out that God, the creator of all things, Who in His eternal wisdom made all things, 'disposed all things in number, measure, and weight' (Wisdom 2:21), explaining which saying Augustine says in his *Concerning Genesis*, bk. 4, ch. 3, that 'the measure of everything refers to mode, and the number of everything refers to species, and weight brings everything to quiet and stability.' Therefore, even as everything in its species has a limited and terminated nature, wherefore the definition of a thing is called the term for it, so it has an inclination to a fixed end and terminus, that in that end it may come to rest and be quiet, and this inclination in bodies is called weight, whence gravity in the earth and in earthly bodies draws them downward, but levity draws the fire upward. But in spiritual beings that inclination is love, whence Augustine says in *The City of God*, bk. 2, ch. 28, 'The masses of the weights of bodies are like love, whether they strive downward by gravity or upward by levity. For as the soul is pulled by love, so the body is pulled by its weight.' Moreover, even as all heavy things are naturally moved to the centre by their gravity, so that there is not one centre for all heavy things and another for one single heavy body, so there is no other end for the individual man than for the whole human race. And thus all men generally and each man individually desire the same last end, namely, beatitude. Moreover, the beatitude that terminates the rational desire is none other than the vision and enjoyment of the highest truth and of the highest goodness; and therefore the human heart can rest in no created thing. . . . And if some say that there can be a political beatitude in this life which consists in the operation of the moral virtues, let them hear Augustine in *The City of God* saying that 'there is no one who can adequately tell the miseries of this world, in which no beatitude is possible.' And there he says that 'moral virtue fights a perpetual war with the vices in this life.' Far be it from us, so long as we are in this war, to call ourselves blessed!

Moreover, the argument from the diversity of parts avails nothing, since the parts of a man are different in species from one another, as the hand from the foot and the eye from the ear. Not thus, however, differs man from man. Whence the ultimate end of one man does not differ from the ultimate end of another man, nor from the ultimate end of the whole human race. Whence it appears that the writer shamefully erred through the fallacy of equivocation, because the nature of an integral part, such as are the eyes and hands in respect of a man, differs from the nature of a subjective part, such as are Peter and Paul in respect of all mankind. Moreover, it should be noted that the diverse beatitudes of diverse men, such as Peter and Paul, differ indeed in number but do not differ in species nor in regard to the object which is the supreme good for all.

John of Turrecremata

[John of Turrecremata was born in Valladolid in 1388 and began his education there. He entered the Dominican order while still very young and became noted for his learning. He accompanied his general to the Council of Constance in 1415. Later, he studied at Paris and received his doctorate in 1423. In 1431, he was made Master of the Holy Palace by Eugenius IV. His able support of the papal cause at the Council of Basel won him a cardinalate in 1439. He died in 1468.

He was the author of several theological and legal works, but his most important writing was his *Summa contra Ecclesie et Primatus Apostoli Adversarios*. Directed particularly against the heresies of Wyclif and Hus and the radical constitutional principles of the conciliarists, and defending in the strongest terms the thesis of illimitable papal supremacy over the church, it may be taken as the most authoritative statement of the principles of the papalist reaction of the fifteenth century. But it is not mere polemic. In its comprehensive scope, in its assured and effective scholarship, in its firm articulation and sharp, clean argument, it can also be taken as worthily representing the culmination of the dominant trend of medieval thought on the nature and structure of the church.

The selection translated below is taken from book 2, ch. 71. I have used the edition printed at Rome in 1489. Turrecremata's definition of the unity of the church is a premise for a series of conclusions directed against the conciliarist view of the whole church as the subject of ecclesiastical power. The thought of the leading conciliarists was founded in a nominalism which required an even more individualistic conception of the church than did Aquinas's moderate realism: the power which they claimed for the eclesiastical community was conceived as vested in 'all taken collectively.' Turrecremata's argument (see pp. 425–429 below) aimed to reduce this idea to an absurdity.]

. . . . Fourthly, it is to be noted that, although the mystic body of the church somewhat resembles the natural body of a man, specifically, in the multiplicity of its members, and in a kind of union binding them to one another, and in the diversity of their offices, in accordance with the saying of the Apostle in Romans 12: [4, 5], 'Even as we have many members in one body, so we, being many, are one body in Christ, and all are members one of another,' nevertheless there are many differences and dissimilarities. One is that, as St. Thomas says in Part III [of the *Commentary on the Sentences*, di. 13, q. 2, a. 2], the members of the natural body are all members at the same time, but the members of the mystic body are not all members at the same time, either in regard to natural existence, since the body of the church is composed of men who exist at various times from the beginning to the end of the world, or in regard to existence in grace, since, even among those who exist at the same time, some lack grace while others already have it. The second difference is that members of the human body constitute a real whole, numerically one, which, subjectively in itself as a whole, is capable of receiving a form, or character, or real influx; and this whole is the human body itself. Not so, however, are the so-called members of the mystic body, since although the faithful are, as Augustine says, united by faith, hope, and charity, yet, since they are distinguished in person and place, they are not said to constitute a real whole, numerically one, which subjectively in itself is capable of receiving a form, or character, or any influx of a real effect. Therefore, when the church is called one by the unity of faith, hope, and charity, it ought not to be understood that the character, numerically one, of faith; the character, numerically one, of hope; the character, numerically one, of charity is in that whole body itself, since the body of the church cannot itself be the subject of such forms, whence also the jurists say that a corporation has no soul . . . ; but there are as many numerically distinct characters of the virtues of faith, hope, and charity as there are believers. Therefore, when one says, 'one faith of the church, one hope, one charity,' the unity is not with respect to a single subject of these characters, since no such subject exists, but with respect to the object, since all the faithful who are deservedly reckoned in the body of the church believe the same thing, hope the same thing, love the same thing. Thus says St. Thomas in Part III, distinction 13. Through this consideration, it is clear, many fantasies of adversaries, innovators, masters, doctors, and canonists vanish. . . .

Chapter Five

THE STRUCTURE OF GOVERNMENT
IN THE STATE

EDIEVAL thought on the structure of government re-
volved, from the beginning, around the figure of the
king. The medieval preference for monarchic government was, of course, primarily the result of the historic fact that
monarchy actually was under medieval circumstances, for large territorial units, the only form of government. It was for centuries the only
alternative to chaos, and, on the whole, justified itself by its fruits. It
enjoyed, moreover, the prestige of old tradition and the sanction, as
countless Scriptural passages testified, of divine approval. Thus the
desirability of kingship was almost an axiom for the medieval mind.
Systematic defences of government by a single man appeared in
medieval political theory only after the study of Aristotle had
acquainted philosophers with arguments for alternative forms of
power and challenged them to a rational justification of their familiar
convictions. But while medieval thought was oriented toward kingship from the beginning, the content and boundaries of royal power
and the relations of the king to the community and to other wielders of
public authority were clarified only as the result of a slow and painful process of experience and reflection.

In early medieval thought,[1] the relation of the king to the kingdom
was ambiguous. If his position was considered in terms of feudalism,
then the kingdom was dissolved into the feudal hierarchy. Of that
hierarchy the king was unquestionably the apex: the supreme lord,

sovereign in the sense that he had no human superior. But he was enmeshed in the hierarchy; for every vassal was in a sense the peer of his lord, bound to him in a mutual contract which could be enforced through the collective judgment of the vassals in the court of the lord or if necessary by armed revolt.

But the king could also be considered supreme in a different sense, which tended to lift him above his kingdom and relate him to the entire body of subjects as their ruler. The teachings of religion, classical influences, and the long tradition of Germanic kingship favoured this interpretation, which ultimately triumphed over the more personal feudal concept. These traditions in turn carried with them a miscellany of special ideas which were only gradually reconciled with one another. The king was conceived as judge and protector of the kingdom, a trustee for its interests, endowed from above with authority over it. He was also conceived to represent it, in the original medieval sense of the term; that is, he acted on its behalf. And finally, though he ruled the kingdom and in a sense was the kingdom, he was also its servant, for his power was granted him for its advantage rather than his own.

The fundamental law belonged to the community, and the kingship belonged to the community. Thus the community had collective rights not absorbed by the kingship: it had the right to participate in the formal definition of law and in the choice or deposition of the king. But these rights of the community lacked regular institutional forms for their expression, and tended either to lapse or to be exercised by miscellaneous private individuals. Deposition became scarcely distinguishable from feudal insurrection. Succession became gradually hereditary in England and France and the right of election in the Empire was confined to a few great lords. The king's great council of vassals exercised the community's role in the promulgation of law. The right—or duty—of performing these essentially public functions thus became a matter of personal status and personal power; yet the magnates involved were always dimly felt to represent the community.

Scarcely more clear than the relationship between king and kingdom was the content of royal authority. Theory was not at all precise; fact was constantly changing and rarely reached the boundaries theory sketched. But it is possible to make a few generalizations.

The king was expected to enforce the law of the land, administer justice, maintain peace and order, defend the land against external and internal foes. In modern language, his role was essentially judicial and administrative; but that role was far less mechanical, far more creative, than these terms often imply. The law which he enforced had to be 'found,' defined, and promulgated; it had to be adjusted to constantly changing circumstances through supplementary decrees. The machinery of justice and peace had to be gradually built up out of practically nothing. The maintenance of public order with inadequate personnel and finance, embryonic rules of procedure, and uncertain cooperation from the subjects necessarily involved a constant choice between alternative objectives and methods, which amounted to the making of vital policy. The prince's opportunities for initiative in government, even within the framework of a relatively rigid customary law, are vividly illustrated in the actual careers of rulers who took their duties seriously and were generally regarded as satisfactory kings: Henry II of England, for example, or Louis IX of France.[2]

On the other hand, the common thought of the early Middle Ages sternly marked off certain areas as immune from the ruler's normal interference. In the relation of the king to customary law were to be found the principles which limited his power. The king, as Bracton put it, must be under the law 'because the law makes the king.' 'The king ... can do nothing on earth which is not according to law.'[3] The terms of the earliest coronation oaths stressed this relationship.[4] Public opinion, quick to resent a breach of ancient custom, strove to enforce it.

The limitation of the king by customary law meant, in the first place, that the king had no right to alter its basic principles, though he was expected to enforce them and supplement them by executive legislation. In practice, of course, enforcement might gradually alter the law. In the terms of promulgation, in the emphases of administrative action, in the decisions of royal courts, there was involved at the very least a choice among customs and not infrequently an interpretation that amounted to a permanent modification. The development of the English common law out of a vast variety of local customs is a striking illustration of the degree of change that could be made in this indirect way. But this path was uncharted by theory. In principle, the often-quoted rule of St. Augustine was maintained: 'It is not for kings to judge of the law, but according to the law.'[5]

As the king could not alter the law, so his authority did not extend to the violation of the rights which the law protected. The property of his subjects and all the attributes of status which medieval thought conceived as property were outside his competence, except as the forfeiture of such rights might be imposed as a penalty in the exercise of jurisdiction. The immunity of property rights from royal infringement meant that the king had no power to tax at will. The king was expected to 'live of his own,' and it was assumed that his private revenues from his domain, plus the incidental perquisites of government and such taxes as had become customary, would be adequate for the support of his government. If they were not, then any further revenues could be properly secured only by the voluntary grant of those who would pay.

The problem of the relation of the king to the property of his subjects was at first complicated by the fact that many functions we would label governmental had passed, through infeudation, into the category of private rights. Popular resistance to royal infringements on property meant that the early recovery of governmental functions from private hands often had to proceed indirectly. Moreover, even agencies created by the king might, in the course of a few generations, come to be conceived as the property of the holders and thus protected by custom from royal interference. Or, as particularly occurred in the empire, the demands of greedy magnates might force the fresh infeudation of jurisdictional rights which the ruler had recovered with difficulty. But the dominant tendency even in early medieval political theory was to sharpen the distinction between property and government and to insist that government must be concentrated in the single figure of the king.

The history of the medieval development of systematic thought on the structure of authority is the history of the development of these basic and characteristically medieval ideas. But that development was profoundly affected by other influences. In general, the study of Roman law worked to strengthen the distinction between private rights and public authority and to elevate the position of the king as the single holder of all public power. It introduced the idea that human law proceeded from the ruler's authoritative will and the idea that the prince himself was in some sense 'released from the laws.'[6] On the other hand, in its concepts of natural law and the law of peoples, it introduced principles for the potential limitation of the ruler more solidly based than mere customary right; and in coupling the notion of the legislative supremacy of the emperor with the idea that his authority had been originally granted him by the people, it laid foundations for an ultimate construction of all royal authority as representative and delegated. In the medieval history of the famous passage, 'What has pleased the prince has the force of law, because by the *lex regia* the people has transferred to him all its command and authority,'[7] the first clause had the more immediate and conspicuous impact, but the influence of the second was, in the long run, more powerful and more enduring.

Second only to the influence of Roman law was the influence of Aristotle. As we have seen,[8] his conception of the positive role of government potentially expanded medieval thought on the proper scope of the ruler's authority. He also offered to medieval thought his own classification of types of government[9]—not too clear, and quite remote from medieval patterns, but none the less to be coped with. His arguments in defence and criticism of each type, his preference for the mixed 'polity,' his thesis that the government of laws was preferable to that of man, and his counterbalancing insistence on the role of equity in modifying the application of laws all played their part in medieval theory.

The developing philosophical and legal speculation of the Middle Ages had to use these materials from alien cultures to guide it in interpreting, systematizing, and evaluating familiar institutions. The process involved inevitable difficulties: a good deal of medieval political writing seems often to have been quite oblivious of medieval political fact and, on the other hand, many of the concepts of the ancient *polis* and the ancient empire were unrecognizably distorted in the attempt to fit them to medieval institutions. Moreover, as medieval institutions themselves developed, they demanded new formulations and new interpretations of the classical terms.

In the formal theory of the twelfth and thirteenth centuries, the idea that jurisdiction and government must be gathered into the hands of the monarch developed slowly and unevenly. The world reflected in Beaumanoir's thirteenth-century *Coutumes de Beauvaisis* was still a world of independent jurisdictions, in which Beaumanoir struggled to distinguish the king's authority from that of lesser lords: 'Every baron is sovereign in his barony, but it is true that the king is sovereign above all and has by his own right the general care of the kingdom . . . .'[10] But John of Salisbury had already written that, because the prince was responsible for the whole community, 'the power of all his subjects is gathered together in him. . . . The prince is, as some define him, a public power and a certain image of the divine majesty on earth.'[11] And by 1256 Bracton had distinguished between the private rights of the king, which could be freely alienated, and 'the administration of justice and peace, and the things annexed thereto,' which could not be separated from the crown, because 'they make the crown what it is.'[12]

Vaguely and with some inconsistency in the *Policraticus,*[13] more clearly in Bracton's treatise *De Legibus et Consuetudinibus Angliae,* we can see the first pattern of medieval thought on government taking form. The king is under the law and limited by the law; but the machinery of jurisdiction and government must be controlled by his authority alone; he is 'guided solely by the judgment of his own mind.'[14] The juxtaposition of these two principles immediately raised a fundamental problem.

Our modern notion of limited government implies the existence of institutional restraints to prevent the misuse of concentrated power. We take it for granted that the first line of defence against tyranny must be a system of checks and counter-checks within the governmental machinery itself. But up to the early fourteenth century political philosophers increasingly assumed that since the exercise of all public power must be concentrated in the king alone, no institutional means of enforcing his responsibility for its proper exercise would be available. The best legal opinion was moving in the same direction. It seemed impossible to avoid the conclusion that, if the essence of the king's office consisted in his absolute control of the machinery through which the laws were enforced, no one else could use that machinery to enforce the laws against the king. It might seem an abuse that the law courts should be closed to individuals injured by the king[15]; but they were the king's courts, and if he did not choose to be liable in them, the subject had no recourse except a petition to his grace. 'No writ runs against the king,' Bracton discovered. Roman law had described the prince as '*legibus solutus.*' Medieval thought shrank from interpreting the difficult phrase in its apparent literal sense, as if kings could ever be free from their obligation to act in accordance with the laws. But it was evident that the king's subjection to law could be secured only through his voluntary acquiescence in its dictates. 'The prince,' John of Salisbury explained, 'is said to be loosed from the bonds of law, not because unjust deeds are permitted him, but because he ought to be one who cultivates equity from love of justice rather than from fear of punishment.'[16] Bracton drew the same conclusion. 'The king has no peer in his kingdom . . . still less . . . a superior. . . . He ought to be under no man, but under God and under the law.' The king must be subject to the law, 'for there is no king where will rules and not law.'[17] But that subjection could be achieved only through the condescension of the king. '. . . . Lest his power be unbridled, let him put on the bridle of temperance, and the reins of moderation.'[18]

Even while Bracton was asserting the freedom of the king from any human restraint, an older opinion was still maintained by some lawyers: that the court of the king's vassals could, in accordance with the typical feudal practice, do justice between king and subject. Bracton's insistence that 'the king has no peer in his kingdom' was countered by an anonymous interpolator with the statement that the counts and barons of his court were the superiors of the king because they were his partners, and therefore 'if the king be without a bridle . . . they ought to put a bridle on him.'[19] A similar doctrine was expressed by the author of another treatise on English law[20]; and it sounded in *The Song of Lewes*, which was the anthem of the Barons' Revolt of the middle of the century.[21] But this was a dying idea; so long as the rights of the great council were construed in feudal, private-law terms, its claims to judge the king could not easily be harmonized with the developing idea of the king as the supreme bearer of public office. Nor was the great council so closely organized within itself that it could satisfactorily act as bridle to the king. There were indeed in thirteenth-century England several experiments in the bridling of the king by the baronage. But they ran counter to the prevailing trend of theory. Innocent III released John from his oath to maintain Magna Carta because it involved 'a loss of regal right.' Louis IX, acting as arbitrator between king and barons, condemned the Provisions of Oxford (which granted a baronial committee the right to control the appointment of ministers) because the king ought to have 'full power and free government in his realm and in the things pertaining thereto.'[22]

Thus there seemed to be no institutional solution for the paradox that the king was at once bound by law and free from it. Under these circumstances, medieval writers naturally devoted a great deal of energy to an effort to persuade the king to accept voluntarily the bridle that could not be forced upon him—to convince him that, as a famous sentence from the *Corpus Juris* nobly phrased it, 'It is a thing greater than empire that a prince submit his government to the laws.'[23] Much of the formal political theory of the Middle Ages appeared embedded in treatises which were designed primarily to teach a king the duties and inspire him with the ideals appropriate to his position. Elaborate analyses of the kingly virtues, enlivened with examples from sacred and classical history and jewelled with quotations from authoritative writers, appeared in profusion in the Middle Ages and perhaps seemed more impressive to their intended readers than they seem to us.[24]

The most important sanction behind these exhortations was the influence of God, who, as the Scriptures abundantly proved, would not allow tyranny to go unpunished. But if the king refused to bridle himself and God failed to intervene at once, must one simply endure the tyranny? Augustine and Gregory the Great had emphasized the possibility that the wicked king was sent by God as a punishment for human sins, in which case it was one's duty to submit.[25] Echoes of this doctrine continued to sound in medieval writings. But medieval thought, once it had clearly distinguished between the man and the office, was in general reluctant to draw this extreme conclusion from the doctrine that royal power was ordained by God. The very majesty of the true king emphasized the difference between the king and the tyrant, and abuse of power appeared not only cruel to man but blasphemous to God. The Germanic idea of the supremacy of law had long been coupled with the idea of a right of resistance. Later, feudalism had made men familiar with the idea of a contingent authority based on contract, and had justified the withdrawal of allegiance by injured vassals; it had even approved the vassal who took up arms against a lord in defence of his threatened rights. Thus the *diffidatio*, or feudal uprising, was generally regarded as an informal but not illegal means of bringing pressure to bear on the tyrannical king and of protecting legitimate interests from his unhallowed grasp.[26]

Even the assassination of the tyrant met with some approval. Scriptural and classical examples had shown tyrannicide in a favourable light and suggested that assassination was the normal conclusion of a tyrannical career. John of Salisbury's defence of tyrannicide may seem at first glance inconsistent, since he stressed the doctrine that the king was responsible to God alone. His glorification of the king as vicar of God and the holder of all public power made it impossible for him to conceive of any public action against the king. But his insistence that those who suffered under tyranny must wait for divine justice was entirely consistent with his praise of tyrannicide, since he regarded the assassin as the agent, not of an outraged community, but of an avenging God.

In the recognition of insurrection and tyrannicide as rightful sanctions against a ruler, medieval political thought faced and accepted the fact that the ultimate judge of the legitimacy of authority must be the conscience of private individuals. This doctrine was not incompatible with the doctrine of the absolutism of the king. The man who took up arms against a tyrant did not act as a political sovereign or as an officer endowed with public power, but as a private individual whose rights had been violated by one against whom he had no recourse but self-help. He was justified not by a superior authority in himself but by a deficiency of authority in the ruler. The whole position was based on the assumption of the supremacy of law to any human authority and the further assumption that the precepts of that law 'were definite and uniform and were as accessible to private persons as to officials.'27 Granted these assumptions, the problem of the use of private sanctions against the ruler could, as Aquinas was soon to suggest, be debated only in terms of expediency. And in an age in which a state of insurrection was not totally dissimilar from a normal state of peace, the argument of expediency did not point decisively toward a duty of submission.

In Aquinas's political theory, the location of authority was rather a *datum* than a conclusion; he was much more interested in its use. There are, accordingly, many ambiguities in his comments on desirable types of government. But his thought seems to have developed on the characteristic medieval framework, with modifications due to his philosophic approach or the influences—not easily harmonized—of Roman law and Aristotle. In his treatise on law in the *Summa Theologiae*, he pointed out that coercive authority might be located either in the community as a whole or in 'the public person who has the care of the multitude.'[28] Both in the treatise on law and in the *De Regimine Principum*, he recognized the historical existence and the possible legitimacy of states in which the authority to make the civil law by enactment and by custom and to govern themselves by magistrates whom they elected and could depose belonged to the people.[29] But he nowhere elaborated the plan of such a state; his illustrations of it were taken from ancient times, and in particular from Rome; at one point he suggested that such a constitution was possible and desirable only under special circumstances.[30] In another passage in the *Summa*,[31] he defended the constitution recommended to the Israelites in the Old Testament[32] as the best, on the rather surprising grounds that it was a mixture of Aristotle's three best forms: monarchic because 'Moses and his successors governed the people as single rulers,' aristocratic because they were assisted by 'wise and noble men,' democratic because the aristocracy was chosen by election. This commendation of 'mixed' government was to be influential in the later Middle Ages, and some modern commentators have made much of it as representing Aquinas's own preference. But there is no allusion to this scheme anywhere else in his writings, and its unique appearance can easily be accounted for as an exegetical expedient. In another context, he commended as 'the best' another kind of mixture, implied in Isidore's definition of law as 'what the nobles together with the people have sanctioned.'[33] Finally, in the *De Regimine Principum* he argued that government by one man was the best.[34]

Aquinas's defence of rule by one man, though supported by analogies from the natural universe and the human body, consisted essentially in the proposition that unity of decision could proceed only from unity of will, and that unity of will could be most securely attained by focusing the power of decision in one person. He recognized the force of Aristotle's argument that concentration of authority might facilitate a transition to tyranny. But he was apparently more willing to run the risk of tyranny than the risk of deadlock, confusion, and civil strife, which seemed to him (and medieval experience at that time would have supported his belief) the probable results of locating authority in a democratic or aristocratic group. He also believed that 'tyranny more often results from the rule of many than from the rule of one.'[35]

In spite of his expressed preference for one-man rule, Aquinas suggested in the *De Regimine Principum*[36] that 'the government of the kingdom ought to be so ordered that the opportunity of tyranny is taken away from the king when he is instituted. And at the same time his power should be tempered, so that he cannot easily fall into tyranny. The things to be done will be considered later.' Since he never finished the book, Aquinas never developed this idea—a fact which has not prevented some modern commentators from assuming that he was on the verge of proposing a modern type of constitutional government in which other governmental institutions with independent power would act as a check upon the king.[37] Such an interpretation would directly conflict with his insistence on unity. The passage just quoted was immediately followed by a discussion of what should be done if the king should nevertheless lapse into tyranny. For this Aquinas offered two remedies, both illustrated by examples from ancient history: if the people had the right to provide themselves with a ruler, they might appropriately overthrow him; if the ruler was given them by some superior, they might appeal to that superior for action;[38] if neither of these conditions prevailed, there was no recourse except to God. If, even for the ultimate crisis, Aquinas had no notion of any regular institutions through which the community could act upon the tyrant, it would seem that his 'tempering' of the royal government, whatever it might imply, could not consistently have implied the provision of other organs with public authority for the continuous bridling of the king. Aquinas might have been thinking of advisory councils; the safest guess, perhaps, is that he was thinking, as he characteristically did, of constitutional principles rather than constitutional machinery: royal authority should be ordered and tempered by a recognition of limits on its rightful scope.[39]

Among all the uncertainties of Aquinas's statements on the location of authority, one certainty persistently asserts itself: the necessary cohesion of all aspects of governmental power. The authority to make law is a corollary of the authority to enforce it[40]; 'the interpretation of laws and dispensation from their observance belongs to him who made the law'[41]; a 'free people' with the right of legislation can make and abrogate custom by its own authority, but if the people does not have legislative authority, its customs are valid only through the tolerance of the ruler[42]; 'it pertains to a king to be over all human offices and to direct them through the authority of his rule'[43]; even a qualified right to determine taxes belongs to royal authority.[44] Moreover, the ruler himself is *legibus solutus*, so far as human law is concerned; for, although he can never be released from law as a 'directive force,' in the sense that he should voluntarily conform to its precepts, it has and can have no 'coercive force' against one who himself rightfully controls all the instruments of coercion.[45]

This idea of the necessary unity of authority was in harmony with his view of government in terms of absolute alternatives. In commenting on the opening sentences of Aristotle's *Politics*, he wrote: 'A state may be ruled in two ways: namely, by political or by regal government. Regal government is that in which he who is over the state has plenary power. Moreover, a political government is that in which he who is over the state has a power restricted in accordance with certain laws of the state.'[46] In the systems described in the *Politics* and in the ancient Roman republic, he was acquainted with instances of 'political government'; he recognized its legitimacy, given a people capable of making good use of such freedom; he equally recognized the legitimacy of the Roman empire, in which the pleasure of the prince had the force of law; but for his own day, he regarded regal government as normal and as the best of all forms; and regal government was to him a government of 'plenary power'.

What substantive boundaries might appropriately limit the area of regal absolutism in his thought, it is hard to say. Seeing in the rationality and justice of law its essential claim to validity, he had no final respect for the sanctity of custom as such. Though he included 'the custom of the country' among the circumstances which a wise ruler would take into account in framing his laws and urged that it be not lightly set aside, he clearly expected that human law would change with changing times and with the growth of human wisdom,[47] and thus his theory potentially exposed customary law, except in so far as it embodied the rational principles of the law of peoples, to cautious and occasional legislative modification. Whether or not he was conscious of the fact, the net effect of his system was to weaken the boundary between the law and the king and to substitute general principles of justice and utility for the more definite legal barriers to authority recognized in medieval constitutional practice. Bracton had twisted the maxim, '*Quod principi placuit legis habet vigorem*,' with its reference to the *lex regia*, into an assertion of the constitutional qualifications of the king's will.[48] But Aquinas's comment on the same maxim was: 'It is necessary that the will be regulated by some reason in regard to those things that are commanded, if this volition is to have the character of law.'[49]

Aquinas's 'regal' government was not a system of arbitrary sovereignty: however broadly construed, it was subject to the rational principles of law not made by man, and these principles were conceived as objective standards against which the commands of the ruler might be measured. Thus Aquinas came face to face with the familiar medieval dilemma; and his solution was the familiar medieval solution, tempered by a new appreciation of the value of stability. If there was no public power superior to the king, private individuals must be recognized to have an ultimate right to judge, to disobey, and to resist. In his early commentary on the *Sentences* of Peter Lombard, he recognized a right of disobedience to commands that exceeded the scope of the ruler's authority and a positive duty of disobedience to commands contrary to the purpose of his office.[50] His analysis of the question in the *Summa Theologiae* betrayed a growing sense of the complexity of the problem. Commands of the king which were *extra vires*, which were not directed to the common good, which distributed burdens inequitably on the people, were 'acts of violence rather than laws' and therefore laid no obligation on men's consciences 'unless perhaps for the sake of avoiding scandal or disturbance, a purpose to which a man should yield his right.'[51] Sedition was a mortal sin, because it was contrary to 'the unity of law and the common good.' But those who revolted against a tyrant were not guilty of this sin; rather 'it is the tyrant that is guilty of sedition, since he encourages discord and sedition among his subjects.' Revolt became sedition only if it brought about greater disaster to the common good than that caused by the tyrant.[52] In a shrewd discussion in the *De Regimine Principum*, Aquinas condemned tyrannicide because, and apparently only because, it was likely to bring about worse evils than those entailed by tyranny itself.[53]

The most emphatic of medieval defences of kingship was made in the *De Regimine Principum* of Aegidius Romanus. The book as a whole is saturated in Aristotelianism, and Aegidius did full justice to Aristotle's arguments for the superiority of the government of laws to the government of man and for the rule of the many. Like Aquinas, he saw regal and political governments as clear-cut alternatives; but his own preference, clearly stated, was for the 'regal lordship, in which someone rules according to his own discretion and the laws which he himself has instituted.'[54] The king must 'abound in civil power'[55]; he was the 'head of the realm' and a 'living law,' superior to inanimate laws as the animate was always superior to the inanimate[56]—superior precisely in the flexibility of an unfettered discretion which was able to adjust natural law principles to specific instances with a precision which no enacted code could emulate. All positive laws, except in so far as they derived their virtue from natural law, must lean on the prince for their authority, as he in turn must lean on the ultimate authority of natural law.[57] The unity of the state and, therefore, its strength demanded unity of rule; it was a principle of nature to reduce multiplicity to unity through a single head; empirical evidence showed that states not ruled by a king tended to poverty and disintegration. While there was value in the pooling of many opinions and wishes, this value could and should be attained through the king's consultation of his council; it was not an argument against the concentration of ultimate authority in the hands of a single man.[58] Finally, as Aegidius urged in an interesting argument based on empirical, psychological considerations, hereditary succession was preferable to election of the ruler.[59]

A preference for the rule of one man and the assumption that such rule would involve a monopoly of public authority was, in fact, typical of the political theory of the theologians of the late thirteenth century and the beginning of the fourteenth. Engelbert of Admont and Dante expanded the case for unity of rule into a justification of universal empire[60]; the same arguments supported the theory of the *plenitudo potestatis* of the pope.[61] There was, however, a minority report. In the anonymous continuation of Aquinas's *De Regimine Principum*, presumably written by his pupil, Tholommeo of Lucca, the alternative which had not aroused Aquinas's interest was defended as the only form of government suitable for free men.

Tholommeo represented a new influence in political thought: that of the Italian communes, which had developed a type of government essentially different from the monarchic pattern of most of Europe. That pattern was neatly summarized by Aegidius Romanus:

'In the Italian cities the many, as the whole people, dominate; the consent of the whole people is sought in establishing statutes and in electing the authorities and also in correcting the authorities. For, although one may observe an authority or some lord who rules the city, yet the whole people dominates more than he, in this respect: that it belongs to the whole people to elect him and to correct him if he does ill and that it belongs to the whole people to establish statutes which the lord is not permitted to transgress.'[62]

This background, reflected in Tholommeo's treatise, gives it an importance to modern scholars which it could scarcely derive from its intellectual merits. Its importance in the Middle Ages was based on the fact that it was generally believed to have been written by Aquinas himself; but Tholommeo's thought and preferences were remote from those of his teacher. Categories sharply distinguished by Aquinas were thrown into confusion when Tholommeo searched the Scriptures and miscellaneous history to find examples and definitions of the despotic, regal, and political constitutions mentioned by Aristotle. He emerged with the conviction that there was very little difference between kingship and despotism. Kingship must mean the exercise of arbitrary control. Such a dominion, he implied, might be the necessary result of human sin; it might be the only kind of government possible for large units; it might even be most like the government of God; and it might enjoy the practical advantage of a flexibility impossible to governments bound by the rule of law. But the recognition of human freedom was achieved only through 'political' dominion, which was found in Israel under the judges, in the Roman republic, and in the Lombard communes, and which was characterized by an elective and responsible magistracy whose power was narrowly confined to the enforcement of laws laid down by the citizenry itself.

A greater mind than that of Tholommeo was also fertilized by Italian experience. In the *Defensor Pacis*, the principles underlying the government of the Italian communes were generalized into a system of authority which was conceived as applying to every true state, whatever its apparent form. In every 'perfect community,' Marsiglio argued, the authority to make fundamental law, determine the form of government, and institute the governing head must belong ultimately to the organized body of the citizens, though for convenience it might be exercised by a smaller body which represented them and acted by their authority. The actual control of government was conveyed by this *legislator* to a *pars principans*, or 'ruling part,' and the *pars principans* in turn instituted and directed the lesser offices of the state. The *pars principans* might be elective or hereditary, a single individual or a governing board small enough to achieve the requisite unity of decision,[63] but in any case the authority by which the *pars principans* acted was an authority delegated to it by the *legislator*, and an authority which must be exercised in accordance with the law which rested on the original authority of the corporate community. Within the area of his competence, the *pars principans* was the specialist in government, empowered to regulate all the civil life of the state. But, if he abused this power, he might be corrected and punished, even deposed, by the *legislator* or the representatives that it appointed for this purpose.

The thesis that in all states, whether regal or republican, the ultimate authority continued in the community made possible constructions not possible in Aquinas's or Tholommeo's scheme of alternatives. And in Marsiglio's theory one does indeed find the embryo of the idea that the community could act through a plurality of institutions. It was represented in its ruling part, whose authority might be as broad or as narrow as the community had chosen to make it; it could also be represented in a legislative body, which could make, amend, abrogate, and supplement the laws by an authority derived directly from the community; and it could be represented in a body specifically charged with the responsibility of restraining the excesses of the *pars principans*. The concept of representation here was, of course, not the modern concept of representation. The institutions through which the community acted were not controlled by the community except formally, by the framework of law which instituted them and within which they were expected to act; their delegated authority was delegated absolutely and carried with it no specific mandates from the popular will. The responsibility of the *pars principans* was a responsibility to the terms of his office, not to a programme dictated even broadly by the *legislator*. The community's power to restrain him through the officers established for that purpose was a latent power, called into action only if he transgressed the conditions of his appointment; in the area of his competence, his authority was absolute, his will supreme.

Thus Marsiglio's pattern was a pattern of formal relations of authority, but not a pattern for a process of actual control and responsibility. In this respect it fell short of modern theories of popular sovereignty. It also, as we have already suggested,[64] fell short of some modern theories in the fact that he did not conceive his community as an arbitrary

sovereign. Its role, like that of Aquinas's legislative king, was an inter-
pretive one, guided by principles of abstract justice more fundamental
than its own desires, principles which it 'discovered' and embodied in
specific form to suit its own particular circumstances, and to which it
gave the stamp of its own unique coercive authority.

Moreover, Marsiglio's system was not, in the modern sense, a
system of separation of powers.[65] The modern doctrine of separation
of powers was an attempt to answer the problem of the potential
tyranny of all authority through the demarcation of types of authority
and through the balancing and continual checking of one type of authority with another. Marsiglio was scarcely aware of this problem; he felt
some concern over the possible tyranny of the *pars principans* but had
no notion of the possible tyranny of the *legislator*. Thus his system was
vague at precisely the points where, if he were really anticipating
modern ideas, it would have been most specific. His *legislator* sometimes appears as a special body; at other times it blurs with the community. It is not clear whether it is a continually functioning institution
or simply the constituent organ which has established 'the form of the
state' once and for all. Although Marsiglio clearly preferred that the
ruler be bound by detailed and specific laws and limited to something
like a mere executive and judicial function, he also accepted the
alternative possibility of a wide range of discretion. He nowhere gave
a precise definition of the content of the authority of the *pars principans*;
he certainly did not distinguish between executive and judicial
authority; in *dictio* 2, particularly, he indiscriminately assigned actions
that are only conceivable as executive or judicial to 'the *legislator* or
him who acts by its authority.' He repeatedly asserted that, whether
broad or narrow, the authority of the *pars principans was* the authority
of the *legislator*; in *dictio* 2, he was quite willing to use the term *legislator*
for the emperor himself.[66]

Thus it is possible for McIlwain, who does not accept the hypothesis
that *dictio* 1 was based upon Italian experience, to argue that the scheme
of the *Defensor Pacis* was simply a rationalization of the northern
monarchy, in which the king was presumed to derive from a constituent people an indeterminate area of control within wide boundaries
set by laws presumed to have emanated from them.[67] This interpretation seems not to give due weight to the passages in *dictio* 1 which
envisage the *legislator* as a continuing institution, nor to its frequent

recommendation of precise legislation narrowly restricting the *pars principans*. However, the ambiguity which makes possible divergent interpretations of the constitutional theories of the *Defensor Pacis* becomes intelligible if one remembers that in the overall plan of the work those theories are subordinate to the compelling issue of Marsiglio's anticlericalism. What he was really looking for was a concentration of rightful authority to which he could assign an ultimate control over ecclesiastical affairs. The principles for such a concentration must be principles applicable to every type of Christian state. If the authority of all government could be recognized as in principle the authority of the community, the particular allotment of powers through which that authority was exercised was, for Marsiglio, a matter of comparative indifference. His real theme was not the separation of powers but their ultimate unity.

Although Marsiglio's theory was born of Italy, the fact that it was expressed in these general terms gave it significance for the main stream of medieval theory and, in particular, made it usable by later conciliarists. For the free Italian institutions that made an intellectual background for Tholommeo and Marsiglio were already passing; the future belonged to the kingdoms, but to kingdoms which were becoming more complex and more institutionalized than those of the early Middle Ages. The theory which paralleled that development can best be studied in terms of general tendencies rather than through the detailed analysis of the work of particular theorists, though the thought of William of Occam is in some ways particularly significant for its early stages and that of Nicholas of Cusa and Sir John Fortescue for the later.

There were three main tendencies in the political thought of the fourteenth and fifteenth centuries. On the one hand, when the notion of the corporate community as the constituent source of all political authority became widely accepted as a general principle, it became the basis of a series of conclusions on the nature of kingly power, its substantive limits, and the continuing rights of the community. This development led to the recognition of a type of governmental structure that was 'political' as well as 'regal.' But, since it was also 'regal' as well as 'political,' this tendency was not incompatible with a continuing and clarified assertion of the absolutism and formal irresponsibility of the king within his proper sphere. Finally, in the fifteenth century we may detect a counter-tendency, never fully explicit or systematically related to the others: a tendency to a pluralistic construction of government as a structure of several semi-autonomous and interacting offices.

The principle that all government had been originally established by the people was combined in Occam's thought with the related idea that the people had also established its own pre-governmental law, which continued to stand as a boundary normally circumscribing the authority of its prince. A pure regal monarchy, limited by no human laws, was for Occam a conceivable legitimate form of government—even 'the best, when it was at its best.' This type of monarchy he sharply distinguished from proprietary, or despotic, lordship, in which the ruler properly used his subjects and their goods for his own advantage; for regal lordship was a government over free men and therefore was intrinsically limited by the requirement that it serve the common utility. But, as Occam clearly recognized, this pure type of monarchy had no contemporary significance: 'in these days there is, perhaps, not in the whole world any instance of the regal principate.' The kingship of his own day was 'a principate according to law,' in which the ruler was 'bound by certain laws or customs introduced by men,' a regal principate which fell short of the pure type.

Thus, in Occam's thought, the Aristotelian categories used by earlier thinkers as alternatives were brought closer to medieval reality by the definition of a type of government which blended the regal with the political, and by the recognition that all medieval kingship belonged to this intermediate category. A century later, a similar idea appeared even more explicitly in the thought of another Englishman. When Sir John Fortescue attempted to define the constitution of his own country, he was forced to the conclusion that the government which had 'burst forth' in England was a 'lordship both political and regal,' a government in which the regal authority was established by the community and was limited by the rights of the people and by the body of laws which had flowed from the people themselves.

' For in the kingdom of England the kings do not establish laws nor impose taxes on their subjects without the consent of the Three Estates of that realm; and also the judges of that realm are all bound by their oaths not to render judgments against the laws of the land even if they receive commands of the prince to the contrary. Cannot this lordship, then, be called political—that is, regulated by the control of the many—but does it not also deserve to be called a regal lordship, since the subjects themselves cannot establish laws without the royal authority, and since the kingdom subject to the regal dignity is held by kings and their heirs in consequence by hereditary right, as is not the case with lordships ruled only politically?'[68]

Fortescue's concept differed from Occam's in so far as an intervening century of institutional development allowed him to envisage a continual interaction between agencies of the community and the king.

These twin conceptions, of royal power originating in the people and of royal power circumscribed by a popular law, involved a number of implications.

In the first place, it must be noticed that in northern Europe the idea of the popular origin of law was not originally coupled with a concept of continuing popular legislation. While Occam thought it possible that the pre-governmental law might be changed 'if all mortals unanimously agreed to contradict it,'[69] and although at times he speculated on the possibility of fundamental changes,[70] he had no notion of any institutional machinery through which such changes might be made. The making or changing of the basic law was for him necessarily an informal and silent process: it was the gradual development of custom by 'the whole community of mortals' rather than the deliberate act of 'the corporation of citizens.' Moreover, he thought of the pre-governmental law, although it rested at least partially on consent, as a quasi-natural law which could reasonably be altered only as a result of a basic change in human conditions. Thus even for Occam, exceptional in his speculative agility and relativist temper, changes in the popular law would be abnormal and necessarily rare; other publicists were even less attentive to the possibility.

Thus even though the development of estates provided an institutional form through which the community might have been conceived as making and abrogating its law, this conception developed very slowly and only in certain countries. English practice from the fourteenth century demanded the participation of the estates in the promulgation of statutes, which, as distinguished from the king's ordinances, were recognized as involving the basic law; and by the fifteenth century English law courts were reluctantly recognizing that new statutes sometimes made new law.[71] But the notion of a representative legislating body was only very gradually distilled from the notion of the representative body which knew what the law of the land already was and therefore must assist in its authoritative finding. In France, where the distinction between statute and ordinance was much less clear, the estates did not necessarily participate in the promulgation of law; acceptance by the courts was regarded as more important for its validation. In medieval Europe, in general, alterations in the substantive law, when they occurred, took place under the guise of a presumed return to the old law or its adjustment to new circumstances; and, in general, alterations in the substantive law were extremely rare. It is significant that for Fortescue the consent of the estates to new taxes was the most conspicuous example of the way in which the community might participate in legislative innovation.

The pre-governmental law was generally conceived as including the whole structure of private property, and this idea, as we have seen,[72] provided a theoretical basis for the protection of proprietary rights from the ruler and the exclusion of private-law relationships from the normal area of his legislative power. This old idea was attacked in the later Middle Ages by the philosophical and civilist idea that the right to determine extraordinary taxes and to expropriate property in case of emergency was part of the content of rulership. In practice, the issue over taxation was variously fought out and variously resolved in terms of the relative strength of the kings and estates of various countries. But in that struggle the claim of the estates to be consulted on new taxes was strengthened by the development of the theory which allowed them to appear not as mere representatives of a totality of private owners but also as spokesmen for the entire community, which had a vested interest in the preservation of its own law within which the proprietary rights of individuals were imbedded.

Not only the private law but also the forms and customs of the government itself were construed as derived from the original authority of the people. Thus Occam[73] and Lupold of Bebenburg,[74] opposing the papal claim to have instituted the electors of the Holy Roman Empire, asserted that the electors had been set up by the people of the empire to represent them in the choice of the emperor. This interpretation, in turn, supported the assertions that the duly-elected emperor needed no further papal confirmation in order to exercise his imperial authority, and that due election, in accordance with the rules of corporation law, need involve no more than a majority decision. The hereditary monarchies of other countries were similarly assumed to rest on the popular choice of a ruling dynasty and a popular determination of the laws of succession. And it could plausibly be argued, as it was at the meeting of the French Estates General at Tours in 1484, that the right to insure its own good government was always latent in the community and that therefore, in such an abnormal situation as the minority of the heir, the right to choose the regency council was inherent in the community and in the Estates General as representing it.[75] Finally, in accordance with this general conception, the rights of the king as such were considered as rights established by the community in its own interest; and this principle supported the distinction between the king's private proprietary rights, which he could freely alienate, and the rights inherent in the kingship, which could never legally be separated from the kingship itself.

The doctrine of the inalienability of the *iura regni*[76] was one of the most significant of the constitutional ideas developed in the Middle Ages. In particular application to the empire and buttressed by maxims from Roman law, twelfth-century civilists used it to support the Hohenstaufen attempts to recover traditional imperial rights in Italy. Later civilists used the same arguments to demonstrate that the Donation of Constantine could have had no validity; their arguments were borrowed and quoted again and again by fourteenth-century publicists opposing the papal claim to sovereignty over the empire and the papal doctrine of ecclesiastical immunities within other kingdoms. The belief that there existed no lawful way in which imperial rights could be detached from the empire provided a serious legal problem for fourteenth-century lawyers and publicists who tried to grapple with the fact that cities and kingdoms on once-imperial soil were exercising all the rights of independent sovereignty and recognized no superior. But on the whole the principle of the inalienability of the rights of the crown was most significant in the support it gave to the consolidation of national kingdoms. In proportion as it was accepted, it was an answer to the persistent feudal tendency toward the infeudation of governmental functions. It was also an answer to the persistent medieval attempts to find a bridle for the king through the control of his expenditures or his appointments. It was on the basis of this principle that Innocent III annulled

Magna Carta and Louis IX asserted the invalidity of the Provisions of Oxford. Thus in its immediate effects this principle supported the irresponsible absolutism of the medieval king; yet, by defining that absolutism as official rather than proprietary and by basing it on the ultimate interests and rights of the community, it was an essential step toward the limited and responsible government of modern times.

Other steps toward that conclusion were taken in the new construction of the role of other public institutions which resulted from the general conception of the corporate community as the basis of political life. For even though the king's inalienable monopoly of jurisdiction and government remained unshaken, the idea that his representation of the community was unique—that 'the power of all his subjects was gathered together in him'—was challenged by the development of other institutions which also seemed to represent the underlying community. Thus Lupold of Bebenburg, in opposition to the canonist Hostiensis, insisted on the representative role of the imperial electors. Similarly, the estates of various countries, although they were formed by royal initiative and continued to be composed partly on the basis of personal, feudal status, were increasingly regarded as representing each kingdom as a whole.[77] Earlier medieval theory could balance the rights of the king only against the rights of individuals; later medieval theory could relate them to the fundamental rights of the community, exercised by representative institutions.

The medieval idea of representation did not carry with it the modern implication of popular control over the popular delegates.[78] In general, medieval thinkers tended to underestimate the dangers of irresponsibility because of their incorrigible hope that reason would narrow the field of debate and that disputes would centre on questions of expediency rather than on a conflict of desires. But, whether or not this hope was well grounded, medieval thought had to grant a discretionary authority to the representative because no other alternative was available. Medieval society had not developed the modern devices for organizing the will of the community, transmitting it to a delegate, and holding him responsible for carrying it out. The whole point of the doctrine of representation lay in the belief that the multitude had no way of coming to a decision except through reposing the power of decision in the hands of representatives. Therefore, just as in the early Middle Ages the notion of the trusteeship of the divinely-established king had been fused with the notion that he also represented the people, so in the later Middle Ages the representation of the community was easily transmuted into a sort of trusteeship.[79]

Thus the idea of representation was not necessarily connected in medieval thought with the idea of election. An hereditary king could represent the entire realm, certain magnates with a customary right or duty of attendance could represent the entire estate of nobles, and their representation was conceived to be no less complete than if they had been elected. No one elected the electors of the Holy Roman Empire. As time went on, the opinion grew that election was the best way of filling representative offices. The act of election was felt to be the formal means by which the power of the community was properly conveyed to its representatives; but hereditary authority could be made compatible with this conception through the assumption that the community had originally elected a family and set the terms on which its representative right was transmitted from son to son.[80] Accordingly, the development of the idea of representation did not mean the democratization of medieval political thought.

The best illustration of this paradox can be found in the theory of Nicholas of Cusa. No other medieval writer so clearly and forcefully asserted the principle that all coercive authority must be based on the consent of free men; and his *De Concordantia Catholica* was avowedly an attempt to reconstruct the government of church and empire on this principle. But when one examines the practical applications which Cusa deduced from it, one is struck by the way in which the requirement of consent evaporates into a system of legal fictions. There is, indeed, a stress on election as the appropriate means of transmitting popular consent to ecclesiastical and secular officers. But such elections, of course, could be popular only through an assumption that the people were already represented in the actual electors. Moreover, the authority transmitted by election was to be complete and final: when the representatives of various parts of the empire 'all meet together in one representative compendium, the whole empire is gathered together'; '. . . all who are subject to the pastoral curia are understood to be united . . . in him who presides, as if he were one soul, and they the body which the soul has to animate. . . . The church is in the bishop through union and thus the bishop symbolizes and represents them. . . .'[81] Finally, though Cusa's plan for reforming the empire through the cooperation of the emperor with general and regional councils was based on the theory that such councils represented the community, he was quite willing to include in them non-elected magnates—appointed judges and hereditary lords.[82]

These characteristics of the medieval idea of representation were partly responsible for the fact that the late medieval tendency to trace all authority to the original authority of the community did not necessarily conflict with the acceptance of a sphere of absolute authority for the king. This conception continued to dominate the thought of the later Middle Ages on kingship: the only basic disputes concerned the scope of that authority and the possibility of action against the ruler who clearly overstepped or abused it.

In discussing the nature of royal authority we must, of course, distinguish between what we may call the indigenous medieval ideas and the theory of the *Corpus Juris*, as interpreted by the civilists and by philosophers influenced by them. For the former, as we have already suggested, the absolutism of the ruler was an absolutism within and under the fundamental law of the land—the absolutism of a supreme judge and administrator who controlled the machinery of government at his discretion but did not control the law itself. The civilists found in the Roman tradition a contrasting picture of rulership, in which the making and unmaking of law was the prominent feature. The idea of the ruler as legislator could be supported philosophically by the principles which we have found in Aquinas's writings: that changing circumstances and the development of human wisdom required changes in the law and that such changes must be made valid by the will in which public authority was located. For the lawyers, seeking for clear-cut criteria of legality, the idea that there must be a single focus of all public authority was naturally a convincing principle. The maxim *quod principi placuit*, as well as the testimony of the Roman laws themselves, taught them that the Roman people had transferred all their authority to the emperor. And when men learned to think that 'every king was emperor in his kingdom,' one obvious implication was that the pleasure of every king could make law. 'Know that the King of France, who is emperor in his kingdom, can make ordinances which have the force of law and can ordain and enact all statutes (*constitutions*).'[83]

From this approach it could logically follow that the participation of representative councils in the making or promulgation of law was not essential to its validity, that the basic private law was submitted to the ruler's discretion no less than matters of immediate policy and procedure, that the validity of custom depended on the tolerance of the ruler and that custom could accordingly be overturned by deliberate legislative enactment, and finally that the prince himself was 'released from the laws' not only because no coercion could reach him but also because he could not be conceived as bound by laws that rested on his own will. The civilists were by no means unanimous in drawing all these conclusions, but civilist thought clearly moved in this direction in the fourteenth and fifteenth centuries. In the middle of the fifteenth century, the brilliant humanist Aeneas Sylvius, who was then in the employment of Frederick III, set forth a theory of the legislative authority of the emperor in a sharp, consistent statement which scarcely fell short of the classic doctrine of sovereignty which Bodin was to formulate in 1576.[84]

Another school of civilist thought, however, dominant in the thirteenth century and important throughout the medieval period, found in the Roman law itself phrases which tended to harmonize the notion of the ruler's legislative absolutism with medieval traditions. Civilists of this school stressed the texts which presented the Roman emperor as legislating with the consent of the senate. The maxim, 'What touches all should be approved by all,'[85] was expanded from its original private-law significance to become also a public-law principle for legislation that affected property rights or basic custom. The validity of such legislation might be construed as resting finally on the ruler's authority; he might even have the right to compel approval not freely granted; but his authority must be expressed formally through regularized procedures of consultation and consent.

Civilist influence was undoubtedly important in shaping constitutional practice on the continent. But, whatever far-reaching implications might be drawn by the more extreme civilists from the Roman doctrine of legislation, in fact the private law of the empire and of France, as of every medieval kingdom, remained virtually intact: the actual legislation of the emperor and of those who were emperors in their kingdoms consisted mainly of the authoritative promulgation of codes of existing custom or the implementing and supplementing of the fundamental law through specific administrative and procedural orders and specific determinations of crimes and penalties.[86] It is significant that the resounding Roman law phrases which frequently prefaced the ordinances of French kings from the time of Philip the Fair were used mainly to rationalize the dispensing power.[87] The widest expansion of royal power appeared in the developing principle that in case of national emergency it was the prerogative of the king to define the new taxes or other abnormal measures required for the welfare of the state entrusted to his care; but this principle, however frequently employed, still carried with it an assumption of an exceptional situation, a temporary instance of the necessity which knows no law. Thus in practice the civilist theory of the legislating ruler did not revolutionize medieval kingship but rather reinforced and expanded the indigenous medieval tradition of the absolutism of the king as administrator and judge within the permanent framework of the customary law.

The point at which classical ideas of rulership were most fully integrated into traditional medieval thought and practice was in the acceptance of the theory of the ruler's power to dispense from or temporarily overstep the law. The dispensing power and the power to violate the laws in an emergency might be rationalized by *quod principi placuit* or *princeps legibus solutus* or by conceptions of the ruler as the guardian of the common utility or the fount of equity, but the practical reason for the increasing emphasis on these powers in the later Middle Ages was the actual obsolescence of medieval law, an obsolescence the more conspicuous because medieval laws were usually rigidly concrete in form. The alternative, which to modern eyes would seem the obvious solution, would have been the continual revision of the fundamental laws by legislative enactment; but this was scarcely imaginable by medieval minds. Thus in medieval political thought there was a constant tension between rationality and custom, between the common good and the common law. Perhaps it is no exaggeration to say that the resolution of that tension was for medieval minds the final meaning of the royal office, as the existence of that tension was the strongest argument for kingship.

At all events, even theorists who by no means subscribed to the conception of kingship as a government of 'plenary power' were among those who refused to regard the law of the community as an utterly impermeable barrier to royal authority. Marsiglio preferred that the legislation of the community should bind the ruler most precisely; yet he granted his *pars principans* the power of dispensation when the exact enforcement of the law would conflict with equity.[88] William of Occam recognized the possibility of emergencies in which the ruler would rightfully violate the human law which was the normal boundary of his authority.[89] And even Fortescue presented, as part of his description of the ideal 'political and regal' lordship, a clear-cut defence of a wide executive and judicial discretion for the ruler combined with an equally clear-cut warning against legislative innovation.[90]

The theory of dispensation and emergency action did not demand the concept of a ruler with supreme legislative power. It only needed the assumption that the office of the king must be adequate to insure the fulfilment of the higher law when it conflicted with the lower. The inevitability of occasional conflicts could be explained by the Aristotelian doctrine, transmitted by Aquinas,[91] that laws are inevitably defective for specific instances in proportion as they descend from general principles to particular formulations. Thus the very rule that the king was always subject to the higher law must at times release him from the lower. But it is important to remember that the dispensing power and the right to violate the laws in an emergency were, in the typical medieval pattern of thought, simply an extreme application of the general idea that the authority of the prince was in essence a discretionary authority.

In recognizing that government and jurisdiction can never be completely reduced to the rule of law but must include an area of interpretation and action in which the government of man must be decisive, medieval thinkers were, perhaps, political realists. However closely government is circumscribed by law, it still consists in the making of concrete and immediate decisions which in the last analysis can be determined only by the reason and will of the person entrusted with the authority to make them. Medieval circumstances and the medieval intellectual heritage made this truth particularly conspicuous to medieval thinkers, but it is, of course, applicable to every governmental system. The only differences are differences in the breadth of the areas left to specific decision and the very important difference, which is the heart of modern constitutionalism, between the concentration of all decisions in a single office and the distribution of decisions through a complex structure.

We have seen the logic of circumstance and theory which led most medieval thinkers to the conclusion that, although the area of decision should be limited, the power to decide was best located in a single man. Given the medieval situation, the conclusion was doubtless unavoidable. But the theory which supported it had a flaw of which medieval men were well aware: as Aristotle had long since pointed out, the only thing wrong with monarchy is that it requires a good king. Since the monarchic system does not automatically tend to the production of good kings, medieval men continued to face the practical and theoretical problem presented by the ruler who abused the freedom which they recognized to be essential to his office.

To this problem no one gave the answer of Machiavelli or of Hobbes. No one denied that the ruler was subject to the moral obligations of divine and natural law, and only Marsiglio questioned the legal status of those obligations. The most extreme position was that suggested by Bracton and elaborated by some of the later civilists and by Aeneas Sylvius: the ruler who had no earthly superior could not be held to account for his actions except by God; since it was his function to adapt the higher law to specific circumstances, his interpretation must be held valid; there was no public power that could judge him, and no private person could question his decisions; whether it was so or not, his will must be presumed to be good.[92] This was a lawyers' answer, rounding out a doctrine of formal sovereignty and gaining added weight from a growing respect for stability and legal order; the old patristic argument that evil rulers might well have been ordained by God for the punishment of His erring people continued to haunt medieval minds and led to the same practical results.[93]

Those who were unwilling to sacrifice the cause of justice to formal legitimacy, or to make the providence of God solely responsible for the misdeeds of rulers, sought other answers. They emphasized the distinction between the king and the tyrant and asserted that tyranny had no inherent claim to obedience. Even if there existed no public authority to bring the tyrant to account, he might still be judged, disobeyed, and resisted by private individuals or by the mass of the community subject to him. This was the position of William of Occam. '. . . . There can be no law which is repugnant to the higher law or to manifest reason; therefore any civil law which is repugnant to divine law or manifest reason is not law; and in the same way the words of canon or civil law, if they are repugnant to divine law (that is, the Holy Scriptures) or to right reason, are not to be observed.'[94] 'The subjects of the emperor are not bound to obey him in all things, but only in those which pertain to the governing of the people: that is, in those things which are necessary to ruling justly and expediently the people subjected to him.' 'No one ought to obey in illicit and unjust things.'[95] 'The king is superior to the whole kingdom, yet under certain circumstances he is inferior to the kingdom, because in case of necessity it can depose him and hold him prisoner in a castle; for it has this right by natural law, as it is a principle of natural law that it is permitted to repel force with force.'[96] The idea here is not a concept of a superior authority to which the ruler is normally responsible: it is a concept of the inherent limitations of the authority or rulership, of the supremacy of natural and divine law, and of the ultimate right of the people, singly or collectively, to protect themselves against injustice. In Occam's flexible system, even the pope might intervene against the abuse of power by the emperor: not as a political superior, but 'casually,' in the same way as 'a rustic can casually used the material sword against the emperor.'[97] In either instance, Occam implied, it was the circumstances that must be appealed to for justification of the action, and papal action stood on the same theoretical basis as private tyrannicide.

The old tradition that approved tyrannicide was thrown into disrepute when it was furbished up by the mediocre mind of an undistinguished Dominican, Jean Petit, to justify the assassination of the Duke of Orleans in 1407. The case of Jean Petit's theses became a *cause célèbre* for the Council of Constance.[98] The attack which ultimately resulted in a somewhat ambiguous condemnation of the theses was led by Gerson—who, as his leadership of the conciliarists had abundantly proved, was himself no advocate of passive submission to misused authority. In his careful examination of the problem, Gerson did not entirely condemn tyrannicide; but he argued that if it were permissible it could only be as a last resource, if the tyranny was notorious and intolerable, if no legal means of removing or reforming the tyrant were available, if it was probable that the tyrannicide would not lead to worse consequences than the tyranny, and even then only if the motives of the killer were impeccable and if he avoided the use of means evil in themselves.[99]

Though tyrannicide had come to be regarded as a dubious and dangerous remedy, disobedience to tyrannical commands and resistance to the tyrant continued throughout the Middle Ages to be supported by a large body of opinion. The case was strongest when the command of the ruler conflicted with the law of God; no one denied that 'it is better to obey God than man.' But even some of the civilists also maintained the nullity of the ruler's actions when they conflicted with natural law, tended to diminish the rights of the crown, or without 'just cause' violated the private rights of the subjects.[100] Among theologians and canonists, Aquinas's analysis of the limits of the duty of obedience continued to be quoted.[101] Conciliarist thought, particularly, stressed the subjects' right—even, perhaps, their duty—to resist tyrannical control.[102]

There was, however, a tendency in later medieval thought to institutionalize resistance to abused authority. The thesis that all power originated in the community was easily extended to the idea that the community still retained the right to secure its own good government through the withdrawal of power from a tyrannical ruler: thus the doctrine of a private right of insurrection merged into the idea of a public right of deposition.[103] Bodies which could be construed as exercising the latent rights of the community—the imperial electors or the estates—were accordingly regarded as agencies which might properly represent the community in the formal deposition of a ruler. This theory, widely held and sometimes put into practice, did not, of course, imply a normal superiority of the community or its representative agencies to the ruler, or their right to dictate his actions in any way so long as those actions conformed to the conditions on which authority had been granted. The right of the community came into play only when the ruler forfeited his claim to authority.

A more continuous institutional check on the ruler was provided by the theory that the king's officers themselves should refuse to enforce his illicit commands.[104] This, in particular, was the remedy envisaged by those civilists who were unwilling to ascribe an absolute sovereignty to the emperor on the grounds that he alone had the right to interpret the higher law and that his will must be presumed to be just. To varying degrees, and often with the qualification that the deliberateness of an imperial command established the presumption of justice, many civilists asserted the duty of judges to disregard commands inherently void by higher law standards or to reinterpret them into conformity with the higher law.[105] A similar pattern of thought supported the refusal of the French Parlement to register edicts that conflicted with fundamental law, unless by the ceremony of the *lit de justice* the king deliberately brought to bear on them the full weight of his final authority. And in England, according to Fortescue, 'the judges are all bound by their oaths not to render judgments against the law of the land even if they receive commands of the prince to the contrary.'[106]

In this theory one can find the embryo of the doctrine of the independence of the judiciary which finally became a cardinal feature of the theory of separation of powers and of modern constitutionalism. But one must be careful not to read into it the full-fledged doctrine. Its medieval expressions were tentative and debatable and never fully detached from the matrix of theory which insisted that the king was charged with supreme jurisdiction and government in his realm, that the judges were his officers and derived their powers solely from his authority, and that their resistance might finally be overborne by his unquestionable prerogative.

A similar ambiguity attached to the relations between the king and his ordinary council and between the king and the estates. Early and late medieval political writings alike stressed the principle that it was the duty of the king to seek the advice of his council on matters of policy; and there was at least the implication that he should not only seek it but follow it. As the estates became self-conscious bodies, they frequently asserted their claims to be consulted.[107] So long as theory insisted on the focussing of full authority in the king, the duty of consultation presented a difficult logical problem; some lawyers and philosophical publicists consistently classified it as a moral rather than a legal obligation. Moreover, as both councils and estates owed their existence and many of the details of their composition to royal initiative, they obviously appeared from one point of view as instruments of the king's discretion and the king's will. On the other hand, the sheer pressure of fact required that councils and estates represent the weightiest elements in the kingdom; thus, though consultation might not be an obligation, it was very often a necessity. Finally, as medieval thought tended to assume a close relationship between *right* and *rights* and tended to find in formalized procedures its best solution for the paradox of the absolute but not arbitrary king, the king's moral duty of consultation was sometimes transformed into the legal principle that the determination of policy must be made through consultation with the council or the estates, although the ruler was not necessarily bound to follow the advice that he received.

This never fully rationalized attitude was a breach in the consistency of the theory of the king's sole responsibility for good government; still more questionable were the recurrent attempts of the estates in England, France, and Spain to arrogate to themselves the right to nominate the king's ministers or to control the spending of the king's revenues.[108] These attempts to influence the day-to-day government of the kingdom were born of specific discontents rather than of general theory. In such crises, the moral advantage lay with the kings, who were able to pose as the defenders of ancient constitutional tradition against dangerous innovation; moreover, the practical result of the experiments was only too often a vivid demonstration of the familiar thesis that unity of action was best attained by unity of will. Accordingly, though these experiments at times were useful in putting an end to immediate abuses, they laid no foundation for permanent institutional or theoretical change. More significant for the future were the techniques of bargaining that derived from the estates' recognized control of the purse-strings; but the revolutionary effect of such bargaining rested on a thoroughly conservative theory.

The late-medieval discontent with unitary monarchic government in the state was of course paralleled by a much more emphatic dissatisfaction with a similar situation in the church. Thus among conciliarist writings one finds some inchoate attempts to buttress a reinterpretation of the structure of ecclesiastical government with a corresponding reinterpretation of the structure of secular government. Gerson and d'Ailly, with the dubious help of Aristotle and Aquinas, declared the 'mixed government' the best of all forms and claimed to have discovered it in France. Their proof that France was a mixed monarchy lay in the assertion that 'the King of France has a Parlement, by which he does not refuse to be judged.'[109] This very statement reveals the vagueness of their conception; for the Parlement, even when it judged the king, was the king's Parlement. In Cusa's prescriptions for the empire, the emperor's council, his appointed officers, and the Diet seem to have a similar ambiguity: they are agencies both of the ruler and of the community, through whom and with whom the emperor should act; they are representative even when they are appointive; they are all members essential to the health of the empire and should not be 'amputated' unless they are hopelessly diseased; but their authority is not legally defined as independent of the imperial authority which creates and presides over them. As in their ecclesiastical theory, so in their allusions to secular government the conciliarists were inhibited from a full development of their conception by their inability to distinguish sharply between different kinds of governmental power; the medieval notion of the necessary unity of political authority offered no tenable alternatives in theory between a more or less limited monarchic absolutism and outright popular republicanism. In the secular theory of the conciliarists there was dimly present the idea that the community's interest in good government required the interplay of a complex of offices, and that that very necessity endowed each one with a right to the unhampered performance of its own function; but this idea was still centuries away from the modern idea of responsible, constitutional government and separation of powers.

Something of the same hesitant groping underlies the work of Fortescue and is responsible for the various ways in which his idea of 'political and regal government' has been interpreted. He has been proclaimed as a spokesman of modern constitutionalism;[110] that he certainly was not. His definition of political and regal government turned on the extent to which the discretion of the king was hemmed in by the national law; it involved no explicit theory of royal responsibility or institutional checks upon the king within the sphere of his properly regal power. On the other hand, there is more than a difference in atmosphere between Fortescue and Bracton, or between Fortescue and Occam. For Fortescue, the national law had ceased to be inert custom, and in the making of new law and the amending of the old the cooperation of king and representative parliament had become an established rule. Thus he was 'the first writer to abandon merely feudal and pre-feudal notions of the monarchy, and to affirm boldly that it was not only limited, but parliamentary in character.'[111] Finally, though Fortescue's suggestions for the reform of the Privy Council aimed primarily at increasing its efficiency as the king's instrument, his recommendation that privy councillors be removable only for cause and with the consent of a majority of their colleagues[112] suggests that he also thought of it as a quasi-autonomous institution. 'In an inchoate fashion' he recognized the necessity of such corporately organized bodies as Parliament, the Privy Council, the courts, and the jury system 'to guarantee rights or maintain restraints upon royal authority.'[113] Each had put down roots into constitutional tradition; each in its own way was necessary to the public welfare; they were thus endowed with a dignity not entirely derived from the authority of the king.

Thus the cardinal ideas of early medieval thought on government— the subordination of the king to a restricting law, the supremacy of the king within his own sphere of authority, the balancing of the public authority of the king against the private rights of individuals—continued to dominate the medieval centuries but were modified and complicated by the growth of other ideas whose implications were not all fully realized within that period. In the sixteenth century, the constitutional treatises of Claude de Seyssel, of Hotman, and of Bodin, and the theoretical systems of the Huguenot author of the *Vindiciae* and of the Jesuits Suarez and Mariana provided systematic syntheses of much of the medieval tradition, but still left unanswered the persistent medieval question, how to enforce the community's interest in the good governing of its king. The right of insurrection and deposition and even the right of private tyrannicide still appeared in some of these treatises as the only sanctions on monarchy fully consistent with the terms in which it was conceived. In the sixteenth century, also, those strands of medieval thought which stressed the independence and formal irresponsibility of the king were gathered together in the doctrine of divine right as enunciated by Barclay and by James I. But the idea that all authority was delegated by the community and limited by the community's law continued to survive; and, where conditions favoured it, the idea of the necessary complexity and mutual interaction of governmental offices gained strength. Then in the England of the Stuarts the inconsistencies inherent in medieval belief and precedent became explicit when courts and Parliament attempted to put a bridle on the king. In this struggle, and in the age of revolutions that it opened, one can trace the gradual evolution of the medieval tradition into the principles of modern constitutionalism.

John of Salisbury

[John discusses tyranny and tyrannicide in the following selections from the *Policraticus* (translated from the Webb edition), book 3, ch. 15, and book 8, chs. 17–21. The complete text is illustrated with stories of Scriptural and classical tyranny.]

BOOK III, CHAPTER XV

.... To kill a tyrant is not only licit but fair and just. For he who has taken up the sword deserves to die by the sword. But this is understood to refer to him who by his own audacity usurps the sword, not to him who receives from God the authority to use it. Surely he who receives authority from God preserves the laws and is a friend of justice and right. But he who usurps authority tramples on rights and submits the laws to his will. Therefore deservedly rights are armed against him who disarms the laws, and the public power rages against him who attempts to weaken the public hand. And although the crimes of *lèse-majesté* are many, there is none graver than this, which is exercised against the very body of justice. Therefore tyranny is not only a public crime, but, if this is possible, more than a public crime. For if the crime of *lèse-majesté* admits all men as prosecutors, how much more the crime committed against the laws which ought to have empire over emperors themselves! Certainly he who does not pursue the public enemy and take vengeance on him injures himself and the whole body of the earthly commonwealth.

BOOK VIII, CHAPTER XVII

.... The tyrant, as the philosophers have painted him, is one who oppresses the people by violent domination, as the prince is one who rules them by laws. ... The prince fights for the laws and the liberty of the people; the tyrant thinks he has accomplished nothing until he has done away with the laws and reduced the people to slavery. The prince is a kind of image of Divinity and the tyrant is the image of the strength of the Enemy, of the wickedness of Lucifer, inasmuch as he imitates him who aspired to set his throne at the north and to be like the Most High, save for His goodness. ... The prince, image of the Deity, ought to be loved, honoured, and cherished; the tyrant,

image of the Evil One, ought usually even to be killed. The origin of
the tyrant is iniquity, and from the poisoned root grows and flourishes
an evil and poisonous tree, which ought to be cut down by any axe. . . .

CHAPTER XVIII

Yet I do not deny that tyrants are ministers of God, Who by His
just judgment has willed them to exist in both primacies, that of souls
and that of bodies, that the wicked may be punished through them, and
the good corrected and disciplined. For the sins of the people cause a
hypocrite to reign [Job 34:30] and, as the Book of Kings testifies, the
faults of priests brought tyrants on the people of God. For the early
fathers and the patriarchs followed nature, the best guide of life. Then
came leaders, beginning with Moses, who kept the law, and judges
who ruled the people by the authority of the law; and we read that
there were priests. Yet in the rage of the Lord kings were given: some
good, but others evil. For Samuel was old, and since his sons did not
walk in his ways but pursued avarice and vice, the people, who perhaps
had deserved that such priests should be in authority over them, ex-
torted a king for themselves from God, Whom they had despised.
Therefore Saul was elected, but with the predicted right of a king:
that is, that he would take their sons and make them charioteers, and
their daughters to become his bakers and his cooks, and their fields
and farms to be distributed to his servants at his pleasure, and that he
would oppress all the people with the yoke of slavery. Yet he was
called the Lord's anointed; although he practised tyranny he did not
lose the honour of a king. For God struck fear into all, that they should
reverence him as minister of the Lord, Whose image, in a way, he
bore. I shall even add that the tyrants of the gentiles, who have been
condemned to death from eternity, are ministers of God and are called
the Lord's anointed. . . . For all power is good, because it comes from
Him from Whom alone are all things and only good things. Yet sometimes it is not good, but evil to the user or to him who suffers it,
although in the broadest view it is good, since it is caused by Him who
uses our ills to good purpose. For even as in a picture a dusky black
colour or something else is considered unlovely in itself and yet adds
beauty to the picture as a whole, so certain things which are perceived
to be ugly and evil in themselves appear good and beautiful when they
are related to the whole, since He whose every work is exceeding good

adapts all things to Himself. Therefore the power even of the tryant is good, yet nothing is worse than tyranny.

CHAPTER XX

. . . . The Books of Kings and of Chronicles are a famous history in which . . . it is shown how Israel suffered under tyrants from the beginning, and that Judah, except for David, Josiah, and Hezekiah, had none but wicked kings. . . . And I shall easily be persuaded that that stiff-necked and hard-hearted people who always resisted the Holy Spirit . . . and provoked God . . . to wrath had deserved tyrants for princes. For penitence blots out, excludes, and destroys the tyrants whom sins require, introduce, and raise to power. And indeed, before their kings, as the story of the judges tells, the children of Israel often served under tyrants, being afflicted at many and various times by divine dispensation; and often, crying to God, they were delivered. For when the time of that dispensation was finished it was permitted to them to cast off the yoke from their necks by the slaughter of the tyrants; and no blame rests on any one of those by whose courage a penitent and humbled people was set free, but he is rather remembered as the minister of God by the happy memory of posterity. . . . [This proposition is illustrated by the story of Ehud in Judges 3:14–24, of Jael in Judges 4:17–26, and of Judith in the Apocryphal book of that name.] The histories teach, however, that no one should attempt the slaying of a tyrant to whom he is bound by the obligation of fealty or an oath. . . . And, although I see that it is sometimes used by unbelievers, I do not read that any licence of poison has been granted by any right. . . . And indeed this is the most useful and safe way of destroying tyrants: that those who are oppressed should flee humbly to the protection of God's mercy, raising pure hands to the Lord in pious prayer, that they may turn aside the scourge with which they are afflicted. For the sins of the wicked are the strength of tyrants. . . .

CHAPTER XXI

. . . . The end of tyrants is confusion, leading to destruction, indeed, if they persist in wickedness; to forgiveness if they reform. For fire awaits the scourge itself when the Father has used it for the correction of His sons. . . . Moreover, wickedness is always punished by God; but sometimes He uses His own weapon and sometimes that of a man for the punishing of the unrighteous.

Bracton

[The following passages are translated from the Woodbine edition of *De Legibus et Consuetudinibus Angliae.* The corresponding passages in the Twiss edition are indicated. The section enclosed in pointed brackets is an interpolation by another hand, conceivably by the author of *Fleta,* who expressed a similar view.]

[Folio 5b–folio 6; Woodbine, vol. II, pp. 32–33; Twiss, bk. 1, ch. 8, sec. 5.]

What the sword signifies

. . . . There are other powerful ones under the king, who are called barons. . . . There are also others who are called vavassors. . . . Also, the knights are under the king. . . . There are also under the king free-men and serfs and those subject to his power, and indeed everyone is under him, and he himself is under no one save God alone.

The king has no peer

Moreover, the king has no peer in his kingdom, because thus he would lose his headship, since an equal has no command over his equal. Again, and all the more strongly, he ought not to have a superior, nor to have anyone more powerful, because thus he would be inferior to his own subjects, and inferiors cannot be equal to the more powerful. Moreover, the king ought not to be under man, but under God and under the law, because the law makes the king. Therefore let the king attribute to the law what the law has attributed to him, namely, domination and power. For there is no king where will rules and not law. And that he ought to be under the law, since he is the vicar of God, appears evidently through his likeness to Jesus Christ, Whose place he occupies on earth. Because the true mercy of God, when many ways were available to Him for the recovery of the human race, ineffably chose the most preferable way, by which He would use not the force of power but the reason of justice for the destruction of the devil's work. And thus He wished to be under the law, that He might redeem those who were under the law. For He did not wish to use force, but judgment. Likewise also the blessed bearer of God, the Virgin Mary,

Mother of the Lord, who by a singular privilege was above the law, yet to show an example of humility did not refuse to be subject to legal institutes. Thus, therefore, the king, that his power may not remain unbridled. Therefore, there ought not to be anyone greater than he in his own kingdom in the administration of law; however, he ought to be the least, or as if he were the least, if he seeks to obtain judgment. But if judgment is sought from him, since no writ runs against him himself, there will be place for a supplication that he may correct his act and amend it, and if he does not do so it suffices for his punishment that he await the vengeance of God. Let no one, indeed, presume to dispute his deeds, much less to oppose his acts.

[Folio 34—folio 34b; Woodbine, vol. II, pp. 109-110; Twiss, bk. 1, ch. 16, sec. 3.]

That the judges ought not to dispute about or judge royal charters

Neither the judges nor private persons can or ought to dispute about royal charters and the deeds of kings; nor, if some doubt arise in regard to them, can they interpret it. Also, in doubtful or obscure matters, or if any expression may contain two meanings, the interpretation and wish of the lord king ought to be awaited, since interpretation belongs to him whose it is to establish. And even if it is altogether false because of an erasure or because the seal affixed is forged, it is better and safer that the judgment proceed in the presence of the king himself. ⟨Likewise, no one can judge the deed or charter of the king so that the king's act is made void. But someone will be able to say that the king might have done justly and well, and if, by the same reasoning, he has done this, that it is ill done; and will be able to impose upon him the obligation of amending the injustice, lest the king and his justiciars fall into the judgment of the living God on account of the injustice. The king has a superior, namely, God. Likewise the law, through which he was made king. Likewise his court, namely, the counts and barons, because the counts are called, as it were, the partners of the king, and he who has a partner has a master. And therefore, if the king be without a bridle, that is, without law, they ought to put a bridle on him, unless they themselves are, with the king, without a bridle.⟩

[Folio 55b; Woodbine, vol. II, pp. 166-167; Twiss, bk. 2, ch. 24, sec. 1.]

Of franchises, and who can grant them, and what things belong to the king

.... Now, moreover, we should discuss franchises: who can grant them, and to whom, and how they are transferred, and how they are possessed or virtually possessed, and how they are retained by use. Who can grant them? The lord king himself, it should be known, who has ordinary jurisdiction and dignity and power over all men who are in his kingdom. For he has in his hand all the rights which belong to the crown, and the secular power, and the material sword which pertains to the governance of the realm. He also has justice and judgment, which belong to jurisdiction, that by his jurisdiction he may as minister and vicar of God assign to each what is his. He also has those things that belong to peace, that the people entrusted to him may be quiet and tranquil in peace and that no one may strike or wound or maltreat another, that no one may take away or carry off the goods of another by violence and robbery, and that no one may maim or slay any man. He also has the coercive power, that he may punish and coerce wrongdoers. He also has it in his power that he may himself in his own person observe and make his subjects observe the laws and statutes and assizes which have been provided and approved and sworn in his kingdom. For it is of no avail to establish rights unless there be someone to protect the rights. Therefore the king has rights and jurisdictions of this sort in his hand. He also has, before all others in his kingdom, privileges belonging to him by virtue of the law of peoples in the things which ought by natural law to belong to the finder, as, for instance, treasure trove, wrecks, the great fish, sturgeon, and castaways, which are said to be the property of no one. He also has in his hand by virtue of the law of peoples those things which by the law of nature ought to be common, as, for instance, wild beasts and wild birds, which ought to be common by natural law, through apprehension and capture and hunting. Likewise through the occupation and apprehension of the property of another, as when something is cast away or considered to have been abandoned. But the administration of justice and peace, and those things which are annexed to justice and peace, belong to no one save only the crown and the royal dignity, nor can they be separated from the crown, for they make the crown what it is. For the crown is to make justice and judgment, and to maintain peace, and without these things the crown can not consist nor hold. Moreover, rights or jurisdictions of this sort cannot be transferred to persons or tenements, nor possessed by a private person, nor can the use or execution of right, unless this were given from above, even as jurisdiction cannot be delegated in such a way that ordinary jurisdiction does not remain with the king himself. Those things which are called privileges of the crown, however, although they belong to the crown, can be separated from the crown and transferred to private persons. . . .

[Folio 107—folio 107b; Woodbine, vol. II, pp. 304–306; Twiss, bk. 3, ch. 9, secs. 1–3.]

Of the organization of the jurisdictions of the kingdom. . . .

. . . . We should examine, in regard to those things which belong to the kingdom, who first and principally ought to and can judge them. And it should be known that the king himself and none other can and ought to judge, if alone he is adequate to this, since he is considered bound to this by virtue of his oath. For in his coronation, the oath having been presented, he ought in the name of Jesus Christ to promise these three things to the people subjected to him:

Of the oath which the king ought to make in his coronation

First, that he will command and, so far as he can, see to it that for the church of God and all the Christian people a true peace may be preserved throughout his time. Secondly, that he will forbid plunderings and all iniquities in all ranks. Thirdly, that in all his judgments he will prescribe equity and mercy, that the clement and merciful God may impart His mercy to him, and that through his justice all men may enjoy a firm peace.

For what the king was created, and of his ordinary jurisdiction

Moreover, the king was created and chosen for this: that he should make justice for all, and that in him the Lord should sit, and that he himself should decide his judgments, and that he should sustain and defend what he has justly judged, because if there were no one to make justice peace could easily be wiped out, and it would be vain to establish laws and to do justice if there were no one to protect the laws. Moreover, since the king is vicar of God on earth, he ought to separate right from unright, fair from unfair, that all those who are subjected to him may live honestly and that no one may injure another, and to each may be rendered by a just award what is his own. But he ought to surpass all his subjects in power. Moreover, he ought to have no peer, still less a superior, especially in the administration of justice, that it may truly be said of him, 'Our great lord, and his great virtue,' etc. Although in the receiving of justice he may be compared to the least person of his kingdom, although he excels all in power, yet since the heart of a king ought to be in the hand of God, lest his power be unbridled let him put on the bridle of temperance and the reins of moderation, lest if it be unbridled he be drawn towards injustice. For the king, since he is minister and vicar of God, can do nothing on earth save only that which is according to law, nor is this contrary to the saying that 'what pleases the prince has the force of law,' since there follows after 'law' 'since by the *lex regia* which was made concerning his rule, [etc.]' [*Digest*, 1, 4, 1]: that is, not what is rashly presumed to be the king's will but what has been duly defined with the counsel of his magnates, the king warranting its authority after deliberation and discussion upon it [*Codex*, 1, 14, 8]. Therefore his power is of right and not of unright, and since he is the author of right there ought not to be born occasion of unrights thence whence rights are born; and he who by virtue of his office must prohibit unright to others ought not to commit it himself in his own person. Therefore the king ought to exercise the power of right as God's vicar and minister on earth because that power is from God above; but the power of unright is from the Devil and not from God, and the king will be the minister of that one of the two whose works he does. Therefore, when he does justice he is the vicar of the Eternal King, but he is the Devil's minister when he falls into injustice. For a king (*rex*) is so called from ruling (*regendo*) well and not from reigning, because when he rules well he is a king, but he is a tyrant when he oppresses with violent domination the people entrusted to him. Therefore, let him temper his power by law, which is the bridle of power, that he may live according to the laws, since a human law has stated that laws bind the lawgiver himself, and else-where in the same source, 'It is a saying worthy of the majesty of rulers that the prince profess himself bound by the laws' [*Codex*, 1, 14, 4]. Again, nothing is so proper to empire as to live by the laws, and 'it is greater than empire to submit the principate to the laws,' and deserv-edly he ought to give back to the law what the law has given to him, for the law makes him king. Again, since it is not always fitting that a king be armed with arms, but with laws, let the king learn wisdom and maintain justice, and God will grant it to him, and when he has found it he will be blessed if he has kept it, since in the speech of the sensible there is honour and glory, and in the tongue of the imprudent there lurks his overthrow; and the principate of the wise man is firm, and the sapient king will judge his people. . . .

[Folio 171b; Woodbine, vol. III, pp. 42–43; Twiss, bk. 4, ch. 10.]

Against whom the assize of novel disseisin is applicable, and how one becomes liable to the assize

. . . . Likewise, among other things, it is to be seen who it was who did the dispossessing. . . . But if it be a prince or a king, or another who has no superior save the Lord, there will be no remedy against him by an assize; on the contrary, there will only be place for a supplication that he will correct and amend, and if he will not do so, one must be content to await the Lord the Avenger, who says, 'Vengeance is mine, I will repay' [Romans 12:19]; unless there be someone who will say that the corporation of the kingdom and its baronage can and ought to do this, in the court of the king himself.

Thomas Aquinas

[The following passages are from the *De Regimine Principum*, bk. 1, chs. 2, 6. I have used the text ed. Mathis (Turin, 1924).]

CHAPTER II

. . . . We must inquire whether it is more expedient for a province or city to be ruled by many or by one. Moreover, we can consider this by considering what the end of government is. For the objective of a ruler should be to procure the welfare of that which he undertakes to rule. The objective of a pilot should be to preserve his ship from the perils of the sea and bring it, unharmed, to the harbour of safety. Now the good and welfare of an associated multitude is the preservation of its unity, which is called peace, without which the utility of social life perishes—nay more, the discordant multitude becomes a burden to itself. This, therefore, is the special function of the ruler: to procure the unity of peace. . . . Now it is manifest that what is itself one can more effectively bring about unity than can a plurality, even as the most effective cause of heat is what is itself hot. Therefore, the government of one man is more useful than the government of many. Further, it is manifest that a plurality of men disagreeing about everything would not preserve the unity of a multitude at all. For there has to be a certain union among the many if they are to be able to rule at all, even as many helmsmen, unless they agree in some way, cannot bring a ship to one harbour; now a plurality is said to be united as it approximates unity. Therefore, one man rules better than a plurality, because of approximation to unity. And again, things are at their best when they most resemble nature; for in each individual case nature does what is best; now the common natural rule is by one; for among the many parts of the body there is one, namely, the heart, which moves all the others, and among the parts of the soul one force, namely, reason, presides as ruler. And the bees have one king, and in the whole universe there is one God, Maker and Ruler of all. This is rational, for all multiplicity is derived from unity. Wherefore, if those things that are produced by art imitate those that follow nature, and since a work of art is better in proportion as it copies what is natural, it is necessarily best for the human multitude to be ruled by one man. This is also apparent from experience. For the provinces or cities that are not ruled by one man suffer dissensions and vacillate without peace. Thus the lamentation seems to be fulfilled that the Lord made through His prophet, saying: 'Many shepherds have destroyed My vineyard.' On the contrary, however, provinces and cities that are ruled by one king enjoy peace, flourish in justice, and rejoice in an abundance of riches. Whence the Lord promised through His prophets, as a great gift to His people, that He would give them one head, and one prince would be in the midst of them.

CHAPTER VI

Therefore, because the government of one man, which is the best, is to be preferred, and because it may happen that this is changed into tyranny, which is the worst, . . . diligent care should be used to provide a king for the multitude in such a way that they will not fall under a tyrant. First, from among those eligible to this office there must be chosen for the kingship a man of such character that he is not likely to lapse into tyranny. . . . Next, the government of the kingdom should be so arranged that the opportunity of tyranny is withdrawn from the king when he is instituted. And at the same time his power should be tempered, so that he cannot easily lapse into tyranny. The things to be done will be considered later.

But now we should consider how the situation could be met if the king should turn to tyranny. And, indeed, if the tyranny is not excessive, it would be more expedient to endure a lax tyranny for a time rather than to bring about many dangers graver than the tyranny itself by opposing it. For it may happen that those who oppose the tyrant cannot prevail, and the tyrant, provoked by their opposition, grows more cruel. But if some one is able to prevail against the tyrant, this very fact often leads to the most serious dissensions in the people, either in the course of the rebellion or when, after the tyrant is overthrown, the multitude breaks into factions over the ordination of the government. It also sometimes happens that when the multitude expels a tyrant with the help of a certain leader, he in turn seizes tyrannical power and in the fear of sharing the fate of his predecessor he may oppress his subjects with even heavier servitude. . . .

If the tyranny is extreme beyond endurance, some people have thought that it is appropriate to the virtue of brave men to kill the tyrant and to expose themselves to the risk of death for the liberation of the multitude; and there is an instance of this in the Old Testament. For a certain Ehud killed Eglon, king of Moab, with a dagger thrust into his side, because he was oppressing the people of God with heavy servitude; and he became a judge of the people [Judges 3]. But this does not agree with the teaching of the apostles. For Peter teaches us to be reverently subject 'not only to good and moderate rulers, but also to the harsh' [I Peter 2:18]. . . . Moreover, if people should attempt the death of rulers, even of tyrants, by private presumption, it would be dangerous to the multitude and to its rulers. For evil men expose themselves to risks of this sort more often than the good, and the dominion of kings, no less than of tyrants, is generally burdensome to evildoers. . . . Therefore, such presumption would be more likely to result in the loss to the multitude of a good king than in the beneficial abolition of a tyrant.

Thus it seems that action against a tyrant should not be taken by the private presumption of individuals but rather by public authority.

First, if the multitude has the right to provide itself with a king, it can justly depose its king or restrain his power if he tyrannically abuses his royal authority. And in this case the multitude should not be considered to act disloyally in deposing a tyrant, since if he does not bear himself faithfully in the government of the multitude, as the office of king requires, his subjects are no longer bound by their contract with him. . . . If, however, some superior has the right to provide the multitude with a king, they should look to him for a remedy against the evildoing of the tyrant. . . . But if no human aid at all can be obtained against the tyrant, recourse must be had to God, King of all, Who gives aid in time of tribulation. . . .

Aegidius Romanus

[The following passages are translated from bk. 3, pt. 2, chs. 5 and 29 of the *De Regimine Principum* written by Aegidius Romanus in 1285 for the instruction of the future king Philip IV of France, whose tutor he was. I have used the edition printed at Rome in 1482.]

CHAPTER V. *That it is better for a kingship to be conveyed by inheritance or the succession of sons than by election*

It seems, perhaps, to some people that it is altogether better and more worthy that the royal lordship and principate be conveyed by election than by inheritance. For when the truth of the question . . . is superficially considered, there seems to be doubt whether it is better to constitute lordship by art or by chance. For if some one is set up as king by election, it seems that such a kingship is not exposed to chance and fortune but is made by art, since a better and more diligent man is set at its head. But if this is done by inheritance, the kingship is to some extent exposed to luck, chance, and fortune, for it is uncertain what kind of son may be expected to inherit the royal dignity. Therefore, speaking in the abstract, it is better that the prince be set up by election than by inheritance; also, because most men have corrupt desires. But if we consider the deeds and conditions of men which we observe empirically, it seems that we ought to decide that it is more expedient for a kingdom or a city that its lord be set up by inheritance rather than by election.

Moreover we can show in three ways that when the conditions of men are considered it is better that such a government be conveyed by inheritance.

The first way is based on consideration of the ruling king himself.

The second is based on consideration of the son who is to succeed to this heritage.

The third is based on consideration of the people which is to be governed by such a rule.

The first way proceeds as follows. According to the Philosopher, II *Politics*, [ch. 2], 'It is inexpressible how much delight one feels and what a difference it makes to know that something is one's own.' For what is natural can not naturally be indifferent and purposeless; moreover, everyone feels friendship toward himself. It is natural, therefore, that the more a king thinks of the kingdom as his own private affair, the more solicitous he will be for its good. Wherefore, if the king sees that he is to be prince over the kingdom not only for his own lifetime, but also, through inheritance, through his sons', the more he will regard the good of the kingdom as his own good. Nay, more: since every hope of the father rests in the sons, and fathers are moved by excessive love toward the pleasure of the sons, he will be moved to seek the welfare of the kingdom with all possible care, if he believes that it will pass to the lordship of his sons.

The Philosopher touches on this point in III *Politics*, [ch. 10], where, discussing this, he says that it is difficult for fathers thus to be able to bequeath the government of a kingdom to their own sons. For he hints that this involves a quasi-divine virtue, above the level of human virtue. But perhaps the Philosopher says this because in ancient times most kings changed into tyrants and the succession of sons to the paternal heritage did not last long; or he says that this is divine in the sense that, unless kings and princes have the right relationship toward divine matters, it rarely happens that sons reign after their father, and if the sons reign, the sons' sons will scarcely or never reign. From the point of view of the king, therefore, that he may be more solicitous for the good of the kingdom, we can argue that it is expedient that the royal government pass to the sons by inheritance.

The second path to this same investigation begins with the son who is to undertake the charge of the kingdom; for even as the behaviour of the newly rich is usually worse than the behaviour of those who have been rich for a long time, so the behaviour of the newly powerful and of those who are newly elevated by acquisition of civil power is worse than the behaviour of others, for they do not know how to carry such fortune. For to be newly exalted to the kingship involves, as one might say, a lack of education for the royal dignity. Such men, indeed, usually become tyrants and reign amateurishly with puffed-up hearts. But if the royal rule is conveyed by inheritance, the sons do not become puffed up nor elated thereby, because they do not think it a great thing to have what their fathers had possessed; therefore, from the viewpoint of the sons who are to succeed to the paternal heritage, it is expedient that the royal dignity should be bequeathed to the descendants through inheritance, lest the kingdom be clumsily ruled, and the royal rule be turned to tyranny.

The third path begins with the people which is to be ruled by this government. For custom is, as it were, another nature, so that custom makes governments quasi-natural. Therefore if the people through long-enduring custom has obeyed the fathers, it is quasi-naturally inclined voluntarily to obey the sons and the sons' sons; and since what is voluntary is less onerous and difficult, it is expedient that there be hereditary succession to the royal dignity, that the people may obey the king's commands more willingly and easily. Therefore the determination of the house and stock from which the king is to be taken calms strife, abolishes tyranny, and brings about a quasi-natural lordship.

. . . . From this follows the further conclusion, that not only is it expedient for the kingdom to determine the stock from which the lord is to be established, but it is also necessary to determine the person, for even as dissensions and disputes arise if it is not known from which line the king is to be taken, so disputes also arise if it is not determined what person in that line ought to rule. . . .

CHAPTER XXIX. *How a city or kingdom is better ruled: whether it is better ruled by the best king or by the best law*

The Philosopher in III *Politics*, [ch. 10], asks whether a city or kingdom is better ruled by the best king or by the best law, and gives two reasons why it is better that the polity of the kingdom be ruled by the best law rather than by the best king. The first is based on the proposition that the king ought to be a sort of organ and instrument of the law; the second on the proposition that it is easier to corrupt a king than a law. The first argument proceeds as follows: as it is said in V *Ethics*, [ch. 6], the prince ought to be the guardian of justice, that is, of just law. He is therefore a prince if he duly rules as a kind of organ of just law, so that what just law commands the king through his civil power causes to be observed. Therefore, if that which is more primary in government is more to be desired than its organ and instrument, to be ruled by the best law is more to be desired than to be ruled by the best king. This, therefore, is what the Philosopher says [III *Politics*, ch. 11]: that it is more desirable that law should rule, because it ought to be established that kings or princes are servants and ministers of the law.

The second path for exploring this question begins with the premise that it is easier for a king to be perverted than the law. For the king, since he is a man, declares not only an apprehended good, but an apprehended good mingled with desire. Granted, therefore, that the king be not perverted in his understanding, yet he can be perverted by the lust annexed to his understanding. Therefore it is said in III *Politics*, that sometimes rage and greed finally destroy and pervert the best man. . . . But law, because it is a matter of reason, seems to declare a rational apprehension only. Therefore it is said in III *Politics*, [ch. 11], that 'he who orders that the understanding rule orders that God and the law shall rule, but he who orders that a man rule . . . appoints a beast to rule also.' By these arguments, therefore, it seems to be shown that it is better that a kingdom or city be ruled by the law rather than by a king.

But that this ought not be said without qualification the Philosopher also shows in the same place. For, as he says, law prescribes as universally just that which is not universally just; for human laws, however much they may be refined, fail in some cases; therefore it is better that a kingdom be ruled by a king rather than by the law, that through the king the defects of the law may be corrected.

Therefore, to say what should be said on this question, it should be known that a king or any ruler is a mean between natural and positive law; for no one rules rightly unless he acts as right reason dictates. For reason ought to be the rule of human actions. Therefore, if the name of *rex* is derived from *regendo*, and it befits a king to rule others and to be a ruler of others, a king must necessarily in ruling others follow right reason and, consequently, follow natural law, since he rules rightly only in so far as he does not deviate from natural law; yet he is above positive law because he constitutes it by his authority. Therefore, even as a king never rightly rules unless he leans on natural law and acts as right reason dictates, so positive law never rightly binds unless it leans on the authority of the [natural] law or of a ruler. For, as was said above [in bk. 3, pt. 2, ch. 24], that which is just by positive law is originally a matter of indifference; however, it is determined when it is promulgated, because of the authority of him who promulgates it. Therefore positive law is below the ruler, even as natural law is above him. And if it is said that some positive law is above the ruler, this is not in proportion as it is positive, but in proportion as there is preserved in it the force of natural law.

Therefore, when it is asked whether it is better that a city or kingdom be ruled by the best king or by the best law, if we are speaking of natural law it is evident that this is more primary in ruling than is the king himself, since no one is a right king except in so far as he leans upon that law. And thus the Philosopher speaks wisely when he suggests in III *Politics*, [ch. 11], that in a right government not a beast, but God and the understanding should rule; for a beast rules when a king tries to rule others not by reason, but by passion and lust, in which we share with the beasts; but God rules when in ruling others the king does not deviate from right reason and from natural law, which God instilled in the understanding of everyone. But if we are speaking of positive law, it is better to be ruled by the best king, especially in those cases in which the law is at fault and sets forth universally that which ought not to be universally observed; in this sense, accordingly, reason leads us to the opposite conclusion: that it is better to be ruled by a king than by the law, since the law cannot determine particular cases. Therefore it is expedient that a king or some other ruler, through right reason and through natural law, which God impressed on the mind of each man, direct the positive law, and be above legal justice, and not observe the law where it ought not to be observed.

Tholommeo of Lucca

[Tholommeo was born in 1236, of a noble Lucchese family. He became a Dominican and pursued the study of theology as a pupil and follower of

Thomas Aquinas. He held a series of ecclesiastical offices in Italy, finally becoming Bishop of Torcella. He died in 1326 or 1327.

He wrote a number of historical and publicistic works, of which one of the most important was his *Determinatio Compendiosa de Jurisdictione Imperii* (1281), the first work by a theologian to develop analytically the theory of papal sovereignty over the empire which had earlier taken legal form in the writings of canonists and in particular of Innocent IV. It was widely used by later writers on both sides of the great controversy. But his continuation of Aquinas's unfinished *De Regimine Principum* (written between 1298 and 1308) was perhaps even more influential in later medieval thought, since it was believed to be the work of the master himself. To modern scholars, its interest lies in the fact that it represents a view seldom encountered in medieval political writings, directly reflecting Italian communal experience in its strong preference for republican rather than monarchic government.

The following selections are from the *De Regimine Principum*, book 2, chs. 8, 9; book 3, chs. 11, 20; and book 4, ch. 1. I have used the editions printed in Leyden in 1602 and 1630.]

BOOK II, CHAPTER VIII

. . . . In his *Politics* [bk. 1, ch. 1], Aristotle has described two kinds of government: . . . namely, the political and the despotic. Political government is that in which a region, province, or town, or a citadel, is ruled by one or more men in accordance with its own statutes, as occurs in the regions of Italy and as particularly occurred in Rome, which was ruled by senators and consuls for the greater part of its history after the city was founded. . . . In such a lordship there are two reasons why the subjects cannot be so rigorously controlled as in a regal lordship. One reason is that the government of the ruler is temporary, and as a result his interest in those subjected to him is lessened by the consideration that his lordship will soon be at an end. . . . Moreover, political lordship is mercenary, for political rulers are attracted through salaries. Now, where payment is provided, rulers give less zealous attention to the governing of their subjects, and consequently the rigour of their discipline is moderated. . . . The second reason why political lordship is necessarily moderate and exercised with moderation concerns the subjects, since their disposition is naturally proportionate to such a system. For Ptolemy proves in the *Quadripartitus* that in regard to systems of morals the regions of men are distinguished in accordance with various constellations. . . . Thus the regions of the Romans which he places under Mars, are less easily brought to subjection. . . . Moreover, the self-confidence of the subjects, whether because they have been free of the lordship of rulers or because they have had experience of governing one another in turn, makes them bold for liberty and unwilling to bow their necks to rulers; thus political lordship is necessarily gentle. Furthermore, this form of ruling is in accordance with the form of the communal or municipal laws by which the ruler is bound; thus, because the prince is not free, his discretion is eliminated and is less like the divine providence. And although the laws are derived from the law of nature, and the law of nature from the divine law, yet they fail in regard to particular cases, since the legislator, ignorant of the future, could not provide for all cases. And this fact leads to a weakness in the political government which does not exist in the regal, for the political ruler judges his people by the laws only, whereas under regal lordship the prince decides through that which is in his heart, and therefore regal lordship more closely resembles the divine providence. . . . The characteristics of the political principate and the manner in which it rules are now apparent; let us next examine the despotic principate.

CHAPTER IX

It should first be noticed that the term *despotic* is applied to the rule of a lord over his slaves, and that it is a Greek word. . . . The Holy Scriptures show that we can identify this principate with the regal. A question arises here, since the Philosopher in I *Politics*, [ch. 1], distinguishes between regal and despotic government; but we shall clear up this difficulty later. . . . Meanwhile, let it suffice to prove through the divine writings what we have said. For the regal laws were described by the Prophet Samuel to the people of Israel, and they imply servitude. For when the people of Israel had sought a king from Samuel, . . . he consulted the Lord, Who answered thus: 'Harken unto the voice of the people in all that they say unto thee, yet protest solemnly with them, and tell them the rights of a king. He will take your sons and appoint them to his chariots, and he will have chariots and horsemen, and men to run before his chariots; and he will make them plough his fields and reap his harvests; and he will make armourers of them; and of your daughters he will make cooks and bakers,' and so on, concerning other conditions of servitude, which are set forth in I Samuel, 8:[7-18]: as if He wished to show by this that the political government of judges, which He had ordained, was more advantageous to the people. And yet the contrary has been argued; and to clear up this difficulty it should be explained that political lordship is preferable to regal lordship in two ways.

First, we may discuss lordship in relation to the righteous condition of human nature, which is called the state of innocence: in this there was political government but not regal, for at that time there was no lordship involving servitude but merely pre-eminence and subjection in disposing and governing the multitude in accordance with the merits of each one, so that each one was disposed in accordance with his nature, both in influencing and in receiving influence. Thus, among wise and virtuous men, such as the ancient Romans were, the political government which imitated the state of nature was preferable. But, since the wicked are restrained only with difficulty, . . . in corrupt nature the regal government is the more advantageous, since the erring nature of men, prone to wickedness and folly, needs severe restraint, which the dignity of kings provides. . . . Therefore the yoke of a discipline which everyone fears and the rigour of justice are necessary in governing the world, because through such discipline the untaught multitude are better regulated. . . . Therefore, in this respect the regal lordship excels the political.

Secondly, geographic location disposes a region in accordance with the aspect of the stars, as was said above; and from this fact we can see that certain regions are suited to servitude, others to liberty. . . .

BOOK III, CHAPTER XI

Now let us proceed to regal lordship. . . . First, in the Holy Scriptures the laws of regal lordship are described in one way by Moses in Deuteronomy and in another way by the Prophet Samuel in I Samuel; and the former, as the mouthpiece of God, differs from the latter in that he ordains the king to the utility of the subject, which is, as the Philosopher says in VIII *Ethics*, [ch. 10], proper to kings. When the king has been set up, Moses says, 'he will not multiply horses for himself, nor lead the people back to Egypt; . . . he will not have many wives, who pervert the soul, nor immense weights of silver and gold; . . . and he will write down for himself a copy of this law of Deuteronomy, and he will keep it with him, and will read it all the days of his life, that he may learn to fear the Lord his God and to keep His words and ceremonies, and that he may direct the people according to the divine law' [Deuteronomy 17:16–19] . . . . But in I Samuel [8:11–18] there are set forth laws of a kingdom more to the utility of the king, as appeared in Book II of this work; for there appears a description of a completely servile constitution, and yet Samuel said that the laws which he described were regal, though they are thoroughly despotic. Moreover, the Philosopher in VIII *Ethics*, [chs. 10, 11], agrees more with the former laws. For in this book he sets forth three things concerning a king: namely, that a lawful king is one who principally intends the good of the subjects, and who has independent resources and excels all in wealth, so that he will not exploit his subjects, and who cares for his subjects like a shepherd, so that things may be done well. And from all this it is obvious that, by such a definition, despotic government is very different from regal government, as the Philosopher seems to say in I *Politics*, [ch. 1]. Moreover, it is said that the kingdom is not for the king, but the king for the kingdom, since God has provided kings for this: that they may rule the kingdom and govern it and protect everyone in his right; and this is the end of government, because if they act for some advantage to themselves, distorting that end, they are not kings but tyrants. . . . But, because no one ever goes to war at his own expense, and everyone by a kind of natural right ought to receive payment for his labour, as the apostle testifies in I Corinthians [9:7; 3:8], princes are permitted to take tributes and annual taxes from their people. . . .

We conclude, therefore, that a lawful king ought to rule and govern according to the description given in Deuteronomy. And we are shown this by examples also, since those who did otherwise came to a bad end. . . . And from these we learn that princes should be content with their own revenue and not exact levies from the property and possessions of their subjects except for two reasons: namely, in case of crime, and for the common good of the realm. For, by reason of crime, he deprives vassals of their fiefs for disloyalty and deprives others of their wealth on the basis of that justice for which lordships were established. . . . And that he can make exactions for the good of the commonwealth (for example, for the defence of the realm or for any other cause rationally belonging to the good of his lordship) is based on evident reason, because if human society is natural, . . . all things that are necessary to the common conservation of that society will belong to natural law. . . . Thus, therefore, in a lawful regal lordship the king can exact from his subjects what is required for their own good. . . .

Thus in these two ways the despotic principate is identified with the regal, but especially by reason of crime, on account of which servitude was introduced, as Augustine says in *The City of God*, book 18. For although there was lordship in the first state of man, it was only by the office of advising and directing, not by the desire of dominating or by the intention of subjecting servilely, as was said above. But the laws set down by the Prophet Samuel for the people of Israel were given under these circumstances, because that people, being ungrateful and stiff-necked, deserved to bear such laws. For sometimes when a people does not recognize the benefit of good government it is expedient to exercise tyranny, because tyranny also is an instrument of divine justice; and for this reason certain islands and provinces, as the histories tell, always have tyrants on account of the wickedness of the people, since they cannot be ruled otherwise than by an iron yoke. Therefore in such unruly regions a despotic regal principate is necessary, not indeed because of the nature of regal lordship but because of the deserts and obstinacy of the subjects. And thus Augustine reasons in the aforesaid book. The Philosopher, also, in III *Politics*, [ch. 9], where he distinguishes kinds of kingdoms, shows that among some barbarous nations regal lordship is completely despotic, since they could not be otherwise ruled. . . .

CHAPTER XX

. . . . Imperial lordship ought now to be compared with regal and political lordship, since . . . it has some aspects in·common with each. It has three things in common with political lordship: first, that it is based on election. . . . Second, that the ruler is not always noble, but sometimes from an obscure family. . . . Third, there is another likeness, in that the lordship of these rulers does not pass to their posterity, so that the lordship expires with the death of the ruler. . . . But there is also a threefold likeness to regal lordship. First, the manner of ruling, since emperors have jurisdiction like kings, and for them, as for kings, by a kind of natural right, tributes and taxes have been established . . . which consuls do not have, nor any other rulers of cities in Italy who rule by political government. . . . The second similarity of emperors to kings is the crown, for emperors are crowned like kings. . . . And the third similarity by which emperors resemble kings and differ from consuls or political rulers is their right to institute laws and the arbitrary power which they have over their subjects. . . . For this reason the imperial and regal lordship is called majesty, a term not appropriate to consuls and political rulers, since consuls and political rulers are not permitted to act except in accordance with the form of laws which has been given them by the will of the people, beyond which they cannot judge. . . .

BOOK IV, CHAPTER I

'Constitute them princes over all the earth; they will be mindful of Thy name, O Lord' [Psalm 45: 16–17]. Although every lordship or principate was instituted by God . . . yet diverse kinds of lordship are described by the Philosopher and in the Holy Scriptures. Thus, since in the previous book we dealt with the monarchy of one man, . . . now we appropriately deal with the lordship of a plurality, which we call by the common name, political. Aristotle has described this for us in its two aspects: first, the manner in which it is assumed; second, the manner in which it is exercised. Now the manner in which this kind of lordship is assumed is election, without regard to family, not through natural origin as in the case of kings; and this is implied by the word 'constitute.' 'Constitute them princes,' it says, and then adds 'over all the earth,' thus showing that it is a general rule for the political principate that the princes are established by election; and it is also a general rule that they should be virtuous, whence it adds, 'They will be mindful of the name of the Lord,' that is, in the consideration of God and His precepts, which are the true plan for the actions of all rulers. . . . Moreover, in the present book we shall discuss the principate which the Philosopher defines in III Politics, [ch. 5] . . . because if in such a constitution a few virtuous men govern, it is called aristocracy: for instance, the government by the two consuls, or the two consuls and a dictator, in the city of Rome in the beginning after the expulsion of the kings.

If, however, many govern—for instance, consuls, dictator, and tribunes, as happened later in that same city, and afterwards senators, as the histories tell—such a constitution is called a polity, from polis, which is a plurality or a city, because this constitution properly belongs to cities, as we especially see in parts of Italy and formerly in Athens, where it flourished after the death of Codrus. . . . For then they ceased to have a regal lordship and used magistrates of the commonwealth as in a city. But whether it is an aristocracy or a polity, it is distinguished from a kingdom or monarchy. . . . And, because both involve plurality, these two types compose the political as distinguished from the regal or despotic lordship, as the Philosopher explains in the first and third books of the *Politics*. And this is what we are to discuss here. . . .

The differences between the political government and the regal and imperial or monarchic can first be somewhat seen with the help of the aforesaid first and third books; but now another distinction is to be added, since political rulers are bound by the laws and cannot go beyond them in the administration of justice. And this is not the case with kings and other monarchic princes, since the laws are hidden in their breasts to cover cases as they arise. And what pleases the prince is held as law, as the law of peoples says. But this is not true of political rulers, since they dare not make any innovation aside from the written law. . . . And it should be recognized that cities everywhere, whether in Germany or in Scythia or in France, live politically, but are circumscribed by the authority of the king, to whom they are bound under definite laws. There is also another difference: that in political lordships the rulers are more often exposed to scrutiny to find out whether they have judged well and have ruled in accordance with the laws given them; and if they have not, they are subjected to punishment. . . .

Marsiglio of Padua

[In *dictio* 1, ch. 18, secs. 3 ff. of the *Defensor Pacis*, Marsiglio provides an institutional check on the ruler. In many Italian communes, the *podesta* was held to account by an investigation at the end of his term of office; Venice provided a continuous check like that which Marsiglio describes.]

3. Because the ruler, being a man, . . . is capable of false judgements or perverse desires, or both, which result in his doing things which are contrary to the determinations of the law, therefore the ruler is made accountable for such actions to someone who has authority to judge and regulate him in accordance with the law. . . ; otherwise his principate would become despotic, and the life of the citizens would become servile and insufficient. . . .

Moreover, the judgment, decision, and execution of any correction of the ruler in accordance with his deserts or his transgression ought to be made by the legislator or by some person or persons appointed to this office by the authority of the legislator. . . . Also, the office of the prince who is to be corrected ought to be temporarily suspended, particularly in relation to the person or persons who are to judge of his transgressions, lest a schism and disturbance and conflict occur in the community because of the plurality of ruling authority, and because the ruler is not corrected as such but as a subject who has transgressed the law.

4. Accordingly, . . . let us say that the offence of the ruler is either serious or trivial; further, it concerns matters that can occur frequently or those that can occur but seldom; further, it concerns matters determined by law or not so determined. Now, if the offence of the ruler is serious—for instance, an offence against the commonwealth, or against an important person, or against any other person, so that scandal or popular disturbance may easily result from the omission of correction —then, regardless of whether it concerns matters of frequent or rare occurrence, the ruler ought to be corrected on this account. For if this offence is not punished, the result may be disturbance of the people and the disorder or dissolution of the polity. And if it concerns a matter determined by law, he ought to be corrected in accordance with the law; but if not, then in accordance with the decision of the legislator; and it ought to be determined by the law as far as possible. . . .

5. But if the offence of the ruler is trivial, either it concerns matters which occur seldom and is seldom committed by the ruler, or else it concerns matters which may occur frequently and is often committed by the ruler. But if this offence is or can be seldom committed by the ruler, it ought to be ignored and passed over. . . . For if the prince is corrected on account of every little fault, however rare and trivial, he will be rendered contemptible; and this will redound considerably to the common injury by leading the citizens to show less reverence and obedience to the laws and to the ruler. And also, if the prince is unwilling to undergo correction for any trifle whatever because he regards it as unimportant, the result may be a grave scandal; and such a sore should not be scratched. . . .

7. If, however, the offence of the ruler is of no great importance but capable of frequent occurrence, it should be determined by law, and a ruler often at fault in this respect should be restrained by an appropriate penalty. For an offence of this sort, however trivial, may injure the polity if committed to a noteworthy extent. . . .

William of Occam

[In *Dialogus*, pt. 3, tr. 1, bk. 2, ch. 6 (Goldast, *Monarchia* . . . , vol. II, pp. 794–795), Occam gives a precise classification of different types of government.]

TEACHER: There are two primary species of polities, even as there are also two proper species of principates or prelacies and of princes or prelates or rulers. For every principate is either ordained principally to the common good, namely, that of the ruler or rulers together with that of the subjects, or it is not ordained to the common good. If it is ordained to the common good, then it is a temperate and right principate. If it is not ordained to the common good, it is a vitiated and perverted principate, since it is a corruption and perversion of the temperate and right and just principate. . . .

Now there are three primary and distinct species of the moderate and right polity. The first is that in which the ruler is one man, and this is called a regal monarchy: in this, one man alone rules for the sake of the common good and not primarily for the sake of his own desires and advantages. And a polity of this sort, according to Aristotle in VIII *Ethics*, [ch. 10], is the best when it is at its best; for there are several kinds of regal monarchy, as Aristotle says in III *Politics*, [ch. 9]; but the most powerful kind of regal monarchy seems to be that in which some one reigns and governs in a kingdom not in accordance with law, but in accordance with his own will. And some men interpret this in the following way. He is said to govern and reign in accordance with his own will and not in accordance with law who reigns for the sake of the common good of all and is bound by no purely positive human laws or customs, but is above all laws of this sort, although he is bound by natural laws. And therefore such a king does not have to swear or promise to maintain any existent human laws or customs whatsoever, although it would be desirable for him to swear to maintain the natural laws for the common utility and, in all things which concern the office he has assumed, to seek the common good rather than his private good. Such a king can be said to have plenitude of power in regard to those things that tend to the common good rather than his private good.

Moreover, a principate of this sort differs from a tyrannic principate since it exists for the sake of the common good; it also differs from a despotic principate, since a despotic principate exists principally for the sake of the private good of the ruler. Now the regal principate exists for the sake of the common good, and therefore it is not properly called a despotic principate; and yet such a king is, in a way, lord of all things, but in a different way from the ruler of a despotic principate. For in a despotic principate the ruler has such great lordship that he can use his slaves, and any other things whatever that belong to his principate, not only for the sake of the common good, but also, so long as he attempts nothing contrary to divine or natural law, for his private good. But the ruler in the regal principate, as we have described him, cannot use his subjects and their property for his private good in whatever way pleases him; and thus the subjects of a regal principate are not slaves but enjoy natural liberty. For it is in keeping with natural liberty that no one can use free men for the utility of the user; but it is not contrary to natural liberty that one should reasonably use free men for the common good, since everyone is bound to prefer the common good to his private good.

PUPIL: According to what you have said, a despotic principate would be greater and more perfect than a regal principate of this sort, since it would involve greater power. . . .

TEACHER: The answer is that a despotic principate is greater in a way, since its extent is, in a way, greater, but for this very reason it is more imperfect, either because the good of the many is better than the good of one, or because injury to the good of the many does not imply perfection but imperfection. . . .

Besides the regal principate that we have described, there are others that fall short of it in various ways, although they are also kinds of monarchy. . . . The principate of one man sometimes falls short of the regal principate in regard to power, since it does not have that plenitude of power which characterizes the regal principate already described. And this kind of regal principate is called a principate according to law, because, although one man rules, yet he does not rule in accordance with his will but is bound by certain laws and customs introduced by men, which he is obliged to maintain; and he is obliged to swear and promise that he will maintain them; and the more such laws and customs he is obliged to maintain, the more he differs from the regal principate first described and therefore in these days there is, perhaps, not in the whole world any instance of the first regal principate. According to Aristotle [VIII *Ethics*, ch. 10], no one is worthy of such a kingship unless he excels in wisdom and virtue and all goods, both corporeal and spiritual, and also in such external goods as friends and riches. For otherwise there would be danger of his becoming a tyrant; and therefore he ought to have resources of his own, either from his own property or assigned to him by his subjects, so that he may never appropriate to himself the property of free men, nor take it in any way, unless evident utility or manifest necessity requires it.

The very opposite of this regal principate is tyranny, which is a corruption and perversion of it and the first and worst species of vitiated polity, since the tyrant does not seek the good of the subjects, unless incidentally, but in principle seeks his own good, regardless of whether his good be good or ill for others. . . . Kings may become tyrants, because, as Aristotle says in VIII *Ethics*, [ch. 10], a bad king becomes a tyrant, for if in accordance with the law he begins to rule his subjects against their will for his own good, he becomes a tyrant; but if he begins to rule them with their consent for his own good, he becomes, properly speaking, a despot. The latter principate is sometimes called a tyranny by Aristotle, on account of its great likeness to tyranny; but, as appears from what has been said, there is a distinction between despotism and tyranny. In summary, we may say that not only tyranny, in the correct sense, but also the despotic principate is in a way the opposite of the royal principate, especially of the most powerful type; or at any rate the two are so different that no one principate can be both royal and despotic with respect to the same subjects. . . .

[In another part of the *Dialogus*, Occam examines the nature and limits of the power of the emperor, using distinctions like those set forth in the passage above to qualify and re-interpret the more absolute assertions derived from the Roman law: *Dialogus*, pt. 3, tr. 2, bk. 2, chs. 20, 23, 26–28 (Goldast, vol. II, pp. 917–918, 920–921, 922–934.)]

CHAPTER XX

PUPIL: . . . . Now let us investigate what power the emperor has over his subjects, to see whether all are bound to obey him in all things.

TEACHER: It is answered that no one ought to obey him in illicit and unjust things.

PUPIL: Do you mean that they ought to obey him in all licit things, so that they sin who refuse to obey him in anything licit?

TEACHER: It is answered that someone who does not obey in what is licit is not necessarily to be judged as sinning, for if he commands someone to fast, or not to drink wine, or something of that sort which does not belong to the office of emperor, no one is bound to obey him; but in temporal matters which belong to the temporal government of the people everyone is bound to obey him.

PUPIL: In such matters, is everyone bound to obey the emperor in preference to anyone else: for example, his king, or duke, or marquis, or some other immediate lord? . . .

TEACHER: It is answered that . . . the emperor is immediate lord in the temporal affairs of all men, so that in those matters that belong to the government of mortals the emperor is to be obeyed rather than any inferior lord. . . .

PUPIL: From these premises two unsatisfactory conclusions seem to follow. The first is that all men are slaves of the emperor and no one is more his slave than is anyone else, and in relation to the emperor no one is more free than anyone else, since those who are equally bound to obey are equally his slaves or equally free. Therefore, if all men who are subject to the emperor are bound to obey him as immediate lord in all things that belong to the government of the people, all are equally his slaves or equally free. The second unsatisfactory conclusion that follows is that anyone who goes to war for his lord against the emperor would commit the crime of *lèse-majesté*, since, if any immediate subject of the emperor commits the crime of *lèse-majesté* if he contemplates the death of the emperor, what about the subject who goes to mortal war against the emperor? Tell me what is said about these inferences.

TEACHER: It is said that the first does not follow from the foregoing premises, since, as was said before, the subjects of the emperor are not bound to obey him in all things, but only in those that concern the government of the people: that is, in those things that are necessary for ruling justly and usefully the people subjected to him, and thus the slaves of the emperor and the free men are not bound to obey him equally; but the slaves are bound to obey him in many things in which the free men are not bound, for at the sole command of the emperor, without any claim of common utility, the slaves are bound to give up to him all the property that they have; but free men are not bound to do this, nor can the emperor command them to do it unless it is useful to the common good—indeed, not unless it is manifestly useful and necessary. Moreover, the slaves of the emperor are bound to obey him in many other respects in which the free men are not bound at all. For it would detract from the dignity of the human race if all were slaves of the emperor, and therefore it would detract from it if the emperor could in all things treat free men like slaves; therefore, since the emperor is bound to procure those things that belong to the dignity and utility of the whole human race, he ought by no means to wish to treat free men as slaves; and therefore the free men are not bound to obey him in all the things in which slaves are bound to obey. To the second inference it is said that whoever goes to unjust war against the emperor with any lord does commit the crime of *lèse-majesté*, and the penalty of the crime of *lèse-majesté* is to be punished and chastised.

CHAPTER XXVI

PUPIL: .... I now ask, in general, whether the emperor has as much plenitude of power in temporal affairs as the pope, in the opinion of many, has in spiritual affairs.

TEACHER: There are various opinions on this point: one is that the emperor has plenitude of power in temporal affairs in the sense that he can command all things not contrary to divine or natural law, so that in all such things his subjects are bound to obey him.

PUPIL: Please give the arguments that support this opinion.

TEACHER: In support of this opinion many arguments can be given. For he who is bound by no human law, but is restrained only by divine and natural law, can command all things not contrary to either of these laws; but the emperor is bound by no human law, but only by divine and natural law, since, as we read in the *Digest*, 1, 3, 31, and in the Gloss on the *Decretals*, bk. 1, tit. 2, ch. 1, the emperor is 'released from the laws'; therefore, in temporals he has plenitude of power in the sense that he can command all things not contrary to divine and natural law.

Further, he whose wish, in regard to a law of this sort, has the force of law has plenitude of power in temporal affairs; but 'what has pleased the prince' (especially, the emperor) 'has the force of law' [*Digest*, 1, 4 1]; therefore, in matters of this sort, the emperor has plenitude of power.

Again, he whose very error makes law in temporal affairs has plenitude of power in temporal affairs; therefore, the emperor has plenitude of power in temporal affairs.

Also, if any subject could justly resist a command of the emperor dealing with temporal affairs and not contrary to divine or natural law, he would have to be able to resist it on the basis of some legal right, because we can do righteously what we can do on the basis of some legal right. . . . But he could not resist on the basis of divine or natural law, for, as was said, the command was not contrary to either of these laws; nor could he resist on the basis of human law, for, as we read in the *Decretum*, c. 1, di. 8, human laws are not contrary to the law of the emperor, since God gave these human laws themselves to the human race through emperors and secular kings. Therefore, no one can resist an imperial command on the basis of imperial law, since the emperor is omnipotent in all matters of this sort.

Besides, human society is obliged to maintain that to which it has bound itself; but human society binds itself to obey kings in general and, consequently, the emperor even more. For Augustine says in the third book of the *Confessions*, as quoted in the *Decretum*, c. 2, di. 8, 'There is assuredly a general compact of human society to obey its kings.' Therefore, the emperor ought to be obeyed in temporal matters generally, so that he can command all things not contrary to divine and natural law.

CHAPTER XXVII

PUPIL: Give the contrary opinion.

TEACHER: The contrary opinion is that the emperor does not have such plenitude of power in temporal affairs that he can command everything not contrary to divine or natural law; but his power is limited so that, in regard to the free men subjected to him and in regard to their property, he can command only those things that further the common utility.

PUPIL: Give the arguments that support this opinion.

TEACHER: In support of this opinion, the following arguments are made. He whose laws ought to be made not for his private advantage but for the common utility does not have such plenitude of power that he can command all things; for, if he had such plenitude of power, he could establish laws not only for the common utility but also for the private utility of himself or someone else, and indeed for any purpose whatever, so long as it was not contrary to divine or natural law. But the imperial laws, and other laws, ought to be made not for private advantage but for the common utility, as Isidore testifies when he says, as quoted in the *Decretum,* c. 2, di. 4, 'Moreover, law will be . . . made, not for private advantage, but for the common utility.' Therefore, the emperor does not have such plenitude of power that he can command all things, but only those that tend to the common utility.

Further, if the emperor had such plenitude of power in matters of this sort, all other kings and princes and other laymen subject to him would be merely his slaves; for a lord has no greater power over his slaves than that he can command them to do anything not contrary to divine or natural law; indeed, his power over them is not so great as this. If, therefore, the emperor could command not only those things that tend to the common utility but also anything whatever, in temporal affairs, not contrary to divine or natural law, all others subject to him would be, in truth, his slaves.

Again, the pope has not plenary power in spiritual affairs, since he cannot command anyone to perform works of supererogation; as, for instance, virginity, fasting on bread and water, entering religion, and the like. Therefore, still less does the emperor have plenitude of power in temporal affairs.

Again, the emperor does not have greater power in temporal affairs than the people had, since the emperor derives his power from the people. . . ; for the people could not transfer to the emperor more jurisdiction and power than it had itself. But the people never had such plenitude of power that it could command one of its members to do anything not contrary to divine or natural law, since it could not command anything which was not necessary, for, as the Gloss on the *Decretals,* bk. 1, tit. 2, ch. 6, bears witness, in such cases nothing can be done unless all consent. Therefore, if the people commands one of its members to do something that necessity does not require, he is not bound to do it unless he wishes; therefore it follows that the emperor has no such plenitude of power.

Besides, to diminish, alienate, sell, give, or bequeath the imperial rights is not contrary to divine or natural law; but the emperor cannot do this; therefore he does not have plenitude of power.

Again, the emperor does not have such power as is dangerous to the common good; but such plenitude of power would be dangerous to the common good, for he could reduce all the subjects to poverty which would be contrary to the common good.

Again, power that is established only for the sake of the common utility extends only to such things as are ordained to the common utility, and consequently does not extend to everything not contrary to divine or natural law. But the imperial power was established only for the sake of the common utility; therefore it does not extend to those things that do not pertain to the common utility. . . .

CHAPTER XXVIII

PUPIL: Because this second opinion seems to favour the community of mortals and the common good, on whose behalf one is bound to be zealous, I wish to know how one answers the arguments in support of the other opinion. Tell me, therefore, how one answers the first argument. . . .

TEACHER: This is answered by making a distinction in regard to human laws, some of which are laws of emperors and of other persons or particular communities subjected to the emperor; and these can be called civil laws. Some, in a way, are laws of the whole community of mortals, which seem to belong to the law of peoples and which in one way are natural and in another way are human and positive, as can be gathered from what we have said in chapters 10 and 11 of part 3, [tr. 1, bk. 1]. Although it is proper that the emperor should live in accordance with his own laws, he is not necessarily bound to do so, provided that he keep those laws that belong to the law of peoples, since all peoples, and especially all who are rational and live by reason, use this law, even as the emperor is bound to it; and he is not permitted to transgress this law irregularly except in a case in which he sees that it is harmful to the common utility. . . . Moreover, it belongs to the law of peoples that the emperor does not have such plenitude of power that he can in temporal affairs command everything not contrary to natural law in the strict sense. . . . Also, that some men are free and not mere slaves is considered to belong to the law of peoples, and the one principle follows from the other. Therefore the emperor is bound by this law, which, however, is human, since, if all mortals unanimously agreed to contradict it, the contrary could be maintained as law.

PUPIL: Tell me how the second argument is answered.

TEACHER: That argument is answered by saying that what pleases the prince, or the emperor, reasonably and justly for the sake of the common good has the force of law, when this is manifestly expressed. If, however, something pleases him not for the sake of the common good but for the sake of private good, it does not therefore have the force of law: that is, not justly, but unjustly and inequitably. . . .

PUPIL: Tell me how the third argument is answered.

TEACHER: It is said that the error of the prince probably makes law, and therefore all are required to obey it unless it appears to them that the error of the prince is contrary to divine or natural law or the common good, because if so, the error of the prince does not make law.

PUPIL: What is the answer to the fourth argument?

TEACHER: It is answered by those things which were said above in answer to the first argument, because one can often resist the order of the emperor, even when it is not against divine or natural law, by virtue of human law—not, indeed, civil law, but the law of peoples, as was said. In reply to the argument, it is said that it speaks of human civil laws, not of the law of peoples; the civil laws are laws of emperors and kings, but the law of peoples is not a law of emperors and kings through their institution of it, although it can be a law of emperors and kings through their approbation and maintenance of it.

PUPIL: Tell what those who hold this opinion think in regard to the last argument.

TEACHER: They think that there is a general pact of human society to obey its kings in those things that tend toward the common good, and therefore human society is bound to obey its emperor in general in those things that further the common good, but not in those in regard to which there is no doubt that they will by no means advance the common good.

[In *Dialogus*, pt. 3, tr. 2, bk. 2, ch. 23 (Goldast, vol. II, pp. 920–921), Occam shows how the authority of the emperor is limited in regard to the *iura regni* and the private property of his subjects. The analysis is made in terms of the concept of divided lordship (see pp. 91–93, 101, above).]

TEACHER: There is an opinion that the emperor is not lord of temporal things, even of those which do not belong to the church, in such a way that at his pleasure he is permitted or is able to ordain for himself what he wishes concerning all things of this sort; yet that he is, in a way, lord of all things: in this respect, that he can use all things of this sort and apply them to the common good, no matter who may oppose him, whenever he sees that the common good ought to be preferred to private utility. And for the evidence of this opinion it should be known that some things are movable and some immovable, and certain things of both kinds belong to the emperor alone, and of these things no one else has lordship or administration unless by a special commission of the emperor, and these things can be called imperial things and things of the *fiscus*. And there are certain things which pertain to others, and these things in some way belong to the lords of these movable things.

Of the things that belong especially to the emperor, the emperor is lord in the following way: he can ordain anything he wishes concerning them without being held to any restitution, and he can sell, grant, bequeath, and alienate gold, silver, and precious stones, clothing, arms, animals, and all other movable things as he wishes, without being held to any restitution; for although the king would sin in unlawfully alienating things of this sort for a bad cause, yet he is not obliged to restore them to the empire or to others. In a similar way he is also lord of certain immovable things, so that he can give or alienate certain castles, fields, vineyards, and cities; therefore, in such things he has lordship and the most complete right. However, of some immovable things he does not have such complete right and lordship, because he cannot sell, grant, bequeath or alienate them: for instance, the imperial and royal rights, the alienation of which would redound to the notable detriment of the empire, and therefore he cannot alienate them; and if he should alienate them *de facto*, such alienation would not be valid *de jure*, but all the things would be recalled to the right of the empire; and, if he could, he would be obliged to restore them; yet he is in a certain way the lord of such things, in as much as he can claim and defend them in law, and can use them for the common utility; nor is anyone else deemed to have a right in them.

He has also lordship of the things belonging to others, to the extent that, for cause, and on behalf of the common utility of the people, and on account of a crime of the possessors, he can take them away from the possessors and appropriate them for himself or grant them to others. Yet, because he cannot do this arbitrarily at his will, but for the guilt of the possessors, or for cause: namely, for the common utility; therefore he does not have in them such complete lordship as in the former things, which he can, at his pleasure, alienate as he wishes in such a way that, however he has alienated them (at least, if he has granted them to the obedient), the alienation thereafter holds, and cannot be revoked by anyone.

Lupold of Bebenburg

[Lupold was one of the German ecclesiastics whose patriotic support of Lewis of Bavaria helped to secure the ultimate independence of the empire from papal control. Born of a wealthy ministerial family, Lupold studied at Bologna under the celebrated canonist Johannes Andreae and held a number of clerical offices in Germany. From 1325 to 1352, he was attached to the cathedral of Würzburg; in 1353, he became bishop of Bebenburg, or Bamberg. In the early stages of his ecclesiastical career, he supported the papal diplomacy in Germany, but in the crisis of 1338 he shifted to support Lewis's claim that the emperor duly chosen by the electoral princes needed no papal confirmation or consecration to assume the full imperial rights in Germany and Italy. Lupold took an important part in the negotiations which led to the Declarations of Rense and Frankfort (see below, p. 459) and was under the ban of the church thereafter. He died in 1363.

His *Tractatus de Juribus Regni et Imperii Romani* was completed in 1340 and dedicated to the archbishop Baldwin of Trier, one of the signers of the Declaration of Rense. The treatise, written, as Lupold tells us, 'out of fervent zeal for Germany my fatherland,' is remarkable for its penetrating and comprehensive definition of issues, for its cogent argument, and for the way in which that argument is permeated by the conviction that the empire was the affair of the German people. It is a cool and erudite work, showing Lupold's control of civil as well as canon law and of historical materials.

Lupold has been called 'the first systematizer of German constitutional law.' The following extract from chs. 5 and 6 is a significant application of the general principles of corporation law to the interpretation of the imperial constitution. The assertion of the principle of majority decision against the old unanimity rule was of fundamental importance for imperial elections, where the almost inevitable failure of unanimity had maintained an open door to papal interference. There is some evidence that Lupold later participated in the composition of the Golden Bull (1356), which formally established the majority vote as decisive in imperial elections.

I have used the text in Schard, *De Jurisdictione* (Basel, 1566), pp. 328–409, at pp. 352 ff.]

CHAPTER V. . . . . *That he who has been elected King or Emperor of the Romans by the Electoral Princes unanimously can by virtue of that election itself legitimately assume the name of King and administer the rights and goods of the Kingdom and Empire in Italy and in the other provinces subject to the Kingdom and Empire. . . .*

. . . . Any people lacking a king can elect a king for itself by the law of peoples, by which law kingdoms were founded . . . (*Digest*, 1, 1, 5); and consequently the king so elected can, by the same right, by virtue of his election by the people, reign in name and substance: which is not other than to assume the name of king and administer the rights and goods of that kingdom, as is self-evident. But in the Kingdom and Empire, when the King or Emperor is dead, the people of Germany, Italy, and the other provinces of the Kingdom lack a king, since hereditary succession does not in these days occur there. And the Electoral Princes, by reason of their [original] institution [by the people of the Empire], have the function of electing the King or Emperor, representing in this all the provinces and people of Germany, Italy, and of the other provinces of the Kingdom and Empire, making the election, as it were, in the name of all, as will be more fully explained in the next chapter. Therefore we conclude that he whom they unanimously elect can by the law of peoples by virtue of this election licitly reign in name and in substance. . . . And from this law of peoples, I think, can be verified the saying of the blessed Jerome, who says that the army makes the Emperor (*Decretum*, c. 24, di. 93). Because at that time the army represented the whole Roman people subject to the Empire, and thus it was able to make the Emperor. But today the princes, by reason of the said institution, represent the people. . . .

CHAPTER VI. . . . . *That he who has been elected King or Emperor by the Princes, even if they have not been unanimous, can, so long as he has been elected by the majority, legitimately assume the name of King by virtue of this election. . . .*

It should be known that Hostiensis, in his gloss on the *Decretals of Gregory IX*, bk. 1, tit. 6, ch. 34 (*Venerabilem*), makes this comment: that the election belongs to the Electoral Princes not as a college but as individual persons. But, saving the reverence due so great a man, I do not believe this to be true. For I believe that this election belongs to them as a college or corporation, for this reason, namely, that, if the institution of the Electoral Princes had not been made, all the princes and other representatives of the people who are subject to the Roman Kingdom and Empire could have the function of electing the King and Emperor. But the Electoral Princes are considered to elect in the place of and by the authority of the corporation of the princes and people of the aforesaid Kingdom and Empire. And hence their election ought to be regarded in the same way as if the whole corporation of the princes and people had done it, as is proved by the text in *Digest*, 3, 4, 6, and by the gloss on *Liber Sextus Decretalium*, bk. 3, tit. 4, ch. 41. It could not, therefore, be said that this election belongs to them as individuals, but rather as a college or as the corporation of all the princes and people aforesaid. . . . This premise having been established, the truth of our proposition is proved as follows. In every corporation, what is done by the majority of the members of the corporation prevails; and thence it is to be regarded as if done by the whole corporation. And this natural reason, as it were, dictates among all men. Because since men are by nature prone to disagree, . . . if the majority vote of a corporation were not decisive nothing could be done or completed by corporations, which would be absurd. And thus, even if canonical and civil law be disregarded, this seems to be, as it were, a principle of the law of peoples (*Digest*, 1, 1, 9). It is also proved by the canon law and the civil law, as in *Digest*, 50, 1, 19; *Decretals*, bk. 1, tit. 6, ch. 21; *Decretals*, bk. 3, tit. 11, ch. 1; etc. Now, in the case with which we are concerned, when the Electoral Princes elect a King or Emperor of the Romans, this election is considered to be made by the corporation of all the princes and people subject to the Kingdom and Empire, as has been said already. Therefore an election by a majority of the Electoral Princes is valid; and hence it is to be regarded as if it were a unanimous election. But, when they all agree in an election, he who is elected by this unanimous election can legitimately rule, etc., as was fully proved in the preceding chapter. Therefore also in the case under discussion—namely, when anyone is elected by a majority of the Electoral Princes—he can likewise, by virtue of this quasi-unanimous election, legitimately assume the name of King and administer the rights and goods of the Kingdom and Empire in Italy and in the other provinces of the Kingdom and Empire.

Somnium Viridarii

[The following passage from the *Somnium Viridarii*, bk. 2, ch. 293, is part of the Knight's argument that the clergy cannot be exempt from royal authority, which is by its very nature inalienable. To this argument, the Cleric characteristically replies that clerical exemption is not a renunciation of royal right but a recognition of the pre-existing and superior right of the pope. The Knight's argument, with its references to principles gleaned from the civil law, feudal law, and canon law, is an excellent summary of one phase of the constitutional theory of the fourteenth century.]

Further, are these rights ... imprescriptible? For they are regalian rights (*Codex*, 7, 39), and the prince can not alienate such rights, since he has sworn in his coronation oath not to alienate the rights of the kingdom and to recover those that have been alienated (*Decretum*, c. 4 and c. 5, di. 10, with the notes thereon), so that the king of France can not alienate his jurisdiction or any case in which the subjects have a right of appeal to him. Hostiensis has noted, in regard to the decretal 'Dilecti' (*Decretals*, bk. 1, tit. 33, ch. 13), that if any lord wishes to subject his land to a strange lord, his vassals can legally prevent it, since it is to their interest not to have many lords and not to change their lord (*ibid.*, ch. 17; *Digest*, 49, 1, 6): because 'what touches all must be approved by all.' And it is explicitly said in the *Libri Feudorum*, bk. 2, bk. 2, tit. 55, that a lord may not transfer his fief to another without the consent of his vassals. And it seems that there is a specific case on this point in the *Decretals*, bk. 1, tit. 24, ch. 33. Further, in the matter which we are discussing custom seems to have no weight; for custom must be rational if it is to have the effect of custom, and a custom by which the subject is deprived of his subordination to his head is not rational. Again, this would have to be the result of prescription. But prescription cannot apply here, since prescription cannot occur without possession, and no one can prescribe obedience for himself. Again, this would have to originate with the knowledge of him who has the right to make the law in this respect. Further, if the church in such matters alleges prescription on the mere grounds of the negligence of the king, such an allegation cannot be made, since there is no such thing as prescription against obedience, and this is set forth in a summary note on 'Cum inter vos' (*Decretals*, bk. 4, tit. 4, ch. 5), where the compiler says that even if the ordinary judge did not use his rights over his subjects for a thousand years, he would not therefore be deprived of them; or else, enjoying that liberty through resistance, the church was a possessor in bad faith; and in such a case prescription does not occur. Besides, the clergy commonly say and allege that they have been exempted from secular jurisdiction; thus it necessarily follows from their own admission that they were at some time subject to it. Further, that the King of France could not alienate such rights to the church, nor the right to hear appeals, of which we spoke above, is clearly shown. For in that case the King of France, who is called true emperor in his kingdom, could not be called *Augustus*, as one who augments his realm, but rather *Angustus*, as one who diminishes it; but any emperor or king should be the opposite of a diminisher and should, in intention at least, augment his realm, as appears in the Preface of the *Institutes* and the *Digest*. Again, in alienating such rights the king cannot bind his successor, because no one has empire over his peer (*Digest*, 36, 1, 13; *Decretals*, bk. 1, tit. 6, ch. 20; *Sext*, bk. 1, tit. 3, ch. 15; *Decretum*, c. [?], C. 16, q. 1). This opinion was held, for the foregoing reasons, by Accursius, glossator of the civil law, in regard to the donation made by Constantine to the Roman church, and this opinion is commonly maintained by the legists of old. And, in regard to the Emperor, it can be argued most strongly that he could not have made that alienation to Silvester, the Roman Pontiff, because he could not give up his jurisdiction and authority except into the hands of the people, from whom he had received it (*Digest*, 1, 18, 21; *ibid.*, 1, 2, 2), even as a guardian, although he has the right to administer, can nevertheless not alienate his wardship, although he may appoint an agent, and for the same reasons we say the same in regard to a bishop (*Decretals*, bk. 1, tit. 1, ch. 10; *ibid.*, bk. 1, tit. 7 throughout). And the King of France could not either tacitly or expressly make such alienations to the church, to the prejudice of his realm; and, for the same reasons, he cannot today abdicate his jurisdiction so long as he remains king; for this is impossible for him by divine law and human law alike.

Nicholas of Cusa

[In the third book of the *De Concordantia Catholica*, Cusa proposes a number of remedies for the evil condition of the empire. In chapters 32–35, he recommends a novel system of royal courts distributed throughout the empire (a proposal which in some ways anticipates the later organization of imperial circles) and regular meetings of the imperial diet, augmented by his new judges, for the general purpose of instigating reform and in particular reforming the obsolete, inequitable, and locally divergent judicial procedures. In other chapters, he urges that the election of the emperor be reformed, with provisions against bribery and a secret, preferential ballot of the electors; he recommends the establishment of a standing army supported by taxation to maintain internal peace, and various specific changes in judicial procedure.

Although this third book begins with a restatement of Cusa's thesis that all government should rest on the consent of the subjects, it is conspicuous in these chapters that the requirement of consent would easily be satisfied by the use of traditional machinery. Moreover, when Cusa comes to specific propositions, consent seems less important in his mind than expertise.

In the concluding chapter of the book, Cusa sets forth his general recommendations for concord in church and empire in terms of a most elaborate physiological analogy. The priesthood is the soul in the body, hierarchically arranged from head to feet; the concord of the church is secured through the flow of its vital spirit through the arteries and veins which represent the canon law. In his description of concord in the empire, two points of some interest seem to be extricable from the intricacies of the analogy: an emphasis on the final responsibility and discretion of the emperor is combined with an emphasis on his duty to consult his regular and greater councils—to secure, not their consent, but their wisdom.

The translations are from the text printed in Schard, *De Jurisdictione*: bk. 3, chs. 4, 32–33, 35, and 41.]

CHAPTER IV

. . . . It was said above that every instance of ordained superiority arises from the elective concordance of voluntary subjection; that there is in the people a divine seed-bed [for authority] through the common equal needs of all men and their equal natural rights; and that accordingly all authority, which is principally from God. . . , is regarded as divine when it arises from the subjects through their common concordance. Thus the ruler established in this way, bearing in himself, as it were, the will of all, is called a public and common person and the father of his individual subjects, governing in right, regular, ordained power, without pride of arrogance; since he knows himself to be, as it were, the creature of all his subjects collectively, he is the father of his subjects as individuals. . . . And since the roots of this divine and human law have been discussed above, I do not repeat them here; it is enough to know that free election, depending on natural and divine law, does not originate in positive law nor in any man whomsoever in such a way that the validity of an election would in any respect depend on his will; and this is especially true in the case of the election of the emperor, whose being and authority do not depend on any one man. Thus the electors, who were constituted at the time of Henry II by the common consent of all the Germans and the others who were subjects of the empire, derive their essential force from that same common consent of all those who, by natural right, could constitute an emperor for themselves. . . .

CHAPTER XXXII

. . . . For the deformities and perils with which the commonwealth is now afflicted a remedy should be diligently and soon provided, since a mortal illness has come upon the German empire; and unless a salutary antidote is immediately found, death will undoubtedly follow. . . . And this remedy cannot better be provided than through the already beaten paths, ancient and tried, to which we must needs come in making a reform. Thus the first step is to institute annual general assemblies, and to begin in this holy Council of Basel, and to make a plan for future meetings. Therefore let the most pious emperor act with his accustomed diligence: that through his holy summons all the greater princes of the empire, both spiritual and temporal, may come together; let the emperor with his admirable industry display the lamentable, universally diminished condition of the empire; let him reveal what he has discovered in Italy and Lombardy about the condition of the imperial forces; let him add a description of the Kingdom of Arles and of all Germany; and when he has disclosed the miserable condition of what was once a flourishing and tremendously powerful empire, let him add what will happen next unless a remedy is applied; and let him demand a remedy from those who were and are most loyal and who are bound to this duty by vow and oath; and let a plan be made concerning the succession, with the concurring providence of his imperial highness.

CHAPTER XXXIII

And since so serious a decline cannot easily be restored to pristine health, let there be given a plan for the cure, and, in the first place, a plan for annual imperial councils and for the maintenance of justice. I find . . . that Constantine the Great used such an assembly and judges in providing for Gaul. For nearly all the deformities were introduced after the imperial courts and assemblies ceased. Therefore it seems that it ought to be ordained that twelve or more benches be established, distributed throughout the provinces subject to the empire, in such a way that each bench is composed of three judges corresponding to the three estates of men: namely, from the nobility, the clergy, and the people. These judges should have cognizance of all cases arising in the territory assigned to them among all kinds of persons—even the clergy, in regard to temporalities dependent on the empire—either as a court of appeal from the proper ordinary court, or as a court of first instance if the plaintiff or the defendant is not subject to an ordinary court—as, for instance, if he is a prince, or if the one is subject to such a court but it is suspect to the other—and not otherwise. The decision of these judges should be final in all cases brought to them by appeal, but the decision of a case brought to them in the first instance can be postponed by appeal to the next session, if it is a great case or involves great persons. Each of these judges should pronounce and cite according to the estate of the various persons: the noble among the nobility, the ecclesiastic among the clergy, and the popular among the people; but no final decision should be made except by the common deliberation of all three, who in difficult cases require the advice of the most expert. If, however, they disagree, the opinion of the majority should be decisive. Moreover, the judges should be authorized to entrust the execution of their decisions to the *bannum* and the secular arm, yielding fines and penalties to the public treasury. And a salary from the public treasury ought to be assigned to these and all other judges. . . .

CHAPTER XXXV

Moreover, an annual assembly should be established, about the Feast of Pentecost, in Frankfurt, which seems in its location and other circumstances to be the most appropriate place. To this should come all the judges and electors of the empire in person, without pomp or heavy expenses. And the lord emperor should preside, if he can, in person; otherwise the first of the electors in his name. And in this assembly the condition of the empire should be dealt with, and also particular matters which have occurred to the judges; and what needs reforming should be reformed. If, however, a difficult matter demands that there be a full assembly of all the princes, there or elsewhere, so be it as it is most expedient. But the ordinary annual council of the lords judges and electors should never be omitted; and in this the cases of the princes can be decided through a common decision.

And since it is wise to introduce a reform by examples, I shall quote an imperial letter, believed to have been written by Constantine, who commanded that a similar meeting of the judges of Gaul should be held in Arles. . . . It should be noticed that it was fitting that not only the judges but also those who held posts of honour in individual cities should, in person or through their delegates, be added to the assembly. . . .

Following this example, there should be established in Frankfurt an annual council to be held for at least a month either in May or in September; and, together with those mentioned above, there should come at least one man from every city and metropolis and the great imperial towns. And the prince electors and the nobles should bring with them whomever they wish as advisers; and they should all be bound with an oath that their counsels should be given in accordance with the right judgment of reason for the public good. There the provincial customs should be examined and as far as possible revised to common observances; and devious forms, especially, should be abolished everywhere. . . ; and certain very bad customs . . . should be abolished; and there are very many very bad customs in Germany, contrary to true justice, which breed wickedness; and since no one would know how to list them all, the judges of the provinces ought to meet and formulate the customs of their provinces in writing and present them for examination to the council.

CHAPTER XLI

. . . . Let his imperial highness consider those aspects of the structure of the body that apply to the empire. For the body is constructed of bones, nerves, and flesh. Now the nerves, being in their nature midway between the two others, have a common connection in the cerebrum, which is one seat of reason; and they go around binding all the parts of the diverse joints of the body to the unity of one body. And these are the imperial laws, constituted midway between hard and soft, binding all members concordantly to one; nor is the head, which represents the emperor, excepted, since all these nerves flow from a rational and natural discourse to which no one is superior. Therefore the supreme power itself has to consider whether these nerves are either relaxed or contracted too much. . . . For it is necessary that law, like a bowstring, be neither too taut, lest the bow be broken, nor too loose, lest when it is relaxed it be unable to give force to the arrow. Also he ought to pay attention to this: that even as the nerves cling firmly to the bones even when the flesh is corrupted, so the laws of a country in regard to the perpetual government itself and the rights of the country ought to be preserved incorruptibly. The country, indeed, is rightly compared to the bones, which have a sweet marrow and are very durable; but the flesh to transitory men who, being human, often fail on account of softness, ignorance, or infirmity; with them it is fitting that the prince act as a father, now succouring, now dispensing, now punishing, as may be suitable for the welfare of each, while the law above remains firm. For if the law is in any part infected, it dies: even as if a nerve is injured in any part of the body the whole body sickens. It is necessary also that he reform each particular law, which is like a small particular vein, that it may not obstruct the common law which provides for the public good and especially that it may not obstruct the fontal source of laws, namely, the rational and natural law; otherwise, that member, intruding the disease of contrariety, could easily by its connection infect the whole body. Therefore the king ought to be a lute-player and one who knows how to preserve harmony among all the strings great and little, and not stretch them too little or too much: that the common concord may resound through every chord.

Therefore let this be the care of the emperor, rightly to preserve the body in health like an expert physician. . . . For when he shall observe that . . . the body is ill . . . let him seek a remedy, and hear the books and counsels of certain most expert physicians of the commonwealth; let him concoct a prescription and test through taste, sight, and smell whether it is suitable to time and place. If it seems that it is, let him confide it first to his privy council, namely, the teeth, that they may chew it and find out whether there is anything comforting and wholesome in the prescription. If the privy council, after chewing it well, finds that there is indeed something salutary in it, let him send it to the stronger and greater examination of his greater council, namely, the stomach, that it may be digested, refined, and the pure separated from the impure. After this, let him send the purified prescription to the consistory of judges, namely, the liver, that the healthful medicinal law may be distributed to each member in accordance with its needs. And let him show paternal care in all things to every part and member, now by a soothing ointment, now by wiping the wound or cauterizing it, and by all other preserving medicines; and let him never yield to the amputation of a member except with compassionate grief, and only when no other method is effective and there is danger of infection. . . .

Aeneas Sylvius

[The career of Aeneas Sylvius Piccolomini was a colourful one, even for an age of colourful careers. He was born in 1405 near Siena, the oldest of eighteen children in a humble family. He worked on the family farm till a priest helped him to go as a poor student to Siena, where he divided his efforts between intensive humanistic studies and pleasures much less arduous. He also studied at Florence. With the help of a series of patrons and the opportunities open to talent at the Council of Basel, he established himself as a skilful and influential diplomat; in 1436, although still a layman, he had a seat in the Council; his activity continued at Ferrara, and his assistance in the election of Felix V was rewarded with the position of papal secretary. In 1442, on a mission for the Council, he met the emperor Frederick III, who made him his poet laureate and private secretary; in the succeeding years he made himself very useful to the emperor in various negotiations and wrote a good deal of lively literature. He made his peace with Eugenius in 1445, and a year later took orders as a sub-deacon, 'forsaking Venus for Bacchus,' as he said. His skill in diplomacy pleased both emperor and pope; he was rewarded by being made bishop of Siena and, in 1448, a prince of the empire and a cardinal. In 1458, he was himself elected pope.

As Pius II, Aeneas Sylvius was not only a noted patron of humanists but also a serious enemy of conciliarism (in the bull *Execrabilis* in 1460 he declared that the idea of conciliar superiority to the pope was heretical) and a serious advocate of a crusade against the Turks. He himself started out with the crusade in 1464, but died in the same year in Venice.

Most of his literary works are thoroughly secular: he wrote poems, a novel, a play, a history of his own times, and so forth. His short treatise, *De Ortu et Auctoritate Imperii Romani* (Schard, *De Jurisdictione . . .*, pp. 314–328), dates from the period of his service to the emperor (1445); it is written in fine rhetorical humanist style and is significant as an extreme statement of the doctrine of absolute imperial authority which developed from civilist analysis of the principles of Roman law. The following passages are taken from chapters 16–23.]

CHAPTER XVI. *That the Emperor is not bound to give the reason for his actions, but that this is presumed to be good*

Since a reasonable cause is to be presumed for every action of the prince, when it happens that the prince either unjustly abrogates privileges or derogates from them, although it may be licit to inform him by way of supplication and humbly to seek restitution, yet it is not lawful to protest, or to blame or attack him if he persists, since there is no one who can take cognizance of his temporal acts. What the prince does, however unjust, must be patiently endured; and one must await amends from his successor, or the correction of the Supreme Judge, Who does not permit violence and injury to exist for ever. . . .

CHAPTER XVII. *That Caesar can also take away temporal goods, both from the evil and from the good*

Something further ought to be said, which will perhaps seem harsh and absurd to some people; but it ought not to be kept silent, because it is a true and useful saying. Why do you thwart me, my pen? Why do you resist me? Why do you not allow the ink to flow? Set forth the privilege of Caesar and do not fear, when what you write is true. Assuredly, the emperor is free to take away—not only from a bad man, but even from a good man and one who has deserved well of the commonwealth—his own land, his own houses, and his own possessions, if the necessity of the commonwealth demands this. Hence we see rustic farms, which when wars threaten are dangerous to the city, burned with their buildings, the fields ploughed up, the vines cut down, the grain from private granaries and the cattle from the stalls given to public use; and although this may seem injurious to individuals, yet it is a lesser evil that single men should suffer than that the commonwealth should be destroyed.

CHAPTER XVIII. *That the commonwealth should be preferred by everyone to private wealth or welfare*

For private wealth cannot endure unless the commonwealth is safe. However, those men who for the sake of the commonwealth undergo individual injuries should be compensated from the public treasury; and thus care should be taken that the injuries of war should not seem to fall upon one, or a few, but upon all equally. But if the condition of the commonwealth does not permit this, it is more tolerable that one should suffer than all. For if a citizen will give everything, whatever he has, for his own safety, how much more will he do it for the safety of the commonwealth, since we are born not only for ourselves, but also for the commonwealth, for which no less than for ourselves we ought to provide riches. Sailors, when the tempest has risen, throw out whatever goods are in the ship for the sake of the safety of their persons. But if they think that some man is the cause of the shipwreck, they throw him also to the waves of the sea. . . . For it is expedient that one man die for the people lest the whole race perish, and this fate a good citizen will endure with a calm mind for the sake of the safety of the commonwealth. . . .

CHAPTER XIX. *That to establish, abrogate, and interpret laws belongs to the emperor*

To establish the most sacred laws, which bind men's lives and are laid upon the necks of the whole world, belongs only to the emperor, whose pleasure has the force of law. It is certain that whatever the emperor has established by letter and signature, or has knowingly decreed, or has interlocuted out of court, or has orally commanded, is law. Moreover, if anything in the established laws seems ambiguous, it should be referred by the judges to the imperial throne, that it may be made clear by the august authority of him to whom alone is entrusted the making and interpreting of laws. Nor will anyone of sound mind deny that laws can be abrogated by him who established them; and, since it is the emperor who gives force and authority to laws, it is certain also that he can modify and abrogate the laws when there is a reasonable cause. . . .

CHAPTER XX. *That emperors are not subject to the laws, yet that it is proper for them to judge according to the laws*

Yet since there is found nothing so attentive to all things as is the authority of the laws, which dispose well both divine and human things and expel every iniquity, it is proper that the prince should both live and judge according to the laws. For law is a certain discovery and gift of God, an eye from many eyes, an intellect without passion. Nor should that which has been carefully digested by many and introduced with great deliberation be easily dissolved. Hence an emperor was used to say, 'It is a saying worthy of the majesty of a ruler that the prince should profess himself bound by the laws' [Codex, 1, 14, 4]. And although this is beautiful to say, yet it ought not to be asserted that the emperor is subject to the laws, since he is free. For there is something else to which, more than to the laws, the emperor is subjected. This is equity, which is not always found in writing. For equity is that which is just, aside from the letter of the law. But if the written law commands one thing and equity urges the other, it is fitting that the emperor control the rigour of the law with the bridle of equity, for he alone is permitted to interpret between equity and law, and on him lies the duty of investigation: especially since no command of law, however much it be weighted with collective wisdom, suffices for the varieties of human nature and its unimaginable contrivances.

CHAPTER XXI. *That human laws can sometimes be changed, sometimes abrogated*

And since human law runs on for ever to infinity, and there is nothing in it which could stand perpetually (for the same nature hastens to produce many new forms, and human institutions vary in accordance with the times), it becomes manifest in the course of time that laws which once were just are rendered unjust and made now useless, now harsh, now inequitable. The control of these is the task of the prince, who is lord of the laws. For if anything set forth in them has become, perhaps, more obscure, it is proper for the emperor to clarify it, and to amend the severity of laws, which does not befit their humanity. For the saying that 'a law, although harsh, must be maintained' refers to inferior judges, not to Caesar. For in him is that force of moderating the laws which is called *epieikeia*, which is so united to the supreme prince that it can be taken from him by no human decrees. But it is not fitting that the prince should use this supreme power without great and urgent cause. . . . For although the law of the empire has released the emperor from the restraints of law, yet nothing is so proper to empire as to live by laws. Nor are the laws to be changed without cause, nor new laws instituted without evident utility; and although it is proper for us, who cannot escape his pleasure, to believe that a legitimate cause underlies every action of the prince, yet the emperor should beware lest he follow his unreasonable desires rather than just laws and become accused by that greatest God, in Whose realms mighty torments are endured by the mighty ones who strayed from the path of law and equity.

CHAPTER XXII. *From the decision of the emperor there can be, and ought to be, no appeal*

Now, in conclusion, we shall discuss appeals; and we shall confute those who assert that there ought to be an appeal from the decision of the supreme prince. For, if an appeal to the *praetorium* from the prefects who are under Caesar is not admissible, how much less ought it to be admitted when Caesar himself, who has no superior in a temporal case, has handed down the decision! . . . But certain persons appeal again to Caesar with the princes added, as if the emperor were greater with them than without them. But if this were true, it would be lawful to appeal again from the emperor with the electors to the same with other princes added, and so the process would continue to infinity. . . . But vain and worthless are their premises. For there is as great a power in Caesar without the princes as with them. For supreme power loves unity and of its own accord flees from the many to the one.

CHAPTER XXIII. *That the emperor is doubly offended by him who appeals from his decision*

Since the highest power is in Caesar, and the highest plenitude of authority, no authority is added by the addition of the princes: because nothing can be added to the highest, nor can what is full be made fuller. But he who appeals must appeal as to a superior who may correct the unjust decision made against him. Thus he injures the imperial majesty with twofold temerity. For he tries to assign a superior to him who is superior to all princes, and he also ascribes injustice to him whom we ought always to consider fair and just. Therefore, those who attempt such things ought to be not only prohibited but also coerced by due penalties and censures. . . . For although injustice does sometimes proceed from the highest throne, yet this fact does not provide grounds for an appeal, since there is no judge who has the right to examine the temporal acts of Caesar. Besides, it is more useful to the commonwealth, in order to bring lawsuits to a close, that the benefit of an appeal be denied to the few who are unjustly oppressed than that the gates of complaint be open to the many who make false accusations after they have been justly ruled. Since those who regard themselves as justly condemned are most rare, the lesser evil must be endured, that the greater may be avoided.

Sir John Fortescue

[In his *De Natura Legis Naturae*, bk. 1, chs. 24, 25, Fortescue argued that the concepts of regal and political lordship were not antithetical; his defence of dispensation and extra-legal action even in a political ruler helps to explain his concept of 'lordship both regal and political'.

The selection from *De Laudibus Legum Angliae*, chs. 9–13, describing the characteristics and supposed origin of England's regal and political lordship, should be read in conjunction with chapters 15–18 on the English law, tr. above, pp. 85–87, and ch. 36 on taxation, tr. above, pp. 135 f.

The text of *De Natura Legis Naturae* is in *The Works of Sir John Fortescue, Knight*, ed. Thomas Lord Clermont (London, 1869), vol. I, pp. 63–333; the selection from *De Laudibus Legum Angliae* is translated from the Latin text edited by S. B. Chrimes (Cambridge, 1942).]

De Natura Legis Naturae

CHAPTER XXIV. *In which the political ruler is advised that he should also, in certain cases, govern regally*

O king ruling politically, rule your people also regally when the case requires, for not all cases can be embraced by the statutes and customs of your realm, and thus the remaining cases are left to your discretion; moreover, always rule all criminal matters at your will, and moderate or remit all penalties, so long as you can do this without harm to your subjects or offence against the customs and statutes of your realm. Equity, too, is left to your wisdom, lest the rigour of the words of the law, confounding its intention, injure the common good. . . . The superior is thought to have absolute power, not indeed that he can dissolve a perfect law, but that, by reason of the law of nature, which is natural equity, he can himself better fulfil the law of his kingdom. For written law often lies like a corpse beneath its cloak of words, yet is not wholly lifeless, and then through equity the prince, as it were, rouses from sleep its vital intention, even as a physician revives one who lies in a stupour or swoon, so that then, as if of two laws lying under one veil, can be said the word of the Gospel: 'There will be two in one bed; one will be taken, the other left' [Matthew 24:40]. And often the mind of the legislator did not fully perceive all that should be embraced by the words of the law, and in that case it is the office of the good prince, who is called a *living law*, to make good the defect of the written law, which otherwise would have remained motionless as a corpse. For this reason the Philosopher properly says that a kingdom is better ruled by the best king than by the best law [*Politics*, bk. 3, ch. 10]. But let the king who rules politically be always wary lest he repudiate the laws of his kingdom, pregnant with justice, and establish new laws without consulting the chief men of his kingdom, or introduce foreign laws, refusing longer to remain a political ruler, and crushing his people with regal law.

CHAPTER XXV. *In which are added other cases in which the political ruler will necessarily govern regally*

Moreover, there are also very many other cases in which it is sometimes licit and expedient for a king with political lordship to rage regally against some of his people: for instance, if his people has risen against him, or a foreign people has invaded his kingdom, so that the time does not allow that all the things necessary for resistance and repulsion be done in the legal form or through the legal processes that are used in that kingdom in time of peace. For this reason it will then be licit for the king at his own discretion to take the sons of the inhabitants of his realm and put them in his chariots, and to make them grooms of his horses, and to do all those other things which the Prophet foretold to the people of Israel as the right of a king [I Samuel 8:11–17]. For even as a physician has charge over the sick, so the king has charge over his kingdom. . . . A physician often binds a patient . . . lest he refuse to take a bitter medicine and thus flee from his own health; and sometimes a surgeon amputates an infected limb, when he cannot otherwise preserve the rest of the body from harm; in such a case the physician or surgeon does not sin, so long as he restores his patient to health even if by crippling him. Neither does the good king sin if, when such disaster has come upon his realm, he takes the goods of his subjects and exposes some of them to inevitable dangers and oppresses them with burdens and toil for the safety of his kingdom, which he could not otherwise preserve. . . .

De Laudibus Legum Angliae

CHAPTER IX

. . . . The king of England cannot at his will change the laws of his kingdom, for he rules his people by a principate not only regal, but also political. If he ruled them by a regal principate only, he could change the laws of his realm and also impose talliages and other burdens on them without consulting them; and this kind of lordship is denoted by the Civil Laws when they say, 'What has pleased the prince has the force of law.' But the case is very different when a king rules his people politically, since he can neither change the laws without the consent of his subjects, nor burden his subjects against their will with strange impositions; thus his people freely enjoys its property under the rule of the laws which it desires, and it is not despoiled by its king nor by anyone else. Yet a people likewise rejoices under a king who rules only regally, so long as he himself does not lapse into tyranny. Of such a king the Philosopher said in III *Politics*, [ch. 10], that 'it is better that a city be ruled by the best man than by the best law.' But because it does not always happen that the ruler of a people is this kind of man, St. Thomas, in the book which he wrote for the king of Cyprus, *De Regimine Principum*, prefers that a kingdom be so instituted that the king is not able freely to govern his people tyrannically; and this can be the case only when regal power is restrained by political law. . . .

CHAPTER X. *The Prince's Question*

The Prince said to him: Whence comes it, Chancellor, that one king can rule his people with pure regal power, while such power is denied to another? Since both kings are of equal dignity, I cannot help wondering why they are unequal in power.

CHAPTER XI. *A Reference to Another Treatise*

Chancellor: That the king who rules politically has no less authority than the king who rules his people regally as he wishes has been sufficiently shown in the aforesaid little book [*De Natura Legis Naturae*], yet I by no means denied there, nor do I now, that they have different kinds of authority over their subjects; and I shall now explain to you as best I can the cause of that diversity.

327

CHAPTER XII. *How Kingdoms Ruled Only Regally First Began*

Formerly men who excelled in power, being greedy for dignity and glory, often subjected neighbouring peoples to themselves by force and compelled those peoples to serve them and obey their orders, which orders they then established as laws for those men. And by long endurance of this situation, the people thus subjected consented to the dominion of the conquerors, since by those conquerors it was defended from the injuries of others; for it thought that it was more advantageous to be under the empire of one man, by. which it would be defended against others, than to be exposed to the oppression of all who might wish to molest it. And so certain kingdoms were begun, and the conquerors who thus ruled the subject people usurped for themselves the name of *rex*, from *regendo*, and their kind of lordship was called purely regal. Thus Nimrod first provided himself with a kingdom, yet in the Holy Scriptures he is not called a king but 'a mighty hunter before the Lord' [Genesis 10:9], because he forced men to obey him as a hunter forces the beasts who enjoy liberty to obey him. Thus Belus the Assyrian and Ninus subjected a great part of Asia to their command; thus also the Romans usurped the empire of the world; and thus kingdoms began among nearly all peoples. Wherefore, when the children of Israel demanded a king such as all peoples then had, the Lord, offended thereby, commanded that the Prophet explain to them the regal right, which was nothing else but the pleasure of the king who would be over them, as is more fully set forth in the First Book of Kings [I Samuel 8:7-18]. Now, if I am not mistaken, Prince, you have the form of the origin of kingdoms possessed regally. Wherefore I shall also try to explain how the kingdom ruled politically first began, that you may know the origins of both kinds of kingdoms; and· from this it will be very easy for you to infer the cause of the diversity which you are asking about.

CHAPTER XIII. *How Kingdoms Ruled Politically First Began*

Saint Augustine, in book 19 of *The City of God*, chapter 23, said that 'a people is an association of men united by a common sense of right and common interests.' So long, however, as such a people is acephalous (that is, headless); it does not deserve to be called a body, because, as in the case of natural bodies when the head is cut off we call the rest not a body but a trunk, so also in the case of political bodies without a head the community is by no means incorporated. Wherefore, in I *Politics*, [ch. 2], the Philosopher said that 'whenever one whole is constituted from many parts, there will be among these one part which rules and others which are ruled.' Thus it is always necessary that people who wish to form themselves into a kingdom or other political body set up one part to rule that whole body, which, through analogy with kingdoms, it is customary to call *rex* from *regendo*. In this way, even as a physical body ruled by one head develops from an embryo, so from the people there breaks forth a kingdom, which is a mystic body governed by one man as head. And, even as in the natural body the heart, as the Philosopher said, first comes to life, having in itself the blood which it sends out to all the members, by which they are quickened to life, so in the political body the intention of the people first comes to life, having in itself the blood—namely, the political provision for the utility of that people—which it transmits to the head and to all the members of that body, by which that body, in its own way, is also quickened. Moreover, the law under which an association of men becomes a people corresponds to the nerves of the physical body; for, even as the structure of the body is fastened together by the nerves, so the mystic body is fastened together and maintained in one whole by law, which takes its name from *ligando*; and the members and bones of this body, which signify the solidity of truth by which the community is sustained, preserve their rights by means of the law, as does the natural body by means of the nerves. And even as the head of a physical body cannot change its nerves, nor deny to its members their proper energies and proper aliment of blood, neither can the king who is head of the political body take from the people against their will what is properly theirs. You now have, Prince, the form of institution of the political kingdom, by which you may measure the power which its king can exercise in regard to the law and the subjects of such a realm. For such a king was set up in order to preserve the law of the subjects and their lives and property, and his power has flowed to him from the people, so that he can not rightly dominate his people by any other power. Wherefore, to give a brief answer to your question about the origin of the diversity of kingly powers, I firmly believe that the sole cause of that distinction lies in the different ways in which these dignities were instituted, as you may logically infer from what has been said. For thus the kingdom of England, which began with the band of Trojans which Brut led from

Italy and the regions of the Greeks, burst forth into political and regal lordship; so also Scotland, once subject to it as a duchy, grew into a kingdom political and regal. By a similar origin, many other kingdoms have also attained the right to be ruled both politically and regally. . . .

Jean Masselin

[The following extract is from a speech supposedly made by Philippe Pot, Sieur de la Roche, at the meeting of the Estates General at Tours in 1484. One wing of the Estates General was asserting the right of the Estates General to name a regency council during the minority of Charles VIII, in opposition to the claim that the regency would naturally pass to the Princes of the Blood. Whether or not this speech is authentic in detail, it represents a widely-accepted concept of the constitution of France at the time. The text is in *Journal des États Généraux de France tenus à Tours en 1484, rédigé en Latin par Jehan Masselin*, ed. Adhelm Bernier (Paris, 1835), pp. 146–148.]

My argument rests on the fact that the kingship is a dignity, not an inheritance, and that it ought not like inheritances to pass directly to natural guardians, namely, to near relatives. What then? Shall the commonwealth remain without a ruler and exposed to all comers? Certainly not; but it will first be submitted to the deliberation of the Estates General: not that they may administer it themselves, but that it may be administered by those who, in the judgment of the Estates, are most worthy.

And—to clarify the matter—the histories say and I have learned from my elders that in the beginning kings were created by the vote of the people, who were lords of their own affairs, and that those who surpassed the rest in virtue and ability were set at the head. For each people chose rulers for itself for its own utility. Indeed, princes do not have command in order that they may enrich themselves at the expense of the people, but that, forgetful of their own interests, they may enrich the commonwealth and improve its condition. But if they sometimes do otherwise, certainly they are tyrants and not shepherds, since when they themselves devour the flock they adopt the manners and name of wolves rather than of shepherds. Therefore the choice of the law and of the ruler by whom the commonwealth is led involves the deepest interest of the people; for if the king is very good then their condition is very good; if otherwise, it is deformed and poor. Have you not often read that *res publica* is *res populi*? But if it is the people's business, how can it neglect and not take care of its business? How can omnipotence be attributed by flatterers to the prince, when he is made by the people? Among the ancient Romans, was not each magistrate made by the choice of the people? Nor was any law promulgated unless it had first been submitted to the people and approved by them. And in many lands the kingship is still elective by old custom. But I do not now wish to discuss the power of a prince who, being of age, administers the commonwealth by right. Let our discussion deal only with the immediate situation: when the king, because of minority or for some other reason, is prevented from taking over the government. And first I wish you to agree that the public business is the people's business, and that it is entrusted to kings by the people, and that those who hold it by force or otherwise, without the consent of the people, are considered tyrants and usurpers. Now it is clear that our king cannot administer the commonwealth himself. Therefore it is necessary that it be administered by the care and service of others. But I have said that it does not revert to any one prince, nor to several, nor to all together, in this case. Therefore it must return to the people who gave it and who resume it as their own, especially since either a long vacancy or a bad regency would always redound to their damage alone. Yet I do not mean to say that the quality of reigning or the lordship itself can pass to any other than to the person of a king; but the administration and guardianship— not the right or property—is rightly assigned for a time to the people, or to those who are elected by them.

NOTES TO CHAPTER ONE *pages* 1 *to* 31

1. H. M. V. Reade, 'Political Theory to c. 1300,' *Cambridge Medieval History*, vol. VI, p. 616.

2. John Dickinson, *The Statesman's Book of John of Salisbury* (New York, 1927), intro., p. liv, n. 164.

3. Cf. Edward Jenks, *Law and Politics in the Middle Ages* (New York, 1898); a suggestive essay; Siegfried Brie, *Die Lehre von Gewohnheitsrecht*, vol. I (Breslau, 1899), pp. 202 ff.: an excellent technical study of the Germanic theory of customary law.

4. Text in William Stubbs, ed., *Select Charters* (8th ed., Oxford, 1905), p. 478.

5. C. H. McIlwain, 'Magna Carta and Common Law,' in *Magna Carta Commemoration Essays*, ed. H. E. Malden (London, 1917), pp. 122–179.

NOTES

6. Cf. Paul Viollet, *Histoire des institutions politiques et administratives de la France* (Paris, 1890–1903), vol. II, pp. 199 ff., for an analysis of this pattern in France.

7. '*Consuetudines* are customs held from antiquity, approved by the princes and maintained by the people, which determine, in regard to something, whose it is and to whom it belongs. *Leges*, however, are decrees, made by princes and kept by the people of the province, through which particular disputes are decided; for *leges* are, as it were, legal instruments for the declaration of the truth of contentions.' *Summa de Legibus*, bk. 10, tit. 1, quoted R. W. and A. J. Carlyle, *A History of Mediaeval Political Theory in the West* (New York, 1903 ff.), vol. III, p. 147, n. 1. 'Moreover the authority of the Roman laws is no mean authority, but their force does not extend so far as to overthrow use and custom. However, the busy lawyer, when a case occurs which is not covered by feudal custom, may, without scandal, use the written law.' *Libri Feudorum*, bk. 2, tit. 1, quoted McIlwain, *op. cit.*, p. 126, n. 2. '. . . . The English laws, although not written, may apparently without any absurdity be termed *leges* (since this itself is a law, that that which pleases the prince has the force of law); I mean, those laws which, it is evident, were promulgated by the advice of the nobles and the authority of the prince, concerning doubts to be settled in their assembly. For if, from the mere want of writing only, they should not be considered laws, then unquestionably writing would seem to confer more authority upon laws themselves than either the equity of the persons who constituted them or the reason of those who framed them. But to reduce the laws and rights of the realm, in every instance, into writing would be, in our times, absolutely impossible, as well on account of the ignorance of writers as because of the confused multiplicity of the laws.' Glanville, *Tractatus de Legibus et Consuetudinibus Regni Angliae*, ed. John Rayner, reprinted with translation by John Beames (Washington, 1900), preface, pp. xxxvii–xxxix.

8. Ulpian, in *Digest*, bk. 1, tit. 1, sec. 10.

9. Cf. Aristotle's distinction between natural (*physikon*) and positive or conventional (*nomikon*) justice, *Nicomachean Ethics*, bk. 5, ch. 7.

10. *Rhetoric*, bk. 2, ch. 53.

11. *Digest*, bk. 1, tit. 1, sec. 9.

12. *Ibid.*, bk. 41, tit. 1, secs. 1, 3, 5, 7; bk. 1, tit. 6, sec. 1.

13. *Ibid.*, bk. 1, tit. 1, sec. 5.

14. *Ibid.*, bk. 1, tit. 1, sec. 1.

15. *Ibid.*, bk. 1, tit. 1, sec. 4. Ulpian's threefold classification was repeated in the *Institutes*, bk. 1, tit. 2, with his definition of natural law, Gaius's definition of *jus gentium*, and a list of *jus gentium* institutions based on Hermogenian.

16. *Epistolae*, XIV, 2.

17. The phrasing is that of the eighth-century encyclopedist Bishop Isidore of Seville. His discussion in the *Etymologiae* presents a fine muddle of the rational, the instinctive, and the primitive natural law. Enshrined in the *Decretum*, his guileless paragraph gave medieval canonists and theologians a worse problem in clarification

than that which the civilists met in trying to sort out Gaius and Ulpian. For a careful and documented analysis of juristic, Stoic, and patristic definitions, see Carlyle, *op. cit.*, vol. I, chs. I–III, IX.

18. Cf. *ibid.*, vol. II, ch. III, for the relevant texts.

19. For the decretists in general, cf. *ibid.*, vol. II, chs. III, IV, and the excellent study of Dom Odon Lottin, *Le droit naturel chez saint Thomas et ses prédécesseurs* (Bruges, 1926), pp. 7–19; for the decretalists, see Walter Ullmann, *Medieval Papalism* (London, 1949), ch. II.

20. Lottin, *op. cit.*, pp. 20–40.

21. *Summa Theologiae*, pt. 3, q. 27, member 3, art. 2, cited Lottin, *op. cit.*, p. 29, n. 34.

22. *Ibid.*, p. 38.

23. Cf. Ewart Lewis, 'Natural Law and Expediency in Medieval Political Theory,' *Ethics*, L (1940), 144–163.

24. Nor does it mark off, in eighteenth-century fashion, a list of inviolable private rights. Maurice de Wulf, 'L'Individu et le groupe dans la scolastique du xiiie siècle,' *Revue néo-scolastique de philosophie*, XXII (1920), 348, calls Aquinas's list a list of the natural rights of the individual; but there is a difference. For the relation between natural law and individual rights, see ch. IV below.

25. Cf. Lottin, *op. cit.*, pp. 71–72. Aquinas's sense of the utility of private property, servitude, and government obviously owes much to Aristotle. For his demonstration of the utility of property, see pp. 108 f. below. In discussing slavery, he sometimes, e.g., *Summa Theologiae*, I, q. 96, art. 4, slips back to the patristic notion that slavery is the result of sin; elsewhere he maintains the Aristotelian position that for certain kinds of men slavery is useful and appropriate and therefore indirectly blessed by nature: *ibid.*, 1a 2ae, q. 57, art. 3.

26. Cf. p. 192 below. An interesting use is cited by Sir Frederick Pollock, 'History of the Law of Nature,' in his *Essays in the Law* (London, 1922), p. 48: an ordinance by Philip the Fair in 1311 enfranchising bondmen on the Valois domain on the grounds that 'the human creature who is formed in the image of our Lord ought generally to be free, by natural law.'

27. See ch. II below.

28. His most extensive discussion of natural law is in *Dialogus*, pt. 3, tr. 2, bk. 3, ch. 6, tr. below. Occam's theology stressed the final dependence of the universe on God's free will (rather than on God's reason, as with Aquinas); his epistemology reduced man's direct knowledge of the external world to the intuition of contingent, individual phenomena. His system, accordingly, gave no final guarantee that the constructs of human reason would correspond to an inherent rationality of the universe. But man's direct intuitive knowledge of himself included the categorical imperatives of his own nature (natural law in the first sense); and further knowledge of God's will was attained through faith in divine revelation. Occam assumed, though he could not

prove, that God willed a universe in which the findings of human reason would have a probable validity; in which, accordingly, there would be no conflict between the commands discovered by self-intuition, the revealed precepts of God, and the conclusions of human reason working upon contingent phenomena; rather, each would supplement the others and could be used to interpret the others. For two views of the technical and controversial question of the relation between Occam's general philosophy and his political thought, see Georges de Lagarde, *La naissance de l'esprit laïque* . . . , vol. VI, *L' Individualisme Ockhamiste: la morale et le droit* (Saint-Paul-Trois-Chateaux, 1946), esp. pp. 143–158; Richard Scholz, *Wilhelm von Ockham als politischer Denker und sein Breviloquium de principatu tyrannico* (Leipzig, 1944), intro., esp. pp. 18–28.

29. Note that the illustrations given suggest Scriptural commands.

30. *Dialogus*, pt. 3, tr. 2, bk. 2, ch. 28.

31. His comment on the relation between *jus gentium* and natural law is significant for what it does not say. 'The custom [of the *jus gentium*] is contrary to that natural equity that existed in the state of innocence, and indeed to that natural equity that ought to exist among men who follow reason in all things. But that custom is not contrary to the natural equity that exists among men prone to dissension and acting badly: and thus the contradiction is in the *genus* of nature rather than that of morals, since this custom is not iniquitous or evil.' *Opus Nonaginta Dierum*, ch. 92.

32. Max Shepard, 'William of Occam and the Higher Law,' *American Political Science Review*, XXVI (1932), 1013; the entire article is excellent. Lagarde, *loc. cit.*, goes further, claiming that Occam regarded all human law, including *jus gentium*, as purely positive; 'natural law in the third sense,' he says, was for Occam a mere rational construct in the realm of the morally indifferent; it had no necessary relation to human law. This was in keeping, according to Lagarde, with Occam's ethics, in which moral force attached only to divine commands. Lagarde's interpretation stresses an absolute contrast between Occam and Aquinas and in my opinion fails to do justice both to the elements of relativism and positivism in Aquinas's theory of human law and to the extent to which Occam continually assessed the rightfulness of human institutions in terms of their rationally argued service to the common utility. Whether or not his basic philosophy supported this, Occam certainly wrote as if reason was the criterion of right and a clue to God's will; cf. Scholz, *loc. cit.*

33. *Dialogus*, pt. 3, tr. 2, bk. 2, ch. 28.

34. See pp. 463 f., 495–500 below.

35. *Dialogus*, pt. 1, bk. 6, ch. 62.

36. *Ibid.*, pt. 3, tr. 2, bk. 3.

37. It has been claimed that the *Defensor Pacis* is an exception to this general rule, but see pp. 17, 217 f. below.

38. Pollock, *op. cit.*, p. 45.

39. *Ibid.*, pp. 54–59.

NOTES

40. See ch. VI below.

41. Pollock, *op. cit.*, p. 47.

42. *Ibid.*, p. 32.

43. Cf. Gerson, *De Unitate Ecclesiastica*, pt. 2, consid. 2, for an interesting miscellaneous list of some of the 'rules' of divine and natural law.

44. Lagarde, *op. cit.*, vol. II, *Marsile de Padoue....* (1934), pp. 164–174; but Lagarde thinks that Marsiglio's reverence for Aristotle kept his positivism from becoming fully explicit and consistent. Cf. Richard Scholz, 'Marsilius von Padua und die Genesis des modernen Staatsbewusstseins,' *Historische Zeitschrift*, CLVI (1937), 99–100, for a thoughtful criticism of Lagarde and a position close to that taken here.

45. A. Passerin d'Entrèves, *The Medieval Contribution to Political Thought* (Oxford, 1939), pp. 61–64.

46. *Ibid.*, p. 62. Passerin d'Entrèves argues that the dualism of Marsiglio's definition of law was more apparent than real, since the legislator itself defined what justice was: 'Only what the community has laid down in the form of law can and must be the supreme measure of justice. Human decision is raised to nothing less than a standard of truth.' But is there any evidence that Marsiglio held this Hobbesian position? Cf. Alan Gewirth, *Marsilius of Padua* (New York, 1951), pp. 134–135, for the argument that Marsiglio's doctrine was 'a positivism . . . with respect not to justice but to law.'

47. Medieval scholars disregarded his thoroughly Greek notion of a correspondence between systems of legal justice and types of political constitutions.

48. As we have seen, this not entirely satisfactory explanation of the law of peoples was not generally followed.

49. *Summa Theologiae*, 1a 2ae, q. 95, art. 2. Elsewhere he wrote: 'Just and good things can be considered in two ways. In one way formally, and in this way they are always and everywhere the same, because the principles of right which exist in the natural reason are not changed. In another way materially, and in this way the same things are not just and good everywhere and among all men, but must be determined by law. And this happens because of the mutability of human nature and the diverse conditions of men and things, according to the diversity of places and times. For instance, it is always just that in buying and selling there be an exchange of equal values, but it is just that at one place or time so much is paid for a measure of grain, and at another place or time not the same amount, but more or less.' *De Malo*, q. 2, art. 4, in *Opera* (Parma ed.), vol. VIII, p. 243.

50. *Decretum*, c. 2, di. 4; cf. Aquinas, *Summa Theologiae*, 1a 2ae, q. 95, art. 3.

51. *Nicomachean Ethics*, bk. 5, ch. 6.

52. *Defensor Pacis*, dictio 1, ch. 10, sec. 5; cf. *Defensor Minor*, ch. 1.

53. Cf. Brie, *op. cit.*, pp. 131–133, 168 ff.

54. Its boundaries changed as the theory of papal absolutism expanded, but a special prestige always attached to the commands of the Bible and the decrees of the first four general councils.

55. Bk. 1, tit. 4, sec. 1; cf. *Institutes*, 1, 2, 6. The terms *imperium* and *potestas* were originally technical and limited in meaning, but the medieval scholars took them as expressing the complete sovereign authority of the Roman people.

56. *Politics*, bk. 3, chs. 10, 11.

57. See below, pp. 322–324.

58. Aegidius Romanus, *De Regimine Principum*, bk. 3, pt. 2, ch. 27, repeats this alternative without emphasis.

59. The form of government favoured by Aquinas has been the subject of much dispute, but cf. McIlwain, *The Growth of Political Thought in the West*, (New York, 1932), pp. 330–331, and pp. 249–253 below.

60. Even with us, the pressure of facts is forcing a new conception of the executive's role and a growing realization that there are certain kinds of legislating which only the executive can satisfactorily do. The quasi-legislative, quasi-judicial administrative agencies of the American government are good modern parallels to Aquinas's prince: like the prince, they receive from a higher source norms stated in loose and general terms and translate them into detailed and enforceable law by a process which, if Congress happened to do it, we should certainly call legislation. The 'usurpation' of a policy-forming role by the British Cabinet or the American President, or by the American Supreme Court, is another illustration of the tendency of legislative activity to gravitate toward the individual or group which has direct control over the machinery of enforcement.

61. *De Regimine Principum*, bk. 3, pt. 2, ch. 29.

62. Brie, *op. cit.*, pp. 78–82, 92–94, 188–201.

63. *Ibid.*, pp. 118–125, 156–160.

64. *Politics*, bk. 3, ch. 10.

65. Cusa, who takes the original freedom of man as a major premise, is nearer to modern democratic thought; yet if Cusa's system is examined closely it becomes evident that popular participation in legislation is for him less intimate, more formal, than for Marsiglio and is, in fact, little more than a theoretical basis for the right of an assembly of irresponsible representatives; cf. pp. 222, 264 f. below.

66. *Defensor Pacis*, dictio 1, ch. 13.

67. Cf. Lagarde, *op. cit.*, vol. II, pp. 164–174, 177–178, 183–194.

68. See bibliography below for references.

69. Cf. C. W. Prévité-Orton, 'Marsilius of Padua,' *Proceedings of the British Academy*, XXI (1935), pp. 152 ff.

70. This position is defended by McIlwain, *The Growth of Political Thought in the West*, pp. 297–308.

71. 'Marsilius von Padua . . . ,' p. 101. Gewirth's attempt to show that Marsiglio was unique in advocating a *real* popular participation in legislation (*op. cit.*, ch. V) seems to me to give inadequate weight to these considerations.

72. Cf. McIlwain, *op. cit.*, pp. 390–392; Walter Ullmann, *The Mediaeval Idea of Law* . . . (London, 1946), *passim*, esp. pp. 183 ff.

73. *Dialogus*, pt. 3, tr. 2, bk. 3, ch. 12.

74. *Ibid.*, pt. 1, bk. 6, ch. 100.

75. The relation of divine law to human law remains finally ambiguous in Marsiglio's thought: where both conflict, he frequently asserts, it is better to obey God' than man; but he offers no suggestions for the juridical or the practical problem. For a long list of references, from both the *Defensor Pacis* and the *Defensor Minor*, see Lagarde, *op. cit.*, vol. II, pp. 248–249; cf. also pp. 217–219, 540–545, below.

76. Scholz, 'Marsilius von Padua . . . ,' p. 100.

NOTES TO CHAPTER TWO *pages* 88 *to* 108

1. Paul Girard, *Manuel élémentaire de droit romain* (7th ed., Paris, 1924), pp. 267 ff.

2. Edouard Meynial, 'Notes sur la formation de la théorie du domain divisé du xiie au xive siècle dans les Romanistes,' in *Mélanges Fitting* (Montpellier, 1908), vol. II, pp. 413 ff.; Rudolf Huebner, *A History of Germanic Private Law* (tr. Francis Philbrick, Boston, 1918), bk. II, chs. V and VI.

3. The feudal view is admirably defined in the selection from Fitzralph, *De Pauperie Salvatoris*, bk. 1, ch. 2, tr. below, pp. 121–124.

4. The following summary is based upon Meynial, *op. cit.*, pp. 409–461; cf. also Otto von Gierke, in Holtzendorff's *Encyklopädie der Rechtswissenschaft* (6th ed.), vol. I, pp. 488–490; Adhémar Esmein, *Cours élémentaire d'histoire du droit français* (11th ed., Paris), pp. 241–242; Huebner, *op. cit.*, bk. II, ch. VI.

5. 'I ask what lordship may be? and the term can be used most broadly to cover every incorporeal right, as, for instance, I have the lordship of some obligation, of usufruct, for example. . . .' Bartolus, *De Acquirendi Possessione*, I, 17, *si quis vi*, §*Differentia*, ╪4, quoted Meynial, *op. cit.*, p. 447.

6. ' . . . . And I have said that, however many they are, they have the lordship of use in various respects, and each one is lord of another, even if the fief descends through many hands. And this is proved as follows: you grant me that a vassal can infeudate his holding; I now show that the vassal himself, who makes the grant to another, holds a right in regard to the thing. . . . It is clear that by its very nature the feudal relation is such that he who grants may retain certain rights, namely, that he can expel his vassal if he defaults . . . and other rights. Therefore, from what the feudal contract allows him, it follows that the aforesaid rights still continue. Nor is it an obstacle that there cannot be several lords of use over a single object, nor several direct lords, because this is true from one point of view, but from various points of view it is as I have said; whence it follows that the first vassal is considered lord of the second, and the second of the third, from the point of view of their relations to one

NOTES

another. . . .' Joannes Faber, *Institutiones, De Locatione et Conductione, Adeo autem,* #4, #5, quoted Meynial, *op. cit.,* pp. 459–460.

7. Georg Meyer, *Das Recht der Expropriation* (Leipzig, 1868), pp. 85–94, 97–115.

8. For specific citations, see Carlyle, *A History of Mediaeval Political Theory in the West,* vol. I, pp. 51–54.

9. *Ibid.,* pp. 23–25.

10. *Ibid.,* vol. I, pp. 132–143; Vernon Bartlett, 'The Biblical and Early Christian Idea of Property,' in *Property, Its Duties and Rights,* ed. Charles Gore (London, 1915); Carlyle, 'Property in Medieval Theology,' in the same collection.

11. See above, pp. 34 f.

12. *Politics,* bk. 2, ch. 2.

13. *Nicomachean Ethics,* bk. 5, ch. 5.

14. The Franciscan rule included the obligation of individual and collective poverty, supposedly imitating the poverty of Christ and the apostles. This position was approved by Nicholas III and Clement V. But problems of interpretation developed. On the one hand, the order developed a technique of providing for its future necessities through vesting in the pope the title to properties donated to it, appointing trustees to administer such properties in the name of the pope, while reserving to itself a simple right of 'actual use.' On the other hand, a more rigid wing of the order, the Spiritual Franciscans, condemned all planning in advance, even for bare necessities, and defied papal attempts to reconcile them to a more lenient interpretation; and a yet more radical group, the Fraticelli, insisted on the most rigorous poverty for the order and also condemned the church in general for its wealth. The quarrels within the order, the scandal of actual Franciscan wealth cloaked by a formal poverty, the general criticism of ecclesiastical wealth by the radical Fraticelli, the defiance of papal authority by all factions—all seemed to call for stern papal action, and John XXII resolved to solve the situation, at a time when the Spiritual Franciscans were in the ascendant, and a Spiritual Franciscan, Michael of Cesena, was general of the order. He refused to hold title to property destined for Franciscan use, and asserted that in the case of goods whose use entailed their consumption there could be no distinction between a right of 'actual use' and ownership. Reversing previous papal decisions, he declared that it was heresy to say that Christ and the apostles had no property either individually or collectively. Ownership itself was established by divine law; the poverty of Christ and the apostles consisted not in any abnegation of ownership, but in an attitude of indifference to worldly goods. The Spiritual Franciscans retorted by refusing to recognize the authority of John XXII himself. The debate, which continued for more than half a century, had innumerable ramifications which cannot interest present-day readers. But it did involve a thorough examination of every aspect of property-theory, which produced some statements of general importance.

15. See above, p. 38 f.

16. *Summa Theologiae,* pt. 3, q. 27, m. 3, art. 2, and m. 4, art 3, quoted Carlyle, *A History of Mediaeval Political Theory in the West,* vol. V, pp. 14, 15.

NOTES

17. *Apparatus ad Quinque Libros Decretalium*, bk. 3, tit. 34, ch. 8, quoted Carlyle, *A History of Mediaeval Political Theory in the West*, vol. V, p. 16, n. 2.

18. George O'Brien, *An Essay on Medieval Economic Teaching* (London, 1920), is a careful and thorough study of the development of the theory which supported economic regulation in the Middle Ages; cf. his bibliography for other references.

19. *Summa Theologiae*, 2a 2ae, qs. 77–78.

20. Aquinas's doctrine of usury is based on Aristotle's theory of money as a commodity whose use entailed its consumption. Thus the theory of the just price would not allow the use of money to be charged for as separate from the money itself; and the just price of the money would obviously be an equal amount of money. But modern readers sometimes forget that the theory of the just price allowed compensation for loss brought upon the seller; thus the money-lender was permitted to demand, besides the return of the money, a penalty for payment delayed beyond the appointed date and also compensation for any loss he incurred through being without the money. These compensations, and that which later writers added, the compensation for opportunities of gain missed on account of the loan, were approved as *interest* and sharply distinguished from *usury*, which was a charge made for the use of the money itself without regard to the lender's circumstances. Although it was recognized that the possession of the money might involve an opportunity of gain for the borrower, the lender was conceived as having no right to be compensated for this gain, which was entirely due to the borrower as the reward of his labour expended on otherwise sterile money. See O'Brien, *op. cit.*, pp. 159–213; W. J. Ashley, *An Introduction to English Economic History and Theory* (London, 1923), vol. I, pt. II, pp. 427–439; B. N. Nelson, *The Idea of Usury* (Princeton, 1949).

21. Notably the permission of interest in compensation for opportunities of gain missed by the money-lender; cf. Ashley, *op. cit.*, vol. I, pt. II, pp. 400–402; O'Brien, *op. cit.*, pp. 187–191.

22. 'The law may justly fix the price of things which are sold, both movable and immovable, in the nature of rents and not in the nature of rents, and feudal and non-feudal, below which price the seller must not give, or above which the buyer must not demand, however they may desire to do so. As therefore the price is a kind of measure of the equality to be observed in contracts, and as it is sometimes difficult to find that measure with exactitude, on account of the varied and corrupt desires of man, it becomes expedient that the mean should be fixed according to the judgment of some wise man. . . . In the civil state, however, nobody is to be decreed wiser than the law-giving authority. Therefore it behoves the latter, whenever it is possible to do so, to fix the just price, which may not be exceeded by private consent, and which must be enforced. . . .' Gerson, *De Contractibus*, pt. 1, ch. 19, cited O'Brien, *op. cit.*, p. 106.

23. *Dialogus*, tr. 3, pt. 2, bk. 2, ch. 23, tr. below, pp. 308–310.

24. See Meyer, *op. cit.*; Otto von Gierke, *Political Theories of the Middle Age*, tr. F. W. Maitland (Cambridge, 1900), pp. 79–80 and notes; Gaines Post, 'Plena Potestas

NOTES

and Consent in Medieval Assemblies,' *Traditio*, I (1943), 335–408, and 'The Theory of Public Law and the State in the Thirteenth Century,' *Seminar*, VI (1948), 42–59, at pp. 49 ff.; for typical discussions, the passages from the *Somnium Viridarii* and from Aeneas Sylvius reproduced below. In harmony with these general ideas was the frequently upheld doctrine that privileges freely granted by the ruler to private individuals and thus resting simply on civil law could be easily abrogated, while claims resting on contracts between ruler and subject could be abrogated only *ex justa causa*, since contracts derived their force from the law of peoples; cf. Gierke, *op. cit.*, pp. 80–81 and notes.

25. See below, pp. 294–296.

26. 'Lordship' (*dominium*) meant to medieval thinkers a power based on right over some subordinate person or thing. It served as a common denominator for both political and proprietary authority; see the excellent analysis in McIlwain, *The Growth of Political Thought in the West*, pp. 250–251. The theories about to be discussed were therefore much more than theories of property, but for convenience we shall treat them here as theories of property, leaving their political aspects to be discussed below in chs. III and VIII.

27. E.g., James of Viterbo, *De Regimine Christiano*, bk. 2, ch. 7; Alvarus Pelagius, *De Planctu Ecclesiae*, bk. 1, ch. 40. For the relation of Aegidius's theory to canonist thought, see Walter Ullmann, *Medieval Papalism* (London, 1949), pp. 129 ff.

28. For a convenient brief statement, see pp. 610–612 below.

29. *De Pauperie Salvatoris*, passage reproduced below and bks. 1–4, *passim*.

30. 'God is lord not mediately, through the rule of subject vassals, as other kings rule, but immediately and through Himself He makes, sustains, and governs all that He possesses and aids it to perform its work according to other uses which He requires.' *De Dominio Divino*, bk. 1, ch. 5 (p. 33).

31. *De Civile Dominio*, bk. 1, chs. 1–6, 18–21, 35–36.

32. *Ibid.*, bk. 1, chs. 37–42; see below, pp. 127–130.

33. *Ibid.*, bk. 1, ch. 30 (p. 218).

34. This fact did not prevent leaders of the social revolts of 1381 from quoting Wyclif in support of their aims—even as Luther's paradoxes on Christian liberty were later misinterpreted as encouragements to the peasant revolts of his time; cf. R. L. Poole, *Illustrations of the History of Mediaeval Thought and Learning* (2nd ed., London, 1920), pp. 261 ff.

NOTES TO CHAPTER THREE *pages* 140 *to* 164

1. Cf. Fritz Kern, *Gottesgnädentum und Widerstandsrecht im früheren Mittelalter* (Leipzig, 1914).

2. *Petri Crassi Defensio Heinrici IV. Regis*, in *MGH, Libelli de Lite*, vol. I, pp. 432–453.

3. Romans 13:1–5; cf. I Peter 2:13, 14.

NOTES

4. Genesis 10:8.

5. I Samuel 8:4–22.

6. For analysis and illustrations of patristic thought, see Carlyle, *A History of Mediaeval Political Theory in the West*, vol. I, chs. X, XI, XIII, XIV.

7. 'Those who murmur against the rulers set over them speak not against a human being, but against Him Who disposes all things to divine order.' *Libri Moralium in Job*, bk. 22, ch. 24, quoted Carlyle, *op. cit.*, vol. I, p. 153, n. 1; cf. Augustine, *De Civitate Dei*, bk. 5, chs. 19, 21.

8. *Etymologiae*, bk. 9, ch. 3; cf. *Sententiae*, bk. 3, chs. 47–51.

9. Cicero, *De Re Publica*, bk. 1, ch. 25; Augustine, *op. cit.*, bk. 19, ch. 21.

10. *Ibid.*, bk. 4, ch. 4; bk. 19, ch. 21; cf. McIlwain, *Growth of Political Thought in the West*, for the demonstration, vs. Figgis and Carlyle, of the interpretation of Augustine followed here.

11. *De Civitate Dei*, bk. 19, ch. 3.

12. 'The dispensation of divine providence established diverse ranks and distinct orders for this purpose: that while the less should show reverence for the more powerful and the more powerful should impose their will upon the less, one fabric of concord would be made from diversity and the administration of individual offices would be rightly performed. For a whole could in no way exist unless a great order of difference of this sort should preserve it. And the example of the celestial hosts shows us that in truth created beings cannot be governed nor live in one and the same equality, because, since there are angels and archangels, it is clear that they are not equal, but one differs from the other in power and order, even as we do. If, therefore, among these, who are without sin, there is established such distinction, what man shall refuse to submit himself willingly to this disposition which he knows that even angels obey?' *Epistolae*, bk. 5, no. 59, quoted Carlyle, *op. cit.*, vol. I, p. 127, n. 2.

13. *Confessions*, bk. 3, ch. 8, quoted *Decretum*, di. 8, c. 2, tr. above, p. 35 f.

14. Letter to Hermann of Metz, 1076, *Registrum*, ed. P. Jaffé, *Bibliotheca Rerum Germanicarum*, vol. IV, p. 2.

15. Letter to Hermann of Metz, 1081, *ibid.*, vol. VIII, p. 21.

16. Cf. other statements of Gregory quoted Carlyle, *op. cit.*, vol. III, pp. 94–96, and Carlyle's general conclusion, p. 105; Gregory's words seem to echo some expressions of Augustine: e.g., *De Doctrina Christiana*, bk. 1, ch. 23, quoted Carlyle, *op. cit.*, vol. I, p. 126, n. 3, and *De Civitate Dei*, bk. 19, ch. 15.

17. See below, pp. 512 f., and tr., pp. 558–562.

18. *Sententiae*, bk. 3, ch. 51, sec. 4.

19. The consecration of the king tended to maintain that aura; Byzantine etiquette, introduced into the empire under Otto III, and influences from the *Corpus Juris Civilis*, which became important under the Hohenstaufens, reenforced the early medieval tradition with the older ideas of the special majesty and holiness of the

Roman emperor. From the time of Frederick Barbarossa, the empire was referred to as 'holy' or 'consecrated' ('*sacrum*' as distinguished from '*sancta*,' the epithet applied to the church). The late twelfth century also saw the introduction of the majestic 'we' for the English king, and the revival of this form, disused since the tenth century, in France. Kern, *op. cit.*, pp. 123–139.

20. *Ibid.*, ch. I, sec. 3 and notes.

21. Especially in the *Tractatus Eboracenses* and Hugh of Fleury, *Tractatus de Regia Potestate et Sacerdotali Dignitate*; on the other hand, Honorius Augustodunensis, *Summa Gloria*, MGH, *Libelli de Lite*, vol. III, pp. 63–80, at p. 69, specifically argues 'that the king is a layman.'

22. *Policraticus*, bk. 4, chs. 2, 1, tr. below.

23. *Ad Gebehardum Liber*, sec. 47.

24. *De Legibus et Consuetudinibus Angliae*, bk. 3, ch. 9, sec. 3.

25. Manegold, *op. cit.*, sec. 43.

26. Bracton, *loc. cit.*

27. *Policraticus*, bk. 4, ch. 3.

28. Gaines Post, 'The Theory of Public Law and the State in the Thirteenth Century,' *Seminar*, VI (1948), 42–59.

29. *Digest*, 1, 4, 1; *Institutes*, 1, 2, 6.

30. *Digest*, 1, 4, 1; 1, 1, 5.

31. *Codex*, 5, 59, 5.

32. *Summa contra Gentes*, bk. 3, ch. 83; cf. Robert Linhardt, *Die Sozial-Prinzipien des hl. Thomas von Aquin* (Freiburg im Breisgau, 1932), pp. 162–173.

33. *Summa Theologiae*, 1a 2ae, q. 91, art. 2, tr. above, p. 49.

34. A convenient formula for the process, entirely in the spirit of Aquinas, is given by James of Viterbo: the secular kingdom is 'from God through the mediation of human nature, which tends thereto, and through the mediation of human institution, which carries out the tendency of nature.' *De Regimine Christiano*, pt. 2, ch. 3. See Aquinas's commentary on the *Politics*, bk. 1, *lectio* 1 (Parma ed., at p. 366), for an analysis of the relation of nature and will in the making of the state.

35. 'Infidelity is not in itself incompatible with lordship' for the distinction between believers and infidels is a matter of divine law 'through which human rights are not abolished'; *Summa Theologiae*, 2a 2ae, q. 12, art. 2; cf. also q. 10, art. 10.

36. *In De Regimine Principum*, bk. 1, ch. 13, he suggested that even as God created the world and the soul gives form to the body, so the prince might make the state; but cf. pp. 205 f. below.

37. *Ibid.*, bk. 1, ch. 14, tr. below.

38. *Summa Theologiae*, 1a 2ae, q. 1.

39. See below, pp. 522 f.

40. *Summa Theologiae*, 1a 2ae, q. 92, art. 1.

41. *De Regimine Principum*, bk. 1, ch. 15, tr. below.

NOTES

42. *Summa Theologiae*, 1a 2ae, q. 97, arts. 1, 2, tr. above, pp. 62 f.

43. Carlyle, *op. cit.*, vol. III, pp. 5–6, denies that Aquinas had much influence; contrast Passerin d'Entrèves, *The Medieval Contribution to Political Thought*, pp. 15–16; cf. Lagarde, *La naissance de l'esprit laïque. . .* , vol. III, ch. V, on the assimilation and development of Aquinas's Aristotelianism by Pierre d'Auvergne, Godefroid de Fontaines, Aegidius Romanus, Remigio de' Girolami.

44. E.g., Tholommeo of Lucca, *Determinatio Compendiosa de Jurisdictione Imperii*, ch. 17; Fitzralph, *De Pauperie Salvatoris*, bk. 2, chs. 24–32; Cusa, *De Concordantia Catholica*, bk. 3, pref.; Fortescue, *De Natura Legis Naturae*, pt. 1, ch. 18; pt. 2, ch. 60.

45. E.g., by Aegidius Romanus, *De Ecclesiastica Potestate*, bk. 1, ch. 3; cf. a similar distinction in the regalist *Quaestio de Utraque Potestate*, art. 2.

46. *De Potestate Regia et Papali*, ch. 18.

47. *De Monarchia*, bk. 3, ch. 16, tr. below, pp. 592–594.

48. *Op. cit.*, ch. 20.

49. *Op. cit.*, bk. 2, ch. 6, tr. below, pp. 580 f.

50. E.g., Aristotle's discussion of the hierarchic relations of sciences serving different ends, *Ethics*, bk. 1, chs. 1–2, was pressed into service.

51. *Op. cit.*, bk. 3, ch. 1.

52. For further analysis of this controversy see ch. II above and ch. VIII below.

53. *Defensor Pacis*, dictio 1, ch. 9, sec. 2.

54. *Ibid.*, dictio 1, ch. 2, sec. 3; the Augustinian idea of peace is of course most obvious here.

55. Cf. Lagarde, *op. cit.*, vol. II, pp. 155–164, and Alan Gewirth, *Marsilius of Padua* (New York, 1951), pp. 54–67, 92–98, 305–310. Lagarde, I think correctly, finds a basic, unconscious contradiction between elements of finalism and of simple empiricism in Marsiglio's thought; Gewirth defends Marsiglio's consistency.

56. See ch. VIII below.

57. *Loc. cit.*; cf. *Somnium Viridarii*, bk. 1, ch. 183 (misnumbered by Goldast 163): 'The electors do not give power [to the emperor] but make him capable of receiving this dignity immediately from God'; cf. Gierke, *Political Theories of the Middle Age*, n. 140.

58. See above, ch. II, n. 30; but cf. also below, ch. VII, n. 56.

59. Bk. 3, pt. 1, chs. 1–6.

60. *Op. cit.*, chs. 1, 11, 16.

61. Although lordship began 'from a certain ambition for grandeur and lust for domination, through usurpation,' it was 'permitted and provided' by God, 'for the punishment of the wicked and the governance of the good'; *op. cit.*, chs. 17–18; cf. his continuation of Aquinas's *De Regimine Principum*, bk. 4, ch. 3.

62. Beaumanoir, *Coutumes de Beauvaisis*, ch. 45, sec. 1453; Engelbert of Admont, *De Ortu et Fine Romani Imperii*, ch. 2; Aeneas Sylvius, *De Ortu et Auctoritate Imperii Romani*, chs. 1, 2. A single illustration, from Beaumanoir, must suffice: 'While there

are several estates of people now, it is true that in the beginning all were free and of the same freedom, for everyone knows that we all descended from one father and one mother. But when the people began to increase, and wars and ill-will had been begun by pride and envy—which, then as now, ruled more than need be the community of the people—those who wanted to live in peace saw that they could not live in peace so long as everyone thought himself as great a lord as everyone else; so they elected a king and made him their lord and gave him the power of judging their misdeeds and of making commandments and laws over them.'

63. Engelbert of Admont, *op. cit.*, ch. 2: 'as if instigated by nature and by reason and by compelling experience of a natural need'; Aeneas Sylvius, *op. cit.*, ch. 1: 'from the reason itself of human nature'; cf. Gierke, *op. cit.*, ns. 303, 306.

64. See references in Gierke, *op. cit.*, ns. 54, 55; cf. ch. VII below.

65. Based on *Decretum*, c. 8, di. 1.

66. Pp. 25–28 above.

67. *Op. cit.*, *dictio* 1, ch. 15, sec. 3.

68. Occam, *Dialogus*, pt. 3, tr. 2, bk. 1, chs. 8, 26–29, and *Octo Quaestionum Decisiones*, q. 2; Lupold of Bebenburg, *De Jure Regni et Imperii Romani*, chs. 5, 6, partly tr. below, pp. 310–312; other references in Gierke, *op. cit.*, ns. 138 ff.

69. Occam's general approach is illustrated in *Dialogus*, pt. 3, tr. 2, bk. 3, ch. 6, tr. above, pp. 80–85; for other uses of this canon-law maxim, see Gierke, *op. cit.*, n. 139.

70. *Summa contra Ecclesie et Primatus Apostoli Petri Adversarios*, bk. 2, ch. 41.

71. Gewirth, *op. cit.*, pp. 219–225, argues that the notion that human freedom requires 'self-legislation' was an important pillar of Marsiglio's system; Marsiglio's rather loosely constructed arguments including 'the state is a community of free men' and a variant of *quod omnes tangit* (tr. above, pp. 76 f.) do not seem to me to bear the weight of Gewirth's emphasis: see below, pp. 216 f. An association of the idea of freedom with the basis of authority flickers through a great deal of medieval thought (cf., e.g., Beaumanoir as quoted above, n. 62), but it does not seem to me that it becomes a distinct philosophical premise for the establishment of legitimate authority before the work of Occam, at the earliest. Freedom was regarded as a circumstance which conditioned the rightfulness or the utility of a certain structure of authority long before it was clearly regarded as a moral imperative of human nature as such.

72. George Sabine, *A History of Political Theory* (rev. ed., New York, 1950), p. 320. The seventeenth-century meaning of consent, Sabine acutely says, was 'hardly possible' in the fifteenth century, 'for the right of private conscience and inward conviction had not the force that it had after the unity of the church was broken. Nor had the breaking-up of traditional social and economic institutions produced the "masterless man" who can be conceived to act only from his own internal motive-power'; *ibid.*, p. 319.

73. *Op. cit.*, bk. 3, pref.

NOTES

74. *Breviloquium* (ed. Baudry), p. 121.

75. Lagarde, *op. cit.*, vol. VI, pp. 183–192.

76. *Vivat Rex*, in *Opera*, vol. IV, p. 597.

77. *The Governance of England*, ch. 8; McIlwain, *The Growth of Political Thought...*, pp. 354–363.

78. *De Regimine Principum*, bk. 3, pt. 2, ch. 29, tr. below, pp. 289–291.

79. *De Regimine Principum*, bk. 2, ch. 8.

80. Cf. e.g., Occam, *Octo Quaestionum Decisiones*, q. 3, ch. 6: '.... Many functions are proper to the prince: namely, to assign to each his rights and to maintain them, to establish necessary and just laws, to constitute inferior judges and other officers, to prescribe what arts ought to be carried on in the community subject to him and by whom, to command acts of all the virtues, and many other things; yet he seems to be constituted most principally for this purpose: that he may correct and punish delinquents. For if in any community no one had to be punished for his crime or guilt, a teacher and monitor for good would suffice and a prince would seem altogether superfluous'; this passage is reproduced *Somnium Viridarii*, bk. 1, ch. 185 (misnumbered 165); cf. also James of Viterbo, *op. cit.*, pt. 2, ch. 4, tr. below.

NOTES TO CHAPTER FOUR *pages* 193 *to* 224

1. Cf. Ewart Lewis, 'Personality in the Chansons de Geste,' *Philological Quarterly*, XV (1936), 273–286.

2. Romans 12: 4–8; 1 Corinthians 12: 4–31.

3. 'Peace between man and God is the well-ordered obedience of faith to eternal law. Peace between man and man is well-ordered concord. Domestic peace is well-ordered concord between those of the household who rule and those who obey. Civil peace is a similar concord among citizens. The peace of the heavenly city is the perfectly-ordered and harmonious enjoyment of God and of one another in God. The peace of all things is the tranquillity of order. Order is the distribution which allots all things, equal and unequal, each to its own place.' *De Civitate Dei*, bk. 19, ch. 3.

4. Hans Liebeschütz, 'John of Salisbury and Pseudo-Plutarch,' *Journal of the Warburg and Courtauld Institutes*, VI (1943), 33 ff., argues that 'Plutarch' was John himself.

5. This interpretation reflects the influence of Otto von Gierke, who, in the section from vol. III of his *Das deutsche Genossenschaftsrecht* (4 vols., Berlin, 1868–1913) tr. F. W. Maitland as *Political Theories of the Middle Age* (Cambridge, 1900), argued that 'truly medieval' theory was an organic theory which only failed of complete systematic development through its failure to formulate the concept of the real personality of the group. Gierke's general thesis has been attacked: see Maurice de Wulf, 'L'Individu et le groupe dans la scolastique du xiiie siècle,' *Revue néo-scolastique de philosophie*, XXII (1920), 341–357; Ewart Lewis, 'Organic Tendencies in Medieval Political

22*

Thought,' *American Political Science Review*, XXXII (1938), 849-876 (some over-simplification in this article is, I hope, corrected here); cf. also the careful analysis of Robert Linhardt, *Die Sozial-Prinzipien des hl. Thomas von Aquin* (Freiburg im Breisgau, 1932), to which I owe a great deal; Georges de Lagarde, *La naissance de l'esprit laïque* . . . , vol. III (1942), *passim*, and 'Individualisme et corporatisme au moyen âge,' in *L'Organisation corporative du moyen âge* (*Études* . . . *pour l'histoire des assemblées d'états*, II; Louvain, 1937).

6. *Policraticus*, bk. 6, chs. 20, 22.

7. See the excellent discussion, with references, in John Dickinson, *The Statesman's Book of John Salisbury* (New York, 1927), intro., pp. xlii–xliv.

8. E.g., bk. 5, ch. 4.

9. 'It is easy to glide into the view that [in Aristotle's theory] the state and its "well-being" . . . are . . . made into a higher end to which the individual and his personal development are sacrificed. Generally speaking, such a view is erroneous: it involves a return, in another form, of that antithesis between political society and the individual which Plato and Aristotle refuse to recognize. The state (they believe) exists for the moral development and perfection of its individual members: the fulfilment and perfection of the individual means—and is the only thing which means—the perfection of the state; there is no antithesis.' Ernest Barker, intro. to his translation of *The Politics of Aristotle* (Oxford, 1946), pp. l–li.

10. Gierke, 'Ueber die Geschichte des Majoritätsprinzip,' in Paul Vinogradoff, ed., *Essays in Legal History* (Oxford, 1913), pp. 312–335.

11. *Defensor Pacis, dictio* 1, ch. 12, secs. 3, 4; ch. 13, sec. 8: tr. above, pp. 74 f., 78; Alan Gewirth, *Marsilius of Padua* (New York, 1951), pp. 182–199, gives an admirable detailed analysis of Marsiglio's concept.

12. The phrase was first coined by Innocent IV for the church; it was later taken up by the civilists and applied to all corporations.

13. Quoted Gierke, *Political Theories of the Middle Age*, p. 70.

14. I am here following the interpretation given by Pierre Gillet, *La personnalité juridique en droit ecclésiastique* . . . : University of Louvain dissertations, 2nd ser., vol. XVIII (1927), pp. 141–169. Gierke argued in *Das deutsche Genossenschaftsrecht* that medieval canon law recognized in the corporation a suprapersonal unity which was the real subject of rights and duties and that it only failed to define this subject as a real person. Without claiming to be an expert in canon law, I find Gillet's documented criticism of this thesis plausible.

15. *De Regimine Principum*, bk. 1, ch. 1, tr. above, pp. 176 f.; cf. Dante, *De Monarchia*, bk. 1, ch. 15: 'All concord depends on the existence of unity in the wills. . . . But this unity cannot exist unless there be one will, the mistress and regulator of the others to unity'; for other references, see Lewis, 'Organic Tendencies . . . ,' pp. 856–857, ns. 35–37.

16. *Political Theories of the Middle Age*, pp. 31–32.

NOTES

17. Even in Aquinas's writing, allusions to this metaphysical problem are rare and fragmentary. Besides the section from the commentary on the *Nicomachean Ethics* tr. below, see *Summa Theologiae*, 1a 2ae, q. 96, art. 1, and *Quodlibeta* 8, art. 5 (*Opera*, Parma ed., vol. XVIII, p. 577): '.... Even as in a commonwealth men, diverse in number, belong to a community, and when some die, others take their place, and thus it does not remain one commonwealth in respect of its matter, since its matter is a succession of different men, but it remains numerically one in respect of its species or form because of the unity of order in the separate offices. ...' This passage is part of a discussion of the nice technical question whether the food eaten by man turns into real human nature.

18. 'In human affairs there is a common good, which is the good of a city or a people. ... There is also a human good which does not consist in the community but pertains to each individual as a self'; *Summa contra Gentes*, bk. 3, ch. 80.

19. 'The brothers are the Order and the Order is the brothers. From which it follows that the Order is not an imaginary and represented person, but the Order is true real persons. ... The Order is not a single true person, but it is true persons, even as a people is not one man but is many men ... , even as the church is true persons.' *Opus Nonaginta Dierum*, ch. 62; this and the other quotations from Occam are cited from Léon Baudry, 'Le philosophe et le politique dans Guillaume d'Ockham,' *Archives d'histoire doctrinale et littéraire du moyen âge*, XIV (1939), 209–230.

20. There is a good deal of suggestive material in Ernst Troeltsch, *The Social Teachings of the Christian Churches* (tr. O. Wyon, New York, 1921), vol. I, *passim*; cf. also Gillet, *op. cit.*

21. *De Sacramentis Fidei Christianae*, bk. 2, pt. 2, ch. 2 (Migne, *PL*, vol. 176, p. 416).

22. *Commentum in Quatuor Libros Sententiarum Magistri Petri Lombardi*, bk. 3, di. 13, q. 2, art. 2, *quaestiuncula* 2; cf. *Summa Theologiae*, pt. 3, q. 8, art. 3.

23. Besides the passage tr. below, see bk. 1, chs. 60–63.

24. Gerson, *De Potestate Ecclesiastica*, consids. 1. 7, tr. below, pp. 408–410.

25. *De Aequitate*, ch. 2 (ed. H. Fitting in *Quaestiones de Iuris Subtilitatibus des Irnerius*, Berlin, 1894, p. 88).

26. *De Regimine Principum*, bk. 1, ch. 14, tr. above, p. 178.

27. E.g., Aeneas Sylvius, *De Ortu et Auctoritate Imperii Romani*, chs. 17, 18, tr. below, pp. 321 f., sometimes cited as an extreme instance of the medieval attitude; but what does his fine talk really amount to?

28. *Confessions*, bk. 2, ch. 8.

29. Linhardt, *op. cit.*, p. 151; Aristotle's statement is in the *Nicomachean Ethics*, bk. 1, ch. 2.

30. The most extreme statement seems to have been that of Remigio de' Girolami, who, with some reservations, asserted that a citizen, while remaining personally guiltless, should accept eternal punishment if that were an alternative to the damnation of his country: according to Ernst H. Kantorowicz, '*Pro Patria Mori* in Medieval

NOTES

Political Thought,' *American Historical Review*, LVI (1951), 472–492, at p. 489.
Remigio was a follower of Aquinas, trained in Paris, later a teacher of the Dominicans
in Florence, perhaps a teacher of Dante. His treatise *De Bono Communi*, extracts from
which have been published ed. Richard Egenter, 'Gemeinnutz vor Eigennutz,'
Scholastik, IX (1934), 79–92, was written to persuade the turbulent Florentines to
love the common good better than their own. Almost anything could happen in
Florence, but Remigio's excursion into fantasy need scarcely be regarded as significant.
In contrast, Henry of Ghent strongly defended temporal death for one's country but
not spiritual death: 'One ought to prefer one's own salvation to that of the whole
universe'; quoted Lagarde, *La naissance* . . . , vol. III, p. 256; Lagarde analyses Remigio's general position, together with that of other followers of Aquinas's analysis,
ibid., ch. V.

One may note that, in comparison with modern men, medieval men were rather
casual about death and very much disturbed about the possibility of dying suddenly
'in one's sins' and thus facing possible damnation. This fear was met by the unofficial
development of the idea that death in a just war for one's country was a martyr's
death blessed by God and a parallel to the death of a crusader, for which the church
promised absolution from sins; cf. Kantorowicz, *op. cit.*

31. *Digest*, I, 1, 2; *Institutes*, I, 1.

32. Gaines Post, 'The Theory of Public Law and the State in the Thirteenth
Century,' *Seminar*, VI (1948), 42–59.

33. In addition to Remigio de' Girolami and Henry of Ghent: especially Aegidius
Romanus in his *De Regimine Principum*, Pierre d'Auvergne, Godefroid de Fontaines;
cf. analyses of these and other writers in Lagarde, *La naissance* . . . , vol. III, chs.
V–VIII.

34. *De Regimine Principum*, bk. 1, ch. 1, tr. above, pp. 176 f.

35. 'The common good is greater than private good if it is of the same genus, but
it can happen that private good is better in accordance with its genus'; *Summa Theologiae*, 2a 2ae, q. 152, art. 4.

36. *Ibid.*, 2a 2ae, q. 58, art. 9.

37. *Summa contra Gentes*, bk. 1, ch. 86.

38. *Ibid.*, bk. 3, ch. 129; *Summa Theologiae*, 2a 2ae, q. 47, art. 10; *Commentum in
Quatuor Libros Sententiarum* . . . , bk. 4, di. 2, q. 1, art. 3.

39. *Summa Theologiae*, 1a 2ae, q. 58, art. 7; in his commentary on the *Nicomachean
Ethics*, Aquinas had treated the distinction between common good and private good
as merely quantitative: bk. 1, *lectio* 2 (*Opera*, Parma ed., vol. XXI, p. 5).

40. *De Regimine Principum*, bk. 1, ch. 2, tr. below, p. 284.

41. Linhardt, *op. cit.*, p. 147; Linhardt's general conclusion (p. 156) is that it is much
more accurate to call Aquinas a liberal than an organicist, and that the position taken
by de Wulf, though over-simplified, is substantially nearer the truth than that of
Gierke. There is an excellent brief discussion to the same effect, in Alexander Passerin

NOTES

d'Entrèves, *The Medieval Contribution to Political Thought* (Oxford, 1939), pp. 26–29. Lagarde, *La naissance* . . . , vol. III, ch. 3, presents a carefully worked out interpretation, with a somewhat greater stress on the organic aspects of Aquinas's thought.

42. 'Comme ce "bonum commune," distinct spécifiquement du bien individuel, ne peut être réalisé en définitive que *par* les personnes groupées au sein de la société, il faut bien admettre que *dans cette perspective* ce sont les personnes individuelles qui se subordonnent au bien social.' The common good is 'le résultat—et la *condition*' of the good of individuals. Lagarde, *La naissance* . . . , vol. III, pp. 98–99.

'The application of the principle, "*omnes partes sunt propter perfectionem totius*" (1a 2ae, q. 90, art. 2), is legitimate in the measure in which the individual, putting certain activities at the service of the community, is considered as part of this whole. But he has in addition a moral value of his own. He is *more* than a simple part of the whole.' De Wulf, *History of Medieval Philosophy*, tr. E. C. Messenger (London, 1932), vol. II, p. 143, n. 1.

43. *Op. cit.*, bk. 1, ch. 3; see pp. 487 f. below for the context.

44. *Political Theories of the Middle Age*, pp. 10, 21; for recent opinion on the meaning of the passage and the general question of Averroist influence on Dante, see Passerin d'Entrèves, *Dante as a Political Thinker* (Oxford, 1952), pp. 47–50 and the bibliography in n. XI; on Averroist political theory, see Lagarde, *La naissance* . . . , vol. III, ch. II.

45. *Op. cit.*, bk. 1, ch. 5.

46. *Politics*, bk. 2, ch. 1; cf. Aegidius Romanus, *De Regimine Principum*, bk. 3, pt. 1, ch. 8.

47. Chs. I, II above; chs. V, VIII below.

48. *Summa Theologiae*, 2a 2ae, q. 40, art. 2; 1a, q. 108, art. 1.

49. *Op. cit.*, *dictio* 1, ch. 2, sec. 3; ch. 17, sec. 2; tr. below.

50. Ch. II above.

51. Cf. *Summa Theologiae*, 1a 2ae, q. 94, art. 2, tr. above, p. 53; Aegidius Romanus, *op. cit.*, bk. 3, pt. 2, ch. 25, tr. above, pp. 68 f.; note also the universal recognition of the natural-law or quasi-natural-law principle that 'it is permitted to repel force with force.'

52. Compare the concepts of freedom implied in the selections from Occam and from Tholommeo of Lucca tr. below, pp. 292–298, 300–308.

53. See ch. V below.

54. This was the case of those who argued, as did some of the later civilists and Aeneas Sylvius, that the will of the prince must be presumed to be good and that the error of the prince established a right; the very phrases recognized that an error was still an error and a presumption only a presumption, and those who used them still regarded natural and divine law as more than mere morality; cf. Gierke, *Political Theories of the Middle Age*, pp. 84–87.

NOTES

55. E.g., Passerin d'Entrèves, *The Medieval Contribution* . . . , pp. 61–62; but cf. pp. 17, 30, above.

56. Above, pp. 26 f., 75–78.

57. In developing Aristotle's contrast between the rule of law and the rule of man, Marsiglio asserted that 'in law, what is just and unjust, beneficial or harmful, in regard to every one of the civil acts of men is determined all but perfectly'; *op. cit.*, *dictio* 1, ch. 11, sec. 3. Marsiglio's example of coercive commands lacking 'a true concept of justice and civil good' and therefore not truly law is taken from 'the countries of the barbarians'; *op. cit.*, *dictio* 1, ch. 10, sec. 5. Note also that the *Defensor Pacis* is not a complete treatise on political theory; Marsiglio's primary purpose in *dictio* 1 was to lay a foundation for the theory of the Christian *legislator* which appears in *dictio* 2. Note also that all medieval thinkers agreed in assuming that the law of peoples achieved an embodiment of rational principles.

58. *Summa Theologiae*, 1a 2ae, q. 21, art. 4.

59. See the long list of references cited Lagarde, *La naissance* . . . vol. II, pp. 248–249.

60. See ch. VIII below.

61. See chs. VI, VIII below.

62. Note Turrecremata's objection to the conciliarist statement that the object of ecclesiastical power was 'the edification of the church'; p. 424, below.

63. *Reflections on the Revolution in France* (Everyman), p. 56. Burke's blend of organic and individualistic ideas has a good deal in common with medieval thought.

64. Cf. Troeltsch, *op. cit.*, vol. I, pp. 275–299, and n. 123 on pp. 407–408.

NOTES TO CHAPTER FIVE *page* 241 *to* 275

1. See R. W. and A. J. Carlyle, *A History of Mediaeval Political Theory in the West*, vol. I, pt. IV, and vol. III; Fritz Kern, *Gottesgnädentum und Widerstandsrecht im früheren Mittelalter* (Leipzig, 1914); C. H. McIlwain, *The Growth of Political Thought in the West*, pp. 172–175, 186–200; Georg von Below, *Der deutsche Staat des Mittelalters* (1st ed., Leipzig, 1914), vol. I, pt. 2, ch. 5; Émile Chénon, *Histoire générale du droit français public et privé des origines à 1815* (Paris, 1926), vol. I, pp. 174–179; Jacques Flach, *Les origines de l'ancienne France* (Paris, 1886 ff.), vol. III, pp. 329–364.

2. 'A do-nothing king, or a king who is merely a moderator between contending parties, or a king who merely executes the expressed desires of Parliament, is not the ideal king of the Middle Ages. He is the ruler of the nation, the commander of its armies and its fleets, the national treasure is his treasure and in very general terms does parliament interfere with his expenditures; it is for him to keep the peace, the peace is his peace; all public officers, high and low, with but few exceptions, are appointed by him, dismissible by him. . . .' F. W. Maitland, *The Constitutional History of England* (Cambridge, 1908), p. 197.

NOTES

3. *De Legibus et Consuetudinibus Angliae*, bk. 1, ch. 8, sec. 5; bk. 3, ch. 9, sec. 3; all quotations from Bracton in this chapter are from the passages translated below, pp. 279–284.

4. For illustrations, see Carlyle, *op. cit.*, vol. I, chs. 18–20; vol. III, pt. I, ch. 2.

5. *De Vera Religione*, ch. 31, quoted *Decretum*, c. 3, di. 4.

6. *Digest*, 1, 3, 31. The original meaning of *princeps legibus solutus est* was that the emperor was specifically exempted from certain private-law rules from which he could dispense; he continued bound by public and criminal law. Medieval thought interpreted the concept as a general rule. Cf. A. Esmein, 'La Maxime *Princeps Legibus Solutus Est* dans l'Ancien Droit Public Français,' in P. Vinogradoff, ed., *Essays in Legal History* (London, 1913), pp. 201–214.

7. *Institutes*, 1, 2, 6; cf. *Digest*, 1, 4, 1.

8. See pp. 151 f., 162 f., above.

9. *Nicomachean Ethics*, bk. 8, ch. 10, *Politics*, bk. 1, ch. 1; bk. 3, chs. 4, 5.

10. *Coutumes de Beauvaisis*, ch. 34, sec. 1043.

11. *Policraticus*, bk. 4, ch. 1.

12. *Op. cit.*, bk. 2, ch. 24, sec. 1 (Woodbine, vol. II, p. 167).

13. Cf., besides the passage tr. above, pp. 170–172, the excellent analysis, with references, in John Dickinson, *The Statesman's Book of John of Salisbury*, Intro., esp. secs. II, III.

14. *Policraticus*, bk. 5, ch. 6. For this whole pattern of thought, illustrated particularly by analysis of Bracton, see C. H. McIlwain, *Constitutionalism Ancient and Modern* (Ithaca, 1940), ch. IV.

15. So thought the author of the *Mirror of Justices*, quoted Carlyle, *op. cit.*, vol. VI, p. 34.

16. *Op. cit.*, bk. 4, ch. 2.

17. *Op. cit.*, bk. 1, ch. 8, sec. 5 (Woodbine, vol. II, p. 33).

18. *Ibid.*, bk. 3, ch. 9, sec. 3 (Woodbine, vol. II, p. 305).

19. *Ibid.*, bk. 1, ch. 16, sec. 3 (Woodbine, vol. II, p. 110). Bracton himself recognized this current doctrine in bk. 4, ch. 10 (Woodbine, vol. III, pp. 42–43). Kern, *op. cit.*, pp. 268–270, groups this idea with references in thirteenth-century German law books to the court of imperial princes, headed by the Count Palatine, which could judge and depose the emperor and condemn him to death, and with references to the 'Justicia' in thirteenth century Aragon, described as judge between king and people; cf. also Carlyle, *op. cit.*, vol. V, pp. 104–110.

20. *Fleta* (London, 1685), bk. 1, ch. 17.

21. Ed. C. L. Kingsford (Oxford, 1890), ll. 951–954.

22. Texts in Charles Bémont, ed., *Chartes des libertés anglaises (1100–1305)* (Paris, 1892), pp. 41–44; William Stubbs, ed., *Select Charters* (9th ed., Oxford, 1921), pp. 393–397.

23. From the passage known as the '*Digna Vox*,' *Codex*, 1, 14, 4: 'It is a saying

worthy of the majesty of the ruler that the prince profess himself bound by the laws: since our authority depends on the authority of the law. And it is indeed a thing greater than empire that a prince submit his government to the laws.'

24. See Lester K. Born, 'The Perfect Prince, A Study of Thirteenth and Fourteenth Century Ideals,' *Speculum*, III (1928), 470–504; W. Burges, *Die Fürstenspiegel des hohen und späten Mittelalters* (*Schriften des Reichsinstituts für ältere deutsche Geschichtskunde*, II, 1938).

25. Augustine, *De Civitate Dei*, bk. 5, chs. 19–21; Gregory I, *Libri Moralium in Job*, bk. 22, ch. 24, quoted Carlyle, *op. cit.*, vol. I, p. 153, n. 1.

26. Cf. Carlyle, *op. cit.*, vol. III, pt. I, ch. 4; vol. V, pp. 112–116.

27. Dickinson, *op. cit.*, p. lxxviii.

28. *Summa Theologiae*, 1a 2ae, q. 90, art. 3, tr. above, p. 48.

29. *Ibid.*, q. 97, arts. 1, 3, tr. above, pp. 62–64 ; *De Regimine Principum*, bk. 1, ch 4.

30. *Summa Theologiae*, 1a 2ae, q. 97, art. 1, tr. above, p. 62.

31. *Ibid.*, 1a 2ae, q. 105, art. 1.

32. Exodus 18: 21; Numbers 11: 16; Deuteronomy 1: 13.

33. *Summa Theologiae*, 1a 2ae, q. 95, art. 4.

34. *De Regimine Principum*, bk. 1, ch. 2, tr. below; the same opinion is expressed in *Summa Theologiae*, 2a 2ae, q. 50, art. 1.

35. *De Regimine Principum*, bk. 1, ch. 5.

36. *Ibid.*, bk. 1, ch. 6, tr. below.

37. This interpretation is typically related to Aquinas's assumed preference for mixed government, based on the two passages in the *Summa*: e.g., by Carlyle, *op. cit.*, vol. V, pp. 94–95. Considerable legerdemain is necessary to derive a theory of constitutional monarchy from these three passages—quite aside from the problem of harmonizing them with Aquinas's other statements. The mixture approved in q. 105 is a sort of administrative decentralization through elective magistrates; that of q. 95, which most closely corresponds to the medieval situation, anticipates the mixture of regal and political monarchy later defined by Occam and Fortescue; the passage in the *De Regimine Principum* is completely non-committal. For an elaborate attempt to read modern concepts into Aquinas, see Jacques Zeiller, *L'Idée de l'état dans Saint Thomas d'Aquin* (Paris, 1910). My own interpretation has been influenced by that in McIlwain, *The Growth of Political Thought in the West*, pp. 328–333, and Robert Linhardt, *Die Sozial-Prinzipien des hl. Thomas von Aquin* (Freiburg im Breisgau, 1932), pp. 167–173.

38. Zeiller, *op. cit.*, p. 41, and others have interpreted this as implying an appeal to the pope; but if this was Aquinas's meaning, why did he not say so? This interpretation must assume that Aquinas regarded the pope as the normal temporal superior of all earthly rulers—a very dubious assumption: cf. pp. 522 f., below.

39. Notice Occam's use of the term *temperata* in *Dialogus*, pt. 3, tr. 1, bk. 2, ch. 6, tr. below, p. 300.

40. *Summa Theologiae*, 1a 2ae, q. 90, art. 3.

41. *Summa contra Gentes*, pt. 3, q. 76.

42. *Summa Theologiae*, 1a 2ae, q. 97, art. 3.

43. *De Regimine Principum*, bk. 1, ch. 15; *Summa contra Gentes*, pt. 2, q. 15: 'The king is the universal cause of rule in the kingdom, above the governors of the kingdom and of the individual cities'; Commentary on *Sentences*, bk. 4, di. 24, q. 2, art. 1, sol. 1 *ad* 3: ' . . . . In the kingdom . . . complete plenitude of power rests in the king, regardless of the powers of his ministers, which are certain participations of the royal power.'

44. *De Regimine Judaeorum*, tr. above, p. 111.

45. *Summa Theologiae*, 1a 2ae, q. 96, art. 5, above, pp. 60 f. This solution, like that of John of Salisbury, was destined to echo and re-echo in later writings; as McIlwain has remarked (*The Growth of Political Thought in the West*, p. 331), it was the philosophical equivalent of Bracton's 'No writ runs against the king.'

46. Commentary on *Politics*, bk. 1, *lectio* 1 (p. 367 in Parma ed.); cf. Aegidius Romanus, *De Regimine Principum*, bk. 2, pt. 1, ch. 14, and John of Paris, *De Potestate Regia et Papali*, ch. 17.

47. *Summa Theologiae*, 1a 2ae, q. 97, arts. 1, 2, 3.

48. *Op. cit.*, bk. 3, ch. 9, sec. 3; cf. Fritz Schultz, 'Bracton on Kingship,' *English Historical Review*, LX (1945), 136–177, at pp. 155–156, for the interpretation of this passage.

49. *Summa Theologiae*, 1a 2ae, q. 90, art. 1.

50. Commentary on *Sentences*, bk. 2, di. 44, q. 2, art. 2.

51. *Summa Theologiae*, 1a 2ae, q. 96, art. 4; cf. *ibid.*, 2a 2ae, q. 104, art. 6.

52. *Ibid.*, 2a 2ae, q. 42, art. 2.

53. *De Regimine Principum*, bk. 1, ch. 6.

54. *De Regimine Principum*, bk. 2, pt. 1, ch. 14.

55. *Ibid.*, bk. 3, pt. 2, ch. 6.

56. *Ibid.*, bk. 3, pt. 2, ch. 12.

57. *Ibid.*, bk. 3, pt. 2, ch. 29, tr. below.

58. *Ibid.*, bk. 3, pt. 2, chs. 3, 4.

59. *Ibid.*, bk. 3, pt. 2, ch. 5, tr. below.

60. See passages tr. below, pp. 473–477, 488–495.

61. See ch. VI below.

62. *Op. cit.*, bk. 3, pt. 2, ch. 2.

63. *Defensor Pacis*, *dictio* 1, chs. 9, 16, 17.

64. Pp. 17, 26 f., 30, above.

65. As has sometimes been suggested: e.g., by Carlyle, *op. cit.*, vol. VI, p. 42.

66. For analysis and illustration of this point, see Georges de Lagarde, *La naissance de l'esprit laïque au déclin du Moyen Age*, vol. II, pp. 177–183; cf. Richard Scholz,

NOTES

'Marsilius von Padua und die Genesis des modernen Staatsbewusstseins,' *Historische Zeitschrift*, CLVI (1937), 88–103, at p. 101.

67. *The Growth of Political Thought in the West*, pp. 306–308.

68. *De Natura Legis Naturae*, pt. 1, ch. 16.

69. *Dialogus*, pt. 3, tr. 2, bk. 2, ch. 28.

70. E.g., the possibility that world-empire was no longer based on utility and common consent; cf. pp. 463 f., 495–500, below.

71. McIlwain, 'Magna Carta and Common Law,' in H. E. Malden, ed., *Magna Carta Commemoration Essays* (London, 1917), pp. 122–179; S. B. Chrimes, *English Constitutional Ideas in the Fifteenth Century* (Cambridge, 1936), pp. 269–279, 254.

72. Ch. II above.

73. *Octo Quaestionum Decisiones*, q. 8, ch. 3.

74. *De Iuribus Regni et Imperii Romani*, chs. 5, 6, tr. below.

75. Jean Masselin, *Diarium*, pp. 146–148, tr. below.

76. For discussion and illustration of this idea, see Gierke, *Political Theories of the Middle Age*, pp. 43–45, 82–84, and notes; McIlwain, *The Growth of Political Thought in the West*, pp. 379–383; see also *Somnium Viridarii*, bk. 2, ch. 293, tr. below.

77. On the estates, see particularly McIlwain, 'Medieval Estates,' in *Cambridge Medieval History*, vol. VII (1932), ch. 23; Gaines Post, 'Plena Potestas and Consent in Medieval Assemblies,' *Traditio*, I (1943), 335–408.

78. The authority of elected delegates to the estates was often limited to specific matters by the terms of their election and they were often equipped with specific instructions from their constituents; but there was no regular machinery for enforcing responsibility and theory did not demand it. Royal policy continually aimed at securing a blanket mandate for the delegates and was increasingly successful.

79. Kern, *op. cit.*, pp. 4–5.

80. For references, see Gierke, *op. cit.*, ns. 152, 153, 234.

81. *De Concordantia Catholica*, bk. 3, ch. 25; *ibid.*, bk. 1, ch. 6, tr. below, pp. 415–417.

82. See the analysis of Cusa's system in Edmond Vansteenberghe, *Le cardinal Nicolas de Cues (1401–1464): l'action—la pensée* (Lille, 1920), pp. 46–51.

83. Boutillier, *Somme rural*, bk. 2, tit. 1, quoted Émile Chénon, *op. cit.*, vol. I, p. 526, n. 5.

84. Tr. below, pp. 321–325. On civilist thought, see Gierke, *op. cit.*, ch. IX and notes, *passim*; Carlyle, *op. cit.*, vols. V, VI, *passim*; Walter Ullmann, *The Mediaeval Idea of Law as Represented by Lucas de Penna* (London, 1946), esp. pp. 48–57, 93–95, 101–104; Gaines Post, 'The Theory of Public Law and the State in the Thirteenth Century,' *Seminar*, VI (1948), 42–59.

85. *Codex*, 5, 59, 5; see G. Post, ' A Romano-Canonical Maxim . . . in Bracton,' *Traditio*, IV (1946), 197–251 ; McIlwain, *Growth of Political Thought in the West*, p. 302, n. 3.

86. For the relations between king and law in the later Middle Ages, see *ibid.*, pp. 364 ff. and *passim* ; Carlyle, *op. cit.*, vols. V, VI, *passim*; Paul Viollet, *Histoire des institutions politiques et administratives de la France* (Paris, 1890–1903), vol. II, pp. 199 ff.; Chrimes, *op. cit., passim*; F. M. Powicke, 'Reflections on the Medieval State,' *Transactions of the Royal Historical Society*, 4th ser., XIX (1936), 1–18; H. Mitteis, *Der Staat des hohen Mittelalters* (2nd ed., Munich, 1948), *passim*.

87. Viollet, *op. cit.*, vol. II, pp. 228–229.

88. *Op. cit., dictio* 1, ch. 14, sec. 7.

89. *Dialogus*, pt. 3, tr. 2, bk. 2, ch. 28.

90. *De Natura Legis Naturae*, pt. 1, ch. 24, tr. below; for the recognized scope of the dispensing power in England, see Paul Birdsall, ' "Non Obstante." A Study of the Dispensing Power of English Kings,' in *Essays in History and Political Theory in Honor of Charles Howard McIlwain* (Cambridge, Mass., 1936), pp. 37–76.

91. See pp. 50, 54 f., above.

92. Gierke, *op. cit.*, pp. 84–85 and notes; Ullmann, *op. cit.*, pp. 93–95, 112 ff.

93. Cf., e.g., Wyclif, who permitted only passive resistance to royal commands violating Christian duty, and no resistance at all where merely secular interests were at stake: *De Officio Regis*, ch. 1 (pp. 1–9); ch. 8 (p. 201); cf. J. N. Figgis, *The Divine Right of Kings* (2nd ed., Cambridge, 1914), ch. IV. The two positions might be combined.

94. *Dialogus*, pt. 1, bk. 6, ch. 100.

95. *Ibid.*, pt. 3, tr. 2, bk. 2, ch. 20.

96. *Octo Quaestionum Decisiones*, q. 2, ch. 7.

97. *Ibid.*, q. 8, ch. 5.

98. Cf. Alfred Coville, *Jean Petit: la question du tyrannicide au commencement du xvᵉ siècle* (Paris, 1932), for a detailed and careful discussion.

99. *Opera*, vol. V, pp. 364 ff.

100. Gierke, *op. cit.*, ns. 273, 285, 290.

101. E.g. Turrecremata, Commentary on the *Decretum*, di. 8 and di. 10, quoted Carlyle, *op. cit.*, vol. VI, pp. 168–169.

102. For a particularly strong statement, see Wetzel of Groningen, *De Dignitate et Potestate Ecclesiastica* (Goldast, *Monarchia . . .*, vol. 1), ch. 23: 'We must therefore resist the wicked powers unless we wish to share with them in secret partnership.'

103. Lupold of Bebenburg, *op. cit.*, chs. 12, 17; *Somnium Viridarii*, bk. 1, ch. 141; Franciscus de Zabarellis, Commentary on *Decretals*, bk. 1, tit. 6, ch. 34, quoted Carlyle, *op. cit.*, vol. VI, p. 165; Gerson, *De Auferibilitate Papae*, consid. 12; Antonius Rosellinus, *Monarchia seu de Potestate Imperatoris et Papae*, bk. 3, ch. 16; Cusa, *op. cit.*, bk. 3, ch. 4; cf. Carlyle's analyses of the depositions of the Emperor Adolf and of Richard II of England: *op. cit.*, vol. V, pt. I, chs. VII, VIII, and vol. VI, pp. 70–75; G. Lapsley, 'The Parliamentary Title of Henry IV,' *English Historical Review*, XLIX (1934), 423–449, 577–606.

NOTES

104. Cf. McIlwain, *Growth of Political Thought in the West*, pp. 365–367.

105. Gierke, *op. cit.*, n. 296.

106. *De Natura Legis Naturae*, pt. 1, ch. 16.

107. Cf. Carlyle, *op. cit.*, vol. VI, pt. I, ch. VI, and pt. II, ch. VI.

108. We have already mentioned the ill-starred attempt of the Provisions of Oxford; cf. later instances described in Carlyle, *op. cit.*, vol. VI, pp. 95, 105–110, 204–205; cf. McIlwain, *Growth of Political Thought in the West*, pp. 370–378.

109. Gerson, *Sermo Habitus XXI die Julii, 1415*, pt. 3, direction 2; cf. d'Ailly, *De Ecclesiae, Concilii Generalis, Romani Pontificis et Cardinalium Auctoritate*, pt. 3, ch. 4.

110. Charles Plummer, intro. to his ed. of Fortescue, *The Governance of England* (Oxford, 1885), p. 83. This position has been criticized, especially by McIlwain, who emphasizes that Fortescue's theory did not imply 'any popular control over the king in his government. . . . His rights were secured against the encroachment of his subjects by the same law which deprived him of the right to abridge their liberties or immunities'; *Growth of Political Thought in the West*, pp. 357–363. Max Shepard, 'The Political and Constitutional Theory of Sir John Fortescue,' in *Essays in History and Political Theory in Honor of Charles Howard McIlwain*, pp. 289–319, in general accepts McIlwain's interpretation, but finds in Fortescue an embryonic notion of institutional restraint upon the king.

111. Chrimes, intro. to Fortescue, *De Laudibus Legum Angliae* (Cambridge, 1942), p. cii.

112. *The Governance of England*, ch. 15.

113. Shepard, *op. cit.*, pp. 312–315.

88